Introduction

Alan J. Christensen and Michael H. Antoni

The past century has witnessed a dramatic shift in the patterns of physical disease. At the turn of the 20th century, acute disorders (primarily infectious disease) comprised the three leading causes of death in the United States (National Office of Vital Statistics, 1947). By the turn of the 21st century, the impact of acute disease had fallen dramatically whereas the prevalence and impact of chronic disorders had steadily increased. Chronic conditions now account for over 70% of all deaths, including the four most common causes: cardiovascular disease, cancer, cerebrovascular disease, and chronic obstructive pulmonary disease. The cost of managing these and other chronic conditions in the United States stands at well over $400 billion annually, or more than 60% of total healthcare expenditures (CDC, 1999).

Such a dramatic shift in the pattern of health and disease provides both a challenge and an opportunity. A central challenge facing biomedical science and medical practice is the difficulty of applying what is fundamentally an acute disease paradigm (i.e., "the germ theory of disease") to multidetermined, chronic conditions that carry the potential for long periods of patient morbidity or disability. In contrast to the mechanistic, reductionistic view of the traditional medical model, behavioral medicine's approach to health and disease has often adopted a biopsychosocial framework (Smith and Nicassio, 1995). This interactive, multivariate framework views biological, psychological, and social factors as having interrelated influences on health and disease (Engel, 1977). In this book we will argue that the adoption of a biopsychosocial paradigm is crucial to our understanding of how individuals afflicted with chronic medical conditions might be most effectively cared for, and how the tremendous personal and societal burden of chronic disease might be reduced.

This book was written by some of the most prominent figures in the field of behavioral medicine. The intention of the first four chapters is to examine a broad set of theoretical and applied issues that we believe are essential to understanding the role that behavioral medicine research and practice can play in the study and management of all chronic physical conditions. The first chapter in this section, by Kaplan, lays the foundation for the book by articulating the need for an alternative perspective in the way that patient outcomes are conceptualized in chronic disorders. This perspective focuses on quality of life as well as duration, and argues that quality of life measures are essential to the assessment of medical treatment effectiveness. The chapter by

Helgeson and Reynolds examining social psychological aspects of chronic disease includes a review of dispositional factors, social–cognitive processes and theories, and social environment characteristics that have figured prominently in chronic illness research. Carver and Scheier's chapter on coping processes and individual differences illustrates how general principles of coping and self-regulatory theories can facilitate our understanding of the chronic illness adjustment process. Finally, Dunbar-Jacob, Schlenk, and Caruthers examine one of the most pervasive and most costly clinical problems in chronic disease management: patient nonadherence with treatment regimens.

The remainder of the book consists of disorder-specific chapters. Underlying each of these is a fundamental recognition that a biopsychosocial approach is needed to capture the complexities of chronic disease management and outcomes. Included is a basic review of the biomedical (e.g., etiology, treatment, disease course) aspects of each disorder, followed by a review of the primary behavioral, psychological and socioenvironmental issues that are most relevant to a given disorder. Chapters also outline how clinical behavioral medicine practice has been, and can continue to be, informed by both basic and clinical research. Space limitations precluded us from assembling an exhaustive list of the physical disorders that have garnered the attention of behavioral medicine specialists. Instead, we have attempted to target those disorders wherein the foundation of empirical knowledge is relatively well developed, and where the translation of research to clinical practice has been, or has the potential to be, most successful.

The first four chapters in this section examine disorders that have received considerable, sustained attention by behavioral medicine researchers for decades. In many ways the work that has been accomplished with these populations provides a model example of how the talents and unique perspective held by behavioral medicine specialists can have a central and enduring impact in shaping the way a physical disorder is conceptualized and managed. The chapter by Smith and Ruiz on coronary heart disease provides an excellent example of how an understanding of the pathophysiology of a physical disease and an understanding of psychosocial assessment and intervention can mutually and effectively inform one another. The chapter by Andersen and Wells centers on the author's biobehavioral model of cancer stress and disease course, and outlines clearly how psychological, behavioral, and biological mechanisms play a vital role in influencing cancer outcomes and can impact effective cancer management. The chapter on diabetes by Gonder-Frederick, Cox, and Clarke explores the key issues of patient compliance and self-care, emotional adjustment, the neuropsychological impact of the disease, and the application and effectiveness of psychobehavioral interventions in diabetes. The chapter by Turk and Okifuji provides an overview of classic work and theory regarding biopsychosocial influences on chronic pain, as well as detailing the state of the art in chronic pain assessment and management. Highlighting the chapter is a summary of the author's own cutting-edge work involving the psychososcial "profiling" of chronic pain patients.

The final four chapters of the volume reflect areas in which the potential impact of behavioral medicine research and practice is still being realized.

Chronic Physical Disorders

Behavioral Medicine's Perspective

Edited by

ALAN J. CHRISTENSEN

and

MICHAEL H. ANTONI

Blackwell Publishers

© 2002 by Blackwell Publishers Ltd
a Blackwell Publishing company
except for editorial arrangement and introduction © 2002 by Alan J. Christensen and
Michael H. Antoni

Editorial Offices:
108 Cowley Road, Oxford OX4 1JF, UK
  Tel: +44 (0)1865 791100
350 Main Street, Malden, MA 02148-5018, USA
  Tel: +1 781 388 8250

First published 2002 by Blackwell Publishers Ltd

Library of Congress Cataloging-in-Publication Data has been applied for

ISBN 0-631-22075-5 (hardback); 0-631-22076-3 (paperback)

A catalogue record for this title is available from the British Library.

Set in 10/12pt Meridien
by Graphicraft Limited, Hong Kong
Printed and bound in TJ International, Padstow, Cornwall

For further information on
Blackwell Publishers, visit our website:
www.blackwellpublishers.co.uk

Contents

Contributors

Barbara L. Andersen, *Department of Psychology, The Ohio State University*
Michael H. Antoni, *Department of Psychology, University of Miami*
Bruce G. Bender, *University of Colorado, National Jewish Medical and Research Center*
Heather M. Burke, *Department of Psychology, Arizona State University*
Donna Caruthers, *University of Pittsburgh, Center for Research in Chronic Disorders*
Charles S. Carver, *Department of Psychology, University of Miami*
Alan J. Christensen, *Department of Psychology, The University of Iowa*
William L. Clarke, *Behavioral Medicine Center, University of Virginia Health System*
Daniel J. Cox, *Behavioral Medicine Center, University of Virginia Health System*
Thomas L. Creer, *Department of Psychology, The Ohio University*
Mary C. Davis, *Department of Psychology, Arizona State University*
Jacqueline Dunbar-Jacob, *University of Pittsburgh, Center for Research in Chronic Disorders*
Linda Gonder-Frederick, *Behavioral Medicine Center, University of Virginia Health System*
Vicki S. Helgeson, *Department of Psychology, Carnegie Mellon University*
Robert M. Kaplan, *Department of Family and Preventive Medicine, University of California, San Diego*
Akiko Okifuji, *Department of Anesthesiology, University of Washington*
Katherine Raichle, *Department of Psychology, The University of Iowa*
John W. Reich, *Department of Psychology, Arizona State University*
Kerry A. Reynolds, *Department of Psychology, Carnegie Mellon University*
John M. Ruiz, *Department of Psychology, The University of Utah*
Michael F. Scheier, *Department of Psychology, Carnegie Mellon University*
Elizabeth A. Schlenk, *University of Pittsburgh, Center for Research in Chronic Disorders*
Amy S. Schultz, *Department of Psychology, Arizona State University*
Timothy W. Smith, *Department of Psychology, The University of Utah*
Dennis C. Turk, *Department of Anesthesiology, University of Washington*
Sharla Wells, *Department of Psychology, The Ohio State University*
Alex J. Zautra, *Department of Psychology, Arizona State University*

Throughout these chapters you will see examples of how the best research methods and the most innovative clinical procedures are being applied to deal with the novel problems and the many unanswered questions these disorders pose. The chapter by Antoni reviews the central biobehavioral issues in HIV and AIDS and, unlike many previous reviews, emphasizes the emerging chronic nature of the disorder. Christensen and Raichle's review of chronic renal disease illustrates how research involving this relatively understudied population is just beginning to highlight the many ways in which behavioral medicine theory and practice can affect patient outcomes. The chapter on asthma by Bender and Creer details how an interdisciplinary, biopsychosocial approach is uniquely suited to addressing the many provider and patient challenges posed by this potentially debilitating condition. Last, but certainly not least, the chapter by Burke, Zautra, Schultz, Reich, and Davis reviews the central psychosocial issues in the development and progression of, and adaptation to, arthritis-related conditions.

Healthcare is increasingly facing the challenge of dealing with a set of prevalent, debilitating, and economically burdensome chronic physical conditions that, in many ways, defy a traditional or narrowly defined view of health and disease. As we believe this book will show, behavioral medicine theorists, researchers, and practitioners, are clearly and competently taking up this important challenge.

References

Centers for Disease Control and Prevention (1999). *Chronic Diseases and their Risk Factors: The Nation's Leading Causes of Death*. Washington, D.C.: U.S. Department of Health and Human Services.

Engel, G. L. (1977). The need for a new medical model: A challenge to biomedicine. *Science*, 196, 129–136.

National Office of Vital Statistics (1947). *Deaths and Death Rates for the 10 Leading Causes of Death by Sex*. Washington, D.C.: U.S. Department of Health and Human Services.

Smith, T. W. and Nicassio, P. M. (1995). Psychological practice: Clinical application of the biomedical model. In P. M. Nicassio and T. W. Smith (Eds.), *Managing Chronic Illness: A Biopsychosocial Perspective* (pp. 1–31). Washington, D.C.: American Psychological Association.

CHAPTER 1

Quality of Life and Chronic Illness

Robert M. Kaplan

University of California, San Diego

Introduction

The 20th century saw remarkable advances in medicine and medical care, yet at the beginning of the third millennium many challenges remained. One of the major accomplishments of traditional medicine was the reduction in deaths from infectious diseases. Today, people rarely die of diseases such as plague or tuberculosis, which relatively few years ago were feared. Instead, most of the modern medical challenges in the industrialized world involve chronic illnesses that require people to adapt and to modify their lifestyles. Healthcare for people with chronic illness has had to switch from a curing model to a caring model. This has required new thinking about the definition of health and healthcare.

Contemporary healthcare developed to attend to acute disease. Acute diseases can typically be diagnosed and treated successfully (or sometimes they will get better on their own). These problems are often identified through a biological test, and patient reports about the experience are often disregarded as unreliable or unnecessary. Most of the information required to diagnose and treat the condition can be identified in the laboratory. The acute disease model has guided the planning and constructions of hospitals, the development of training programs, and the creation of medical subspecialties (Holman and Lorig, 2000). However, the traditional acute disease model has significant limitations because the major burden on our healthcare system now results from chronic disease rather than acute illnesses.

Supported in part by grants R01 HS 09170 from the AHCPR, P60 AR 40770 from the NIH, TPRH-98-119-01 from the American Cancer Society.

Correspondence concerning this chapter should be addressed to Robert Kaplan Ph.D. Professor and Chair, Mail Code 0628 Department of Family and Preventive Medicine Clinical Sciences Building, Room 240, University of California, San Diego, La Jolla, CA 92093-0628.

Chronic diseases typically have multiple causes, and people who have one chronic condition typically have other chronic diseases as well. The Medical Outcomes Study, for example, recruited patients who had one of six chronic disease states. However, over 90% of the participants had other chronic conditions in addition to the category they represented in the study (Ware et al., 1996). Chronic conditions also differ from acute diseases in that chronic conditions are usually not cured. As a result, patients must adapt to their problems, and psychological or social factors are of key importance. Patient interpretation of the condition and adaptation to the problem cannot be ignored.

A different conceptual model is needed to measure consequences of chronic illness. In contrast to the traditional biomedical model, which requires the identification of basic disease mechanisms, the outcomes model (Kaplan, 2000) emphasizes all behavioral and social determinants of patient outcome. Whereas some may believe that treatments are not of value unless the biological pathway underlying the disease is understood, the outcomes model recognizes that biologic pathways may never be fully understood (Kaplan, 1994a). Further, some behavioral risk factors may affect health outcomes through a variety of different biological pathways. For example, researchers spent years attempting to identify the impact of tobacco use upon specific organs. Separate studies presented the effects of cigarette smoking upon lung cancer, heart disease, emphysema, oral cancers, and so on. By looking at the disease-specific impact of smoking and emphasizing the specific biological models, the total impact of tobacco use was underestimated. The outcomes approach links tobacco use to deaths from all causes and to reductions in quality of life. Considered from this perspective, the impact of tobacco use is huge, accounting for an estimated 19% of all premature deaths (McGinnis and Foege, 1993). Tobacco use is far and away the leading cause of preventable death in the United States.

Outcomes in Chronic Illness

One of the most important differences is in how the two models define a unit of benefit. The traditional biomedical model usually links benefit to a diagnosis. For example, outcome might be assessed by changes in blood pressure, tumor size, or death from a specific disease. The traditional model often focuses on the small picture while neglecting the big picture. Much of contemporary preventive cardiology care is based on observations from the Coronary Primary Prevention Trial or CPPT (Coronary Primary Prevention Trial, 1984a; 1984b). In this experimental trial, men were randomly assigned either to take a placebo or to use a drug known as cholestyramine. Cholestyramine can significantly lower serum cholesterol and, in this particular trial, produced an average total cholesterol reduction of 8.5%. Compared to men using placebo, men in the treatment group experienced 24% fewer heart attack deaths and 19 fewer heart attacks.

One of the crucial features distinguishing the outcomes model and the traditional biomedical model is in how they define patient outcome. The

CPPT showed a 24% reduction in cardiovascular mortality in the treated group. The absolute proportion of patients who died of cardiovascular disease was similar in the two groups. In the placebo group there were 38 deaths among 1,900 participants (2%). In the cholestyramine group there were 30 deaths among 1,906 participants (1.6%). In other words, taking medication for 6 years reduced the chances of dying from cardiovascular disease from 2% to 1.6%. However, the diagnosis-specific medical model focuses on cardiovascular deaths because the medicine was designed to reduce deaths from heart disease. Considering all causes of death, there was essentially no benefit of treatment. At the end of the study, 3.7% of those in the placebo group had died and 3.6% of those in the cholestyramine group had died. Since the publication of the CPPT, most studies have obtained the same result. Cholesterol lowering may reduce the chances of dying of heart disease but does not reduce the chances of dying prematurely. The outcomes model does not take cause of death into consideration. From the outcomes perspective, the focus is on whether or not the patient is alive (Golomb, 1998). If a medication reduces the chances of dying of one disease while increasing the chances of dying of another, it is not regarded as effective (Kaplan, 1990). Because virtually all treatments have the potential to produce harm as well as benefit, the outcomes model may be the most appropriate to evaluate benefits of treatment.

Mortality

Public health statistics concentrate on death rates. One major indicator is life expectancy, defined as the median number of years of life expected for each birth cohort. The second major indicator is infant mortality, which is defined as the number of babies born alive that die within 1 year. Infant mortality is usually expressed per 100,000 live births. Mortality remains the major outcome measure in most epidemiologic studies and clinical trials.

A model of health outcome that excluded mortality would be incomplete. Indeed, many public health statistics focus exclusively on mortality through estimations of crude mortality rates, age-adjusted mortality rates, and infant mortality rates. Death is an important outcome that must be included in any comprehensive conceptualization of health. However, many significant health conditions are not well reflected by mortality information. For example, osteoarthritis, cataract disease, and minor depression may all cause poor health without affecting life expectancy or infant mortality.

Health-Related Quality of Life

The conceptualization and measurement of health status has interested scholars for many decades. Following the Eisenhower administration, a President's Commission on national goals identified health status measurement as an important objective. In his influential book *The Affluent Society*, John Kenneth Galbraith described the need to measure the effect of the healthcare system on "quality of life" (Galbraith, 1958). In recent years there have been many attempts to define and measure health status.

Galbraith's proposal to consider quality of life was followed shortly by the development of quality of life measures. Sullivan (1966) argued that behavioral indicators such as absenteeism, bed-disability days, and institutional confinement were the most important consequences of disease and disability. Ability to perform activities at different ages could be compared to societal standards for these behaviors. Restrictions in usual activity were seen as *prima facie* evidence of deviation from wellbeing. Health conditions affect behavior, and in this chapter health outcomes are conceptualized as observable behavioral consequences of a health state (Sullivan, 1966). Arthritis, for example, may be associated with difficulty in walking, observable limping, or problems in using the hands. Even a minor illness, such as the common cold, might result in disruptions in daily activities, alterations in activity patterns, and decreased work capacity.

Diseases and disabilities are important for two reasons. First, illness may cause a truncation of the life expectancy. In other words, those in specific disease categories may die prematurely. Death is a behavioral outcome. It can be defined as the point at which there is no observable behavior. Second, diseases and disabilities may cause behavioral dysfunctions, as well as other symptoms. Biomedical studies typically refer to health outcomes in terms of mortality (death) and morbidity (dysfunction) and sometimes to symptoms (Kaplan, 1990).

Although important, each of these measures ignores dysfunction while people are alive. The National Center for Health Statistics of the Centers for Disease Control and Prevention provides information on a variety of states of morbidity. For example, it considers disability, defined as a temporary or long-term reduction in a person's activity. Over the last 30 years, medical and health services researchers have developed new ways to assess health status quantitatively. These are often called quality of life measures. As they are used exclusively to evaluate health status, we prefer the more descriptive "health-related quality of life" (Kaplan and Bush, 1982). Some approaches to the measurement of health-related quality of life combine measures of morbidity and mortality to express health outcomes in units analogous to years of life. The years of life figure, however, is adjusted for diminished quality of life associated with diseases or disabilities (Kaplan, 1996).

Modern measures of health outcome consider future as well as current health status. Cancer, for example, may have very little impact on current functioning but may have a substantial impact on behavioral outcomes in the future. Today, a person with a malignant tumor in a leg may function very much like a person with a leg muscle injury. However, the cancer patient is more likely to remain dysfunctional in the future. Comprehensive expressions of health status need to incorporate estimates of future behavioral dysfunction as well as measuring current status (Kaplan, 1994a).

The spectrum of medical care ranges from public health, preventive medicine, and environmental control through diagnosis to therapeutic intervention, convalescence and rehabilitation. Many programs affect the probability of occurrence of future dysfunction, rather than altering present functional status. In many aspects of preventive care, for example, the benefit of the treatment cannot be seen until many years after the intervention. A supportive family that instills proper health habits in its children, for example, may also promote better "health" in the future, even though the benefit may not be realized for years. The concept of health must consider not only the ability to function now, but also the probability of future changes in function or probabilities of death. A person who is very functional and asymptomatic today may harbor a disease with a poor prognosis. Thus, many individuals are at high risk of dying from heart disease even though they are perfectly functional today. Should we call them "healthy?" The term "severity of illness" should take into consideration both dysfunction and prognosis.

Comprehensive models that combine morbidity, mortality, and prognosis have been described in the literature (Kaplan, 1994a). A behavioral conceptualization of health status can represent this prognosis by modeling disruptions in behavior that might occur in the future (Kaplan, 1990).

Measurement of Health-related Quality of Life

A wide variety of measures have been proposed to quantify health-related quality of life (Strömbeck et al., 2000; Van Hoosier, 2000; Weymuller et al., 2000). These are similar in that each expresses the effects of medical care in terms that can be reported directly by a patient. However, the rationales for the methods differ considerably. In the late 1960s and early 1970s, the National Center for Health Services Research funded several major projects to develop general measures of health status. All were guided by the World Health Organization's (WHO) definition of health status, which states that "health is a complete state of physical, mental, and social wellbeing and not merely absence of disease" (WHO, 1948).

The projects resulted in a variety of assessment tools, including the Sickness Impact Profile (Bergner et al., 1981), the Quality of Well-Being Scale (Kaplan et al., 1998), the McMaster Health Index Questionnaire, the SF-36 (Kosinski et al., 1999a), and the Nottingham Health Profile (Lowe et al., 1990). Many of the measures examined the effect of disease or disability on performance of social role, ability to interact in the community, and physical functioning. Some of the systems have separate components for the measurement of social and mental health. The measures also differ in the extent to which they consider subjective aspects of quality of life (Brown et al., 2000).

There are two major approaches to quality of life assessment: psychometric and decision theory. The psychometric approach attempts to provide separate measures for the many different dimensions of quality of life. Perhaps the best-known example of the psychometric tradition is the Sickness Impact Profile (SIP). This is a 136-item measure that yields 12 different scores, each reflecting some aspect of patient functioning, displayed in a format similar to an MMPI profile (Bergner et al., 1981).

The decision theory approach attempts to weight the different dimensions of health in order to provide a single expression of health status. Supporters of this approach argue that psychometric methods fail to consider that different health problems are not of equal concern: 100 runny noses are not the same as 100 missing legs. In an experimental trial using the psychometric approach, some aspects of quality of life may improve while others get worse. For example, a medication might reduce high blood pressure but also produce headaches and impotence. Because components of outcome may be changing in different directions, an overall subjective evaluation is often used to integrate the components and offer a summary of whether the patient is better or worse off. The decision theory approach attempts to provide an overall measure of quality of life that integrates subjective function states, preferences for these states, morbidity, and mortality.

Generic Methods for the Measurement of Quality of Life

A variety of methods have been proposed to measure quality of life, but we cannot review and critique them all here. One useful way of classifying quality of life measures is as either generic or disease targeted. Generic measures can be used to evaluate outcomes for any population. Disease-targeted or disease-specific measures are crafted to measure outcomes for people with a particular health condition. Although most methods cannot be covered in one chapter, we will review some of the more common generic and disease-targeted approaches. Readers interested in more detailed reviews should consult Shumaker and Berzon (1995), Walker and Rosser (1993) or McDowell and Newell (1996).

Profile Methods

SF-36

Perhaps the most commonly used outcome measure in the world today is the Medical Outcome Study Short Form-36 (SF-36). The SF-36 grew out of work by the RAND Corporation and the Medical Outcomes Study (MOS) (Ware et al., 1999; Ware and Gandek, 1998). Originally, it was based on the measurement strategy from the RAND Health Insurance Study. The MOS attempted to develop a very short, 20-item instrument known as the Short Form-20 or SF-20. However, the SF-20 did not have appropriate reliability for some dimensions. The SF-36 includes eight health concepts: physical functioning, role-physical, bodily pain, general health perceptions, vitality, social functioning, role-emotional, and mental health (Kosinski et al., 1999b). The SF-36 can be either administered by a trained interviewer or self-administered, and it has many advantages. For example, it is brief, and there is substantial evidence for its reliability and validity (Keller et al., 1999; Koloski et al., 2000; Scott-Lennox et al., 1999; Ware et al., 1999). The SF-36 can be machine scored and has been evaluated in large population studies.

Despite its many advantages, the SF-36 also presents some disadvantages. For example, it does not have age-specific questions and one cannot clearly determine whether it is equally appropriate at each level of the age continuum.

The items for older retired individuals are the same as those for children (Stewart and Ware, 1992). Nevertheless, the SF-36 has become the most commonly used behavioral measure in contemporary medicine.

Nottingham Health Profile

The Nottingham Health Profile (NHP) is a measure that has been particularly influential in the European Community. It has two parts. The first includes 38 items divided into six categories: sleep, physical mobility, energy, pain, emotional reactions, and social isolation. Items within each of these sections are rated in terms of relative importance, and are rescaled in order to allow them to vary between 0 and 100 within each section.

The second part of the NHP includes seven statements related to the areas of life most affected by health: employment, household activities, social life, home life, sex life, hobbies and interests, and holidays. The respondent indicates whether or not a health condition has affected his or her life in these areas. Used in a substantial number of studies, the NHP has considerable evidence for its reliability and validity.

The NHP is consumer based and arises from definitions of health offered by individuals in the community. Furthermore, this scale uses language that is easily interpreted by people in the community and conforms to minimum reading requirements. Substantial testing has been performed on the NHP. However, the NHP does not provide relative-importance weightings across dimensions. As a result, it is difficult to compare the dimensions directly with one another (McEwen, 1992).

Decision Theory Approaches

Within the last few years, interest has grown in using quality of life data to help evaluate the cost/utility or cost-effectiveness of healthcare programs. Cost studies have gained in popularity because healthcare costs have increased so rapidly in recent years. Not all healthcare interventions return equal benefit for the expended dollar. Objective cost studies might guide policymakers toward an optimal and equitable distribution of scarce resources. Cost-effectiveness analysis typically quantifies the benefits of a healthcare intervention in terms of years of life, or quality-adjusted life years (QALYs). Cost/utility is a special use of cost-effectiveness that weights observable health states by preferences or utility judgments of quality (Kaplan et al., 1999). In cost/utility analysis, the benefits of medical care, behavioral interventions, or preventive programs are expressed in terms of QALYs (Kaplan, 2000).

If a man dies of heart disease at age 50 and we expected him to live to age 75, we might conclude that the disease precipitated 25 lost life-years. If 100 men died at age 50 (and also had a life expectancy of 75 years), we might conclude that 2,500 (100 men × 25 years) life-years had been lost. Yet death is not the only relevant outcome of heart disease. Many adults suffer myocardial infarctions that leave them somewhat disabled for a long time. Although they are still alive, they suffer diminished quality of life. Quality-adjusted life-years take into consideration such consequences. For example, a disease that reduces quality of life by half will take away 0.5 QALY over the course of each year. If the disease affects two people, it will take away 1 year (2 × 0.5) over each year. A medical treatment that improves quality of life by 0.2 for each of five individuals will result in the equivalent of 1 QALY if the benefit persists for 1 year. This system has the advantage of considering both benefits and side-effects of programs in terms of the common QALY units.

The need to integrate mortality and quality of life information is clearly apparent in studies of heart disease. Consider hypertension. People with high blood pressure may live shorter lives if untreated, longer if treated. Thus, one benefit of treatment is to add years to life. However, for most patients high blood pressure does not produce symptoms for many years. Conversely, the treatment for high blood pressure may cause negative side-effects. If one evaluates a treatment only in terms of changes in life expectancy, the benefits of the program will be overestimated because side-effects have not been considered. On the other hand, considering only current quality of life will underestimate the treatment benefits, because information on mortality (death) is excluded. In fact, considering only current function might make the treatment look harmful because the side-effects of the treatment might be worse than the symptoms of hypertension. A comprehensive measurement system takes into consideration side-effects and benefits, and provides an overall estimate of the benefit of treatment.

Of the several different approaches for obtaining QALYs, most are similar (Kaplan et al., 1998). The three most commonly used methods are the EQ-5D, the Health Utilities Index (HUI) and the Quality of Well-Being Scale (QWB).

EQ-5D

The approach most commonly used in Europe is the EQ-5D. This method, developed by Paul Kind and associates, was developed by a collaborative group from western Europe known as the EuroQol group (Kind, 1997). The intention of this effort was to develop a generic "currency" for health that could be used commonly across Europe. The concept of a common EuroQol was stimulated by the desire for a common European currency – the Euro dollar. The original version of the EuroQol had 14 health states in six different domains. The method was validated by postal surveys in England, Sweden, and the Netherlands. More recent versions of the EuroQol, known as the EQ-5D, are now in use in a substantial number of clinical and population studies (Gudex et al., 1996; Hurst et al., 1997). Although the EQ-5D is easy to use and comprehensive, there have been some problems with ceiling effects. Substantial numbers of people obtain the highest possible score.

Health Utilities Index

Another approach has been developed in Canada by Torrance, Feeny, Furlong and associates (Feeny et al., 1999). This method, known as the Health Utilities

Index (HUI), is derived from microeconomic theory. There have been several versions of the measure, typically identified by "Mark." The IIUI Mark I was developed for studies in the neonatal intensive care unit and had 960 unique health states. In 1992, the HUI Mark II was developed and included 24,000 unique health states. The HUI Mark III, released in 1995, had 972,000 health states. Eight components of the HUI Mark III include vision (six levels), hearing (six levels), speech (five levels), ambulation (six levels), dexterity (six levels), emotion (five levels), cognition (six levels), and pain (five levels). Multiplying the number of levels across the eight dimensions gives the 972,000 states. The HUI has been used in many population and clinical studies.

Quality of Well-Being Scale (QWB)

A third method, known as the Quality of Well-Being Scale, integrates several components into a single score. First, patients are classified according to objective levels of functioning. These are represented by the scales of mobility, physical activity, and social activity. Most traditional measures used in medicine and public health consider only whether a person is dead or alive. In other words, all living people get the same score. Yet we know that there are different levels of wellness, and there is a need to quantify these levels. To accomplish this, the observable health states are weighted by quality ratings for the desirability of these conditions. Human value studies have been conducted to place the observable states on to a preference continuum, with an anchor of 0 for death and 1.0 for completely well (Kaplan et al., 1999). Studies have shown that the weights are highly stable over a 1-year period and that they are consistent across diverse groups of raters (Kaplan, 1994a). Finally, one must consider the duration of stay in various health states. Having a cough or a headache for 1 day is not the same as having the problem for 1 year. A health measure must take these durations into consideration. Using this information, one can describe health-related quality of life in terms similar to years of life. For example, 1 year in a state assigned the weight of 0.5 is equivalent to 0.5 of a quality-adjusted life-year.

The QWB combines preference-weighted values for symptoms and functioning. The preference weights were obtained by ratings of 856 people from the general population. These judges rated the desirability of health conditions in order to place each on the continuum between death (0.00) and optimum health (1.00). Symptoms are assessed by questions that ask about the presence or absence of different symptoms complexes. Functioning is assessed by a series of questions designed to record functional limitations over the previous 6 days, within four separate domains (mobility, physical activity, social activity, and symptoms/problems). The four domain scores are combined into a total score that provides a numerical point-in-time expression of wellbeing that ranges from zero (0) for death to one (1.0) for asymptomatic optimum functioning. Table 1.1 summarizes the general quality of life scores for a variety of conditions as assessed by the Quality of Well-Being Scale.

Table 1.1   Mean QWB score by patient group

Condition	Mean QWB	Reference
Well children	0.89	Kaplan et al., 1976
General population, San Diego	0.81	Kaplan et al., 1976
Elderly men, Beaver Dam Wisconsin	0.68	Fryback et al., 1993
Elderly women, Beaver Dam Wisconsin	0.67	Fryback et al., 1993
Adults with COPD	0.66	Kaplan et al., 1984
Osteoarthritis	0.64	Groessl et al., 2001
Depression (inpatients)	0.64	Pyne et al., 1997
Advanced cancer (site varied)	0.63	Anderson et al., 1998
AIDS patients in clinical trial of AZT	0.61	Kaplan et al., 1989
Macular degeneration	0.58	Williams et al., 1998
Fibromyalgia	0.56	Kaplan et al., 2000
Alzheimer's disease	0.51	Kerner et al., 1998
Major nonhead trauma	0.46	Holbrook et al., 1994

Integrating Cost with Outcome Data

Although treatment programs provide health benefits, they also have costs. Resources are limited, and good policy requires that they be used wisely. Methodologies for estimating costs have now become standardized (Gold, 1996). From an administrative perspective, cost estimates include all costs of treatment and any costs associated with caring for the side-effects of treatment. Typically, economic discounting is applied to adjust for using current assets to achieve a future benefit. From a social perspective, costs are broader and may include the cost of family members staying off work to provide care. Comparing treatment programs for a given population with a given medical condition, cost-effectiveness is measured as the change in costs of care for the program compared to the existing therapy or program, relative to the change in health measured in a standardized unit such as the quality-adjusted life year (QALY). The difference in costs over the difference in effectiveness is the incremental cost/effectiveness and is usually expressed as the cost/QALY. Because the objective of all programs is to produce QALYs, the cost/QALY ratio can be used to show the relative health benefits from investing in different programs (Kaplan et al., 1998).

Behavioral service providers must compete with other healthcare providers for limited resources. In order to compete successfully, it will be necessary to document that behavioral services provide a benefit to the consumer. One of the advantages of using QALY outcomes is that the common metric allows for comparisons among very different types of services. All providers in the healthcare system have the common objectives of increasing length of life and improving quality of life. General quality of life outcomes, such as QALYs, allow evaluations of the relative value of investing in each of these specialties in comparison to the resources that they use. Several different countries have proposed allocating resources based on systematic data (Kaplan, 1993; Kaplan and California Policy Seminar, 1993). For example, the Australian government now requires evidence of effectiveness, as do a variety of European governments. Canada has considered the QALY as a basis for making decisions about which drugs would be purchased by the different Provinces (Detsky, 1999). This has also been considered in the United Kingdom (Williams, 1997).

Formal models of resource allocation have been implemented by at least one state in the USA. Oregon has attempted to prioritize the cost utility of different health services in an innovative experiment with their Medicaid Program (Kaplan, 1994b). One of the landmark features of the Oregon experiment was the attempt to give mental and other health services the same priority. In one list, 709 pairs of conditions and treatments were considered. Although it was ultimately not instituted, the cutoff for funding was roughly 600. Top priorities assured of funding included mental health services, such as treatment for rumination disorder of infancy, schizophrenia, AIDs dementia, and treatment for a single episode of major depression. Middle priorities also likely to be funded included services such as psychotherapy for anxiety disorder and panic disorder, and schizophrenia, simple type. However, low priority was given to services such as psychotherapy for antisocial personality disorder, psychotherapy for transsexualism, and psychotherapy for schizoid personality disorder.

The World Bank and the World Health Organization have also recognized that traditional health indicators, such as life expectancy and infant mortality, may be relatively unaffected by many of the investments in public health for the developing world. They used measures of disability-adjusted life-years (DALYs), which are very similar to QALYs (Murray and Lopez, 1996). In order to calculate DALYs, they considered 109 diseases that represent about 95% of all deaths in the world. Using the 1990 mortality data, they estimated the distribution of these diseases by age, sex, and demographic region of the world. Next, they estimated mortality from each of these diseases and created life tables for each condition by region. The next step involved healthy life expectancy estimates for these regions using experts to judge the distribution in disability levels by diagnostic category. Finally, expert judgment was used to create qualitative ratings for levels of disability.

Considering only life expectancy, conditions such as osteoarthritis and depression do not appear to be major public health problems. These conditions affect quality of life but have relatively little impact on life expectancy. Using the DALY methodology, WHO and the World Bank evaluated world health problems and concluded that there was too much effort being directed toward infectious diseases, such as the Ebola virus. In terms of DALYs lost, mental illness is the leading threat to worldwide health. Non-communicable problems, such as smoking and traffic accidents, are second and third. The authors of the study noted that traditional indicators that consider only death tend to ignore some of the most important health problems associated with psychological and psychiatric illnesses. However, using a weighted system that places all outcomes in the same measurement units suggests that these problems should be given much higher priority (Murray and Lopez, 1996).

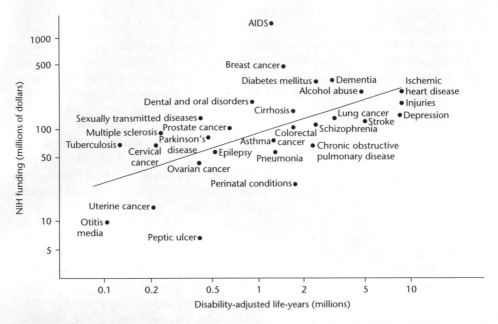

Figure 1.1 Relation between NIH disease-specific research funding in 1996 and disability-adjusted life-years for 29 conditions. From Gross, C. P. (1999), *New England Journal of Medicine*, 340, 1881–1887. Reprinted with permission. Copyright © 1999 Massachusetts Medical Society. All rights reserved.

Recently, Gross, Anderson, and Powe (1999) evaluated the relationship between National Institutes of Health (NIH) funding and burden of disease. They noted that the relationship between incidence, prevalence, and number of hospital days attributed to a variety of diseases was unrelated to NIH funding for these problems. Similarly, the number of deaths and the number of life-years lost were only weakly correlated. However, DALYs lost to each condition were strongly associated with NIH funding for those problems (see figure 1.1). The results suggest that NIH funding decisions are responsive to disease burden (Gross et al., 1999). Of course, there are some unusual cases. For example, HIV and AIDS have only a small effect on DALYs but attract a large amount of NIH funding. However, left unchecked, these diseases might be associated with the loss of many DALYs in the future.

Disease Targeted Measures and their Applications in Selected Chronic Diseases

In addition to generic measures, many QOL measures have been developed for application in specific diseases. In this section, selected disease-targeted measures will be described and compared with generic approaches.

Arthritis

Musculoskeletal disorders are among the most common and most disabling medical conditions. Kelsey and her colleagues have analyzed the Health and Nutrition Examination Survey (HANES) data from 1971 to 1975 in an effort to determine the impact of musculoskeletal disorders on quality of life and role function (Kelsey et al., 1979). Musculoskeletal problems were found to rank first among conditions producing "impairment – a chronic and permanent defect representing a decrease or loss of ability to perform various functions." This was true of both men and women of all age groups (Lawrence et al., 1989). Furthermore, musculoskeletal impairments ranked second regarding number of physician office visits, third regarding number of surgeries, and fourth regarding the number of hospital visits. The category "arthritis and rheumatism" was found to be the most common cause of disability for subjects aged 18–64 years. The total economic cost of musculoskeletal conditions was estimated at $20 billion per year.

Historically, the nonfatal nature of arthritis and related conditions has made it difficult to assess and express the "outcome" of these disorders. Recent improvements in outcome measures have helped portray the impact of arthritis upon function, disability, and quality of life. Data have indicated that over 21% of the population reporting musculoskeletal symptoms experience moderate or severe restriction of activity. Eighteen percent of these patients have a change in their job status (Cunningham and Kelsey, 1984). In one study, 60% of the patients with rheumatoid arthritis (RA) were considered disabled (Yelin et al., 1980). Meenan and colleagues (Meenan et al., 1981) reported that persons with RA who were able to work earned only 50% of their expected income, and 63% experienced major psychosocial changes as a result of their disease. Although RA is a more costly disease to care for than osteoarthritis (OA), OA is more common and the societal costs may be seven times higher (Lanes et al., 1997).

Focus on functional outcomes deviates from the traditional medical model. Even the biopsychosocial model (Engel, 1977) concentrates on sickness and its causes. Attention is directed toward the psychological or environmental etiology and the physiological lesion (Kaplan, 2000). These models have directed measurement toward assessment of disease categories, characteristics of lesions, and disease risk factors. In most areas of medicine measures of blood chemistry, physical characteristics, and blood or tissue sensitivity to medication are given the greatest attention. As Deyo has suggested, outcome measures in studies of rheumatology have been difficult to evaluate because they typically focus on clinical measures such as joint tenderness, grip strength, and joint circumference (Deyo, 1988).

Some studies have shown that the reliability of these clinical outcome measures is often poor (Kaplan, 2000). However, laboratory measures may be even less useful. Fries (1983) questions the relevance and reliability of a variety of traditional outcome measures, ranging from laboratory measures of erythrocyte sedimentation rate (ESR) to latex fixation titer, and hemoglobin (Fries, 1983). In addition, Fries suggested that traditional clinical measures

Table 1.2 Summary of American Rheumatism Association (ARA) functional classification system

Class	Definition
I	Complete functional capacity with the ability to carry on all usual duties without handicaps
II	Functional capacity adequate to conduct normal activities despite handicap of discomfort or limited mobility of one or more joints
III	Functional capacity adequate to perform only few or none of the duties of the usual occupation or self-care
IV	Largely or wholly incapacitated with patient bedridden or confined to wheelchair, permitting little or no self-care

such as grip strength, walking time, and patient global assessment are merely surrogates for true outcome in arthritis. The real outcomes are disability, physical discomfort, and financial impact. Laboratory findings may be predictive of this dysfunction and are only important for that reason. However, serological abnormalities often do not coincide precisely with joint inflammation or any other measured functional outcome (McCarty, 1979).

The American Rheumatism Association (ARA) has promoted functional assessment for many years. In 1949, they introduced a simple scale for the classification of patients with arthritis (see table 1.2). This scale has been used extensively in clinical studies and patient care. It has been shown to have moderate negative correlations with grip strength and positive correlation with ESR and X-rays (Deyo, 1988). However, the ARA scale has well known drawbacks. The major problem is that the four broad categories are very limited for capturing health changes due to treatment. Studies have demonstrated that over half of the patients with RA are in functional class II (Meenan et al., 1981), suggesting that the measure has difficulty in making fine distinctions. Deyo (1988) also criticized the ambiguity of the terms used in the classification system. For example, there is no explication in the definition of "normal activities" or "usual duties." In general, the ARA scale appears far too crude to use as an outcome measure in clinical trials (Deyo et al., 1983).

Arthritis Impact Measurement Scale (AIMS)

The most widely used specific measure for arthritis is the Arthritis Impact Measurement Scale (AIMS). This is a health index designed at the Multipurpose Arthritis Center at Boston University and is intended to measure physical health and social wellbeing for patients with rheumatoid arthritis (Meenan, 1982). The resultant scale includes 67 items, with questions about functioning, health perceptions, morbidity, and demographics (Meenan, 1982; Meenan et al., 1980). The AIMS contains scales for mobility, physical activity, social activity, activities of daily living, depression and anxiety, and arthritis-related symptoms. In effect, it is an adaptation of an early version of the QWB (Kaplan et al., 1998), with a series of items designed to tap more specifically the effect of arthritis upon functioning and the quality of life. Factor analysis of the AIMS has produced three subscales: physical function, psychological function, and pain. Most current applications of the AIMS use composite scores for these three areas.

The psychometric properties of the AIMS were evaluated in a study involving 625 patients with rheumatoid disease. Alpha reliabilities were found to be acceptable (> 0.7) for the various subscales, and the mean test–retest correlation, over an interval of 2 weeks, was 0.87. In order to assess validity, the investigators correlated AIMS scores with physician ratings of health status, and these correlations were found to be highly significant. In addition, AIMS subscores were found to have convergent and discriminant validity when correlated with specific measures used in rheumatology research. For example, the physical activity portion of the AIMS correlated more highly with walking time than with grip strength. A dexterity scale of the AIMS was significantly correlated with grip strength but did not correlate significantly with walking time.

A review of 35 papers on health outcome for arthritis patients suggested that most of the studies were narrowly focused (Coons and Kaplan, 1993). Most did not attempt to measure overall health-related quality of life (and therefore did not define it). Few studies offered any theoretical model of health status or health-related quality of life. The most commonly used disease-specific measure was the AIMS, whereas the most commonly used general measure was the QWB. In contrast to other literatures we have reviewed, most arthritis studies presented at least some evidence for the reliability and validity of the measure. However, the validity criteria varied significantly across studies. Most studies validated measures against clinical judgments or other clinical measures: very few were treatment evaluations. In addition, very few considered the relative importance of the dimensions; the exceptions are: Balaban et al. (1986), Bombardier et al. (1986), Helewa et al. (1982), and Strand et al. (1999).

There have been several applications of the generic measures for the evaluation of surgical interventions, such as total joint replacement. Liang and colleagues compared different outcome measures for the evaluation of total joint replacement in several studies (Liang et al., 1990). In one paper they administered the QWB, along with the AIMS, the Sickness Impact Profile (SIP), and the HAQ to 38 patients with severe arthritis. The instruments were given prior to total hip or knee replacement, and after 3 months, 12 months, and 15 months. All of the instruments demonstrated a significant improvement in functioning following the surgery. For early response to treatment, the QWB demonstrated the largest effect size among the measures that were considered. However, the AIMS showed more sensitivity to global change in long-term follow-up.

HIV

In addition to the opportunistic infections and malignancies that define AIDS, HIV infection may cause a broad range of diseases. These conditions include persistent lymphadenopathy, thrombocytopenia, immune complex disease, wasting, various constitutional symptoms, and HIV neurologic diseases. The impact of HIV infection on functioning is equally diverse. For example, HIV infection may result in fatigue, arthritis, blindness, memory loss, or paraplegia. Treatments for HIV infection should be designed to prevent early mortality and to reduce morbidity during periods before death. The diverse impacts of both HIV disease and its treatment require a general approach to assessment.

There have been several previous attempts to evaluate quality of life in HIV-infected patients. However, most of these have focused only on psychological outcomes. A number of studies have attempted to characterize the health status and economic impacts of HIV infection, and we are aware of only a few that have applied general health-related quality of life scales (Hays and Shapiro, 1992; Kaplan et al., 1997a; Lubeck and Fries, 1993; Nieuwkerk et al., 2000; Revicki et al., 1998; Scott-Lennox et al., 1999). Several brief health status measures derived from the MOS are now being used with HIV-infected patients, including the SF-36 (Stewart and Ware, 1992), the 30-item MOS-HIV (Revicki et al., 1998; Wu et al., 1991); and the 30-item AIDS-HAQ (Lubeck and Fries, 1993) and SF-56 (Hays and Shapiro, 1992) designed for use in ongoing cohort studies.

The MOS measures have been used more extensively in AIDS/HIV clinical trials and cohort studies than any other measure. In general, these studies have shown that the MOS measures are easy to administer, have good reliability and construct validity, and correlate well with known differences in clinical states. The MOS measures have also been used to identify treatment effects in clinical trials of antiretroviral (Jacobson et al., 1997) and antimicrobial agents (Wu et al., 1991). As specific dimensions are measured by sets of overlapping or identical items, these studies provide evidence for the validity of this entire family of instruments for use in HIV disease.

Measures of quality of life have been evaluated in relation to physiologic, neurological, and psychological outcomes for patients with HIV disease. One example study evaluated 514 men who were in four different disease states. All participants in this study had acquired the illness through sexual contact with other males. One group was uninfected controls with a similar lifestyle ($n = 114$). The Centers for Disease Control identifies three levels of disease progression. Group A was infected but asymptomatic ($n = 272$), group B had minor symptomatic complications of HIV disease ($n = 81$), and group C had major symptomatic complications ($n = 47$). General quality of life measures systematically discriminated between these groups. The generic Quality of Well-Being Scale demonstrated that those in the control group had highest quality of life scores, followed systematically by those in the other groups (see figure 1.2). Patients with major symptomatic complications obtained QWB scores that were about 0.14 units of wellbeing lower than the asymptomatic group. This suggests that individuals lose about 1/7 (calculated as 1.0/0.14) of a quality-adjusted life-year compared to the asymptomatic group. Compared to controls, the effect of the illness would be equal to about 1 year of life lost for each seven infected individuals.

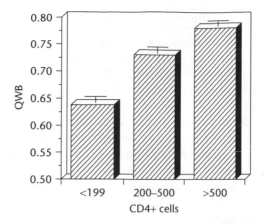

Figure 1.2 Concurrent relationship between CD4+ lymphocytes CDC classification and QWB scores. From Kaplan, R. M., Anderson, J. P., and Patterson, T. (1995), *Psychosomatic Medicine*, 57, 138–147.

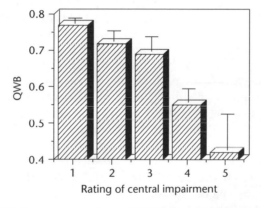

Figure 1.3 Relationship between neurologist global ratings of impairment and QWB scale scores. Higher impairment ratings indicate greater impairment. From Kaplan, R. M., McCutchan, J. A., Navarro, A. M., and Anderson J. P. (1994), *Psychology and Health*, 9, 131–141.

The HIV patients were evaluated on a wide range of physiologic and neurologic tests. The general QWB scale was systematically associated with CD4+ lymphocytes, clinician ratings of neuropsychological impairment, neurologists' ratings of dysfunction, and all scales of the Profile of Mood States (POMS). The relationship between quality of life and neurological function is shown in figure 1.3. Higher scores on the neurological impairment scale were related to lower scores on the QWB Scale. Moreover, baseline scores on the Quality of Well-Being Scale systematically predicted survival over an interval of 2.5 years (Kaplan et al., 1997a). A variety of other studies have also shown systematic relationships between physiologic and quality of life scores for HIV-infected patients (Hays and Shapiro, 1992; Lubeck and Fries, 1993; Revicki et al., 1998). Overall, quality of life appears to be a good predictor of remaining life expectancy for such patients.

Chronic Obstructive Pulmonary Disease

Chronic obstructive pulmonary disease (COPD) is a disease state associated with airflow obstruction due to chronic bronchitis or emphysema. COPD has a profound effect upon functioning and everyday life, and patients experience significant limitations in their daily activities. Current estimates suggest that COPD affects nearly 11% of the adult population and the incidence is increasing. Newer trends indicate that the rate of COPD among women is increasing to reflect the increase in tobacco use among women in the later part of the 20th century. Reviews of the medical management of COPD justify the use of symptomatic measures, including bronchodilators, corticosteroids, and antibiotic therapy. In addition, long-term oxygen therapy has been shown to be beneficial for patients with severe hypoxemia (Edelman et al., 1992). However, it is widely recognized that these measures cannot cure COPD, and that much of the effort in the management of this condition must be directed toward improving symptoms, patient functioning, and quality of life.

Most medical interventions for COPD have little or no effect on measures of pulmonary function, and there is increasing recognition that treatments must be evaluated on the basis of patient experience. A variety of quality of life measures have been used in studies of COPD patients. An example of a disease-specific measure is the University of California, San Diego, Shortness of Breath Questionnaire (SOBQ). This measure includes 25 items that evaluate self-reported shortness of breath during the performance of various activities of daily living. Evaluations of the measure show it is highly correlated with other quality of life measures, such as the Quality of Well-Being Scale and the Center for Epidemiologic Studies Depression Scale. The measure has high internal consistency ($\alpha = 0.96$) and is significantly correlated with performance measures such as the amount of distance that can be walked in 6 minutes (Eakin et al., 1998).

Generic quality of life measures, often used in cost-effectiveness studies, are now being applied in major clinical trials for patients with COPD. One example is the National Emphysema Treatment Trial (NETT), which is a multicenter randomized trial of lung-volume reduction surgery (LVRS). Patients in the trial are randomly assigned to LVRS or to maximal medical therapy. Two of the major questions in this study are whether or not the surgery results in improvements in quality of life and whether it is cost-effective in relation to other alternatives (Ramsey et al., 2000). Four quality of life measures are applied in the ongoing study: the Quality of Well-Being Scale (QWB) (Kaplan et al., 1998), the SF-36 (Ware and Gandek, 1998), the St. George's Respiratory Questionnaire (Jones, 1995), and the UCSD Shortness of Breath Questionnaire (Eakin et al., 1998). Early evidence indicates substantial validity for each of these measures (Kaplan, et al., submitted).

Remaining Challenges for Quality of Life Research

Quality of life research is a relatively new area of investigation. Over the last decade, the number of papers on quality of life measurement has increased dramatically and quality of life measures have become a mainstream component of medical outcomes research. However, there are significant challenges ahead. One of the most challenging questions is in identifying appropriate quality of life measures for research. There has been a remarkable proliferation of disease-targeted measures, and many measures are used in only a few studies. As a result, it is difficult to compare results across studies. On the other hand, the number of well-validated generic measures remains limited. Additional study is needed in order to determine the responsiveness of generic measures for patients in specific disease categories.

Future research also is necessary to identify the clinical meaning of quality of life measures. Although the use of such measures in clinical practice is becoming more common, most clinicians do not know whether the changes they observe on questionnaires are meaningful. More work is needed involving attempts to calibrate QOL measures against clinical and physiological parameters. Finally, evaluations of patient outcomes are important for determining the cost-effectiveness of healthcare. QOL measures can be used to estimate the relative value of investments in various services. These analyses not only consider whether patients improve, but also determine whether investments in particular programs are good uses of healthcare resources. Cost-effectiveness studies are often controversial, and continued refinement of the methodologies will be important.

Summary

Current healthcare is built on an acute disease model. However, most resources are used for chronic illnesses. Measurement of outcomes for chronic illnesses requires a different conceptualization of health. The outcomes model is an alternative perspective that focuses on duration and quality of life. From the outcomes perspective, quality of life measures are essential to the assessment of treatment effectiveness.

Quality of life measures evolve from two different measurement traditions: psychometric theory and decision theory. Psychometric methods, such as the SF-36, typically create a profile of outcomes, whereas decision theory methods, such as the QWB, attempt to portray an integrative summary judgment of health. Decision theory methods are better suited for cost-effectiveness studies.

A review of current outcomes research for chronic diseases such as arthritis, HIV infection, and COPD shows that quality of life measures are now commonly used. There is substantial evidence for the validity of these measures in many chronic illnesses, and quality of life data are now commonly used in major clinical trials and in public policy analysis.

References

Anderson, J. P., Kaplan, R. M., Coons, S. J., and Schneiderman, L. J. (1998). Comparison of the quality of well-being scale and the SF-36 results among two samples of ill adults: AIDS and other illnesses. *Journal of Clinical Epidemiology*, 51(9), 755–762.

Balaban, D. J., Sagi, P. C., Goldfarb, N. I., and Nettler, S. (1986). Weights for scoring the quality of well-being instrument among rheumatoid arthritics. A comparison to general population weights. *Medical Care*, 24, 973–980.

Bergner, M., Bobbitt, R. A., Carter, W. B., and Gilson, B. S. (1981). The Sickness Impact Profile: Development and final revision of a health status measure. *Medical Care*, 19, 787–805.

Bombardier, C., Ware, J., Russell, I. J., Larson, M., Chalmers, A., and Read, J. L. (1986). Auranofin therapy and quality of life in patients with rheumatoid arthritis. Results of a multicenter trial. *American Journal of Medicine*, 81, 565–578.

Brown, M., Gordon, W. A., and Haddad, L. (2000). Models for predicting subjective quality of life in individuals with traumatic brain injury. *Brain Injury*, 14, 5–19.

Coons, S. J., and Kaplan, R. M. (1993). Quality of life assessment: Understanding its use as an outcome measure. *Hospital Formulary*, 28, 486–498.

Coronary Primary Prevention Trial. (1984a). The Lipid Research Clinics Coronary Primary Prevention Trial results. I. Reduction in incidence of coronary heart disease. *Journal of the American Medical Association*, 251, 351–364.

Coronary Primary Prevention Trial. (1984b). The Lipid Research Clinics Coronary Primary Prevention Trial results. II. The relationship of reduction in incidence of coronary heart disease to cholesterol lowering. *Journal of the American Medical Association*, 251, 365–374.

Cunningham, L. S., and Kelsey, J. L. (1984). Epidemiology of musculoskeletal impairments and associated disability. *American Journal of Public Health*, 74, 574–579.

Detsky, A. S. (1999). Economics and cost-effectiveness in evaluating the value of cardiovascular therapies. Terminology I would like to see disappear. *American Heart Journal*, 137, S51–52.

Deyo, R. A. (1988). Measuring the functional status of patients with low back pain. *Archives of Physical Medicine and Rehabilitation*, 69, 1044–1053.

Deyo, R. A., Inui, T. S., Leininger, J. D., and Overman, S. S. (1983). Measuring functional outcomes in chronic disease: A comparison of traditional scales and a self-administered health status questionnaire in patients with rheumatoid arthritis. *Medical Care*, 21, 180–192.

Eakin, E. G., Kaplan, R. M., and Ries, A. L. (1993). Measurement of dyspnea in chronic obstructive pulmonary disease. *Quality of Life Research*, 2, 181–191.

Eakin, E. G., Resnikoff, P. M., Prewitt, L. M., Ries, A. L., and Kaplan, R. M. (1998). Validation of a new dyspnea measure: The UCSD Shortness of Breath Questionnaire. University of California, San Diego. *Chest*, 113, 619–624.

Edelman, N. H., Kaplan, R. M., Buist, A. S., Cohen, A. B., Hoffman, L. A., Kleinhenz, M. E., Snider, G. L., and Speizer, F. E. (1992). Chronic obstructive pulmonary disease. Task Force on Research and Education for the Prevention and Control of Respiratory Diseases. *Chest*, 102, 243S–256S.

Engel, G. L. (1977). The need for a new medical model: A challenge for biomedicine. *Science*, 196, 129–136.

Feeny, D., Furlong, W., Mulhern, R. K., Barr, R. D., and Hudson, M. (1999). A framework for assessing health-related quality of life among children with cancer. *International Journal of Cancer. Supplement*, 12(9 Suppl), 2–9.

Fries, J. F. (1983). The assessment of disability: From first to future principles. *British Journal of Rheumatology*, 22, 48–58.

Fryback, D. G., Dasbach, E. J., Klein, R., Klein, B. E., Dorn, N., Peterson, K., and Martin, P. A. (1993). The Beaver Dam Health Outcomes Study: Initial catalog of health-state quality factors. *Medical Decision Making*, 13, 89–102.

Galbraith, J. K. (1958). *The Affluent Society*. Boston: Houghton Mifflin.

Gold, M. R. (1996). *Cost-Effectiveness in Health and Medicine*. New York: Oxford University Press.

Golomb, B. A. (1998). Cholesterol and violence: Is there a connection [see comments]? *Annals of Internal Medicine*, 128, 478–487.

Groessl, E., Kaplan, R. M., and Cronan, T. A. (2001). Quality of well-being in osteoarthritis. Submitted.

Gross, C. P., Anderson, G. F., and Powe, N. R. (1999). The relation between funding by the National Institutes of Health and the burden of disease [see comments]. *New England Journal of Medicine*, 340, 1881–1887.

Gudex, C., Dolan, P., Kind, P., and Williams, A. (1996). Health state valuations from the general public using the visual analogue scale. *Quality of Life Research*, 5, 521–531.

Hays, R. D., and Shapiro, M. F. (1992). An overview of generic health-related quality of life measures for HIV research. *Quality of Life Research*, 1, 91–97.

Helewa, A., Goldsmith, C. H., and Smythe, H. A. (1982). Independent measurement of functional capacity in rheumatoid arthritis. *Journal of Rheumatology*, 9, 794–797.

Holbrook, T. L., Hoyt, D. B., Anderson, J. P., Hollingsworth-Fridlund, P., and Shackford, S. R. (1994). Functional limitation after major trauma: A more sensitive assessment using the Quality of Well-being scale – the trauma recovery pilot project. *Journal of Trauma*, 36, 74–78.

Holman, H., and Lorig, K. (2000). Patients as partners in managing chronic disease. Partnership is a prerequisite for effective and efficient healthcare [editorial; comment]. *British Medical Journal (Clinical Research Ed.)*, 320, 526–527.

Hurst, N. P., Kind, P., Ruta, D., Hunter, M., and Stubbings, A. (1997). Measuring health-related quality of life in rheumatoid arthritis: Validity, responsiveness and reliability of EuroQol (EQ-5D). *British Journal of Rheumatology*, 36, 551–559.

Jacobson, J. M., Greenspan, J. S., Spritzler, J., Ketter, N., Fahey, J. L., Jackson, J. B., Fox, L., Chernoff, M., Wu, A. W., MacPhail, L. A., Vasquez, G. J., and Wohl, D. A. (1997). Thalidomide for the treatment of oral aphthous ulcers in patients with human immunodeficiency virus infection. National Institute of Allergy and Infectious Diseases AIDS Clinical Trials Group [see comments]. *New England Journal of Medicine*, 336, 1487–1493.

Jones, P. W. (1995). Issues concerning health-related quality of life in COPD. *Chest*, 107, 187S–193S.

Kaplan, R. M. (1990). Behavior as the central outcome in healthcare. *American Psychologist*, 45, 1211–1220.

Kaplan, R. M. (1993). *The Hippocratic Predicament: Affordability, Access, and Accountability in American Medicine*. San Diego: Academic Press.

Kaplan, R. M. (1994a). The Ziggy theorem: Toward an outcomes-focused health psychology. *Health Psychology*, 13, 451–460.

Kaplan, R. M. (1994b). Value judgment in the Oregon Medicaid experiment. *Medical Care*, 32, 975–988.

Kaplan, R. M. (1996). Measuring health outcomes for resource allocation. In Robert L. Glueckauf, Robert G. Frank et al. (Eds.), *Psychological Practice in a Changing Healthcare System: Issues and New Directions* (pp. 101–133). New York: Springer.

Kaplan, R. M. (2000). Two pathways to prevention. *American Psychologist*, 55, 382–396.

Kaplan, R. M., Anderson, J. P., Wu, A. W., Mathews, W. C., Kozin, F., and Orenstein, D. (1989). The Quality of Well-being Scale. Applications in AIDS, cystic fibrosis, and arthritis. *Medical Care*, 27(3 Suppl), S27–43.

Kaplan, R. M., Atkins, C. J., and Timms, R. (1984). Validity of a quality of well-being scale as an outcome measure in chronic obstructive pulmonary disease. *Journal of Chronic Diseases*, 37(2), 85–95.

Kaplan, R. M., and Bush, J. W. (1982). Health-related quality of life measurement for evaluation research and policy analysis. *Health Psychology*, 1, 61–80.

Kaplan, R. M., Bush, J. W., and Berry, C. C. (1976). Health status: types of validity and the index of well-being. *Health Services Research*, 11, 478–507.

Kaplan, R. M., and California Policy Seminar. (1993). *Allocating Health Resources in California: Learning from the Oregon Experiment*. Berkeley, CA: California Policy Seminar.

Kaplan, R. M., Feeny, D., and Revicki, D. A. (1999). Methods for assessing relative importance in preference based outcome measures. In C. R. B. Joyce, Hannah M. McGee et al. (Eds.), *Individual Quality of Life: Approaches to Conceptualisation and Assessment* (pp. 135–149). Amsterdam, Netherlands: Harwood Academic Publishers.

Kaplan, R. M., Ganiats, T. G., Sieber, W. J., and Anderson, J. P. (1998). The Quality of Well-Being Scale: Critical similarities and differences with SF-36 [see comments]. *International Journal for Quality in Healthcare*, 10, 509–520.

Kaplan, R. M., Patterson, T. L., Kerner, D. N., Atkinson, J. H., Heaton, R. K., and Grant, I. (1997a). The Quality of Well-Being scale in asymptomatic HIV-infected patients. HNRC Group. HIV Neural Behavioral Research Center. *Quality of Life Research*, 6, 507–514.

Kaplan, R. M., Reilly, J., and Mohsenifar, Z. (2000). Measurement of health-related quality of life in the National Emphysema Treatment Trial (NETT). *American Journal of Respiratory and Critical Care Medicine*, 161(3 (Suppl.).

Kaplan, R. M., Ries, A. L., Reilly, J. J., and Mohsenifar, Z. (submitted). Measurement of health-related quality of life in the National Emphysema Treatment Trial (NETT). Submitted for publication, November, 2001.

Kaplan, R. M., Schmidt, S. M., and Cronan, T. A. (2000). Quality of well being in patients with fibromyalgia. *Journal of Rheumatology*, 27, 785–789.

Keller, S. D., Ware, J. E., Jr., Hatoum, H. T., and Kong, S. X. (1999). The SF-36 Arthritis-Specific Health Index (ASHI): II. Tests of validity in four clinical trials. *Medical Care*, 37, MS51–60.

Kelsey, J. L., White, A. A. D., Pastides, H., and Bisbee, G. E., Jr. (1979). The impact of musculoskeletal disorders on the population of the United States. *Journal of Bone and Joint Surgery. American Volume*, 61, 959–964.

Kerner, D. N., Patterson, T. L., Grant, I., and Kaplan, R. M. (1998). Validity of the Quality of Well-Being Scale for patients with Alzheimer's disease. *Journal of Aging and Health*, 10, 44–61.

Kind, P. (1997). The performance characteristics of EQ-5D, a measure of health related quality of life for use in technology assessment [abstract]. *Annual Meeting of International Society of Technology Assessment in Health Care*, 13, 81.

Koloski, N. A., Talley, N. J., and Boyce, P. M. (2000). The impact of functional gastrointestinal disorders on quality of life. *American Journal of Gastroenterology*, 95, 67–71.

Kosinski, M., Keller, S. D., Hatoum, H. T., Kong, S. X., and Ware, J. E., Jr. (1999a). The SF-36 Health Survey as a generic outcome measure in clinical trials of patients with osteoarthritis and rheumatoid arthritis: tests of data quality, scaling assumptions and score reliability. *Medical Care*, 37, MS10–22.

Kosinski, M., Keller, S. D., Ware, J. E., Jr., Hatoum, H. T., and Kong, S. X. (1999b). The SF-36 Health Survey as a generic outcome measure in clinical trials of patients with osteoarthritis and rheumatoid arthritis: Relative validity of scales in relation to clinical measures of arthritis severity. *Medical Care*, 37, MS23–39.

Lanes, S. F., Lanza, L. L., Radensky, P. W., Yood, R. A., Meenan, R. F., Walker, A. M., and Dreyer, N. A. (1997). Resource utilization and cost of care for rheumatoid arthritis and osteoarthritis in a managed care setting: The importance of drug and surgery costs. *Arthritis and Rheumatism*, 40, 1475–1481.

Lawrence, R. C., Hochberg, M. C., Kelsey, J. L., McDuffie, F. C., Medsger, T. A., Jr., Felts, W. R., and Shulman, L. E. (1989). Estimates of the prevalence of selected arthritic and musculoskeletal diseases in the United States. *Journal of Rheumatology*, 16, 427–441.

Liang, M. H., Fossel, A. H., and Larson, M. G. (1990). Comparisons of five health status instruments for orthopedic evaluation. *Medical Care*, 28, 632–642.

Lowe, D., O'Grady, J. G., McEwen, J., and Williams, R. (1990). Quality of life following liver transplantation: a preliminary report. *Journal of the Royal College of Physicians of London*, 24, 43–46.

Lubeck, D. P., and Fries, J. F. (1993). Health status among persons infected with human immunodeficiency virus. A community-based study. *Medical Care*, 31, 269–276.

McCarty, D. J. (1979). The management of gout. *Hospital Practice*, 14, 75–78, 83–75.

McDowell, I., and Newell, C. (1996). *Measuring Health: A Guide to Rating Scales and Questionnaires* (2nd edn.). New York: Oxford University Press.

McEwen, J. (1992). The Nottingham Health Profile. In S. R. Walker, and R. M. Rosser (Eds.), *Quality of Life Assessment: Key Issues for the 1990s*. Dordrecht: Kluwer Academic Publishers.

McGinnis, J. M., and Foege, W. H. (1993). Actual causes of death in the United States [see comments]. *Journal of the American Medical Association*, 270, 2207–2212.

Meenan, R. F. (1982). The AIMS approach to health status measurement: Conceptual background and measurement properties. *Journal of Rheumatology*, 9, 785–788.

Meenan, R. F., Gertman, P. M., and Mason, J. H. (1980). Measuring health status in arthritis. The arthritis impact measurement scales. *Arthritis and Rheumatism*, 23, 146–152.

Meenan, R. F., Yelin, E. H., Nevitt, M., and Epstein, W. V. (1981). The impact of chronic disease: A sociomedical profile of rheumatoid arthritis. *Arthritis and Rheumatism*, 24, 544–549.

Murray, C. J., and Lopez, A. D. (1996). Evidence-based health policy – lessons from the Global Burden of Disease Study. *Science*, 274, 740–743.

Nieuwkerk, P. T., Gisolf, E. H., Colebunders, R., Wu, A. W., Danner, S. A., and Sprangers, M. A. (2000). Quality of life in asymptomatic- and symptomatic HIV infected patients in a trial of ritonavir/saquinavir therapy. The Prometheus Study Group. *Aids*, 14, 181–187.

Pyne, J. M., Patterson, T. L., Kaplan, R. M., Ho, S., Gillin, J. C., Golshan, S., and Grant, I. (1997). Preliminary longitudinal assessment of quality of life in patients with major depression. *Psychopharmacology Bulletin*, 33, 23–29.

Ramsey, S. D., Sullivan, S. D., Kaplan, R. M., Wood, D. E., Wagner, J., and Chiang, Y. (2000). Economic analysis of lung volume reduction surgery as part of the National Emphysema Treatment Trial. *Annals of Surgery*, in press.

Revicki, D. A., Sorensen, S., and Wu, A. W. (1998). Reliability and validity of physical and mental health summary scores from the Medical Outcomes Study HIV Health Survey. *Medical Care*, 36, 126–137.

Scott-Lennox, J. A., Wu, A. W., Boyer, J. G., and Ware, J. E., Jr. (1999). Reliability and validity of French, German, Italian, Dutch, and UK English translations of the Medical Outcomes Study HIV Health Survey. *Medical Care*, 37, 908–925.

Shumaker, S. A., and Berzon, R. (1995). *The International Assessment of Health-Related Quality of Life: Theory, Translation, Measurement and Analysis*. New York: Oxford.

Stewart, A. L., and Ware, J. E. (1992). *Measuring Functioning and Well-Being: the Medical Outcomes Study Approach*. Durham, NC: Duke University Press.

Strand, V., Tugwell, P., Bombardier, C., Maetzel, A., Crawford, B., Dorrier, C., Thompson, A., and Wells, G. (1999). Function and health-related quality of life:

Results from a randomized controlled trial of leflunomide versus methotrexate or placebo in patients with active rheumatoid arthritis. Leflunomide Rheumatoid Arthritis Investigators Group. *Arthritis and Rheumatism*, 42, 1870–1878.

Strömbeck, B., Ekdahl, C., Manthorpe, R., Wikström, I., and Jacobsson, L. (2000). Health-related quality of life in primary Sjögren's syndrome, rheumatoid arthritis and fibromyalgia compared to normal population data using SF-36. *Scandinavian Journal of Rheumatology*, 29, 20–28.

Sullivan, D. F. (1966). *Conceptual Problems in Developing an Index of Health*. Washington, D.C.: U. S. Dept. of Health Education and Welfare Public Health Service.

Van Hoosier, G. L. (2000). Principles and paradigms used in human medical ethics can be used as models for the assessment of animal research. *Comparative Medicine*, 50, 103–106.

Walker, S. R., and Rosser, R. (1993). *Quality of Life Assessment: Key Issues in the 1990s*. Dordrecht/Boston: Kluwer Academic Publishers.

Ware, J., Bayliss, M. S., Mannocchia, M., and Davis, G. L. (1999). Health-related quality of life in chronic hepatitis C: Impact of disease and treatment response. The Interventional Therapy Group. *Hepatology*, 30, 550–555.

Ware, J. E., Jr., Bayliss, M. S., Rogers, W. H., Kosinski, M., and Tarlov, A. R. (1996). Differences in 4-year health outcomes for elderly and poor, chronically ill patients treated in HMO and fee-for-service systems. Results from the Medical Outcomes Study [see comments]. *Journal of the American Medical Association*, 276, 1039–1047.

Ware, J. E., Jr., and Gandek, B. (1998). Overview of the SF-36 Health Survey and the International Quality of Life Assessment (IQOLA) Project. *Journal of Clinical Epidemiology*, 51, 903–912.

Weymuller, E. A., Yueh, B., Deleyiannis, F. W., Kuntz, A. L., Alsarraf, R., and Coltrera, M. D. (2000). Quality of life in patients with head and neck cancer: Lessons learned from 549 prospectively evaluated patients. *Archives of Otolaryngology – Head and Neck Surgery*, 126, 329–335; Discussion 335–326.

Williams, A. (1997). Cochrane Lecture. All cost effective treatments should be free . . . or, how Archie Cochrane changed my life! *Journal of Epidemiology and Community Health*, 51, 116–120.

Williams, R. A., Brody, B. L., Thomas, R. G., Kaplan, R. M., and Brown, S. I. (1998). The psychosocial impact of macular degeneration. *Archives of Ophthalmology*, 116, 514–520.

World Health Organization (WHO) (1948). *Constitution of the World Health Organization*. New York: World Health Organization.

Wu, A. W., Rubin, H. R., Mathews, W. C., Ware, J. E., Jr., Brysk, L. T., Hardy, W. D., Bozzette, S. A., Spector, S. A., and Richman, D. D. (1991). A health status questionnaire using 30 items from the Medical Outcomes Study. Preliminary validation in persons with early HIV infection. *Medical Care*, 29, 786–798.

Yelin, E., Meenan, R., Nevitt, M., and Epstein, W. (1980). Work disability in rheumatoid arthritis: Effects of disease, social, and work factors. *Annals of Internal Medicine*, 93, 551–556.

CHAPTER 2

Social Psychological Aspects of Chronic Illness

Vicki S. Helgeson and Kerry A. Reynolds

Carnegie Mellon University

Introduction

Since the later half of the 20th century the leading causes of death have involved chronic diseases, in particular heart disease and cancer. These diseases are complicated because they are not caused by single agents: they are caused by multiple factors, and many of these have to do with a person's lifestyle, such as smoking, diet, and exercise. More importantly for the purposes of this chapter, people not only die of chronic diseases, they live with them – often for a long time.

We begin this chapter by defining the features of a chronic illness and identifying why chronic illness is important to study. The remainder of the chapter is devoted to the adjustment process. We examine the role of three sets of factors for adjustment: dispositional variables, reactions to illness, and social environmental variables. We conclude by commenting on how aspects of the person and the environment interact to predict adjustment to chronic illness.

The Nature of Chronic Illness

We adopt DiMatteo's (1991) definition of a chronic illness: "Chronic illness or handicap involves one or more impairments or deviations from normal structure and functioning that, whether extensive or not, remain permanent. Chronic conditions are not reversible, and they are usually accompanied by some sort of residual disability" (p. 372). The central feature of this definition is that a chronic illness is not curable, which distinguishes it from an acute illness. A chronic illness must be incorporated into the individual's life.

Correspondence concerning this chapter should be addressed to Vicki Helgeson Ph.D. Department of Psychology, Carnegie Mellon University, 5000 Forbes Avenue Pittsburgh, PA 15213.

Chronic illnesses are lasting but they vary in the nature of their progression. Someone with cancer may be treated and appear cancer-free for years; the cancer then re-emerges and is far more resistant to treatment. Other chronic diseases are not characterized by a remission period *per se*, but have periods in which symptoms are more or less severe. Someone with rheumatoid arthritis may have periods in which symptoms are quite severe and periods in which they wane. The flare-ups of symptoms may be quite unpredictable. Other chronic illnesses show a progressive deterioration over time, but even the rate of progression within a single illness is variable across individuals. Multiple sclerosis is a progressive chronic illness but the rate of progression varies tremendously between individuals. One feature that is common to most chronic illnesses is the unpredictability of the progression of disease and/or the exacerbation of symptoms. At some point, recurrences, relapses, new problems, or re-emergences of old problems appear. Thus, the nature of the adjustment process will necessarily change over time because the disease changes over time.

We now turn to some of the factors that influence the adjustment process. We do not describe all of the dispositional variables, illness reactions, or social environmental variables that influence adjustment. Instead, we choose several variables in each category that are illustrative of factors that influence adjustment. The dispositional variables that we examine are sex and gender role. The illness reactions that we examine are self-esteem and perceptions of control, two of the central components of cognitive adaptation theory (Taylor, 1983). We examine multiple aspects of social support in our discussion of the social environment.

Dispositional Variables

Sex

Do men or women adjust more poorly to chronic illness? The evidence on this issue is contradictory. Studies of heart disease show that women adjust more poorly than men. In a review of nine studies, women reported more anxiety and more depression following a heart attack compared to men (Brezinka and Kittel, 1995). In a study of patients who had cardiac surgery, women had lower physical functioning than men over the course of an entire year post surgery (Jenkins and Gortner, 1998).

There is an important methodological issue that many studies neglect when comparing men's and women's adjustment to chronic illness. Investigators often fail to consider differences between men's and women's physical and psychological functioning before the onset of the chronic illness. In the Jenkins and Gortner (1998) study, women had worse functioning than men prior to surgery. Thus, women's lower functioning after surgery may be due to a pre-existing sex difference in functioning. A study of patients after bypass surgery showed that women were more depressed than men 1 year later, but women were older, were more likely to be widowed, had less income, and had more other health problems than men (Ai et al., 1997). When these factors were taken into consideration, the sex difference in depression disappeared. Sex differences in depression following the onset of a chronic illness are especially suspect because women are more depressed than men in general (Culbertson, 1997). A study of patients with congestive heart failure revealed that women were more depressed than men (Murberg et al., 1998) but the size of this sex difference was no larger than that found in the general population. Thus, the authors concluded that there was no reason to believe that women responded more adversely than men to heart failure.

Other research has shown that women adjust better than men to chronic illness. A study of persons with cancer found that females evidenced more positive adjustment than males (Fife et al., 1994). Although men and women reported similar levels of distress, women scored higher on measures of functioning in multiple domains, and women were more likely than men to find meaning in their illness.

There are two ways to determine whether a chronic illness has different effects on men's and women's quality of life. One would be to conduct a prospective study of healthy men and women and follow them until a chronic illness develops and measure their adjustment. Second, one could compare the psychological status of men and women with a chronic illness to a control group of healthy men and women. Few studies have used these procedures.

Another framework for understanding sex differences in adjustment to chronic illness that may be more informative is gender roles. Chronic illness poses different challenges for men and women in terms of their traditional roles in society. The traditional male gender role and the traditional female gender role both have implications for adjustment to chronic illness.

Gender Roles

Male Gender Role

The traditional male gender role may be an advantage or a disadvantage in adjusting to chronic illness. On the negative side, chronic illness undermines characteristics of the traditional male gender role, such as independence and self-control. People with a traditional masculine orientation may find it difficult to depend on others for assistance or to ask others for help. This will be problematic to the extent that help from others is needed. For example, a cardiac patient who refuses to allow others to help with mowing the lawn or shoveling snow is placing him- or herself at risk for a fatal heart attack.

Another feature of the male gender role that might impede adjustment to illness is difficulties with emotional expression. The traditional male role requires that feelings and vulnerabilities be hidden from others. However, the failure to share feelings and difficulties will keep others from providing necessary support.

A chronic illness also challenges the traditional male gender role to the extent that illness is viewed as a weakness and a source of vulnerability. The traditional male gender role emphasizes strength. A chronic illness will be especially threatening to men to the extent that it undermines their bread-winner role, which is the case when women go to work, men retire, or men reduce their workloads in response to their illness (Charmaz, 1995). Because the male gender role is linked to physical strength, men might have more difficulty than women in coping with any physical limitations an illness imposes. In a study of patients with congestive heart failure, Murberg et al. (1998) found that physical limitations were associated with depression for men but not women. The authors suggested that men's overall sense of wellbeing may be more strongly linked to their physical capabilities. That is, men who find it difficult to lift and carry objects, walk, and climb stairs may be more depressed than women with comparable physical limitations. The authors also suggested that women may be more accepting of physical limitations than men because women find it more acceptable to turn to others for assistance.

The traditional male gender role also might be maladaptive to the extent that it interferes with adherence to physician instructions. The traditional male may construe a strict diet, taking medication, an exercise regimen, and orders to refrain from physical exertion or reduce activities as interfering with their personal control. Self-control and independence are features of the traditional male gender role. Strict orders by physicians to adhere to these behaviors may invoke a state of *psychological reactance*, whereby one perceives a threat to freedom and reacts to that threat by doing the opposite of what is demanded (Brehm, 1966). In defying others' instructions, personal control is restored. In the case of chronic illness, personal control may be restored at the expense of taking care of oneself. The traditionally masculine male might be most vulnerable to noncompliance. Research is not clear as to whether there are sex differences in noncompliance because the concept of noncompliance is so broad, but men are clearly more likely than women to engage in risky behavior (Waldron, 1997) and men have less positive attitudes toward authority figures than women (Emler and Reicher, 1987).

On the positive side, characteristics of the male gender role may be quite helpful in coping with chronic illness. Chronic illness can be construed as a problem that is meant to be solved. To the extent that there are clear-cut behaviors that can solve or "control" the problem, men might be especially likely to take advantage of those behaviors. For example, one behavior that is helpful in regulating diabetes is exercise. Exercise, in and of itself, is consistent with the male gender role. Exercise also can be construed as a problem-focused coping behavior. Williams (2000) found that adolescent males with diabetes were more likely than adolescent females to use exercise as a way to control their illness. In general, male adolescents with chronic illness are more likely to perceive that they can control their illness than are female adolescents (Williams, 2000). To the extent that control is possible and control behaviors are helpful in regulating the illness, this perspective is a healthy one.

We have made some specific predictions about how aspects of the male gender role might be maladaptive and adaptive in the adjustment process. What is the evidence for these predictions? To address this issue, we distinguish between two facets of the male gender role – the gender-related traits of unmitigated agency and agency. Agency is a focus on the self and is associated with high self-esteem and positive psychological wellbeing among healthy people (Helgeson, 1994). Unmitigated agency, by contrast, is a focus on the self to the exclusion of others. Unmitigated agency involves a hostile attitude toward others and an absorption in the self (Helgeson and Fritz, 1999). Whereas agency has been linked to positive adjustment to chronic illness, unmitigated agency has been linked to greater adjustment difficulties.

Unmitigated agency has been associated with poor adjustment to chronic illnesses, such as heart disease (Helgeson, 1993a) and prostate cancer (Helgeson and Lepore, 1997). One reason that unmitigated agency is associated with adjustment difficulties is that it is linked to noncompliance. In studies of cardiac patients, unmitigated agency has been associated with the failure to adhere to physicians' instructions to reduce daily activities (Helgeson, 1993a) and to poor health behaviors, in particular smoking (Helgeson, 1995). Unmitigated agency individuals might be the most vulnerable to psychological reactance.

Another reason that unmitigated agency is associated with poor adjustment to chronic illness is that it is linked to impaired social networks (Helgeson, 1993a, 1995). In a study of men with prostate cancer, unmitigated agency was associated with difficulties with emotional expression (Helgeson and Lepore, 1997), and this explained the link of unmitigated agency with poor psychological and physical functioning.

Agency is a positive aspect of the male gender role that has been linked to good adjustment to heart disease (Fritz, 2000; Helgeson, 1993a, 1995; Nir and Neumann, 1990), prostate cancer (Helgeson and Lepore, 1997), and rheumatoid arthritis (Trudeau et al., 1999). One reason may be that agency reflects the positive problem-solving orientation of the male gender role. Agency has been linked to perceptions of control over illness (Helgeson, 1995) and to the exertion of control behaviors, such as eating a healthier diet (Helgeson, 1995). Agency also has been linked to high self-esteem among cardiac patients (Nir and Neumann, 1990).

Thus, there are positive and negative implications of the male gender role for the adjustment process. To the extent that chronic illness threatens aspects of the male gender role, such as independence, self-reliance, and control, recovery will be difficult and may be impeded. Other aspects of the male gender role, such as a problem-solving orientation and a positive self-image, may be used to aid recovery.

Female Gender Role

There are aspects of the female gender role that may impede and facilitate adjustment to chronic illness. The traditional female gender role is passive rather than active. Thus, some people have argued that women will adjust more easily than men to chronic illness because they are more accepting of situations in which they do not have control (Fife et al., 1994). However, to the extent that successful recovery requires active attempts at control, the traditional female gender role may be a barrier to good adjustment. In a study of adolescents with cystic fibrosis, Miller, Willis, and Wyn (1993) found that women were more passive with respect to their illness and felt powerless compared to men.

The female gender role is implicated in the adjustment process to the extent that a chronic illness alters physical appearance. Illnesses that are associated with disfiguring surgery, such as breast cancer, may threaten the feminine self-image. To the extent that concerns with appearance override concerns with physical health, the female gender role is a disadvantage. Miller et al. (1993) found that adolescent women with cystic fibrosis were more concerned with their physical appearance than their physical health. Williams (2000) found that adolescent females with diabetes had particular difficulties following a diabetic diet because of concerns with weight and body image. Dieting can lead to hypoglycemia in people with diabetes, which can be life-threatening.

The female gender role also poses difficulties with adapting to chronic illness when the caregiving role is central to self-esteem and chronic illness interferes with this role. To the extent that caring for oneself undermines caring for others, women may fail to attend to their own healthcare. For example, women might be more reluctant than men to relinquish traditional household responsibilities, which could hinder their recovery. A study of cardiac patients found that women were less likely than men to reduce household responsibilities (Rose et al., 1996). Another study of heart attack survivors found that women were less likely than men to have assistance with household tasks, such as meal preparation and laundry, regardless of whether they were married or not (Young and Kahana, 1993).

The conflict between receiving support and providing support to others may be especially difficult for women who are highly invested in the caregiving role, such as those who score high on unmitigated communion. Unmitigated communion is a focus on others to the exclusion of the self (Fritz and Helgeson, 1998; Helgeson and Fritz, 1998). Defining features include an over-involvement with others and self-neglect. Unmitigated communion has been linked to poor adjustment to chronic illnesses, such as heart disease (Fritz, 2000; Helgeson, 1993a; Helgeson and Fritz, 1999), breast cancer (Helgeson and Fritz, 2000; Piro et al., 1997), rheumatoid arthritis (Trudeau et al., 1999), and diabetes in adolescents (Helgeson and Fritz, 1996). One reason seems to be that these women neglect their own health in favor of helping others. In studies of cardiac patients and women with breast cancer, unmitigated communion has been associated with providing support to others but neglecting oneself in terms of good health behavior (Helgeson and Fritz, 1998). In one study of heart disease, people who scored high on unmitigated communion were less likely to follow physicians' instructions to reduce household activities (Helgeson, 1993a). In another study of heart disease, people who scored high on unmitigated communion were less likely to adhere to physicians' recommended exercise regimens (Fritz, 2000). In a study of adolescents with diabetes, those who scored high on unmitigated communion had poor metabolic control over their diabetes, partly because they were attending to the needs of others instead of themselves (Helgeson and Fritz, 1996).

On the positive side, there are aspects of the female gender role that may facilitate adjustment to chronic illness. One aspect centers on social relationships.

The female gender role permits help-seeking and reliance on others for support. In a study of children with chronic illnesses, Prout (1989) found that illness mobilized support more in girls than in boys. That is, friends came to visit girls who were sick and absent from school, but not so for boys. The traditional female gender role involves the expression of feelings and self-disclosure. Thus, women may be more likely than men to share their illness with others. Communion, formerly referred to as psychological femininity, involves a focus on others and has been linked to the receipt of social support and satisfying social relationships among healthy populations (see Helgeson, 1994 for a review). Although communion has not been directly associated with adjustment to chronic illness, it has been linked to receipt of support following chronic illness (Helgeson and Fritz, 1998).

Thus, there are positive and negative aspects of the traditional female gender role that can affect adjustment to chronic illness. On the negative side, a chronic illness may undermine one's ability to help others. To the extent that the caregiver role is central to self-esteem, as it is among unmitigated communion individuals, adjustment difficulties may follow. On the positive side, the traditional female gender role is associated with a willingness to ask others for help and the availability of support, both of which may facilitate recovery.

Illness Reactions

The way in which one responds to the onset of a chronic illness has implications for adjustment. One framework which has been used to outline these reactions and explain how people adjust to chronic illness is cognitive adaptation theory (Taylor, 1983). According to cognitive adaptation theory, people have a set of assumptions about themselves and the world which are shattered by the onset of a traumatic event, such as the onset of chronic illness. Specifically, a chronic illness may challenge one's sense of self-worth, one's sense of invulnerability, and one's optimism about the future.

One way to successfully adapt to chronic illness is to restore these assumptions (Taylor, 1983). Perceptions of invulnerability can be restored by perceiving control over the future course of the illness. Self-esteem can be restored by engaging in self-enhancing social comparisons, that is, by perceiving that one is coping well compared to other people with the same illness. Optimism can be restored by having a positive outlook about the future course of the disease.

There is evidence that people with a sense of high self-esteem, control, and optimism adjust more successfully to chronic illness. In a study of women with breast cancer, those who were able to feel a sense of control over the future course of their illness and to restore self-esteem by comparing themselves favorably to others evidenced better adjustment (Taylor et al., 1984). These responses to illness also were found to predict adjustment among AIDS patients (Taylor et al., 1991) and among mothers of infants with severe perinatal problems (Affleck et al., 1985). In a study of cardiac patients, Helgeson (1999) created a cognitive adaptation index that consisted of dispositional and situation-specific versions of self-esteem, control, and optimism. This index, measured during hospitalization for a first cardiac event, predicted successful adjustment to cardiac disease 6 months later.

Taylor (1983) refers to the restoration of these beliefs as a process of engaging in mildly positive self-relevant distortions or illusions. One problem with illusions is that they are vulnerable to disconfirmation. Recall that a defining feature of chronic illness is that setbacks, recurrences – basically subsequent health problems – frequently arise. How will someone who perceives control over his or her illness fare in the face of an illness recurrence? Taylor (1983) maintained that people's beliefs are robust and that they will not be disconfirmed in the face of an illness setback. The data appear to support her claim. In the study of cardiac patients described above (Helgeson, 1999), the cognitive adaptation index predicted positive adjustment even among patients who had subsequent cardiac events. In some instances, the benefits of cognitive adaptation were even stronger for patients who faced a subsequent event.

Much of the research on illness reactions has focused on specific components of cognitive adaptation theory. There are separate literatures on the relation of self-esteem, control, and optimism to adjustment. Because optimism will be discussed in another chapter (Carver and Scheier, this volume), we focus on the self-esteem and control literatures.

Self-Esteem

One of the primary challenges the chronically ill person faces is maintaining a positive self-image. People generally operate under the assumption that they are worthy, good, and decent – an assumption that maintains high self-esteem (Janoff-Bulman and Frieze, 1983). A victimizing experience, such as the onset of chronic illness, leads one to question that assumption. It is difficult to reconcile a negative experience such as a heart attack, a cancer diagnosis, or the onset of diabetes with the belief that one is a good person (Thompson and Janigian, 1988). Chronic illness activates negative self-images. The self may be weak, needy, and/or dependent. There are often lasting changes to the physical self. The physical limitations imposed by chronic illness may interfere with daily activities and restrict social activities (Wood et al., 1985). Physical appearance is affected by treatments (e.g., hair loss from chemotherapy) and visible manifestations of the disease (e.g., tremors from Parkinson's disease).

One reason that chronic illness may adversely affect self-image is that some chronic diseases are associated with a stigma. An obvious one is AIDS. Even cancer is still associated with a stigma for some people. A study of patients with AIDS and cancer revealed that feeling stigmatized was associated with lower self-esteem and a poor body image (Fife and Wright, 2000). In that study, people with AIDS felt more stigmatized than people with cancer.

One way to summarize the threat to self-esteem that chronic illness poses is as a "loss of the self" (Charmaz, 1991). Charmaz (1991) says that society acknowledges the physical suffering that results from chronic illness, but that there is a kind of suffering that society neglects – the loss of self that existed prior to illness. Chronic illness undermines former self-images. Adjustment difficulties occur when new, equally valued self-images do not replace the old ones.

What is the evidence that chronic illness affects self-esteem? Janoff-Bulman (1989) conducted a study of victims and nonvictims and compared them on eight assumptions about the self and the world. The one that most reliably discriminated the two groups was perceived self-worth. Victims had lower perceived self-worth than nonvictims. Two studies of people with rheumatoid arthritis showed that those with greater disability had lower self-esteem (Affleck and Tennen, 1991; DeVellis et al., 1990). A study of cardiac patients revealed indirect support for the idea that patients suffered only a temporary loss of self-esteem, by showing that self-esteem increased during the 6 months following diagnosis (Helgeson, 1999). By contrast, in the cancer literature, a number of studies have compared the self-esteem of individuals with cancer to healthy control groups and found no differences (see Katz et al., 1995, for a review). Many of the studies of people with cancer, however, do not examine people immediately after diagnosis. The decline in self-esteem may be temporary: self-esteem may have been restored by the time the people were studied. If self-esteem is affected by chronic illness, the effects are not long-lasting.

One concern with the literature evaluating the effect of chronic illness on self-esteem is that the majority of studies evaluate global self-esteem, which may not be sensitive to the specific aspects of self-concept that are affected by chronic illness (Curbow et al., 1990; Katz et al., 1995). People value different aspects of themselves, and chronic illnesses affect different aspects of one's self-concept. For example, a chronic illness such as asthma that imposes limitations on physical exertion will have a stronger impact on the self-concept of someone who is a runner than someone who is not athletic. One way that people can successfully adjust to chronic illness is to redefine themselves to emphasize domains that are less threatened by the illness.

One specific aspect of self-concept that has been studied is body image. Patients who are medically ill have a lower body image than healthy patients (Katz et al., 1995). Much of the work demonstrating an effect of chronic illness on body image comes from the work on cancer, in particular women with breast cancer (Katz et al., 1995). There may be reason to believe that body image is more important to women's than to men's adjustment.

How are feelings of self-worth restored after the onset of a chronic illness? One way is to compare oneself favorably to others who have the same illness. Thus, a 65-year-old person with heart disease no longer compares him or herself to any 65-year-old person, but to a similarly aged person with heart disease. Indeed, one of the tenets of social comparison theory is that we evaluate our situations by comparing ourselves to similar others (Festinger, 1954).

Within the domain of similar others, meaning others with a similar condition, people restore their self-esteem by engaging in self-enhancing social comparisons, that is, comparing themselves to others who are worse off (Taylor, 1983; Wills, 1981). It can be difficult to measure these downward comparisons, as people are often unwilling to admit that they compare themselves to others (Helgeson and Taylor, 1993), let alone that they compare themselves favorably to others. Our confidence in the role of downward comparisons in adjustment to chronic illness stems partly from the sheer prevalence of spontaneous downward comparisons that are made by people with cancer (Bogart and Helgeson, in press; Wood et al., 1985), rheumatoid arthritis (DeVellis et al., 1990), and heart disease (Helgeson and Taylor, 1993).

Do downward comparisons actually restore self-esteem? Although downward comparisons have been associated with self-esteem among the chronically ill (Helgeson and Mickelson, 2000; Helgeson and Taylor, 1993), the cross-sectional nature of most of the studies has made it difficult to determine whether downward comparisons enhance self-esteem or whether self-esteem leads to the ability to make downward comparisons. In a longitudinal study of women with breast cancer, positive downward comparisons were associated with a subsequent improvement in self-esteem, whereas self-esteem did not predict the making of positive downward comparisons (Bogart and Helgeson, in press). Thus, downward comparisons are indeed one way to restore self-esteem.

Downward comparisons may be more adaptive for individuals who face a more severe threat. In one study, downward comparison was more strongly related to reduced distress among cardiac patients whose event was more recent than distant (Helgeson and Taylor, 1993), whereas in another study, downward comparison was more strongly related to adjustment among cardiac patients who had more severe disease (Helgeson and Mickelson, 2000).

A neglected issue in this area is the idea that self-esteem may increase after chronic illness. Feeling as if one has overcome adversity may enhance one's feelings of self-worth (Katz et al., 1995). Carpenter (1997), in her study of women with breast cancer, found that women reported an increase in self-esteem since diagnosis.

Control

Individuals' perceptions of control are often threatened by the progressive physical deterioration and often unpredictable symptom flare-ups associated with chronic disease. Patients may feel a loss of control over their body, over their ability to work, or over their life in general. However, some chronically ill individuals are able to maintain a greater sense of control than others. Perceived personal control over illness has been associated with better adjustment to heart disease (Bar-on, 1983), rheumatoid arthritis and chronic obstructive lung disease (Scharloo et al., 1998), multiple sclerosis (Fournier et al., 1999), prostate cancer (Eton et al., 1999), type I diabetes (Aalto et al., 1997), and spinal cord injury (Hampton, 2000).

However, perceptions of control are not always associated with good adjustment to illness. The association of control to adjustment depends on the specific domain over which an individual perceives control. Specific domains include symptoms or daily aspects of disease, disease onset, and the course of the disease. Perceived control over symptoms and other daily aspects of the disease experience (e.g., emotions) is clearly associated with positive well-being

(Helgeson and Franzen, 1998; Thompson et al., 1993; Wallhagen and Brod, 1997). However, the effects of perceived control over illness onset and illness course are mixed. Perceived control over the onset of illness has been associated with good adjustment to spinal cord injury (Schulz and Decker, 1985) but poor adjustment to cancer (Newsom et al., 1996). Perceived control over the course of illness has been associated with good adjustment among cancer and AIDS patients (Griffin and Rabkin, 1998; Thompson et al., 1993), but is unrelated to adjustment among patients with Parkinson's disease (Wallhagen and Brod, 1997). One factor that may influence whether a domain of control is associated with adjustment may be the potential for control. There is greater potential for personal control over the symptoms or daily aspects of chronic illness than over the actual onset and course of the disease. This may explain why the former has been more consistently associated with health benefits than the latter.

The self is not the only source of control. Patients may also perceive that someone or something else (e.g., a physician, God) has control over their illness. This type of control has been called external or vicarious. We typically construe an external locus of control as an unhealthy orientation to life, but in the case of chronic illness perceiving that others have control may be helpful. Vicarious control over disease course has been shown to be associated with positive adjustment for patients with good prognoses but negative adjustment for patients with poor prognoses (leukemia: Andrykowski and Brady, 1994; renal disease: Christensen et al., 1991). Other work has suggested that vicarious control may only be beneficial for women (Taylor et al., 1991), who are used to relying on others for assistance. In a study of patients with rheumatoid arthritis, vicarious control over symptoms was associated with poor adjustment (Affleck et al., 1987). There may be some aspects of the illness for which control should not be surrendered.

A construct that is related to vicarious control and incorporates personal control is participatory control. Participatory control involves a collaborative relationship between healthcare providers and patients, in which patients maintain some control over their healthcare, but willingly relinquish some control to medical staff (Reid, 1984). Few researchers use the term participatory control, but some investigators have examined the relation of the combination of high personal control and high vicarious control to adjustment. In a study of adolescents with diabetes, high personal control combined with high vicarious control was beneficial (Helgeson and Franzen, 1998). However, in another study, high participatory control (measured in the same way) was associated with negative mood and adjustment for patients infected with HIV (Jenkins and Patterson, 1998). In the case of HIV, it is possible that any amount of vicarious control negatively impacts adjustment. A study of AIDS patients found that vicarious control was linked to poor adjustment (Taylor et al., 1991). The belief that powerful others (e.g. doctors) have control over health outcomes may be harmful in the context of AIDS because society is not all that sympathetic to the diagnosis.

From the previous discussion, one can discern that the relations of the different kinds of control to adjustment to chronic illness are not always consistent. This may be because of variables that influence the relationship between perceived control and adjustment. Two potential moderators are the severity of the disease and an illness recurrence. We discuss these below.

Severity of Illness

Perceptions of control seem to be more adaptive under conditions of severe threat. Perceived control has been shown to more adaptive under conditions of more severe than less severe threat in the case of rheumatoid arthritis (Banwell and Ziebell, 1985), diabetes (Helgeson and Franzen, 1998), heart disease (Helgeson, 1992), AIDS (Reed et al., 1993), and cancer (Thompson et al., 1993). The severity of the threat, however, may interact with other variables, such as the reality of personal control. Personal control may be more important to maintain when the threat is severe, but personal control in some domains also may be more unrealistic. A study of rheumatoid arthritis patients indicated that perceived control over symptoms was associated with positive mood for those with severe disease, but not for those with mild disease (Affleck et al., 1987). In that same study, perceived control over *illness course* was associated more strongly with negative mood for patients with severe than with mild disease (Affleck et al., 1987). Perceived control over symptoms may be more realistic than perceived control over disease course.

Effect of Recurrence

Several studies have specifically examined whether control perceptions are adaptive in the face of treatment failure or illness recurrence. In one study, researchers examined the adaptiveness of perceived control among renal transplant patients whose treatment had failed. The authors found that an internal health locus of control was related to reduced depression among patients who did not receive a transplant, but more depression among patients whose transplants failed (Christensen et al., 1991). The authors suggested that control perceptions were maladaptive among failed transplant patients because they were violated. The cross-sectional nature of this study makes the interpretation of findings difficult. It is not known whether some failed transplant patients had lower perceptions of control before the transplant, or changed their beliefs to fit the outcome. In a prospective study of patients who sustained a first coronary event, Helgeson (1992) showed that perceived control was more strongly related to adjustment among patients who subsequently sustained a second event than among patients who did not. One interpretation of this finding is that subsequent events increased threat severity.

Do all aspects of control remain adaptive when subsequent threats emerge? Is control ever disconfirmed? In one study of cardiac patients, self-efficacy (perception that one has the ability to influence important outcomes) was associated with worse adjustment among patients who faced a recurrent event and better adjustment among patients who did not (Helgeson, 1999). Because self-efficacy involves specific control efforts aimed at preventing a subsequent event, a subsequent event may directly disconfirm those efforts. Such people may feel frustrated and distressed that they made certain health behavior changes and the changes did not influence the outcome. In that same study, perceptions of control over the treatment decision were associated with greater distress if the treatment failed (subsequent cardiac event) and less distress if the treatment was successful. Thus, the possibility remains that recurrent events may influence whether some control cognitions are adaptive.

Perceived control may not always be harmful when an illness recurrence or setback occurs because people may distort their perceptions of control to fit the outcome. In a study of renal transplant patients, Wagener and Taylor (1986) found that failed transplant patients took less personal responsibility for the decision and felt that there was little else that they could have done. This study was cross-sectional, however, making it difficult to know whether failed transplant patients had different beliefs to begin with, or really changed their beliefs from before to after the transplant. In a prospective study of cardiac patients who had a successful angioplasty, Helgeson (1999) found that patients distorted some features of the treatment decision to fit the outcome. Patients were asked about the treatment decision within 48 hours of the successful angioplasty and then recalled aspects of the decision 6 months later. Patients who sustained a second cardiac event in the intervening 6 months did not take less personal responsibility for the decision, but recalled that their spouse had less influence in the treatment decision than they had initially reported. Patients who sustained a second event also were less likely to believe that angioplasty was the only treatment that was right for them, were more surprised at the treatment outcome, and increased their beliefs in the odds of recurrence.

Taken collectively, it appears that there may be some risk in choosing a treatment that fails, or in believing that one's specific behaviors influence an outcome, but it also appears that people are able to buffer themselves from the adverse effects of subsequent events by altering the way that they view the decision and their perceptions of control.

Social Environment

In the previous sections, we have discussed ways in which personal resources influence the adjustment process. In this section we discuss how social resources influence adjustment. First, we identify the aspects of the social environment that have implications for adjustment. We distinguish between quantitative and qualitative aspects of the social environment, and between positive versus negative interactions with network members. Then, we examine the implications of the illness for the social environment.

Structural vs. Functional Components

Investigators who study the effects of the social environment on health and wellbeing distinguish between structural and functional components. The structural aspects of the social environment are ways of quantifying support.

Structural indices include marital status, number of social roles, amount of contact with network members, and group memberships. In contrast, the functional aspects of the social environment are qualitative – what functions do network members serve? There are numerous typologies of social support functions, but most investigators agree on three: emotional support, informational support, and instrumental support (House, 1981; House and Kahn, 1985). Emotional support involves the communication of caring, understanding, love, and concern. Informational support involves the provision of information or advice. Instrumental support involves the provision of concrete aid or assistance.

Which aspects of the social environment are most strongly related to adjustment to chronic illness? The distinction between the main effects and the stress-buffering effects of support can answer this question (Cohen and Wills, 1985). The main effects hypothesis is that support directly affects wellbeing, regardless of health status or level of stress. The stress-buffering hypothesis states that support buffers one from the adverse effects of stressors, such as a chronic illness. The evidence suggests that the structural features of the social environment exert main effects on wellbeing, whereas the functional aspects exert stress-buffering effects (Cohen and Wills, 1985).

Thus, the most relevant aspects of the social environment for adjustment to chronic illness are support functions. One study demonstrated the importance of functional support in the context of chronic illness and also supported the stress-buffering hypothesis. Penninx, van Tilburg, Boeke, Deeg, Kriegsman, and van Eijk (1998) found that functional support was related to reduced depression among those who suffered from a chronic illness, but was unrelated to depression among healthy people. Stress-buffering also may occur within a group of chronically ill patients who face varying degrees of stress. In a study of patients with breast, colorectal, or lung cancer, the relation of support to good adjustment was stronger among those with worse prognoses (Ell et al., 1989).

Support functions have been related to better psychological and physical adjustment among people with arthritis (Fitzpatrick et al., 1988), cancer (Ell et al., 1989; Molassiotis et al., 1997), end-stage renal disease (Siegel et al., 1987), type I diabetes (Aalto et al., 1997), HIV (Grassi et al., 1999), and heart disease (King et al., 1993). Of the three functions, researchers have considered emotional support to be the most important (Cohen and Hoberman, 1983; House, 1981; Schaefer et al., 1981). To be fair, however, many investigators make this assumption *a priori* and only measure emotional support.

According to the stressor–support specificity model, the most effective form of support depends on the situation-specific needs that arise (Cohen and McKay, 1984; Cohen and Wills, 1985; Cutrona, 1990). One determinant of the needs that arise is the phase of the adjustment process. According to Jacobson (1986), there are three phases of stress that require distinct kinds of support. The first phase is threat recognition or crisis. Emotional support is most helpful at this time because it provides reassurance that others are available to help. If the crisis cannot be resolved by a return to the pre-existing situation (which is the case in chronic illness), the individual moves into the transitional phase to find new ways of coping with the threat. The transition phase is characterized by confusion, and needs are best met by informational support. Information and guidance from others can help one to understand the meaning of and the changes required by the situation. The third phase is a deficit state, in which the individual's situation is character-ized by continued demands that exceed resources. This state is best met with the provision of aid or instrumental assistance.

In a test of the stressor–support specificity model, Helgeson (1993b) hypo-thesized that both cardiac patients and spouses would benefit from emotional support because of the crisis they experienced upon learning of the diagnosis. Helgeson also hypothesized that patients and spouses would have different needs as they began to cope with the illness. Because patients face a major life transition, they need information about how to establish a lifestyle oriented toward the prevention of future heart problems. Spouses face increasing de-mands as they assist patients with healthcare while also taking over the tasks and responsibilities previously performed by the patient. Thus, spouses may be faced with the deficit phase. These hypotheses were largely supported. Emotional support benefited both patients and spouses, informational support benefited patients, and instrumental support benefited spouses.

Another determinant of which function of support is most adaptive is the source of support. In the cancer literature, it is quite clear that informational support is helpful when received from healthcare professionals, but not from family and friends (Helgeson and Cohen, 1996). Emotional support, however, seems to be helpful regardless of the source. In a study of women with recurrent breast cancer, emotional support from partners but informational support from physicians predicted improvements in physical functioning over time (Brady and Helgeson, 1999).

Negative Aspects of the Social Environment

Researchers have recently recognized that support attempts may fail and that support providers may create rather than alleviate tension and stress. The negative aspects of social relationships are often stronger determinants of adjustment to chronic illness than the positive aspects (cancer: Manne et al., 1997; heart disease: Helgeson, 1993b; multiple sclerosis: Wineman, 1990; rheumatoid arthritis: Manne and Zautra, 1990).

Network members do not have to be overtly negative in order for the social environment to have adverse affects on adjustment to chronic illness. Some studies have shown that positive support functions are associated with indic-ators of *poor* health. Receipt of positive support functions may be experienced as aversive because it implies dependence. Shinn, Lehmann, and Wong (1984) have suggested that receiving too much support from network members may become problematic for people who are in dependent roles, such as the chron-ically ill. Patients sometimes report that the support they are receiving is too much and not helpful (Helgeson, 1993b). Penninx and colleagues (1998) found that instrumental support was associated with greater depression among people with diabetes and cancer. They argued that receiving assistance may have undermined feelings of competence and instilled a feeling of dependence.

Support can be intrusive and undermine personal control. In a study of adults with diabetes, directive support, which was defined as intrusive behavior and behavior in which the support provider took responsibility for the patient's behavior (e.g., administered insulin injections), was associated with greater distress (Fisher et al., 1997).

Effect of Illness on Social Environment

Investigations often focus on how the social environment affects the adjustment process, but researchers rarely investigate how the illness affects the social environment. The illness may affect the patient's ability to engage in social activities. Patients who are tired, in pain, or physically limited may not feel up to socializing. Side-effects from treatments also may make it difficult to resume normal social activities. A common side-effect of the treatment for prostate cancer is urinary incontinence. Patients may prefer to cope with incontinence by remaining at home rather than socializing. The treatment regimen associated with a chronic illness also may interfere with social activities. A person with diabetes may not feel comfortable attending the 3:00 Thanksgiving meal because the timing of it disrupts his or her regular eating schedule. An illness also might alter social relations if it is associated with a stigma. Patients might avoid social interactions because of a fear of rejection. Thus, one outcome of a chronic illness may be a reduction in social relations.

The illness itself also might adversely affect the nature of social relationships. We know that social support facilitates adjustment, but what are the implications of the illness for support? One would hope that an illness activates support from the social environment. But the continued and possibly increasing need for support among chronically ill individuals may impose a burden that network members cannot withstand. In a longitudinal study of women newly diagnosed with breast cancer, Bolger, Foster, Vinokur, and Ng (1996) found that patients who were more psychologically distressed received less support over time. In contrast, patients who had more physical impairments received more support over time. Consistent with these findings, Brady and Helgeson (1999) found that women with recurrent breast cancer who were more psychologically distressed received less emotional support from partners over 3 months. These two studies suggest that spouses have difficulty coping with the psychological distress of patients, but may be better able to meet the physical challenges of the illness. However, in both studies the patients were female and the spouses were male. Thus, it may be that men are uncomfortable with spouses who are psychologically distressed, which leads to the withdrawal of support.

Caregiver mental and physical health is another facet of the social environment that should be considered when studying adjustment to chronic illness. Caregivers are faced with the physical stress of caring for a loved one and the emotional stress of the prospect of losing them or watching them deteriorate. Caregivers may be just as or more distressed than patients. Some studies show that male caregivers have a more difficult time coping than female caregivers (Baider et al., 1989, 1995). One reason why women adjust better than men to the caregiver role is that caregiving is consistent with the female gender role. Whereas the caregiving expectations are clear for female spouses, these expectations are not as clear for male spouses. Male spouses may be less certain about how they should behave. Russell (1989) has suggested that there might be a more extreme outcome when men become caregivers. He observed that there was a higher divorce rate among couples in which the woman had MS than among couples in which the man had MS, and suggested that male spouses had a more difficult time than female spouses coping with their spouses' illness.

Conclusions

We have discussed the ways in which dispositional factors, illness reactions, and aspects of the social environment influence adjustment to chronic illness. In our discussions, we have emphasized the fact that variables often interact with one another to predict adjustment. Knowing someone's sex does not predict adjustment as well as knowing aspects of gender roles. Even gender roles do not have a direct relation to adjustment. The relations of traditional male and female gender roles to adjustment depend upon which aspects of roles are threatened by chronic illness. When the caregiving role is threatened, unmitigated communion individuals will have difficulties. When support is needed, people characterized by communion will have an advantage. When physical strength, control, and independence are threatened, unmitigated agency individuals will have difficulties. When problem-focused coping is required, agency individuals will have an advantage. Illness reactions, such as self-esteem and control, sometimes directly influence adjustment, but often interact with aspects of the disease, such as severity and stigma. Whether perceptions of control are adaptive will be determined in part by whether the environment provides opportunities to exert control. The social environment can provide support functions that will aid adjustment to chronic illness, but different kinds of support are needed at different stages of the illness. Thus, to fully understand how someone will adjust to a chronic illness, aspects of the person, the environment, and the disease need to be considered.

References

Aalto, A.-M., Uutela, A., and Aro, A. R. (1997). Health related quality of life among insulin-dependent diabetics: Disease-related and psychosocial correlates. *Patient Education and Counseling*, 30, 215–225.

Affleck, G., and Tennen, H. (1991). Social comparison: Contemporary theory and research. In J. M. Suls and T. A. Wills (Eds.), *Social Comparison: Contemporary Theory and Research* (pp. 369–393). Hillsdale, NJ: Lawrence Erlbaum Associates.

Affleck, G., Tennen, H., and Gershman, K. (1985). Cognitive adaptations to a high-risk infant: The search for meaning, mastery, and protection from future harm. *American Journal of Mental Deficiency*, 89, 653–656.

Affleck, G., Tennen, H., Pfeiffer, C., and Fifield, J. (1987). Appraisals of control and predictability in adapting to a chronic disease. *Journal of Personality and Social Psychology*, 53, 273–279.

Ai, A. L., Peterson, C., Dunkle, R. E., Saunders, D. G., Bolling, S. F., and Buchtel, H. A. (1997). How gender affects psychological adjustment one year after coronary artery bypass graft surgery. *Women and Health*, 26, 45–65.

Andrykowski, M. A., and Brady, M. J. (1994). Health locus of control and psychological distress in cancer patients: Interactive effects of context. *Journal of Behavioral Medicine*, 17, 439–458.

Baider, L., Perez, T., and De-Nour, A. K. (1989). Gender and adjustment to chronic disease. *General Hospital Psychiatry*, 11, 1–8.

Baider, L., Perry, S., Holland, J. C., Sison, A., and De-Nour, A. K. (1995). Couples and gender relationship: A sample of melanoma patients and their spouses. *Family System Medicine*, 13, 69–77.

Banwell, B., and Ziebell, B. (1985). Psychological and sexual health in rheumatic diseases. In W. Kelly, E. Harris, S. Ruddy, and C. Sledge (Eds.), *Textbook of Rheumatology* (pp. 497–510). Philadelphia: WB Saunders.

Bar-on, D. (1983). Patients' theories about their myocardial infarctions. *Family Physician*, 11, 220–232.

Bogart, L., and Helgeson, V. S. (in press). Spontaneous social comparisons among women with breast cancer. *Journal of Applied Social Psychology*.

Bolger, N., Foster, M., Vinokur, A. D., and Ng, R. (1996). Close relationships and adjustment to a life crisis: The case of breast cancer. *Journal of Personality and Social Psychology*, 70, 283–294.

Brady, S. S., and Helgeson, V. S. (1999). Social support and adjustment to recurrence of breast cancer. *Journal of Psychosocial Oncology*, 17, 37–55.

Brehm, J. W. (1966). *A Theory of Psychological Reactance*. New York: Academic Press.

Brezinka, V., and Kittel, F. (1995). Psychosocial factors of coronary heart disease in women: A review. *Social Science and Medicine*, 42, 1351–1365.

Carpenter, J. S. (1997). Self-esteem and wellbeing among women with breast cancer and women in an age-matched comparison group. *Journal of Psychosocial Oncology*, 15, 59–80.

Charmaz, K. (1991). *Good Days, Bad Days*. New Brunswick, NJ: Rutgers University Press.

Charmaz, K. (1995). Identity dilemmas of chronically ill men. In D. Sabo and D. F. Gordon (Eds.), *Men's Health and Illness: Gender, Power, and the Body* (pp. 266–291), Thousand Oaks, CA: Sage.

Christensen, A. J., Turner, C. W., Smith, T. W., Holman, J. M., and Gregory, M. C. (1991). Health locus of control and depression in end-stage renal disease. *Journal of Consulting and Clinical Psychology*, 59, 419–424.

Cohen, S., and Hoberman, H. M. (1983). Positive events and social supports as buffers of life change stress. *Journal of Applied Social Psychology*, 13, 99–125.

Cohen, S., and McKay, G. (1984). Social support, stress, and the buffering hypothesis: A theoretical analysis. In A. Baum, J. E. Singer, and S. E. Taylor (Eds.), *Handbook of Psychology and Health* (pp. 3–22). Orlando: Academic Press.

Cohen, S., and Wills, T. A. (1985). Stress, social support, and the buffering hypothesis. *Psychological Bulletin*, 98, 310–357.

Culbertson, F. M. (1997). Depression and gender: An international review. *American Psychologist*, 52, 25–31.

Curbow, B., Somerfield, M., Legro, M., and Sonnega, J. (1990). Self-concept and cancer in adults: Theoretical and methodological issues. *Social Science Medicine*, 31, 115–128.

Cutrona, C. E. (1990). Stress and social support – In search of optimal matching. *Journal of Social and Clinical Psychology*, 9, 3–14.

DeVellis, R., Holt, K., Renner, B., Blalock, S., Blanchard, L., Cook, H., Klotz, M. L., Mikow, V., and Harring, K. (1990). The relationship of social comparison to rheumatoid arthritis symptoms and affect. *Basic and Applied Social Psychology*, 11, 1–18.

DiMatteo, M. R. (1991). *The Psychology of Health, Illness, and Medical Care*. Pacific Grove, CA: Brooks/Cole Publishing Company.

Ell, K. O., Mantell, J. E., Hamovitch, M. B., and Nishimoto, R. H. (1989). Social support, sense of control, and coping among patients with breast, lung, or colorectal cancer. *Journal of Psychosocial Oncology*, 7, 63–88.

Emler, N., and Reicher, S. (1987). Orientations to institutional authority in adolescence. *Journal of Moral Education*, 16, 108–116.

Eton, D. T., Lepore, S. J., and Helgeson, V. S. (1999, October). *Predictors of Distress in Men Treated for Prostate Cancer*. Paper presented at the Pan-American Congress of Psychosocial and Behavioral Oncology, New York.

Festinger, L. (1954). A theory of social comparison processes. *Human Relations*, 7, 117–140.

Fife, B. L., Kennedy, V. N., and Robinson, L. (1994). Gender and adjustment to cancer: Clinical implications. *Journal of Psychosocial Oncology*, 12, 1–21.

Fife, B. L., and Wright, E. R. (2000). The dimensionality of stigma: A comparison of its impact on the self of persons with HIV/AIDS and cancer. *Journal of Health and Social Behavior*, 41, 50–67.

Fisher, E. B., La Greca, A. M., Greco, P., Arfken, C., and Schneiderman, N. (1997). Directive and nondirective social support in diabetes management. *International Journal of Behavioral Medicine*, 42, 131–144.

Fitzpatrick, R., Newman, S., Lamb, R., and Shipley, M. (1988). Social relationships and psychological wellbeing in rheumatoid arthritis. *Social Science and Medicine*, 27, 399–403.

Fournier, M., de Ridder, D., and Bensing, J. (1999). Optimism and adaptation to multiple sclerosis: What does optimism mean? *Journal of Behavioral Medicine*, 22, 303–326.

Fritz, H. L. (2000). Gender-liked personality traits predict mental health and functional status following a first coronary event. *Health Psychology*, 19, 420–428.

Fritz, H. L., and Helgeson, V. S. (1998). Distinctions of unmitigated communion from communion: Self-neglect and overinvolvement with others. *Journal of Personality and Social Psychology*, 75, 121–140.

Grassi, L., Righi, R., Makoui, S., Sighinolfi, L., Ferri, S., and Ghinelli, F. (1999). Illness behavior, emotional stress and psychosocial factors among asymptomatic HIV-infected patients. *Psychotherapy and Psychosomatics*, 68, 31–38.

Griffin, K. W., and Rabkin, J. G. (1998). Perceived control over illness, realistic acceptance, and psychological adjustment in people with AIDS. *Journal of Social and Clinical Psychology*, 17, 407–424.

Hampton, N. Z. (2000). Self-efficacy and quality of life in people with spinal cord injuries in China. *Rehabilitation Counseling Bulletin*, 43, 66–74.

Helgeson, V. S. (1992). Moderators of the relation between perceived control and adjustment to chronic illness. *Journal of Personality and Social Psychology*, 63, 656–666.

Helgeson, V. S. (1993a). Implications of agency and communion for patient and spouse adjustment to a first coronary event. *Journal of Personality and Social Psychology*, 64, 807–816.

Helgeson, V. S. (1993b). Two important distinctions in social support: Kind of support and perceived versus received. *Journal of Applied Social Psychology*, 23, 825–845.

Helgeson, V. S. (1994). The relation of agency and communion to wellbeing: Evidence and potential explanations. *Psychological Bulletin*, 116, 412–428.

Helgeson, V. S. (1995). Masculinity, men's roles, and coronary heart disease. In D. Sabo and D. F. Gordon (Eds.), *Men's Health and Illness* (pp. 68–104). Thousand Oaks, CA: Sage Publications.

Helgeson, V. S. (1999). Applicability of cognitive adaptation theory to predicting adjustment to heart disease after coronary angioplasty. *Health Psychology*, 18, 561–569.

Helgeson, V. S., and Cohen, S. (1996). Social support and adjustment to cancer: Reconciling descriptive, correlational, and intervention research. *Health Psychology*, 15, 135–148.

Helgeson, V. S., and Franzen, P. L. (1998). The role of perceived control in adjustment to diabetes. *Anxiety, Stress, and Coping*, 11, 113–136.

Helgeson, V. S., and Fritz, H. L. (1996). Implications of communion and unmitigated communion for adolescent adjustment to Type I diabetes. *Women's Health: Research on Gender, Behavior, and Policy*, 2, 169–194.

Helgeson, V. S., and Fritz, H. L. (1998). A theory of unmitigated communion. *Personality and Social Psychology Review*, 2, 173–183.

Helgeson, V. S., and Fritz, H. L. (1999). Unmitigated agency and unmitigated communion: Distinctions from agency and communion. *Journal of Research in Personality*, 33, 131–158.

Helgeson, V. S., and Fritz, H. L. (2000). The implications of unmitigated agency and unmitigated communion for domains of problem behavior. *Journal of Personality*, 68, 1031–1057.

Helgeson, V. S., and Lepore, S. J. (1997). Men's adjustment to prostate cancer: The role of agency and unmitigated agency. *Sex Roles*, 37, 251–267.

Helgeson, V. S., and Mickelson, K. D. (2000). Coping with chronic illness among the elderly. In S. B. Manuck, R. Jennings, B. S. Rabin, and A. Baum (Eds.), *Behavior, Health, and Aging* (pp. 153–178). Mahwah, NJ: Lawrence Erlbaum.

Helgeson, V. S., and Taylor, S. E. (1993). Social comparisons and adjustment among cardiac patients. *Journal of Applied Social Psychology*, 23, 1171–1195.

House, J. S. (1981). *Work Stress and Social Support*. Reading, MA: Addison-Wesley.

House, J. S., and Kahn, R. L. (1985). Measures and concepts of social support. In S. Cohen and L. Syme (Eds.), *Social Support and Health* (pp. 83–108). Orlando: Academic Press.

Jacobson, D. E. (1986). Types and timing of social support. *Journal of Health and Social Behavior*, 27, 250–264.

Janoff-Bulman, R. (1989). The benefits of illusions, the threat of disillusionment, and the limitations of inaccuracy. *Journal of Social and Clinical Psychology*, 8, 158–175.

Janoff-Bulman, R., and Frieze, I. H. (1983). A theoretical perspective for understanding reactions to victimization. *Journal of Social Issues*, 39, 1–17.

Jenkins, L. S., and Gortner, S. R. (1998). Correlates of self-efficacy expectation and prediction of walking behavior in cardiac surgery elders. *Annals of Behavioral Medicine*, 20, 99–103.

Jenkins, R. A., and Patterson, T. L. (1998). HIV locus of control and adaptation to seropositivity. *Journal of Applied Social Psychology*, 28, 95–108.

Katz, M. R., Rodin, G., and Devins, G. M. (1995). Self-esteem and cancer: Theory and research. *Canadian Journal of Psychiatry*, 40, 608–615.

King, K. B., Reis, H. T., Porter, L. A., and Norsen, L. H. (1993). Social support and long-term recovery from coronary artery surgery: Effects on patients and spouses. *Health Psychology*, 12, 56–63.

Manne, S. L., Taylor, K. L., Dougherty, J., and Kemeny, N. (1997). Supportive and negative responses in the partner relationship: their association with psychological adjustment among individuals with cancer. *Journal of Behavioral Medicine*, 20, 101–125.

Manne, S. L., and Zautra, A. J. (1990). Couples coping with chronic illness: Women with rheumatoid arthritis and their healthy husbands. *Journal of Behavioral Medicine*, 13, 327–342.

Miller, R., Willis, E., and Wyn, J. (1993). *Gender and Compliance in the Management of a Medical Regimen for Young People with Cystic Fibrosis.* Paper presented at the BSA Medical Sociology Conference, University of York, UK.

Molassiotis, A., Akker, V. D., and Boughton, B. J. (1997). Perceived social support, family environment and psychosocial recovery in bone marrow transplant long-term survivors. *Social Science and Medicine*, 44, 317–325.

Murberg, T. A., Bru, E., Aarsland, T., and Svebak, S. (1998). Functional status and depression among men and women with congestive heart failure. *International Journal of Psychiatry in Medicine*, 28, 273–291.

Newsom, J. T., Knapp, J. E., and Schulz, R. (1996). Longitudinal analysis of specific domains of internal control and depressive symptoms in patients with recurrent cancer. *Health Psychology*, 15, 323–331.

Nir, Z., and Neumann, L. (1990). Motivation patterns, self-esteem, and depression of patients after first myocardial infarction. *Behavioral Medicine*, 16, 62–66.

Penninx, B. W. J. H., van Tilburg, T., Boeke, J. P., Deeg, D. J. H., Kriegsman, D. M. W., and van Eijk, J. T. M. (1998). Effects of social support and personal coping resources on depressive symptoms: Different for various chronic diseases? *Health Psychology*, 17, 551–558.

Piro, M., Knight, S. J., Zeldow, P. B., Vessey, J., and Mytko, J. (1997). *The Relationship of Agentic and Communal Personality Traits to Psychosocial Adjustment in Breast Cancer.* Paper presented at the American Psychological Association, Chicago.

Prout, A. (1989). Sickness as a dominant symbol in life course transitions: An illustrated theoretical framework. *Sociology of Health and Illness*, 11, 336–359.

Reed, G. M., Taylor, S. E., and Kemeny, M. E. (1993). Perceived control and psychological adjustment in gay men with AIDS. *Journal of Applied Social Psychology*, 23, 791–824.

Reid, D. (1984). Participatory control and the chronic-illness adjustment process. In H. Lefcourt (Ed.), *Research with the Locus of Control Construct: Extensions and Limitations* (Vol. 3, pp. 361–389). New York: Academic Press.

Rose, G. L., Suls, J., Green, P. J., Lounsbury, P., and Gordon, E. (1996). Comparison of adjustment, activity, and tangible social support in men and women patients and their spouses during the six months post-myocardial infarction. *Annals of Behavioral Medicine*, 18, 264–271.

Russell, S. (1989). From disability to handicap: An inevitable response to social constraints? *Canadian Review of Sociology and Anthropology*, 26, 276–293.

Schaefer, C., Coyne, J. C., and Lazarus, R. S. (1981). The health-related functions of social support. *Journal of Behavioral Medicine*, 4, 293–301.

Scharloo, M., Kaptein, A. A., Weinman, J., Hazes, J. M., Willems, L. N. A., Bergman, W., and Rooijmans, H. G. M. (1998). Illness perceptions, coping and functioning in patients with rheumatoid arthritis, chronic obstructive pulmonary disease and psoriasis. *Journal of Psychosomatic Research*, 44, 573–585.

Schulz, R., and Decker, S. (1985). Long-term adjustment to physical disability: The role of social support, perceived control, and self-blame. *Journal of Personality and Social Psychology*, 48, 1162–1172.

Shinn, M., Lehmann, S., and Wong, N. W. (1984). Social interaction and social support. *Journal of Social Issues*, 40, 55–76.

Siegel, B. R., Calsyn, R. J., and Cuddihee, R. M. (1987). The relationship of social support to psychological adjustment in end-stage renal patients. *Journal of Chronic Disease*, 40, 337–344.

Taylor, S. E. (1983). Adjustment to threatening events: A theory of cognitive adaptation. *American Psychologist*, 38, 1161–1173.

Taylor, S. E., Helgeson, V. S., Reed, G. M., and Skokan, L. A. (1991). Self-generated feelings of control and adjustment to physical illness. *Journal of Social Issues*, 47, 91–109.

Taylor, S. E., Kemeny, M. E., Reed, G. M., and Aspinwall, L. G. (1991). Assault on the self: Positive illusions and adjustment to threatening events. In G. A. Goethals and J. A. Strauss (Eds.), *The Self: An Interdisciplinary Perspective* (pp. 239–254). New York: Springer-Verlag.

Taylor, S. E., Lichtman, R. R., and Wood, J. V. (1984). Attributions, beliefs about control, and adjustment to breast cancer. *Journal of Personality and Social Psychology*, 46, 489–502.

Thompson, S. C., and Janigian, A. S. (1988). Life schemes: A framework for understanding the search for meaning. *Journal of Social and Clinical Psychology*, 7, 260–280.

Thompson, S. C., Sobolew-Shubin, A., Galbraith, M. E., Schwankovsky, L., and Cruzen, D. (1993). Maintaining perceptions of control: Finding perceived control in low-control circumstances. *Journal of Personality and Social Psychology*, 64, 293–304.

Trudeau, K. J., Danoff-Burg, S., and Revenson, T. A. (1999). *Accessing Agency and Communion among Women with Rheumatoid Arthritis*. Paper presented at the Association of Rheumatoid Arthritis Professionals, Boston, MA.

Waldron, I. (1997). Changing gender roles and gender differences in health behavior. In D. S. Gochman (Ed.), *Handbook of Health Behavior Research I: Personal and Social Determinants* (pp. 303–328). New York: Plenum Press.

Wagener, J. J., and Taylor, S. E. (1986). What else could I have done? Patients' responses to failed treatment decisions. *Health Psychology*, 5, 481–496.

Wallhagen, M. I., and Brod, M. (1997). Perceived control and wellbeing in Parkinson's disease. *Western Journal of Nursing Research*, 19, 11–31.

Williams, C. (2000). Doing health, doing gender: Teenagers, diabetes and asthma. *Social Science and Medicine*, 50, 387–396.

Wills, T. A. (1981). Downward comparison as a coping mechanism. *Psychological Bulletin*, 90, 245–271.

Wineman, N. M. (1990). Adaptation to multiple sclerosis: The role of social support, functional disability, and perceived uncertainty. *Nursing Research*, 39, 294–299.

Wood, J. V., Taylor, S. E., and Lichtman, R. R. (1985). Social comparison in adjustment to breast cancer. *Journal of Personality and Social Psychology*, 49, 1169–1183.

Young, R. F., and Kahana, E. (1993). Gender, recovery from late life heart attack and medical care. *Women Health*, 20, 11–31.

CHAPTER 3

Coping Processes and Adjustment to Chronic Illness

Charles S. Carver

University of Miami

and

Michael F. Scheier

Carnegie Mellon University

Introduction

This chapter considers the role of coping processes and individual differences in adaptation to chronic illness. We focus initially on coping, then turn to how coping processes emerge in times of adversity, such as confronting chronic illness. Our viewpoint on coping is in some ways very simple: we think coping is efforts at self-regulation under adversity. What we are calling self-regulation here is people's efforts to create and maintain desired conditions in their lives. The conditions can be stable ones (e.g., good health), or they can be dynamic (e.g., helping a child grow into a responsible adult). Whether the person's goal is to maintain a stable picture or to make something happen, the process by which that goal is realized is a process of self-regulation.

Self-regulatory efforts often run smoothly, unimpeded by external impediments or personal inadequacies. Sometimes, however, people have trouble doing what they want to do, being what they want to be, or keeping their lives ordered the way they want them. These are the situations that are experienced as stressful. In this chapter we explore what self-regulation

Preparation of this chapter was facilitated by grants CA64710, CA64711, CA62711, CA78995, and CA84944 from the National Cancer Institute, and grants HL65111 and HL65112 from the National Heart, Lung, and Blood Institute.

Correspondence concerning this chapter should be directed to the author at Department of Psychology, University of Miami, Coral Gables, FL 33124, USA, E-Mail: ccarver@miami.edu, Phone: 305-284-2817, Fax: 305-284-3402.

models tell us about the experience of stress and the processes of coping, and how the latter can influence the management of chronic illness. We begin by describing the principles that form our preferred model of self-regulation, and then consider how they bear on the experience of coping.

Self-Regulation as an Orienting Framework

A common view among today's personality theorists is that behavior is organized around goals (Austin and Vancouver, 1996; Bandura, 1997; Cantor and Kihlstrom, 1987; Carver and Scheier, 1998; Elliott and Dweck, 1988; Emmons, 1986; Higgins, 1987, 1996; Klinger, 1975; Little, 1989; Markus and Nurius, 1986; Miller and Read, 1987; Pervin, 1982, 1989). Such views share the idea that goals energize and direct activities (Pervin, 1982). They convey the sense that understanding a person means understanding that person's goals. Indeed, this view typically presumes that the self consists partly of the person's abstract goals and values and the organization among them.

We should reiterate that although some goals have a static quality, others are quite dynamic. The goal of taking a vacation is not to be sitting in your driveway at the end of the 2 weeks, but to experience the events planned for the vacation. The goal of having a productive career is not just the goal of being "established" or of retiring: it's the full pathway of steps involved in the career.

Goals and Feedback Processes

Obviously, goals would not mean much if they did not relate to actions. But how exactly are goals *used* in acting? Part of the answer concerns the deconstruction of goals into subgoals. We think another part is the engagement of feedback processes (Carver and Scheier, 1998, 1999d). A feedback loop is four elements – input function, reference value, comparator, and output function (figure 3.1) – in a particular organization (cf. Miller et al., 1960).

An input function is a sensor, bringing in information about what exists. For present purposes this means perception. The reference value is information about what condition is desired or intended (i.e., a goal). The comparator is so named because it compares input and reference value, yielding either of two outcomes: either the values are distinctly different or they are not. Following the comparison is an output function. For present purposes, output is behavior, though sometimes the behavior is internal.

The nature of the output varies, depending on what kind of loop is under consideration. There are two kinds of loop, corresponding to two kinds of goal. In a discrepancy-*reducing* loop, the output is aimed at diminishing any discrepancy detected between input and reference value. If the comparison yields "no difference," the output function remains whatever it was. If the comparison yields "discrepancy," the output changes in a way that will diminish the discrepancy. In human behavior, discrepancy reduction (matching of input to reference value) is reflected in attempts to approach desired goals.

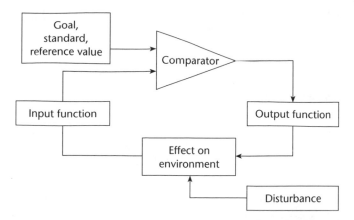

Figure 3.1 Schematic depiction of a feedback loop. In such a loop a sensed value is compared to a reference value or standard, and adjustments are made in an output function as necessary.

The other kind of loop is discrepancy *enlarging*. The value here is not one to approach, but one to avoid. It may be simplest to think of such values as "anti-goals." Examples are public ridicule and speeding tickets. A discrepancy-enlarging loop senses conditions, compares them to the anti-goal, and tries to enlarge any discrepancy sensed between the two. Discrepancy-enlarging processes in living systems are usually constrained by discrepancy-reducing loops (see Carver and Scheier, 1998). To put it differently, the attempt to avoid something often leads to approaching something else. In this chapter we focus largely on approach loops, but it should be recognized that some of the situations we describe also have aspects that can be viewed in terms of avoidance.

Hierarchical Organization of Goals

Goals differ in many ways beyond the distinction between approach and avoidance. They also differ in level of abstraction. A man might have the high level goal of being a good father. He may also have the goal at a lower level of taking his son to his soccer game. The first goal is to be a particular kind of *person*; the second involves completing particular kinds of *action*. It is easy to imagine even more concrete goals, such as executing a left turn on entering the parking lot. Such goals are closer to specifications of individual acts than were the second, which was more a summary statement about the desired outcome of intended action patterns.

These examples of concrete goals link directly to the example of an abstract goal, helping to illustrate the idea that goals can be connected hierarchically. In 1973, William Powers argued that behavior occurs via a hierarchical organization of discrepancy-reducing feedback loops. Inasmuch as such loops imply goals, his argument assumed a hierarchical model of goals. He reasoned that the output of a high-level system consists of resetting reference values at the next lower level. To put it differently, higher-order systems "behave" by providing goals to the systems just below them. Goals are more concrete at

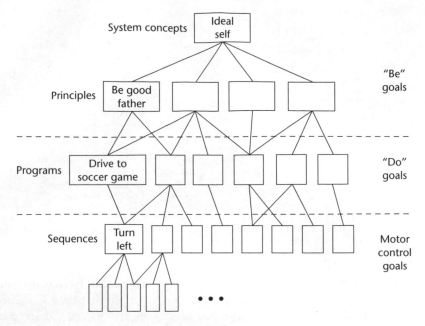

Figure 3.2 A hierarchy of goals (or of discrepancy-reducing feedback loops). Lines indicate the contribution of lower level goals to specific higher-level goals. They can also be read in the opposite direction, indicating that a given higher-order goal specifies more concrete goals at the next lower level. The hierarchy described in text involves goals of "being" particular ways, which are attained by "doing" particular actions.

From C. S. Carver and M. F. Scheier (1998), *On the self-regulation of behavior*, copyright 1998, Cambridge University Press; reproduced with permission of the publisher.

each lower level. Control at each level regulates a quality that contributes to that controlled at the next higher level. Each level monitors input at its own level of abstraction, and each level adjusts output to minimize its discrepancies.

Powers focused mostly on low levels, but he suggested labels for several higher levels. *Sequences* are strings of acts that run off directly once cued. Above sequences are *programs*, activities involving conscious decisions at various choice points. Above programs are *principles*, qualities abstracted from (or implemented in) programs. These are the kinds of qualities represented by trait terms. Powers gave the label *system concepts* to the highest level he proposed. Goals represented there include idealized views of self, of a close relationship, or of a group identity.

Figure 3.2 shows a simplified portrayal of this idea (see also Vallacher and Wegner, 1987). This diagram omits the loops of feedback, using lines to indicate only the links between goals. The lines imply that moving toward a particular lower goal contributes to the attainment of a higher one (or even several at once). Multiple lines to a given higher goal indicate that several lower-level action qualities contribute to its attainment. As indicated previously, there are goals to "be" a particular way and goals to "do" certain things (and, at lower levels, goals to create physical movement).

The notion of hierarchy has implications for several issues in conceptualizing behavior (see Carver and Scheier, 1998, 1999b). In this view, goals at any given level often can be attained by several means at lower levels. This fits the fact that people sometimes shift radically the manner in which they try to reach a goal, when the goal itself has not changed. For example, you can be productive (fulfilling an abstract goal) by building a house, by compiling a report from a set of records, or by thinking through a problem and describing its solution verbally. The quality that constitutes the higher-order goal is implied by each of these lower-order activities.

These particular examples were chosen because the first implies a good deal of physical exertion, whereas the others do not. Physical mobility is an issue that often arises in thinking about the impact of chronic illness. As these examples illustrate, having a chronic illness that impedes physical movement does not in principle remove the capacity to reach abstract goals.

Just as a given goal can be obtained via multiple pathways, so can a specific act be performed in the service of diverse goals. As an example, there are several reasons why you might buy a gift for someone: to make him feel good, to repay a kindness, to put him in your debt, to satisfy a perceived holiday-season role, or to prevent other people from thinking you are stingy. The act can have strikingly different implications, depending on the purpose it is intended to serve.

Goals also vary in importance. The higher in the organization, the more tied to the sense of self are the goals. Thus goals at higher levels tend to be more important than those at lower levels, by their closer links to the core sense of self. At the same time, two goals at a lower level are not necessarily equivalent in importance. There are two ways for importance to accrue to a lower goal. First, one that is more central to attaining a valued abstract goal is more important than one less central attaining the abstract goal. Second, one that contributes to attaining several higher-level goals at once is more important than one that contributes to attaining only one such goal.

Good and Bad Feelings, Confidence and Doubt

An important aspect of experience ignored thus far is feelings. We think feelings arise by another feedback process, the details of which are beyond the scope of this chapter (see Carver and Scheier, 1998, 1999d). One way to characterize what it does is to say it is continuously checking on how well the behavior system is doing at its job. Skipping over the details, the argument is that positive feelings mean you are doing better at something than you need to, and distress or negative feelings mean you are doing worse than you need to. This implies a bipolarity in the affect that might potentially arise with respect to any given action. That is, affect can be either positive or negative, depending on how well the action is going. Because adversity essentially means that things are not going well, it will be no surprise that adversity leads to feelings of distress.

We see feelings as being closely intertwined with the moment-to-moment expectancies that are generated "on-line" as behavior unfolds. As we said earlier, we suspect that one mechanism yields two readouts: affect, and a sense of confidence versus doubt. Thus, what we have said about affect applies also to the confidence and doubt that emerge with ongoing action.

The on-line sense of confidence and doubt does not operate in a vacuum, though. Having one's efforts at goal attainment disrupted by adversity can yield distress emotions and doubtful feelings. But sometimes those immediate reactions are overridden by other information. We have suggested that when people experience adversity in trying to move toward goals, they periodically interrupt their effort and assess in a more deliberative way the likelihood of success (e.g., Carver and Scheier, 1981, 1990, 1998). In effect, people suspend the behavioral stream, step outside it, and judge what outcome is likely. In doing so, they presumably use memories of prior outcomes in similar situations, thoughts about alternative approaches to the problem, and thoughts about other resources they might bring to bear (cf. Lazarus, 1966; MacNair and Elliott, 1992). They also may use social comparison information (e.g., Wills, 1981; Wood, 1989; Wood et al., 1985) and attributional analyses of prior events (Pittman and Pittman, 1980; Wong and Weiner, 1981).

In some cases, people retrieve "chronic" expectancies from memory. In such cases, the information already *is* expectancies, summaries of products of previous behavior. These chronic expectancies may simply substitute for those derived from immediate experience, or they may blend with and color those immediate expectancies. For example, a person with a substantial history of adverse information from medical tests may find himself automatically expecting the worst from a newly conducted test.

In other cases, people think about possible changes in the situation. For such possibilities to influence expectancies, their consequences must be evaluated. This can be done by playing them through mentally as behavioral scenarios (cf. Taylor and Pham, 1996). For example, a cancer patient considering a new therapy may play through a scenario of undergoing the therapy, experiencing limited side-effects, and having an improvement in health. She may derive from that scenario a sense of confidence. Effective mental scenarios emphasize explicit processes needed for reaching a goal, the concrete steps that must be enacted in order to get there (Taylor et al., 1998; see also Cameron and Nicholls, 1998). Simply imagining the goal as having been attained is not enough to facilitate self-regulatory activities, and can even be detrimental (Oettingen, 1996).

Efforts and Giving Up

Whatever their source, the expectancies that people take back to their behavior influence the behavior: if expectations are favorable enough, the person renews their effort. If doubts are strong enough, there is an impetus to disengage from effort, and even from the goal itself. We have argued that these two classes of reaction form a "watershed" (Carver and Scheier, 1981, 1998): that is, one set of responses involves continued efforts at movement forward. The other set consists of disengagement and quitting (see also Klinger, 1975; Kukla, 1972; Wortman and Brehm, 1975).

The fact that goals vary in specificity – from very general, to those pertaining to a particular domain of life, to very concrete and specific – suggests that expectancies also vary in the same way (Armor and Taylor, 1998; Carver and Scheier, 1998). To put it more concretely, a cancer patient can be confident or doubtful about living a long life, about recovering from cancer, about being able to tolerate another course of chemotherapy, about finishing one more day of chemotherapy, or about lifting her arm. A patient with multiple sclerosis can be confident or doubtful about having a long and interesting life, about being able to move around effectively in the work setting, about being able to cross a room unaided, and about being able to stand.

Which sort of expectancies matter? Maybe all of them. Expectancy-based theories often hold that behavior is predicted best when the specificity of the expectancy matches that of the action. Sometimes it is argued that prediction should take into account several levels of specificity at once, inasmuch as many outcomes in life have multiple causes, varying in specificity. It has also been suggested that, in multiply determined situations and in novel situations, generalized expectations are especially useful in predicting behavior and emotions (Scheier and Carver, 1985).

The same principles that apply to focused confidence also apply to the generalized sense of optimism and pessimism. When researchers talk about variables such as optimism and pessimism, the sense of confidence at issue is just more diffuse and broader in scope. Thus, when confronting a challenge, optimists should tend to take a position of confidence and persistence, assuming the adversity can be handled successfully in one way or another. Pessimists should be more doubtful and hesitant, more ready to anticipate disaster.

Scaling Back Goals: Limited Disengagement Yet Remaining Engaged

Sometimes when people give up trying to reach a goal, they do quit. Sometimes, however, something else happens. In some cases people want to quit but don't. Rather, they *trade the threatened goal for a less demanding one*. This is a kind of limited disengagement. They have given up on the first goal at the same time as they are adopting a lesser one. This limited disengagement has an important positive consequence, however: by doing this, people remain engaged in the domain they had wanted to quit (or felt the need to quit). By scaling back (giving up in a small way), they keep trying to move ahead (thus *not* giving up, in a larger way).

An illustration comes from research on couples in which one partner was becoming ill and dying from AIDS (Moskowitz et al., 1996). Some healthy subjects had the goal of overcoming their partner's illness and continuing to have an active life together. As the illness progressed, however, and it became apparent that this goal would not be met, the healthy partner often scaled back their aspirations. Now the goal was to do more limited activities during the course of a day, for example. Choosing a goal that is more limited and manageable ensures that it will be possible to move toward it. The result is that, despite the adversity, the person experienced more positive feelings than would have otherwise been the case, and stayed engaged behaviorally with efforts to move forward with this aspect of life.

We believe this principle of scaling back – partial disengagement without completely abandoning the goal domain – is a very important one. By keeping the person engaged in goal pursuits in particular domains, it keeps them engaged in living.

Self-Regulation Models and Stress-and-Coping Models

The view of self-regulation described above aimed at characterizing the structure and processes of "behavior in general." Although it was not devised as a model of stress and coping, we believe it provides a window on the nature of those experiences (Carver and Scheier, 1999c; Carver et al., 1992). From this point of view, stress occurs when people encounter impediments to attaining their desired goals or avoiding anti-goals. Coping constitutes efforts to create conditions that will foster continued movement toward desired goals (or away from anti-goals), or efforts to disengage from goals that are seen as no longer attainable.

Although it may not be obvious, this line of thought resonates with analyses of stress and coping *per se*. Lazarus and Folkman and their colleagues have argued that stress exists when people appraise threat or loss (e.g., Lazarus, 1966; Lazarus and Folkman, 1984). Threat is a perception of the impending occurrence of something harmful; loss is the perception that harm has already occurred. We would say that threat suggests imminent interference with the pursuit of desired activities, goals, or conditions (e.g., a serious illness threatens one's life goals, one's tennis game, and one's perception of reality). Loss prevents the continued existence of a desired state of affairs (e.g., the death of a spouse prevents the continued relationship). Although we have portrayed these effects in terms of approach goals, it should be clear that issues of avoidance can also be readily applied here.

Another point of similarity between self-regulation models and the Lazarus–Folkman model concerns the continuous re-evaluation of the situation and one's response to it. In the Lazarus and Folkman model, people do not always respond to stressful encounters in a reflexive automatic way. They often weigh options and consider the consequences of those options before acting. Decisions about how to cope depend in part on confidence or doubt about whether a particular strategy of responding will help. Thus, issues of confidence and doubt, as well as the disruption of intended courses of behavior, are embedded in their theoretical model.

Indeed, a disjunction between effort and giving from the self-regulatory model is also implicit in this view of coping. Everyone knows the distinction between problem-focused coping (attempts to remove the obstacle or to minimize its impact) and emotion-focused coping (attempts to reduce the distress caused by the obstacle, by reappraisal of the obstacle and its consequences, or by management of the emotion *per se*; Gross, 1998). What is often termed avoidance coping cuts across this distinction. Avoidance coping sometimes seems intended to avoid acknowledging that the problem exists (via self-distraction, denial, substance use, wishful thinking, etc.); it sometimes reflects giving up the attempt to do anything about the problem (by substance use, giving up goals that are being interfered with, etc.). Avoidance coping seems to be prompted by doubts about being able to deal effectively with the problem or its emotional reverberations.

We also see links between self-regulation and a somewhat different view on stress suggested by Hobfoll (Hobfall, 1989; Hobfoll et al., 1996). He holds that people accumulate resources, which they try to protect, defend, and conserve. These resources can be objects (e.g., a house, a car), conditions of life (e.g., friends, good health), personal qualities (e.g., work skills, social prowess), or others (e.g., knowledge, money). Resources are anything the person values. Stress occurs when resources are threatened or lost, or when people invest resources and do not receive an adequate return on the investment.

We would argue that resources matter inasmuch as they facilitate movement toward desired goals (or avoidance of anti-goals). What is the value of a car? It can take you places, and it can make an impression on other people. What use are friends? They can help you feel better when you are upset, and you can do interesting things of mutual enjoyment with them. What value is good health? It keeps you moving toward a variety of goals. In brief, we think that resources are intimately bound up with the continuing pursuit of goals. Loss of resources threatens continued goal attainment. Once again, we see a strong connection to principles of self-regulation.

Dysfunctional Responses to Threat and Loss

Situations involving threat and loss occur fairly frequently in life, and people do not always react to them well. Indeed, people facing adversity sometimes react in ways that create additional distress. Because we believe such dysfunctional patterns are embedded in some of the ways in which people cope with chronic illness, we outline several of them in this section.

Premature Disengagement of Effort

We said earlier that when people have impediments and doubts about success, they tend to give up. Sometimes people give up too soon from goals that are attainable. Disengaging too fast keeps people from trying their best: it short-circuits potential success. As an example, it is often hard for a person who has never exercised before to start exercising for health promotion (or to rehabilitate from an injury or illness). A person who doubts being able to create a routine pattern of exercise may quit prematurely, never to try again.

A more subtle pattern involves premature withdrawal of *effort*, but continued *commitment* to a goal. People with this pattern no longer try, but the goal remains in mind. Because of the doubts, any attempt to move toward it is sporadic, easily disrupted by withdrawing effort (cf. Carver, 1996; McIntosh and Martin, 1992; Wine, 1971, 1980). Because the person is committed to the goal but not moving toward it, there also is considerable distress (Carver and Scheier, 1990, 1998; Klinger, 1975; Pyszczynski and Greenberg, 1992).

This depiction might reflect the situation of people who receive a diagnosis of a chronic illness and decide that they are going to be unable to perform well at activities they value, and therefore stop engaging in them. They still have those activities in mind, in the form of desires and urges, but they are not engaging in active pursuit of them. They are still psychologically committed, but not making efforts to implement the commitment.

Struggling Too Long Toward Unattainable Goals

If there are drawbacks to withdrawing effort too quickly from goals that might be attained, it can also be bad to keep struggling toward goals that are unattainable. Giving up is an important part of life. People need to be able to retrace steps, back out of corners, free themselves to go elsewhere. Continued commitment to a goal that is unattainable wastes resources in futile effort. If the futile efforts are extensive, so is the waste of resources. It can be important to accept the reality of a permanent change in one's situation (Carver et al., 1993; Scheier and Carver, in press). As an example, paraplegia currently has no remedy. A person who loses the use of his legs and focuses only on regaining the ability to walk may expend extensive resources in a futile effort to do so.

This situation shares two consequences with the case of disengaging effort while remaining committed to the goal. First, both yield distress. The person who is unable to let go, but who cannot move forward (whether because of absence of effort or owing to an impassable impediment) will experience distress. Second, in both cases people fail to take up new, viable goals, because the commitment to the old one keeps them from noticing or responding to new opportunities (cf. Baumeister and Scher, 1988; Feather, 1989; Janoff-Bulman and Brickman, 1982). For example, losing the use of one's legs still permits many goals in life to be attained, but not if the person is unwilling to consider them.

Hierarchicality and Importance Can Impede Disengagement

The inability to disengage from an unattainable goal creates so many problems as to beg the question of why it happens. A key reason stems from the idea that goals are hierarchically organized. Recall that as one moves to higher levels goals are more central to the self. Recall also that some lower-order goals connect to only a few higher ones, whereas other lower-order goals connect to many higher ones. Some lower goals connect intimately to higher ones; other lower goals connect only weakly to higher ones. There are also, of course, individual differences in the organization.

Presumably, disengaging from higher-order goals is always hard. Disengaging from a high-order goal means giving up a core element of the self, which is not done lightly (Greenwald, 1980). Less obvious is the fact that disengagement from a concrete goal is also hard, if the concrete goal is closely linked to a higher-order goal. Under such circumstances, giving up on a lower-order goal means more than simply abandoning the concrete behavior. It also means creating a problem for the higher-order goals to which the lower goal is linked. As a result, disengagement from the concrete goal is difficult.

For example, we know a man for whom being able to play a vigorous game of tennis is very important. It connects to several of his higher-order values, including creating favorable impressions on others, displaying social dominance (by winning), staying in good physical condition, attracting female admirers, and socializing with people he does not get to see in other contexts. Further, the link from his tennis game to his sense of social dominance is quite strong, and that sense of dominance is closely linked to his sense of self. If he were to be told by his cardiologist to give up his vigorous tennis competition because of a heart condition, it would be very hard for him to do so. It would challenge his very sense of himself.

When Is Disengagement the Correct Response?

It will be apparent from the foregoing that a critical question in life is when to stay engaged and when to dissolve a goal commitment (cf. Pyszczynski and Greenberg, 1992). On the one hand, giving up (at some level, at least) is a necessity. It is part of self-regulation. If people are ever to turn away from efforts at unattainable goals, if they are ever to back out of blind alleys, they must be able to disengage, to give up, and to start over somewhere else.

The importance of disengagement is obvious regarding such concrete goals, but it is also important with regard to some higher-level ones. A vast literature attests to the importance of moving on with life after the loss of close relationships, even if the moving on does not imply a complete putting aside of the old (e.g., Cleiren, 1993; Orbuch, 1992; Stroebe et al., 1993). Being stuck in the past instead of moving on has been found to create problems for people who have experienced a variety of life traumas (Holman and Silver, 1998).

We would assert more specifically that giving up is an adaptive response *when it leads to the taking up of other goals*, whether these represent substitutes for the lost one or simply new goals in a different domain. By providing for the pursuit of alternate goals, giving up creates an opportunity to re-engage and move ahead again (Carver and Scheier, 1998; Scheier and Carver, in press). In such cases, giving up occurs in service to the broader function of keeping the person engaged with life. This appears to apply to values that extend fairly deeply into the sense of self. People need multiple paths to such values (cf. Linville, 1985, 1987; Showers and Ryff, 1996; Wicklund and Gollwitzer, 1982). If one path is blocked, people need to be able to shift to another.

It seems likely that substituting a new path for an obstructed one is made easier by having clearly identified values at the more abstract level. For example, consider the case of a highly competitive athlete who loses his mobility. A person in this situation who understands that his core desire is to *compete* can more readily recognize that there are many ways to satisfy that desire than can someone who is less clear about the nature of the core desire. Similarly, it seems likely that a person who already recognizes the multiple paths that exist to a given goal will be better prepared to make such shifts, as necessary.

In any case, it appears that the ability to shift to a new goal, or a new path to a continuing goal, is an important part of remaining goal-engaged. What happens if there is no alternative to take up? In such a case disengagement from an unattainable goal cannot be accompanied by a shift of focus. This is the worst situation: nothing to pursue, nothing to take the place of the unattainable (cf. Moskowitz et al., 1996). There is reason to believe that this situation is implicated in suicide (Beck et al., 1985). There is even reason to suspect that it may be implicated in premature death from natural causes (Carver and Scheier, 1998, Chapter 18).

Coping with Chronic Illness

How do the concepts discussed in the preceding sections relate to patients with chronic illnesses? Chronic illness creates a continuing threat to the continuation of desired activities. It represents an impediment to continued movement toward desired goals or movement away from threatening anti-goals. In brief, a chronic illness and its ramifications represents a central threat to multiple aspects of a person's ongoing life.

An important theme in our discussion of self-regulatory activities and of coping was that expectations play a pivotal role in responses to adversity. When an impediment is encountered (and the experience of stress commences), what happens next depends on whether the person feels the obstacle can be overcome, the problem solved or circumvented. When people expect to succeed (given an opportunity for further effort), they keep trying, and even enhance their efforts. When people believe success is out of reach, they withdraw their effort, even give up the attempt to reach the goal. This difference plays out in various aspects of coping, including coping with chronic illness.

There are, of course, important individual differences in coping. It should come as no surprise that we believe individual differences in expectancies represent an important influence on people's coping under adversity. Although there are many individual differences that might be invoked here, this section of the chapter focuses on research in which expectancies were operationalized in terms of generalized optimism versus pessimism.

Differences in coping between optimists and pessimists have been found in many studies examining a variety of stressors (for reviews, see Carver and Scheier, 1999a, or Scheier et al., 2001). A simple characterization of some of the results of these studies is that optimism tends to relate to problem-focused coping, whereas pessimism tends to relate to attempts to distance oneself from the problem, along with a tendency to give up on goals the stressor is threatening.

Some of the research on optimism and coping deals with populations suffering from one or another chronic illness. To illustrate this research, we here focus on three diseases: coronary artery disease, cancer, and HIV infection. Studies are briefly reviewed in the sections that follow. In each case we try to point to evidence that optimism relates to signs of continued life engagement, whereas pessimism relates to avoidance coping and greater distress.

Coronary Disease

Coronary heart disease creates many complications in people's lives (see Smith, this volume). When the disease is severe, it is sometimes treated surgically. Confronting the need for this major surgery, and experiencing the surgery itself, represent major stressors. Several studies have examined how optimists and pessimists deal with the stress of heart surgery.

One early study in the optimism literature examined men undergoing and recovering from coronary artery bypass surgery (Scheier et al., 1989). Patients completed questionnaires the day before surgery, a week after surgery, and 6 months later. Before surgery, optimists reported less hostility and depression than pessimists. They also reported they were making plans for their future and setting goals for their recovery (remaining engaged with their personal futures). A week later, optimists reported more happiness and relief, more satisfaction with their medical care, and more satisfaction with emotional support from friends. They also were more likely to report seeking out information about what the physician would require of them in the months ahead (again reflecting greater engagement with their lives).

Six months after surgery, optimists reported higher quality of life than pessimists. In a follow-up 5 years after surgery (Scheier and Carver, 1992), optimists continued to experience greater subjective wellbeing and quality of life than pessimists. They also reported greater engagement in the activities of their lives, including cardiac rehabilitation programs to remain healthy.

A later study of optimism and quality of life after coronary artery bypass surgery (Fitzgerald et al., 1993) assessed participants 1 month before surgery and 8 months afterward. Optimism related to less presurgical distress, and to greater postsurgical life satisfaction, even controlling for presurgical life satisfaction. Further analysis revealed that the general sense of optimism influenced feelings of life satisfaction through a more focused sense of confidence about the surgery. That is, the general sense of optimism about life apparently was funneled into a specific optimism regarding the surgery, and from there to satisfaction with life afterwards.

Scheier et al. (1999) recently reported data on yet another sample of bypass patients. This report focused not on psychological adaptation, but on a medical problem that sometimes arises after bypass surgery: the need for rehospitalization, owing to infection from the surgery or to complications from the underlying disease. Scheier et al. (1999) found that optimists were significantly less likely to be rehospitalized, controlling for medical variables and other personality measures. It is not clear whether this effect stems from behavioral differences in coping (e.g., remaining active, complying more fully with medical regimens), from differences in emotional responses, or from concomitant differences in the physical processes inside the patients (e.g., immune function). Nonetheless, the finding suggests an important medical difference related to this personality variable.

Another research group (Leedham et al., 1995) has even explored the effects of positive expectations on experiences surrounding heart transplant surgery (this study did not examine optimism *per se*, but variables conceptually linked to optimism). Patients (and their nurses) completed questionnaires prior to surgery, at discharge, and at 3 and 6 months post surgery. Initial questionnaires assessed patients' confidence about the efficacy of treatment, their expectations about their future health and survival, and broader expectations for the future. Positive expectations related to higher quality of life later on, even among patients who had health setbacks. Importantly, confidence predicted better adherence to the postoperative medical regimen (reflecting engagement), and strongly predicted nurses' ratings of patients' physical health at 6 months after surgery. There was also a tendency for positive expectations to predict longer delays before the development of infection (which is a near-universal side-effect of heart transplantation).

Cancer

Cancer is another chronic illness that has received attention from psychologists (see Andersen, this volume). Several studies have examined the relationships between optimism, coping, and wellbeing among cancer patients. One study focused on women who were scheduled for breast biopsy (Stanton and Snider, 1993). Optimism, coping, and mood were assessed the day before biopsy and (among women who had cancer) 24 hours before and 3 weeks after surgery.

Pessimistic women in this study used more cognitive avoidance in coping with the upcoming diagnostic procedure than did optimists. This avoidance contributed significantly to distress prior to biopsy. Indeed, avoidance proved to be a mediator of the association of pessimism with prebiopsy distress. Cognitive avoidance before biopsy also predicted post-biopsy distress among women with positive diagnoses.

Another study examined adjustment to treatment for early-stage breast cancer (Carver et al., 1992). Breast cancer is life-threatening, but the prognosis for early-stage cancer (stages I and II) is relatively good. There thus is enough ambiguity about the future to permit individual differences to be readily expressed. Optimism, coping, and mood were assessed the day before surgery. Coping and mood were also assessed 10 days post surgery, and at 3-, 6-, and 12-month follow-ups.

Optimism predicted lower distress, above and beyond the effect of medical variables and the effects of earlier distress. That is, prediction of distress at 3, 6, and 12 months after surgery was significant even controlling for the immediately prior level of distress. Thus, optimism predicted not just lower initial distress, but also resilience against distress during the year following surgery.

Both before and after surgery, optimism also related to a pattern of coping responses that revolved around accepting the reality of the situation, placing as positive a light on the situation as possible, trying to relieve the situation with humor, and (at presurgery only) taking active steps to do whatever there was to be done. Pessimism related to pushing the situation away (denial) and to a giving-up tendency at each time point. The coping responses that related to optimism also related strongly to distress. Not unexpectedly, given the pattern of the correlations, the effect of optimism on distress was largely indirect through coping.

The fact that optimists and pessimists differed in their use of problem-focused coping is entirely consistent with the self-regulation model. Not directly predicted, however, was the fact that optimists and pessimists also differed in the way they accepted the reality of this difficult situation. In retrospect, however, the findings fit the self-regulation framework. That is, it probably is easier to accept the reality of a bad situation if one is confident of a favorable eventual outcome. Further, acceptance of a hard situation is the necessary first step in the process of overcoming the threat the situation poses.

Most of the research on optimism among cancer patients deals with subjective quality of life. However, at least some findings link pessimism (and avoidance coping) to survival, although the mechanism for such effects remains highly speculative. Patients in one project (Schulz et al., 1996), all with recurrent cancer, were assessed and then followed for 8 months, by which time approximately one-third had died. Among the younger subset of participants, pessimism predicted mortality: controlling for site of cancer and levels of symptoms at baseline, persons with a pessimistic orientation were less likely to remain alive at the 8-month follow-up.

Another study examined the progression of cancer across the period of a year (Epping-Jordan et al., 1994). Subjects were patients who varied in terms of disease site and prognosis, who completed a variety of measures, and who then were followed. At 1-year follow-up, after controlling for initial prognosis, patients who had earlier reported trying to avoid thinking or talking about the cancer exhibited more disease progression than those who had been less avoidant.

A third study followed a large cohort of early-stage breast cancer patients for a period of 5 years after diagnosis and treatment (Watson et al., 1999). The study examined whether measures collected at the time of diagnosis would predict health outcomes. Reacting to the diagnosis with a response of hopelessness (similar to the disengagement reaction) was associated with an elevated risk of relapse and death over the next 5 years.

Finally, a recent study with early-stage cancer patients has found that a group stress management intervention can have an influence on dispositional optimism, despite the fact that optimism is a stable trait. The intervention significantly increased the levels of optimism reported by the patients, and the elevations remained in place at 3- and 9-month follow-ups (Antoni et al., 2001). It is too soon to know whether these changes will have health benefits, but these patients will be followed for that purpose in the years to come.

HIV and AIDS

Information regarding optimism and coping also comes from research on HIV and AIDS patients (see also Antoni, this volume). In one study (Taylor et al., 1992), optimism related to active coping strategies. Optimism predicted positive attitudes and tendencies to plan for recovery, seek information, and reframe bad situations to see their most positive aspects. Optimists used less fatalism, self-blame, and escapism, and did not focus on the negative aspects of the situation or try to suppress thoughts about their symptoms. Optimists also appeared to accept situations that they could not change, rather than trying to escape those situations.

Two other studies relating to individual differences in disease management examined the development of symptoms in men who were HIV positive but symptom free. The question was whether psychological variables would predict who developed symptoms first. In one study (Reed et al., 1999) an index of stoic acceptance was derived, involving mental preparation for the worst and acceptance of the inevitable. This index, which has been characterized as reflecting adverse disease-specific expectancies (Reed et al., 1994), predicted earlier symptom onset.

Another study (Ironson et al., 1994) followed participants who had no symptoms for 2 years, after informing them of their HIV-positive serostatus. Measures of coping were collected both before diagnosis and again 5 weeks after diagnosis. Participants who after diagnosis reported greater denial (the tendency to try to push the reality of the positive diagnosis away and treat it as though it was not real) and greater disengagement were more likely to have developed AIDS symptoms 2 years later.

Summary

Taken as a group, these various studies indicate that optimists differ from pessimists in the kinds of coping responses they use when confronting health threats. In general, the findings suggest that optimists tend to use more problem-focused strategies than do pessimists. When problem-focused coping is not a possibility, optimists turn to adaptive emotion-focused strategies, such as acceptance, use of humor, and positive reframing. These strategies keep them engaged with the effort to move forward with their lives. Pessimists tend to cope through overt denial and by disengaging from goals with which the stressor is interfering. Moreover, these differences in coping appear to be at least partly responsible for differences between optimists and pessimists in emotional wellbeing. The findings thus implicate elements of self-regulation models in coping with chronic illness.

It is particularly noteworthy that optimists turn in part toward acceptance in uncontrollable situations, whereas pessimists tend toward denial. Denial (the refusal to accept the reality of the situation) means trying to adhere to a world view that is no longer valid. In contrast, acceptance implies a restructuring of one's experience to come to grips with the reality of the situation. Acceptance thus may involve a deeper set of processes in which the person actively works through the experience, attempting to integrate it into an evolving world view (cf. Janoff-Bulman, 1992; Tedeschi and Calhoun, 1995).

The attempt to come to terms with the existence of problems may confer special benefit to acceptance as a coping response. We should be very clear, however, about what we mean. The acceptance we are stressing here is a willingness to admit that a problem exists or that an event has happened – even an event that may irrevocably alter the fabric of the person's life. We are *not* talking about a stoic resignation, a fatalistic acceptance of the negative consequences to which the problem event might lead, no matter how likely those consequences might be. The latter response does not confer a benefit and may even be detrimental (Greer et al., 1979, 1990; Pettingale et al., 1985; Reed et al., 1994; for further discussion of this issue, see Scheier and Carver, in press).

Concluding Comment

In this chapter we have highlighted the links between a model of the self-regulation of action and the experience of stress and coping, and then applied some of those ideas to the experience of having a chronic illness. We believe that understanding the psychological impact of a chronic illness requires having a model of the processes behind behavior more generally. In our attempt to argue for the merits of that belief, we pointed to several conceptual links between elements of the self-regulation model and others' conceptualizations of stress and coping. Although space constraints prevent a deeper discussion of the coping literature, we believe many more aspects of that literature also fit this picture (see Zeidner and Endler, 1996).

In essence, we emphasize that stress is not an all-or-nothing phenomenon, and coping is not fundamentally different in kind from other behavior. Disruptions in life fall along a continuum, ranging from minor threats and frustrations to devastating losses. All disruptions, large and small, raise issues that need to be resolved by the people involved. The approach taken here suggests that the underlying structure of those issues is the same, regardless of the source of the disruption. The person's effort to dissolve the adversity, to dampen its subjective impact, or to accommodate to the new life situation that the adversity brings with it, are the essence of coping – and of self-regulation.

In considering how the concepts discussed in those sections relate to the experience of chronic illness, we began with a simple assumption about how such illnesses intrude into the lives of the people who confront them. Specifically, we assumed that chronic illnesses pose a continuing threat to the carrying out of activities that make up people's lives. They constitute impediments to moving toward desired goals. Any chronic illness threatens multiple aspects of a person's ongoing life. If the behavioral domains that are disrupted constitute core areas of the person's identity, such an illness can threaten the very sense of self.

People respond to such threats in diverse ways, some of which appear more adaptive than others. In discussing this point, we suggested that there are drawbacks to giving up too soon and failing to exert one's best efforts. There are also drawbacks to persisting too long. We believe that the optimal course lies somewhere in between. People must accept the reality of the health threats they confront, and the possibility that chronic illness may mean changes in their lives. The key is to recognize that change in life does not mean the end of life, and it does not even mean the end of one's dreams and aspirations. If the disease hampers one's ability to engage in the relevant activities some of those goals must be scaled back, but the values of greatest importance to people can usually be expressed in many different ways, some of which are not likely to be precluded by chronic illness.

References

Antoni, M. H., Lehman, J. M., Kilbourn, K. M., Boyers, A. E., Culver, J. L., Alferi, S. M., Yount, S. E., McGregor, B. A., Arena, P. L., Harris, S. D., Price, A. A., and Carver, C. S. (2001). Cognitive–behavioral stress management intervention decreases the prevalence of depression and enhances benefit finding among women under treatment for early-stage breast cancer. *Health Psychology*, 20, 20–32.

Armor, D. A., and Taylor, S. E. (1998). Situated optimism: Specific outcome expectancies and self-regulation. In M. Zanna (Ed.), *Advances in Experimental Social Psychology* (Vol. 29, pp. 309–379). San Diego: Academic Press.

Austin, J. T., and Vancouver, J. B. (1996). Goal constructs in psychology: Structure, process, and content. *Psychological Bulletin*, 120, 338–375.

Bandura, A. (1997). *Self-Efficacy: the Exercise of Control*. New York: Freeman.

Baumeister, R. F., and Scher, S. J. (1988). Self-defeating behavior patterns among normal individuals: Review and analysis of common self-destructive tendencies. *Psychological Bulletin*, 104, 3–22.

Beck, A. T., Steer, R. A., Kovacs, M., and Garrison, B. (1985). Hopelessness and eventual suicide: A 10-year prospective study of patients hospitalized with suicidal ideation. *American Journal of Psychiatry*, 142, 559–563.

Cameron, L. D., and Nicholls, G. (1998). Expression of stressful experiences through writing: Effects of a self-regulation manipulation for pessimists and optimists. *Health Psychology*, 17, 84–92.

Cantor, N., and Kihlstrom, J. F. (1987). *Personality and Social Intelligence*. Englewood Cliffs, NJ: Prentice-Hall.

Carver, C. S. (1996). Goal engagement and the human experience. In R. S. Wyer, Jr. (Ed.), *Advances in Social Cognition* (Vol. 9, pp. 49–61). Mahwah, NJ: Erlbaum.

Carver, C. S., Pozo, C., Harris, S. D., Noriega, V., Scheier, M. F., Robinson, D. S., Ketcham, A. S., Moffat, F. L., Jr., and Clark, K. C. (1993). How coping mediates the effect of optimism on distress: A study of women with early stage breast cancer. *Journal of Personality and Social Psychology*, 65, 375–390.

Carver, C. S., and Scheier, M. F. (1981). *Attention and Self-Regulation: A Control-Theory Approach to Human Behavior*. New York: Springer Verlag.

Carver, C. S., and Scheier, M. F. (1990). Origins and functions of positive and negative affect: A control-process view. *Psychological Review*, 97, 19–35.

Carver, C. S., and Scheier, M. F. (1998). *On the Self-Regulation of Behavior*. New York: Cambridge University Press.

Carver, C. S., and Scheier, M. F. (1999a). Optimism. In C. R. Snyder (Ed.), *Coping: The Psychology of what Works* (pp. 182–204). New York: Oxford University Press.

Carver, C. S., and Scheier, M. F. (1999b). Several more themes, a lot more issues: Commentary on the commentaries. In R. S. Wyer, Jr. (Ed.), *Advances in Social Cognition* (Vol. 12, pp. 261–302). Mahwah, NJ: Erlbaum.

Carver, C. S., and Scheier, M. F. (1999c). Stress, coping, and self-regulatory processes. In L. A. Pervin and O. P. John (Eds.), *Handbook of Personality* (2nd ed.) (pp. 41–84). New York: Guilford.

Carver, C. S., and Scheier, M. F. (1999d). Themes and issues in the self-regulation of behavior. In R. S. Wyer, Jr. (Ed.), *Advances in Social Cognition* (Vol. 12, pp. 1–105). Mahwah, NJ: Erlbaum.

Carver, C. S., Scheier, M. F., and Pozo, C. (1992). Conceptualizing the process of coping with health problems. In H. S. Friedman (Ed.), *Hostility, Coping, and Health* (pp. 167–199). Washington, D.C.: American Psychological Association.

Cleiren, M. (1993). *Bereavement and Adaptation: A Comparative Study of the Aftermath of Death*. Washington, DC: Hemisphere.

Elliott, E. S., and Dweck, C. S. (1988). Goals: An approach to motivation and achievement. *Journal of Personality and Social Psychology*, 54, 5–12.

Emmons, R. A. (1986). Personal strivings: An approach to personality and subjective well being. *Journal of Personality and Social Psychology*, 51, 1058–1068.

Epping-Jordan, J. E., Compas, B. E., and Howell, D. C. (1994). Predictors of cancer progression in young adult men and women: Avoidance, intrusive thoughts, and psychological symptoms. *Health Psychology*, 13, 539–547.

Feather, N. T. (1989). Trying and giving up: Persistence and lack of persistence in failure situations. In R. C. Curtis (Ed.), *Self-Defeating Behaviors: Experimental Research, Clinical Impressions, and Practical Implications* (pp. 67–95). New York: Plenum.

Fitzgerald, T. E., Tennen, H., Affleck, G., and Pransky, G. S. (1993). The relative importance of dispositional optimism and control appraisals in quality of life after coronary artery bypass surgery. *Journal of Behavioral Medicine*, 16, 25–43.

Greenwald, A. G. (1980). The totalitarian ego: Fabrication and revision of personal history. *American Psychologist*, 35, 603–618.

Greer, S., Morris, T., and Pettingale, K. W. (1979). Psychological response to breast cancer: Effect on outcome. *Lancet*, 2, 785–787.

Greer, S., Morris, T., Pettingale, K. W., and Haybittle, J. L. (1990). Psychological response to breast cancer and 15-year outcome. *Lancet*, 1, 49–50.

Gross, J. J. (1998). Antecedent- and response-focused emotion regulation: Divergent consequences for experience, expression, and physiology. *Journal of Personality and Social Psychology*, 74, 224–237.

Higgins, E. T. (1987). Self-discrepancy: A theory relating self and affect. *Psychological Review*, 94, 319–340.

Higgins, E. T. (1996). Ideals, oughts, and regulatory focus: Affect and motivation from distinct pains and pleasures. In P. M. Gollwitzer and J. A. Bargh (Eds.), *The Psychology of Action: Linking Cognition and Motivation to Behavior* (pp. 91–114). New York: Guilford.

Hobfoll, S. E. (1989). Conservation of resources: A new attempt at conceptualizing stress. *American Psychologist*, 44, 513–524.

Hobfoll, S. E., Freedy, J. R., Green, B. L., and Solomon, S. D. (1996). Coping in reaction to extreme stress: The roles of resource loss and resource availability. In M. Zeidner and N. S. Endler (Eds.), *Handbook of Coping: Theory, Research, Applications* (pp. 322–349). New York: Wiley.

Holman, E. A., and Silver, R. C. (1998). Getting "stuck" in the past: Temporal orientation and coping with trauma. *Journal of Personality and Social Psychology*, 74, 1146–1163.

Ironson, G., Friedman, A., Klimas, N., Antoni, M., Fletcher, M. A., LaPerriere, A., Simoneau, J., and Schneiderman, N. (1994). Distress, denial, and low adherence to behavioral interventions predict faster disease progression in gay men infected with human immunodeficiency virus. *International Journal of Behavioral Medicine*, 1, 90–105.

Janoff-Bulman, R. (1992). *Shattered Assumptions*. New York: Free Press.

Janoff-Bulman, R., and Brickman, P. (1982). Expectations and what people learn from failure. In N. T. Feather (Ed.), *Expectations and Actions: Expectancy-Value Models in Psychology* (pp. 207–237). Hillsdale, NJ: Erlbaum.

Klinger, E. (1975). Consequences of commitment to and disengagement from incentives. *Psychological Review*, 82, 1–25.

Kukla, A. (1972). Foundations of an attributional theory of performance. *Psychological Review*, 79, 454–470.

Lazarus, R. S. (1966). *Psychological Stress and the Coping Process*. New York: McGraw-Hill.

Lazarus, R. S., and Folkman, S. (1984). *Stress, Appraisal, and Coping*. New York: Springer.

Lecci, L., Okun, M. A., and Karoly, P. (1994). Life regrets and current goals as predictors of psychological adjustment. *Journal of Personality and Social Psychology*, 66, 731–741.

Leedham, B., Meyerowitz, B. E., Muirhead, J., and Frist, W. H. (1995). Positive expectations predict health after heart transplantation. *Health Psychology*, 14, 74–79.

Linville, P. (1985). Self-complexity and affective extremity: Don't put all of your eggs in one cognitive basket. *Social Cognition*, 3, 94–120.

Linville, P. (1987). Self-complexity as a cognitive buffer against stress-related illness and depression. *Journal of Personality and Social Psychology*, 52, 663–676.

Little, B. R. (1989). Personal projects analysis: Trivial pursuits, magnificent obsessions, and the search for coherence. In D. M. Buss and N. Cantor (Eds.), *Personality Psychology: Recent Trends and Emerging Directions* (pp. 15–31). New York: Springer-Verlag.

MacNair, R. R., and Elliott, T. R. (1992). Self-perceived problem-solving ability, stress appraisal, and coping over time. *Journal of Research in Personality*, 26, 150–164.

Markus, H., and Nurius, P. (1986). Possible selves. *American Psychologist*, 41, 954–969.

McIntosh, W. D., and Martin, L. L. (1992). The cybernetics of happiness: The relation of goal attainment, rumination, and affect. In M. S. Clark (Ed.), *Review of Personality and Social Psychology: Volume 14. Emotion and Social Behavior* (pp. 222–246). Newbury Park, CA: Sage.

Miller, G. A., Galanter, E., and Pribram, K. H. (1960). *Plans and the Structure of Behavior*. New York: Holt, Rinehart, and Winston.

Miller, L. C., and Read, S. J. (1987). Why am I telling you this? Self-disclosure in a goal-based model of personality. In V. J. Derlega and J. Berg (Eds.), *Self-Disclosure: Theory, Research, and Therapy* (pp. 35–58). New York: Plenum.

Moskowitz, J. T., Folkman, S., Collette, L., and Vittinghoff, E. (1996). Coping and mood during AIDS-related caregiving and bereavement. *Annals of Behavioral Medicine*, 18, 49–57.

Oettingen, G. (1996). Positive fantasy and motivation. In P. M. Gollwitzer and J. A. Bargh (Eds.), *The Psychology of Action: Linking Cognition and Motivation to Behavior* (pp. 219–235). New York: Guilford Press.

Orbuch, T. L. (Ed.). (1992). *Close Relationship Loss: Theoretical Approaches*. New York: Springer-Verlag.

Pervin, L. A. (1982). The stasis and flow of behavior: Toward a theory of goals. In M. M. Page and R. Dienstbier (Eds.), *Nebraska Symposium on Motivation* (Vol. 30, pp. 1–53). Lincoln: University of Nebraska Press.

Pervin, L. A. (Ed.). (1989). *Goal Concepts in Personality and Social Psychology*. Hillsdale, NJ: Erlbaum.

Pettingale, K. W., Morris, T., and Greer, S. (1985). Mental attitudes to cancer: An additional prognostic factor. *Lancet*, 1, 750.

Pittman, T. S., and Pittman, N. L. (1980). Deprivation of control and the attribution process. *Journal of Personality and Social Psychology*, 39, 377–389.

Powers, W. T. (1973). *Behavior: The Control of Perception*. Chicago: Aldine.

Pyszczynski, T., and Greenberg, J. (1992). *Hanging on and Letting Go: Understanding the Onset, Progression, and Remission of Depression*. New York: Springer-Verlag.

Reed, G. M., Kemeny, M. E., Taylor, S. E., Wang, H.-Y. J., and Visscher, B. R. (1994). "Realistic acceptance" as a predictor of decreased survival time in gay men with AIDS. *Health Psychology*, 13, 299–307.

Reed, G. M., Kemeny, M. E., Taylor, S. E., and Visscher, B. R. (1999). Negative HIV-specific expectancies and AIDS-related bereavement as predictors of symptom onset in asymptomatic HIV-positive gay men. *Health Psychology*, 18, 354–363.

Scheier, M. F., and Carver, C. S. (1985). Optimism, coping and health: Assessment and implications of generalized outcome expectancies. *Health Psychology*, 4, 219–247.

Scheier, M. F., and Carver, C. S. (1992). Effects of optimism on psychological and physical well-being: Theoretical overview and empirical update. *Cognitive Therapy and Research*, 16, 201–228.

Scheier, M. F., and Carver, C. S. (in press). Adapting to cancer: The importance of hope and purpose. In A. Baum and B. L. Andersen (Eds.), *Psychosocial Interventions for Cancer*. Washington, DC: American Psychological Association.

Scheier, M. F., Carver, C. S., and Bridges, M. W. (2001). Optimism, pessimism, and psychological well-being. In E. C. Chang (Ed.), *Optimism and Pessimism: Implications for Theory, Research, and Practice* (pp. 189–216). Washington DC: American Psychological Association.

Scheier, M. F., Matthews, K. A., Owens, J. F., Magovern, G. J., Sr., Lefebvre, R. C., Abbott, R. A., and Carver, C. S. (1989). Dispositional optimism and recovery from coronary artery bypass surgery: The beneficial effects on physical and psychological well being. *Journal of Personality and Social Psychology*, 57, 1024–1040.

Scheier, M. F., Matthews, K. A., Owens, J. F., Schulz, R., Bridges, M. W., Magovern, G. J., Sr., and Carver, C. S. (1999). Optimism and rehospitalization following coronary artery bypass graft surgery. *Archives of Internal Medicine*, 159, 829–835.

Schulz, R., Bookwala, J., Knapp, J. E., Scheier, M. F., and Williamson, G. M. (1996). Pessimism, age, and cancer mortality. *Psychology and Aging*, 11, 304–309.

Showers, C. J., and Ryff, C. D. (1996). Self-differentiation and well being in a life transition. *Personality and Social Psychology Bulletin*, 22, 448–460.

Stanton, A. L., and Snider, P. R. (1993). Coping with breast cancer diagnosis: A prospective study. *Health Psychology*, 12, 16–23.

Stroebe, M. S., Stroebe, W., and Hansson, R. O. (Eds.) (1993). *Handbook of Bereavement: Theory, Research, and Intervention*. Cambridge: Cambridge University Press.

Taylor, S. E., Kemeny, M. E., Aspinwall, L. G., Schneider, S. G., Rodriguez, R., and Herbert, M. (1992). Optimism, coping, psychological distress, and high-risk sexual behavior among men at risk for Acquired Immunodeficiency Syndrome (AIDS). *Journal of Personality and Social Psychology*, 63, 460–473.

Taylor, S. E., and Pham, L. B. (1996). Mental stimulation, motivation, and action. In P. M. Gollwitzer and J. A. Bargh (Eds.), *The Psychology of Action: Linking Cognition and Motivation To Behavior* (pp. 219–235). New York: Guilford.

Taylor, S. E., Pham, L. B., Rivkin, I. D., and Armor, D. A. (1998). Harnessing the imagination: Mental simulation, self-regulation, and coping. *American Psychologist*, 53, 429–439.

Tedeschi, R. G., and Calhoun, L. G. (1995). *Trauma and Transformation: Growing in the Aftermath of Suffering*. Thousand Oaks, CA: Sage.

Vallacher, R. R., and Wegner, D. M. (1987). What do people think they're doing? Action identification and human behavior. *Psychological Review*, 94, 3–15.

Watson, M., Haviland, J. S., Greer, S., Davidson, J., and Bliss, J. M. (1999). Influence of psychological response on survival in breast cancer: A population-based cohort study. *Lancet*, 354, 1331–1336.

Wicklund, R. A. and Gollwitzer, P. M. (1982). *Symbolic Self-Completion*. Hillsdale, NJ: Erlbaum.

Wills, T. A. (1981). Downward comparison principles in social psychology. *Psychological Bulletin*, 90, 245–271.

Wine, J. D. (1971). Test anxiety and direction of attention. *Psychological Bulletin*, 76, 92–104.

Wine, J. D. (1980). Cognitive–attentional theory of test anxiety. In I. G. Sarason (Ed.), *Test Anxiety: Theory, Research, and Application* (pp. 349–378). Hillsdale, NJ: Erlbaum.

Wong, P. T. P., and Weiner, B. (1981). When people ask "why" questions, and the heuristics of attributional search. *Journal of Personality and Social Psychology*, 40, 650–663.

Wood, J. V. (1989). Theory and research concerning social comparisons of personal attributes. *Psychological Bulletin*, 106, 231–248.

Wood, J. V., Taylor, S. E., and Lichtman, R. R. (1985). Social comparison in adjustment to breast cancer. *Journal of Personality and Social Psychology*, 49, 1169–1183.

Wortman, C. B., and Brehm, J. W. (1975). Responses to uncontrollable outcomes: An integration of reactance theory and the learned helplessness model. In L. Berkowitz (Ed.), *Advances in Experimental Social Psychology* (Vol. 8, pp. 277–336). New York: Academic Press.

Zeidner, M., and Endler, N. S. (Eds.). (1996). *Handbook of Coping: Theory, Research, Applications*. New York: Wiley.

CHAPTER 4

Adherence in the Management of Chronic Disorders

Jacqueline Dunbar-Jacob, Elizabeth A. Schlenk and Donna Caruthers

University of Pittsburgh

Introduction

As the population rises and lifespan lengthens, the prevention and management of chronic disorders becomes an increasingly significant focus in healthcare. Estimates are that 85% of older people are affected by one or more of these conditions (McElnay and McCallion, 1998), the most common of which are arthritis and hypertension (Commerce, 1992). The majority of chronic disorders are managed with some combination of pharmacotherapy, dietary modification, and/or exercise. A major requirement for successful management is that the patient adheres to prescribed treatment. Yet data show that poor or nonadherence is a significant problem. Adherence rates average approximately 50%, whether one is examining drug therapy, dietary therapy, or continuation with therapeutic exercise. Inadequate management has contributed to unnecessary disease progression, complications, doctor visits, hospitalization, and even death (Dunbar-Jacob and Schlenk, 1996). Indeed, the impact of poor adherence is reflected in the findings that it may account for as much as 25% of transplant failures (Rovelli et al., 1989) and 50% of treatment failures in hypertension (Stephenson, 1999). The costs are substantial, with estimates running as high as $100 billion per year (Grahl, 1994).

Poor adherence comprises multiple behaviors, each of which may impact upon treatment (Dunbar-Jacob and Schlenk, 2000). First, patients may reject treatment. This can occur initially in therapy or at some later point. In the realm of pharmacotherapy, 20% of patients have been reported to fail to fill

Correspondence about this chapter should addressed to Jacqueline Dunbar-Jacob, University of Pittsburgh, Center for Research in Chronic Disorders, 460 Victoria Building, 3500 Victoria Street, Pittsburgh, PA 15261.

prescriptions (Burns et al., 1992), as many as 7% may fail to pick up filled pre-scriptions (Matsui et al., 2000), and an additional 5–25% may drop out of treatment (Dunbar and Knoke, 1986). In the arena of exercise as many as 50% of persons drop out of exercise programs by the sixth month, with an additional 25% dropping out over the next 6 months (Oldridge, 1988). These rates have been attributed to issues such as failure to perceive the need for treatment, lack of belief in treatment efficacy, cost, as well as inconvenient or adverse experiences with the treatment.

Secondly, patients may adjust the "dosage" of treatment. This can be seen in pharmacotherapy, where the number of drugs taken is reduced, in dietary alterations where the targeted nutrient goal is not met, or in exercise regi-mens where the number of sessions is reduced. Adjustments also include an increase in the dosage of treatment. Such dosage adjustments in pharmaco-therapy have been associated with symptom management, cost, and lack of comprehension of the regimen. Fewer data are available to evaluate the con-tributing factors in exercise and dietary modification.

Thirdly, patients may be quite variable in their regimen management. This is perhaps the most common pattern of poor adherence seen. Variations can include episodic missed or extra doses as well as errors in the timing of treatment. For example, with pharmacotherapy the patient may miss an occa-sional evening dose of medication, take two doses too close together, and/or take a brief holiday from medication taking. With dietary modifications the patient may err during a restaurant meal, skip the modification during a holiday, and/or take a dietary holiday while traveling. With exercise, the patient may exercise on two consecutive weekend days while skipping mid-week bouts, skip exercise on bad weather days, and/or take exercise holidays during periods of demanding work deadlines. The impact of such variability depends upon the frequency with which such patterns occur.

Episodic errors, such as those mentioned above, may occur because of several factors, including such things as the comprehension of the regimen, the ability to self-monitor, memory, inconvenience, as well as deliberate deci-sion making and potentially motivational factors. Our work suggests that interruptions in daily routine may be a major factor, at least in medication taking. In a preliminary study involving 51 persons with rheumatoid arthritis who were less than 40% adherent by electronic event monitor, the primary reasons for missed medications were *change in daily routine* and self-reported memory failure ($R^2 = 0.223$). For the 47 who were 40–80% adherent the primary reasons were running out of medication, *frequency of taking medication at the same time each day*, and being symptom free ($R^2 = 0.18$) (Dunbar-Jacob, 2001, unpublished data).

Unfortunately, little research has been done on these specific areas. Most of the research addressing rates of poor adherence, as well as predictors of adherence, has not separated out the types of errors seen in the management of the treatment regimen. Thus, what we know about adherence is relatively non-specific.

Measurement of Adherence

Part of the problem in identifying the specific types of errors that occur in the management of a treatment regimen lies in the strategies for assessing adherence. The commonly used measurement strategies – self-report, pill counts, and drug levels – typically provide summaries of the extent to which the regimen has been followed, with no detail on the timing and the nature of the errors. A strategy that can provide more information is a daily diary, which has the problems of timely completion and accuracy, as well as electronic measures, which have cost constraints.

The varying strategies for measurement of adherence also contribute to the broad range of adherence rates seen in the literature. Different measurement techniques exhibit differing levels of adherence to a specific regimen across the same population over the same time period (Dunbar-Jacob et al., 1998). Typically the errors are biased such that strategies related to self-report are more likely to overestimate adherence than are electronic methods (Dunbar-Jacob et al., 1996, 1998; Kass et al., 1986). These strategies have relatively poor sensitivity in identifying poor adherers (Sereika et al., 1998), and so many patients with poor adherence are overlooked. Improved identification of poor adherers, as well as improved methods of identifying the nature of the errors made in managing a treatment regimen, calls for improved sensitivity in measurement.

The limited sensitivity in assessment may also contribute to the variability in findings regarding factors associated with poor adherence. In our own work we have found that self-reporting and electronic monitors identify different predictors of medication adherence within the same population monitored over the same period of time (Dunbar-Jacob et al., 1995). Indeed, the predictors were sufficiently distinct that we suspect that the measures may tap different phenomena, e.g. how people report their adherence behavior versus how they actually adhere. Certainly this hypothesis needs further investigation.

Assessment of Medication Adherence

Perhaps the most common method of assessing medication adherence historically has been self-report, which continues to be a primary method of assessment in clinical practice. Yet self-report has been shown to have significant error. These errors may be due to various factors, one of which is the ability to remember one's behavior, particularly habitual behavior, over time. The amount of time that has elapsed influences the ease with which such memories are accessed (Belli et al., 1999). Individuals tend to recall a behavioral occurrence and telescope that behavior over time (e.g. Means and Loftus, 1991; Prohaska et al., 1998). In the case of medication assessment, adherence rates have been shown to be highest just before and immediately after a clinical visit (Cramer et al., 1990). Thus, the patient may recall their behavior at the recent level and telescope that behavior over time to arrive at the estimate that adherence has been consistently at higher levels. In this case adherence is incorrectly inferred in the direction of an overestimate, yet the patient may believe the overestimate is accurate. Patients may also deliberately overestimate adherence, presumably owing to social desirability influences. Indeed, in one study examining adherence to inhaled medication, the associated electronic monitor showed that a proportion of patients triggered the inhaler numerous times in a brief period before the clinical visit (Simmons et al., 2000). Although self-report may provide some detail about dosing errors if the patient acknowledges poor adherence, reports of good adherence may be masking problems.

Drug levels are also utilized in clinical practice to assess adherence. These levels provide little information on the patterns of adherence in terms of both dosing and timing. With studies in pharmacokinetics and in pharmacodynamics, numerous factors other than adherence have been found to affect drug levels. Drug levels have been shown to be affected by individual variations in drug absorption, metabolism, and excretion (Kroboth et al., 1991). Thus, although drug levels may offer some confirmation that drug has been ingested, they are not particularly useful in determining the level of adherence to that drug.

Another form of self-report is the daily diary. Diaries offer the opportunity to identify patterns of poor adherence as well as the circumstances surrounding poor adherence events. However, questions arise about the accuracy and timing of recording. Our own data among patients with rheumatoid arthritis participating in an adherence study, suggested that the relationship between diary and monitored adherence was poor, with both over- and underreporting errors.

Pill counts have been used extensively in clinical trials, but have been less practical in clinical settings. Pill counts have also been shown to overestimate adherence when contrasted with electronic monitoring (Dunbar-Jacob et al., 1996) as well as with drug levels (Mattson and Friedman, 1984). Further, they do not offer information on dosing or timing errors. Pharmacy refills have been used in managed care practices with pharmacies and through the use of Medicare databases. They have similar limitations to the pill count in that dosing or timing errors are not identified.

Electronic monitors have become closest to a gold standard in studies of adherence, although cost is still a barrier to clinical practice. These monitors offer the advantage of identifying dosing and timing errors, as well as patterns of poor adherence (Dunbar-Jacob et al., 1998). Thus, monitors offer the opportunity to identify factors that contribute to poor or nonadherence for the individual. This further offers the opportunity to develop and test interventions tailored to specific regimen management errors.

Measurement of Physical Activity

As with medication adherence, physical activity is commonly measured through self-report, attendance, and, in research settings, electronic monitoring. Although fitness levels are often used, these reflect the outcome of physical activity rather than a measure of adherence to the prescribed exercise itself.

Self-report is the most common method of assessment and occurs through interview, diary, and questionnaire. Diaries are typically used over 1, 3, or 7 days and may collect data on the type of activity as well as its frequency, intensity, and duration. As with medication diaries problems are related to the accuracy and timeliness of completion. Our own work suggests that completion rates are high, with 99.6% of days completed over an 18-week period (Schlenk et al., 2000).

Physical activity questionnaires rely on recall to assess physical activity over variable periods of time, such as the past week, month, year, or lifetime. Those covering 1 year can capture seasonal variation. Patients may be asked to provide detailed accounts of their physical activities or a general estimate of usual or typical activity. The disadvantage of questionnaires is recall bias, in which patients err in reporting because of memory failures over time. For a compendium of physical activity questionnaires with evidence of psychometric studies, see the supplement to *Medicine and Science in Sports and Exercise*, Volume 29 (6), June 1997, prepared by Dr Andrea Kriska.

The two most common estimates for diary and questionnaire data are obtained by summing (a) time spent in physical activity as hours per week, which is the product of the frequency and duration; and (b) energy expended as MET-hours per week (kilocalories/kilogram/week), which is the product of time and intensity, expressed as METs or the metabolic cost of the activity. The latter can be converted to kilocalories per week by computing the product of MET-hours per week by body weight in kilograms (Kriska and Caspersen, 1997). The metabolic cost of various physical activities is available from several sources to compute energy expenditure (e.g. Ainsworth et al., 1993; Lee et al., 1992).

Objective measures have been used to validate physical activity measures in some studies. These include the respiratory chamber and the doubly labeled water technique (LaPorte et al., 1985), as well as a variety of motion sensors. The doubly labeled water technique is a method of measuring total energy expenditure over a period of several days. Patients drink isotopic enriched water, urine samples are collected, and isotope ratio mass spectrometry is performed on the samples.

Motion sensors include mechanical pedometers and, more recently, electronic digital pedometers, which count steps taken, distance walked, and kilocalories expended if stride length and weight are input. Bassett et al. (1996) reported that the DIGI-WALKER™ Step Counter is highly accurate, being within 1% of the actual steps taken. More sophisticated accelerometers estimate the energy expenditure of daily activities by measuring the acceleration and deceleration of movements in a given plane using a ceramic piezoelectric transducer (Rutter, 1994). The rate at which activity is counted is determined by a preprogrammed resting metabolic rate and the extent of bender disturbance from the frequency and intensity of movement. The calorie expenditures are computed from kilocalories from regression equations provided by the manufacturer, considering height, weight, age, and gender (Rutter, 1994). Recent research has shown a relationship between triaxial acceleration output and the metabolic cost of physical activity ($r = 0.95$) (Bouten et al., 1994). We corroborated daily exercise diaries in a study with subjects with fibromyalgia syndrome. During the first 3 days of baseline there was a mean agreement of $88.4\% \pm 31.1\%$ between walking reported in the subjects' diaries and TriTrac-R3D™ accelerometers. The κ statistics were good to excellent (κ = 0.80, P < 0.001; κ = 0.71, P < 0.001; κ = 0.78, P < 0.001). These data suggest that exercise dairies provide an accurate estimate of exercise adherence (Schlenk et al., 2000).

Measurement of Dietary Adherence

Measurement of dietary adherence involves assessing what the subject eats and determining the degree to which food intake approaches the prescribed diet (Burke et al., 1997). This discussion will focus on the first element. Dietary adherence is most frequently assessed by self-report using 24-hour recall, food diaries, food frequency questionnaires, and diet histories (Block, 1982, 1989). The interviewer-administered 24-hour recall may be subject to social desirability and may not be representative of the subject's usual food intake because of the short duration. Food diaries are typically used for 3–7 days and, as with all diaries, are dependent upon the patient's willingness to record accurately. Additionally, the patient must be able to identify food preparation methods and the amount of food consumed. Food frequency questionnaires are convenient, economical, and provide representative data (Willett et al., 1985). However, because they include foods most often consumed by the US population they may not be useful across ethnic groups (Burke et al., 1997). Interviewer-administered food histories provide extensive data, but can be influenced by recall bias and subject fatigue.

Biological measures can be used to assess dietary adherence, such as 24-hour urine assays and urine dipstick tests to estimate sodium intake (Burke and Dunbar-Jacob, 1995), and stool weights to assess fiber (Greenwald et al., 1992). Limitations of biological measures are that they only assess adherence near the assay point, which is often at a follow-up appointment when adherence is at its best (Cramer et al., 1990). Further, they do not provide a precise level of adherence.

Thus there are relatively consistent sets of assessment strategies for assessing adherence to various health behaviors. These include self-report (interview, diary, questionnaire), biological assays, and electronic monitors. The strengths and weaknesses of these are relatively consistent across behaviors, with one exception. The diary has been shown to have limited accuracy when used over an extended period with medication taking, but has shown better accuracy, at least when used over a brief period, with physical activity. Selected unique strategies exist as well, such as the pill count for medication taking and the doubly labeled water method for physical activity. Problems of recall, accuracy of assessment, and willingness to report accurately affect all of the self-report measures. Specificity in identifying adherence levels is an issue with the biological assays. Also, cost is a factor for all of the electronic monitors. Indeed, the level of detail obtained with regard to the nature of adherence and the accuracy of the assessment appears to be inversely related to the cost involved in assessment. Yet detail and accuracy are important if we are to identify the types of errors made and to design and evaluate strategies for intervening on those errors.

Strategies to Improve Adherence

Adherence intervention research has been conducted with various disease models, such as infectious disease, cardiovascular risk factors, pulmonary disease, and others (Haynes et al., 1996; Volmink and Garner, 2000). However, few studies have used theory-directed adherence intervention approaches in randomized controlled trials (Berg et al., 1997; Jeffery et al., 1998; Smith et al., 1997; Smith and Biddle, 1999), although such an approach has been advocated. The intervention studies driven by conceptual frameworks have included cognitive, behavioral, and subject-regulated approaches to enhance treatment adherence for medications, weight management, and exercise.

Behavioral Intervention Studies

Behavioral interventions for enhancing adherence appear to be relatively effective as individual strategies (Roter et al., 1998), although a limited number have a follow-up period sufficient to examine long-term effectiveness. The use of behavioral strategies requires specific skills in behavior shaping and reinforcement (Kaplan et al., 1993; Masters et al., 1987). The interventions may incorporate specific strategies, such as problem solving, relapse prevention, goal setting, incentives, modeling, contracting, and reminders/cuing. Indeed, most studies that have identified a behavioral framework have used multiple components or not specified the specific strategies utilized. A review of those studies that examined individual behavioral strategies and their effect on adherence follows. In most of these, adherence was assessed through self-report.

The use of incentives has shown short-term results in limited studies. Morisky and Tulsky each found an advantage for monetary incentives in improving adherence to tuberculosis medication (Morisky et al., 1990; Tulsky et al., 2000). Using a lottery incentive, short-term attendance to an exercise program was improved, but had no long-term advantage and no impact on weight loss (Jeffery et al., 1998). Verbal reinforcement has also been found to contribute to favorable – though nonsignificant – changes in fat and fiber intake (Beresford et al., 1992). Although reinforcement of some form is a common component of behavioral interventions, there are few randomized, controlled studies that have examined its contribution to enhancing adherence. However, these few studies suggest that, at least for short-term change, incentives may be useful.

Reminders may have some effectiveness in enhancing adherence to appointment keeping, although the results have been variable (Ahluwalia et al., 1996; Keder et al., 1998; Martin, 1998; Morrow et al., 1999a; O'Brian and

Lazebnik, 1998). Work by Morrow suggests that certain dimensions of reminders may enhance their usefulness. Repetition (Morrow et al., 1999b; Morrow et al., 1999a), length (Morrow et al., 1998), and organization (Morrow et al., 1998) appear to be important dimensions of the reminder.

Tailoring is yet another strategy that has been evaluated for its impact on adherence. Tailoring in this arena was first evaluated by Haynes and colleagues in the first randomized, controlled intervention study addressing medication adherence with adherence assessed through pill count (Haynes et al., 1976). More recently tailored newsletters have been paired with goal setting and the combination has been successful in improving daily fruit and vegetable intake (Lutz et al., 1999), whereas tailored feedback has also been effective in lowering fat intake and increasing fruit and vegetable intake (Brug et al., 1998). Tailored advice with a tailored pamphlet has also been superior to standard advice or pamphlets on the promotion of exercise (Bull and Jamrozik, 1998). Thus, this technique for individualizing appears to be effective in the few studies in which it has been evaluated.

Cognitive/Social Cognitive Theories

Perhaps the most common cognitive–behavioral intervention seen in the adherence arena is that of self-efficacy enhancement, an element that has been shown to be a predictor of treatment adherence (e.g., Brus et al., 1999; Kavanagh et al., 1993; Pavone et al., 1998). The theoretical model addresses two primary variables: self-efficacy, or the perception of ability to carry out a behavior under varying conditions, and outcome expectancy, or the perception that engaging in the behavior would have a desired outcome (Bandura, 1997). The theory proposes that efficacy is enhanced through mastery, persuasion, modeling, and/or physiological feedback. In studies on adherence, enhancement of self-efficacy has been effected through self-management strategies (Berg et al., 1997) and motivational interviewing (Smith et al., 1997), or through unspecified strategies. The effectiveness of self-efficacy enhancing interventions has been noted in the case of medication adherence (Berg et al., 1997), dietary modifications (Allen, 1996; Shannon et al., 1997; Smith et al., 1997) as well as exercise (Allen, 1996).

Theory of Reasoned Action and Planned Behavior

The theory of reasoned action and planned behavior has examined predictors of adherence, with a limited examination of the utility of the theory on intervention. This theory considers the intention of behavior, which is viewed as being under voluntary control and influenced by attitudes, beliefs and expectations (Ajzen, 1988). The theory predicted intention in an intervention study on exercise promotion (Smith and Biddle, 1999), but was not associated with appointment keeping for tuberculosis skin testing (Malotte et al., 1998).

Although numerous theories (e.g., Health Belief Model, Transtheoretical Model, Protection Motivation, and various social support models) have been utilized to examine predictors of adherence, few have been used to examine the efficacy of interventions in improving patient adherence to treatment regimens. Patient education has been utilized with varying results (Beresford et al., 1997; Bull and Jamrozik, 1998; Meland et al., 1997; Schapira et al., 1991; Turner et al., 1998; van der Palen et al., 1997), although without a particular theoretical orientation. These interventions seem to be more effective when messages are tailored (Bull and Jamrozik, 1998; Campbell et al., 1994; Lutz et al., 1999).

Unfortunately, the research has had little effect on the rates of adherence in practice. In the 1970s, adherence to medication, to diet, and to exercise was reported to be approximately 50%, with similar rates being reported today (Dunbar-Jacob, 2000). Clearly we need to learn more about how to improve this significant problem.

Summary and Conclusions

Failure to improve the widespread public health problem of poor adherence to treatment regimens requires careful examination of the work that has been carried out over the past 30 years. Overall, the intervention research on adherence is sparse. In the medication adherence arena there have been just 19 randomized controlled studies with at least a 6-month follow-up over the past 30 years (Haynes et al., 1996). The studies that address actual *adherence* to exercise or dietary prescriptions are even fewer. Further, there have been limited theoretical approaches to intervention, thus limiting the ability to develop and test interventions that may have broader applicability. Whereas behavioral strategies appear useful and are based upon extensive scientific data on interventions for other behaviors, the adherence data suggest that multicomponent strategies may be the most powerful (Roter et al., 1998). This may be related to the finding that the intervention studies do not appear to address specific behaviors or problems with adherence.

Intervention strategies in existing research tend to be all-inclusive, attempting to improve adherence without attention to the specific behavioral manifestations or the contributing causes. We may be much more effective in addressing the problems of poor adherence if we address specific behaviors and specific etiologies – the "patient by treatment interaction" approach advocated by Christensen (2000). This requires a much more focused examination of adherence than has been taken so far, by asking such questions as "What is the behavioral presentation of poor adherence?" and "What are the factors contributing to each of the various behavioral presentations?" This kind of approach further requires that measurement strategies be used that provide detailed descriptions of behavior over time and which permit the identification of associated factors with some degree of confidence. Clearly there is considerable work to be done to address the problem of poor adherence to treatment regimen if we are to solve this $100 billion problem in the management of chronic disease.

References

Ahluwalia, J. S., McNagny, S. E., and Kanuru, N. K. (1996). A randomized trial to improve follow-up care in severe uncontrolled hypertensives at an inner-city walk-in clinic. *Journal of Healthcare for the Poor and Underserved*, 7(4), 377–389.

Ainsworth, B. E., Haskell, W. L., Leon, A. S., Jacobs, D. R. Jr., Montoye, H. J., Sallis, J. F., and Paffenbarger, R. S. Jr. (1993). Compendium of physical activities: Classification of energy costs of human physical activities. *Medicine and Science in Sports and Exercise*, 25, 71–80.

Allen, J. K. (1996). Coronary risk factor modification in women after coronary artery bypass surgery. *Nursing Research*, 45, 260–265.

Ajzen, I. (1988). *Attitudes, personality, and behavior*. Chicago: Dorsey Press.

Bandura, A. (1997). *Self–efficacy: The exercise of control*. New York: W. H. Freeman and Company.

Bassett, D. R. Jr., Ainsworth, B. E., Leggett, S. R., Mathien, C. A., Main, J. A., Hunter, D. C., and Duncan, G. E. (1996). Accuracy of five electronic pedometers for measuring distance walked. *Medicine and Science in Sports and Exercise*, 28, 1071–1077.

Belli, R. F., Traugott, M. W., Young, M., and McGonagle, K. A. (1999). Reducing vote overreporting in surveys: Social desirability, memory failure, and source monitoring. *Public Opinion Quarterly*, 63, 90–108.

Beresford, S. A., Curry, S. J., Kristal, A. R., Lazovich, D., Feng, Z., and Wagner, E. H. (1997). A dietary intervention in primary care practice: The Eating Patterns Study. *American Journal of Public Health*, 87, 610–616.

Beresford, S. A., Farmer, E. M., Feingold, L., Graves, K. L., Sumner, S. K., and Baker, R. M. (1992). Evaluation of a self-help dietary intervention in a primary care setting. *American Journal of Public Health*, 82, 79–84.

Berg, J., Dunbar-Jacob, J., and Sereika, S. (1997). An evaluation of a self-management program for adults with asthma. *Clinical Nursing Research*, 6, 225–238.

Block, G. (1982). A review of validations of dietary assessment methods. *American Journal of Epidemiology*, 115, 492–505.

Block, G. (1989). Human dietary assessment: Methods and issues. *Preventive Medicine*, 18, 643–660.

Bouten, C. V., Westerterp, K. R., Verduin, M., and Janssen, J. D. (1994). Assessment of energy expenditure for physical activity using a triaxial accelerometer. *Medicine and Science in Sports and Exercise*, 26, 1516–1523.

Brug, J., Glanz, K., Van Assema, P., Kok, G., and van Breukelen, G. J. (1998). The impact of computer-tailored feedback and iterative feedback on fat, fruit, and vegetable intake. *Health Education and Behavior*, 25, 517–531.

Brus, H., van de Laar, M., Taal, E., Rasker, J., and Wiegman, O. (1999). Determinants of compliance with medication in patients with rheumatoid arthritis: The importance of self-efficacy expectations. *Patient Education and Counseling*, 36, 57–64.

Bull, F. C., and Jamrozik, K. (1998). Advice on exercise from a family physician can help sedentary patients to become active. *American Journal of Preventive Medicine*, 15, 85–94.

Burke, L. E., and Dunbar-Jacob, J. (1995). Adherence to medication, diet, and activity recommendations: From assessment to maintenance. *Journal of Cardiovascular Nursing*, 9, 62–79.

Burke, L. E., Dunbar-Jacob J., and Hill, M. N. (1997). Compliance with cardiovascular disease prevention strategies: A review of the research. *Annals of Behavioral Medicine*, 19, 239–263.

Burns, J. M., Sneddon, I., Lovell, M., McLean, A., and Martin, B. J. (1992). Elderly patients and their medication: A post-discharge follow-up study. *Age and Ageing*, 21, 178–181.

Campbell, M. K., DeVellis, B. M., Strecher, V. J., Ammerman, A. S., DeVellis, R. F., and Sandler, R. S. (1994). Improving dietary behavior: The effectiveness of tailored messages in primary care settings. *American Journal of Public Health*, 84, 783–787.

Christensen, A. J. (2000). Patient-by-treatment context interaction in chronic disease: A conceptual framework for the study of patient adherence. *Psychosomatic Medicine*, 62, 435–443.

Commerce, D. (1992). *Statistical Abstract of the United States* (112th ed.). Washington, DC: United States Government.

Cramer, J. A., Scheyer, R. D., and Mattson, R. H. (1990). Compliance declines between clinic visits. *Archives of Internal Medicine*, 150, 1509–1510.

Dunbar, J., and Knoke, J. (1986, May). *Prediction of Adherence at One Year and Seven Years.* Paper presented at the Society for Clinical Trials Seventh Annual Conference, Montreal, Canada.

Dunbar-Jacob, J. (2000, November). *Behavioral Interventions: State of the Art.* Paper presented at the 73rd Annual Scientific Sessions of the American Heart Association, New Orleans, LA.

Dunbar-Jacob, J., Burke, L. E., Rohay, J., Sereika, S., Schlenk, E. A., Lipello, A., and Muldoon, M. F. (1996). Comparability of self-report, pill count, and electronically monitored adherence data. *Controlled Clinical Trials*, 17, S80.

Dunbar-Jacob, J., and Schlenk, E. A. (1996). Treatment adherence and clinical outcome: Can we make a difference? In R. J. Resnick, and R. H. Rozensky (Eds.), *Health Psychology Through the Life Span: Practice and Research Opportunities* (pp. 323–343). Washington, D.C.: American Psychological Association.

Dunbar-Jacob, J., and Schlenk, E. A. (2000). Patient adherence to treatment regimen. In A. Baum, T. A. Revenson, and J. E. Singer (Eds.), *Handbook of Health Psychology* (pp. 571–580). Hillsdale, NJ: Lawrence Erlbaum Associates.

Dunbar-Jacob, J., Sereika, S., Rohay, J., and Burke, L. E. (1998). Electronic methods in assessing adherence to medical regimens. In D. Krantz and A. Baum (Eds.), *Technology and Methods in Behavioral Medicine* (pp. 95–113). Mahwah NJ: Lawrence Erlbaum Associates.

Dunbar-Jacob, J., Sereika, S., Rohay, J., Burke, L. E., and Kwoh, C. K. (1995). Predictors of adherence: Differences by measurement method. *Annals of Behavioral Medicine*, 17S, S196.

Grahl, C. (1994). Improving compliance: Solving a $100 billion problem. *Managed Healthcare*, June, S11–S13.

Greenwald, P., Witkin, K. M., Malone, W. F., Byar, D. P., Freedman, L. S., and Stern, H. R. (1992). The study of markers of biological effect in cancer prevention research trials. *International Journal of Cancer*, 52, 189–196.

Haynes, R., McKibben, K., and Kanani, R. (1996). Systematic review of randomized trials of interventions to assist patients to follow prescriptions for medications. *Lancet*, 348, 383–386.

Haynes, R. B., Sackett, D. L., Gibson, E. S., Taylor, D. W., Hackett, B. C., Roberts, R. S., and Johnson, A. L. (1976). Improvements in medication compliance in uncontrolled hypertension. *Lancet*, 1, 1265–1268.

Jeffery, R., Wing, R., Thorson, C., and Burton, L. (1998). Use of personal trainers and financial incentives to increase exercise in behavioral weight-loss program. *Journal of Consulting and Clinical Psychology*, 66, 777–783.

Kaplan R. M., Sallis, J. F. Jr., and Patterson, T. L. (1993). Understanding and changing health behaviors. *Health and Human Behavior* (pp. 39–70). New York: Mcgraw-Hill.

Kass, M. A., Meltzer, D., Gordon, M., Cooper, D., and Goldberg, J. (1986). Compliance with topical pilocarpine treatment. *American Journal of Ophthalmology*, 101, 515–523.

Kavanagh, D. J., Gooley, S., and Wilson, P. H. (1993). Prediction of adherence and control in diabetes. *Journal of Behavioral Medicine*, 16, 509–522.

Keder, L. M., Rulin, M. C., and Gruss, J. (1998). Compliance with depot medroxypro-gesterone acetate: A randomized, controlled trial of intensive reminders. *American Journal of Obstetrics and Gynecology*, 179, 583–585.

Kriska, A. M., and Caspersen, C. J. (1997). Introduction to a collection of physical activity questionnaires. *Medicine and Science in Sports and Exercise*, 29, S5–S9.

Kroboth, P. D., Schmith, V. D., and Smith, R. B. (1991). Pharmacodynamic modelling: Application to new drug development. *Clinical Pharmacokinetics*, 20, 91–98.

LaPorte, R. E., Montoye, H. J., and Caspersen, C. J. (1985). Assessment of physical activity in epidemiologic research: Problems and prospects. *Public Health Reports*, 100, 131–146.

Lee, I. M., Paffenbarger, R. S. Jr., and Hsieh, C. C. (1992). Time trends in physical activity among college alumni, 1962–1988. *American Journal of Epidemiology*, 135, 915–925.

Lutz, S. F., Ammerman, A. S., Atwood, J. R., Campbell, M. K., DeVellis, R. F., and Rosamond, W. D. (1999). Innovative newsletter interventions improve fruit and vegetable consumption in healthy adults. *Journal of the American Dietetic Association*, 99, 705–709.

Malotte, C., Rhodes, F., and Mais, K. (1998). Tuberculosis screening and compliance with return for skin testing among active drug users. *American Journal of Public Health*, 88, 792–796.

Martin, E. (1998). Telephone reminders improve compliance with a second dose of hepatitis B vaccine in high risk adults. *Evidence-Based Nursing*, 1, 44.

Masters, J., Burish, T., Hollon, S., and Rimm, D. (1987). *Behavior Therapy* (3rd ed.). New York: Harcourt Brace Jovanovich.

Matsui, D., Joubert, G. I. E., Dykxhoorn, S., and Reider, M. J. (2000). Compliance with prescription filling in the pediatric emergency department. *Archives of Pediatrics and Adolescent Medicine*, 154, 195–198.

Mattson, M. H., and Friedman, L. B. (1984). Medication adherence assessment in clinical trials. *Journal of Controlled Clinical Trials*, 5, 488–496.

McElnay, J. C., and McCallion, R. C. (1998). Adherence in the elderly. In L. B. Myers and K. Midence (Eds.), *Adherence to Treatment In Medical Conditions* (pp. 223–253). Toronto, Canada: Harwood Academic Publishers.

Means, B., and Loftus, E. I. (1991). When personal history repeats itself: Decomposing memories for recurring events. *Applied Cognitive Psychology*, 5, 297–318.

Meland, E., Laerum, E., and Ulvik, R. J. (1997). Effectiveness of two preventive interventions for coronary heart disease in primary care. *Scandinavian Journal of Primary Healthcare*, 15, 57–64.

Morisky, D., Malotte, C., Choi, P, Davidson, P., Rigler, S., Sugland, B., and Langer, M. (1990). A patient education program to improve adherence rates with antituberculosis drug regimens. *Health Education Quarterly*, 17, 253–267.

Morrow, D., Leirer, V. O., Carver, L. M., and Tanke, E. D. (1998). Older and younger adult memory for health appointment information: Implications for automated tele-phone messaging design. *Journal of Experimental Psychology*, 4, 352–374.

Morrow, D., Leirer, V. O., Carver, L. M., Tanke, E. D., and McNally, A. D. (1999a). Repetition improves older and younger adult memory for automated appointment messages. *Human Factors*, 41, 194–204.

Morrow, D., Leirer, V. O., Carver, L. M., Tanke, E. D., and McNally, A. D. (1999b). Effects of aging, message repetition, and note-taking on memory for health information. *Journal of Gerontology*, 54B, 2–11.

O'Brian, G., and Lazebnik, R. (1998). Telephone call reminders and attendance in an adolescent clinic. *Pediatrics*, 101, E6.

Oldridge, N. B. (1988). Cardiac rehabilitation exercise programme: Compliance and compliance-enhancing strategies. *Sports Medicine*, 6, 42–55.

Pavone, R. M., Burnett, K. F., LaPerriere, A., and Perna, F. M. (1998). Social cognitive and physical health determinants of exercise adherence for HIV-1 seropositive, early symptomatic men and women. *International Journal of Behavioral Medicine*, 5, 245–258.

Prohaska, V., Brown, N. R., and Belli, R. F. (1998). Forward telescoping: The question matters. *Memory*, 6, 455–465.

Roter, D. L., Hall, J. A., Merisca, R., Nordstrom, B., Cretin, D., and Svarstad, B. (1998). Effectiveness of interventions to improve patient compliance: A meta-analysis. *Medical Care*, 36, 1138–1161.

Rovelli, M., Palmeri, D., Vossler, E., Bartus, S., Hull, D., and Schweizer, R. (1989). Noncompliance in organ transplant recipients. *Transplantation Proceedings*, 21, 833–834.

Rutter, S. (1994). Comparison of energy expenditure in normal-weight and overweight women using the Caltrac Personal Activity Computer. *International Journal of Eating Disorders*, 15, 37–42.

Schapira, D. V., Kumar, N. B., Lyman, G. H., and Baile, W. F. (1991). The effect of duration of intervention and locus of control on dietary change. *American Journal of Preventive Medicine*, 7, 341–347.

Schlenk, E. A., Dunbar-Jacob, J., Sereika, S., Starz, T., Okifuji, A., and Turk, D. (2000). Comparability of daily diaries and accelerometers in exercise adherence in fibromyalgia syndrome. *Measurement in Physical Education and Exercise Science*, 4, 133.

Sereika, S. Dunbar-Jacob, J., Rand, C., Hamilton, G. Schron, E., Czajkowski, S., Waclawiw, M., Weeks, K., Lew, R., Leveck, M., Huss, K., Farzansar, R., and Friedman, R. (1998). *Adherence in Clinical Trials: A Collaborative Investigation of Self-Reported and Electronically Monitored Adherence*. Paper presented at the 19th Annual Meeting of the Society for Clinical Trials, Atlanta, GA.

Shannon, J., Kirkley, B., Ammerman, A., Keyserling, T., Kelsey, K., DeVellis, R., and Simpson, R. J. Jr. (1997). Self-efficacy as a predictor of dietary changes in a low-socioeconomic-status southern adult population. *Health Education and Behavior*, 24, 357–368.

Simmons, M. S., Nides, M. A., Rand, C. S., Wise, R. A., and Tashkin, D. P. (2000). Unpredictability of deception in compliance with physician-prescribed bronchodilator inhaler use in a clinical trial. *Chest*, 118, 290–295.

Smith, D. E., Heckemeyer, C. M., Kratt, P. P., and Mason, D. A. (1997). Motivational interviewing to improve adherence to a behavioral weight-control program for older obese women with NIDDM: A pilot study. *Diabetes Care*, 20, 52–54.

Smith, R., and Biddle, S. (1999). Attitudes and exercise adherence: Test of the Theories of Reasoned Action and Planned Behavior. *Journal of Sports and Science*, 17, 269–281.

Stephenson, J. (1999). Noncompliance may cause half of antihypertensive drug "failures". *Journal of the American Medical Association*, 282, 313–314.

Tulsky, J., Pilote, L., Hahn, J., Zopola, A., Burke, M., Chesney, M., and Moss, A. (2000). Adherence to isoniazid prophylaxis in the homeless: A randomized controlled trial. *Archives of Internal Medicine*, 160, 697–702.

Turner, M. O., Taylor, D., Bennett, R., and Fitzgerald, J. M. (1998). A randomized trial comparing peak expiratory flow and symptom self-management plans for patients with asthma attending a primary care clinic. *American Journal of Respiratory and Critical Care Medicine*, 157, 540–546.

van der Palen, J., Klein, J. J., and Rovers, M. M. (1997). Compliance with inhaled medication and self-treatment guidelines following a self-management programme in adult asthmatics. *European Respiratory Journal*, 10, 652–657.

Volmink, J., and Garner, P. (2000). Interventions for promoting adherence to tuberculosis management. *The Cochrane Library* (2).

Willett, W. C., Sampson, L., Stampfer, M. J., Rosner, B., Bain, C., Witschi, J., Hennekens, C. H., and Speizer, F. E. (1985). Reproducibility and validity of a semiquantitative food frequency questionnaire. *American Journal of Epidemiology*, 122, 51–65.

CHAPTER 5

Coronary Heart Disease

Timothy W. Smith and John M. Ruiz

University of Utah

Introduction

Coronary heart disease (CHD) is the leading cause of death in the United States and most industrialized western nations, despite recent declines in CHD mortality (American Heart Association, 2001). Each year about 450,000 people in the United States die from CHD, about 1,000,000 experience an initial or recurrent coronary event, and about 12,000,000 are living with documented CHD. Between 40 and 50% of healthy 40-year-old men will later develop CHD, as will between 25 and 35% of healthy 40-year-old women (Lloyd-Jones et al., 1999). Given its seriousness and prevalence, it is not surprising that $100 billion are spent on CHD each year in the United States, in direct medical costs, disability payments, and lost productivity. Of course, these figures do not capture adequately the toll of suffering among the millions of CHD patients and their families.

Throughout the history of behavioral medicine and health psychology, CHD has been a major focus of research and clinical practice. All three major topics in these fields (Smith and Ruiz, 1999) are relevant to CHD. In health behavior and disease prevention, daily habits (e.g., smoking, activity level, diet) are reliable risk factors for CHD, and changes in these risk factors can reduce its incidence (Smith and Leon, 1992). Regarding psychobiologic influences on disease (e.g., stress, negative emotions), a variety of psychosocial character-istics predict subsequent CHD and underlying mechanisms have been identified (Rozanski et al., 1999). Finally, regarding the psychosocial aspects of estab-lished medical illness and care, CHD affects emotional wellbeing and func-tional activity (Swenson and Clinch, 2000), and behavioral interventions are valuable additions to the medical and surgical care of these patients (Dusseldorp et al., 1999). Hence, CHD presents a prototypical challenge for health psy-chology and behavioral medicine. As a result, the application of concepts and

Correspondence regarding this chapter should be addressed to Timothy W. Smith, Ph.D., Depart-ment of Psychology, University of Utah, 390 South 1530 East (room 502), Salt Lake City, UT, 84112-0251, email: tim.smith@psych.utah.edu, phone: 801-581-5087, fax: 801-581-5841.

methods in clinical health psychology and behavioral medicine to CHD (i.e., "cardiac psychology") has grown rapidly (Allan and Scheidt, 1996; Baker and Neuman, 2000).

In this chapter, we review psychosocial influences on the development and course of CHD, and the utility of related psychosocial interventions. Recent declines in CHD mortality reflect changes in behavioral risk factors only to some extent (Kuulasmaa et al., 2000), and appear to reflect mostly improvements in emergency services, medical care, and surgical treatment (Hunink et al., 1997; Tunstall-Pedoe et al., 2000). Hence, the need for research and clinical services in the psychosocial aspects of established CHD is still growing. Yet, given the importance of behavioral risk factors in the initial development of CHD, behavioral approaches to prevention are at least as valuable as psychosocial interventions for persons with clinically apparent CHD (Kaplan, 2000). However, the behavioral prevention of CHD is beyond our present scope. Instead, we review research relevant to the design and implementation of interventions for CHD patients. We are guided by the general biopsychosocial model (Engel, 1977) as it is applied to the assessment and management of chronic disease (Smith and Nicassio, 1995). This approach asserts that the pathophysiology of a disease and its usual medical and surgical management are essential guides to psychosocial assessment and intervention. Hence, after reviewing these aspects of CHD, we turn to research on psychosocial risk factors, adaptation to CHD, and the effects of psychosocial interventions in acute and longer-term management. We conclude with a discussion of the challenges in the clinical implementation of this literature and emerging areas of research and practice.

Etiology, Course, and Management of Coronary Heart Disease

The term coronary heart disease (CHD) refers to the clinical manifestations of advanced coronary atherosclerosis or coronary artery disease (CAD). In the earliest stages of CAD, lipids and related cells (e.g., macrophages, foam cells) accumulate in microscopic amounts within the inner arterial walls. These progress to visible "fatty streaks" (Stary et al., 1994), seen as early as middle childhood (Strong et al., 1999). The initiating events in these stages include cellular responses to plasma-derived lipoproteins and microscopic injury to the arterial inner lining (i.e., endothelium). At these sites, components of the reparative response to injury (e.g., monocytes; smooth muscle cells) foster the progressive deposition of lipoproteins into cellular structures in the arterial wall, especially in the presence of high blood lipid levels. Later stages of CAD are characterized by extensive extracellular lipid accumulation in the arterial wall and a thickening of the structure. Still later, lesions are characterized by fibrous tissues, calcium deposits, and narrowing of the artery opening (the lumen) (Stary et al., 1995).

The growing fatty deposit first thickens the arterial wall, eventually encroaching progressively into the lumen. These more advanced lesions or plaques, often covered by a fibrous, calcified cap, are sometimes seen in early adulthood and even late adolescence (McGill et al., 2000). As lesions intrude into the lumen, blood flow past the site is reduced. Still later, the calcified, fibrous cap may rupture or fragment. The exposed tissues promote blood clotting, thereby further obstructing blood flow (i.e., thrombus). Portions of clots may be dislodged by the force of blood flow and carried "downstream" to narrower portions of the branching arterial tree (i.e., embolus). These events can cause a near or complete blockage of blood flow to myocardial tissues otherwise supplied by the occluded artery (Stary et al., 1995).

Whereas CAD develops without symptoms for years, acute thrombolitic events can occur within minutes. Severe blockage can precipitate the clinical manifestations of CHD – particularly myocardial infarction (MI; death of heart muscle) or unstable angina (i.e., rapidly worsening chest pain of cardiac origin). These two indications of CHD reflect severe and prolonged myocardial ischemia – an insufficient supply of blood (and, as a result, oxygen) to the heart. Other manifestations of CHD or episodes of ischemia occur whenever the demands of the heart muscle for oxygen exceed the available supply. Ischemia typically reflects a combination of limited supply due to reduced flow through occluded coronary arteries, and temporary increases in myocardial oxygen demands, as during physical exertion. This ischemia abates when oxygen demand is reduced or blood supply increased. Another cause of transient ischemia is spasm or temporary contraction of the muscle tissue within the artery itself. This occurs at CAD lesions and causes a temporary but potentially dangerous reduction in blood supply to the heart muscle. Sublingual nitrates (i.e., nitroglycerin tablets) may reduce acute ischemia by promoting dilation of the coronary arteries, but also reduce the pumping activity and oxygen demands of the heart by allowing blood to pool in the peripheral circulation. (For a review, see Scheidt, 1996).

Some episodes of myocardial ischemia are accompanied by angina pectoris – transient, severe chest pain of cardiac origin. Ambulatory studies of ischemia during daily life and studies of ischemia provoked by exercise or other laboratory stressors indicate that many episodes of ischemia are silent (Krantz, et al., 1994). Hence, advanced disease may have few outward symptoms. Ischemic myocardium is also vulnerable to rhythm disturbances. In a severe arrhythmia – ventricular fibrillation (VF) – the heart muscle twitches chaotically, halting systemic circulation and causing death within minutes if adequate rhythm is not restored. In the hundreds of thousands of cases of sudden coronary death (i.e., within 1 hour of symptom onset) that occur in the United States each year, VF is the usual cause (Scheidt, 1996).

Risk factors impact CHD by promoting damage to the coronary endothelium, the development of CAD lesions and inflammation, rupture of plaques and clotting of blood, acute reductions in the flow of blood through diseased arteries (e.g., spasm), or increased myocardial oxygen demands (i.e., a greater rate or force of myocardial contraction) in people with advanced CAD. Risk factors (e.g., smoking, chronic physical inactivity, high blood cholesterol) may influence the incidence and course of CHD through several of these mechanisms. As depicted in figure 5.1, psychosocial risk factors also influence the

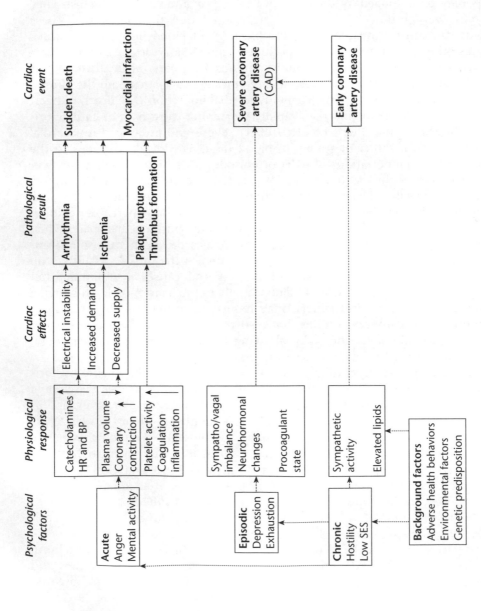

Figure 5.1 Psychophysiological influences on coronary artery disease and coronary heart disease. From Kop, W. J. (1999). Chronic and acute psychological risk factors for clinical manifestations of coronary artery disease. *Psychosomatic Medicine*, 61, 476–487.

development and course of CHD through several physiological processes at several points in its natural history (Cohen et al., 1994; Kop, 1999).

The medical care for CAD and CHD depends on the circumstances of their presentation. Emergency assessment and care differ considerably from routine services. In nonemergency situations, patients with possible symptoms of CHD (e.g., chest pain or pressure, severe shortness of breath during exertion) or elevated risk factors undergo one or more tests. The stress ECG involves electrocardiographic recording during progressively more demanding exertion (e.g., exercise bicycle, treadmill). In patients with advanced CAD, myocardial oxygen demand eventually exceeds the available supply, producing characteristic changes on the ECG. Ambulatory ECG (i.e., Holter monitoring) is used to detect ischemia during daily activities. The "thallium scan" is a more sensitive test, in which the uptake of radioactive thallium by myocardial tissues is examined during and after exercise. Reversible perfusion deficits reflect significant ischemia and advanced CAD; nonreversible deficits reflect prior MI. Other techniques (e.g., blood pool imaging, echocardiography) detect abnormalities in ventricular wall motion caused by ischemia or infarction (see Rozanski, 1998, for a review). Positive test results indicate the need for a definitive assessment of the location and severity of CAD lesions, accomplished via coronary angiography with coronary arteriography. Over 1,000,000 of these procedures are performed annually in the United States (American Heart Association, 2001). Through an incision in the femoral or brachial artery, a catheter is threaded into the coronary arteries. Radio-opaque dye is injected and filmed at high speed, depicting the location and severity of CAD.

A decision may then be made to manage the patient through medication and lifestyle changes, as reviewed below. Table 5.1 lists common drugs used for CHD. The effectiveness of these drugs is well documented (Campeau, et al., 1999; Deedwania, 1995; Pearson and Feinberg, 1997; Shepherd et al., 1995), but adherence to the usage regimen is often poor. Poor adherence is

Table 5.1 Commonly used drugs in the treatment of coronary heart disease

Class	Example	Action
β-Blockers	Propranolol (Inderol)	Reduces heart rate and strength of contraction
Calcium blockers	Diltiazem (Cardizem)	Vasodilators in peripheral and coronary arteries
Nitrates	Sublingual nitroglycerin	Coronary and peripheral vasodilators
Antilipid agents	Lovastatin (Mevacor)	Improve lipid profiles
ACE inhibitors	Catopril (Capoten)	Antihypertensive, primary therapy in CHF
Digoxin	(Lanoxin)	Increases cardiac contraction strength; stabilizes rhythm
Diuretics	Furosemide (Lasix)	Decrease blood volume
Anticoagulants	Warfarin (Coumadin) Aspirin	Reduces blood clotting

associated with subsequent cardiac morbidity and mortality, not only among those taking active medications in placebo-controlled trials, but also among patients taking placebos (Irvine et al., 1999). Hence, psychosocial correlates of problematic adherence may compound the negative impact on reduced levels of therapeutic medications.

After angiography, many patients undergo percutaneous transluminal angioplasty (PCTA). Over 500,000 PCTAs are performed annually in the United States (American Heart Association, 2001). A specialized catheter is positioned at the lesion and its balloon tip briefly inflated to a precise diameter at high pressure. This enlargement of the lumen produces increased blood flow. In a newer variation designed to reduce restenosis, small metal mesh tubes (i.e., stents) are inserted to maintain the lumen diameter (Topol and Serruys, 1998). Controlled trials indicate that PCTA reduces angina, but there is less evidence of effects on cardiac events (Gersh, 1994). After PCTA, patients are typically referred for medical management. Coronary artery bypass graft (CABG) procedures are the main surgical treatment for CAD. Over 500,000 CABGs are performed annually in the United States (American Heart Association, 2001). Usually, a graft from the patient's saphenous vein is attached to the aorta and the diseased artery "downstream" from the lesions. Multiple grafts are often performed, depending on the extent of CAD. As in PCTA, patients undergoing successful CABG are typically referred for medical management following discharge.

Cases where an unfolding MI is suspected are treated as dire medical emergencies. Once the patient is hospitalized, tests are performed to determine whether an infarction has occurred (i.e., ECG monitoring, cardiac enzyme testing) and to evaluate the stability of the heart rhythm and pumping effectiveness, with management by a variety of medications and procedures. For example, in cases of acute MI antithrombolitic medications (i.e., "clot busters") may be administered. Patients may undergo cardiac arteriography and emergency PCTA. After discharge, patients can be referred for medical management.

Behavioral and Psychosocial Risk Factors

Statistical associations between behavioral and psychosocial characteristics and subsequent CHD outcomes (e.g., MI, cardiac death) may reflect the impact of these risk factors on any of several distinct phases of the long and changing pathophysiology. Some risk factors that predict CHD incidence also predict the prognosis of established CHD. Hence, risk factors targeted at the prevention of CHD overlap with those addressed in medical management.

Traditional Behavioral Risk Factors

Three modifiable risk factors have a strong association with CHD – high levels of blood cholesterol (i.e., low-density lipoprotein), hypertension, and smoking. Other modifiable risk factors have smaller, but important effects – obesity, physical inactivity, and diabetes (Stamler et al., 1999; Wannamethee et al.,

Table 5.2 Risk factor goals

Total blood cholesterol	< 180 mg/dl
HDL cholesterol	> 45 mg/dl
Blood pressure	< 120/80 mmHg
Nonsmoking status	
Normal weight for height	+ 10%
Moderate-intensity physical activity	> 30 minutes/day
Vigorous exercise	> 20 minutes/3 times per week
Normal blood sugar level and glucose tolerance	

1998). Desirable levels of these risk factors are presented in table 5.2. Aggressive, population-based efforts to reduce these could reduce CHD incidence, and favorable risk factor profiles are associated with rapid reductions in healthcare costs (Daviglus et al., 1998; Pronk et al., 1999). Hence, enhanced risk reduction efforts could produce not only substantial longer-term improvements in CHD prevalence and related health expenditures, but more immediate savings as well.

It is important to note that these risk factors also predict the course of CHD. For example, in a quantitative review of 12 studies of smokers who suffered an MI, smoking cessation was associated with a 50% reduction in mortality (Wilson et al., 2000). Reductions in blood pressure and plasma lipids have similar, though perhaps less dramatic, effects. Hence, behavioral approaches to smoking cessation, diet, activity level, and weight loss are key components of CHD management, as are interventions to improve adherence to pharmacological treatments for these risk factors (Balady et al., 1994).

Psychosocial Risk Factors

Several psychosocial characteristics are significant predictors of the initial development of CHD, as well as its course (Adler and Matthews, 1994; Rozanski et al., 1999). For example, socially isolated individuals are at increased risk of developing and dying from CHD (Berkman, 1995). Further, structural measures of social isolation (e.g., marital status, living with a confidant) and low levels of reported social support are associated with reduced survival among CHD patients (see Rozanski et al., 1999, for a review). Some of these effects may be mediated by health behaviors, in that socially isolated persons may experience less encouragement to maintain a low-risk lifestyle (e.g., smoking cessation). However, the association between social isolation and CHD events remains significant even when these behavioral factors and potential confounders (e.g., initial health status) are controlled. Therefore, the physiological effects of social support and isolation have been examined as mechanisms underlying these effects (Uchino et al., 1996), consistent with the basic model depicted in figure 5.1. Self-reports of higher social support are generally associated with attenuated cardiovascular and neuroendocrine responses to potential stressors (Uchino et al., 1996), as are experimental manipulations of support (Kamarck et al., 1998; Lepore, 1998). The fact that social isolation predicts the prognosis of clinically apparent CHD suggests that it influences one or more elements of the later stages of CHD pathophysiology (Cohen et al., 1994). Its impact on the development of CAD prior to clinically apparent CHD is less well established.

Perhaps the most widely discussed psychosocial risk factor is the type A, coronary-prone behavior pattern initially described by Friedman and Rosenman (1959). This comprises a hard-driving, competitive, and achievement-oriented style, as well as overinvolvement in work, impatience, easily provoked anger and hostility, and a rapid and forceful vocal style. After several years of supportive findings, an expert panel (Cooper et al., 1981) concluded that type A persons were at significantly greater risk for CHD than more easy-going type Bs. Several studies were consistent with the hypothesis that this effect was mediated by exaggerated cardiovascular and neuroendocrine responses in type As to potential stressors (Houston, 1988). That is, type A individuals display larger increases in heart rate, blood pressure, and circulating catecholamines (e.g., epinephrine, norepinephrine) in response to stressors than do type Bs. These responses, in turn, may promote CAD and CHD.

However, enthusiasm for this risk factor waned under the weight of notable failures to replicate its effects on CHD (e.g., Shekelle et al., 1985; Ragland and Brand, 1988). A subsequent quantitative review indicated that despite these inconsistencies the type A pattern was indeed a reliable risk factor, but only among initially healthy individuals (as opposed to CHD patients and other high-risk groups) and only when assessed through behavioral ratings (as opposed to self-reports; Miller et al., 1991). Nonetheless, the global type A concept received reduced attention in the behavioral medicine and cardiological communities. This is despite the fact that a large, randomized controlled trial of group therapy to modify type A behavior in post-MI patients demonstrated that this behavior pattern could be changed, and that the treatment significantly reduced recurrent cardiac events (Friedman et al., 1986; Powell and Thoresen, 1988).

Inconsistencies in the type A literature prompted studies of components of the multifaceted construct, and they identified hostility as the element most closely related to MI and coronary death (for reviews, see Smith, 1992; Miller et al., 1996). The term hostility is used to refer to individual differences in the tendency to experience anger, cynical and suspicious attitudes and beliefs about others, and aggressive behavior (Smith, 1994). These characteristics are assessed with a variety of self-report instruments and behavioral ratings (Barefoot and Lipkus, 1994). Despite some negative findings (e.g., Leon et al., 1988; Maruta et al., 1993), a quantitative review of studies published through 1994 found that hostility is reliably associated with subsequent CHD (Miller et al., 1996). Additional prospective studies confirmed this association (Everson et al., 1997; Kawachi et al., 1996; Williams et al., 2000). Other studies suggest that hostility is associated with an increased risk of recurrent events among CHD patients – including coronary events and restenosis following PCTA, and transient ischemia during laboratory stressors and daily activities (DeLeon et al., 1996; Goodman et al., 1996; Helmers et al., 1993).

Hostility is associated with increased cardiovascular and neuroendocrine responses to relevant stressors (Houston, 1994; Smith and Gallo, 2001). In response to controlled laboratory stressors (Smith and Gallo, 1999; Suarez et al., 1998) and in ambulatory assessments of blood pressure (Benotsch, Christensen, and McKelvey, 1997; Guyll and Contrada, 1998) and endocrine responses (Pope and Smith, 1991) during daily activities, hostile persons display larger physiological stress responses than do their more agreeable counterparts. These responses may account for the association of hostility with the development of atherosclerosis (e.g., Iribarren et al., 2000; Julkunen et al., 1994; Matthews et al., 1998) and its association with the course of established CHD. Case–control studies suggest that episodes of anger can precipitate MI (Mittleman et al., 1995). In patients with CAD, the arousal of anger can induce transient myocardial ischemia in the laboratory (Ironson et al., 1992) and during daily life (Gabbay et al., 1996; Gullette et al., 1997). Hence, psychophysiological correlates of anger and hostility may underlie their association with both the development of CAD and manifestations of CHD.

Other mechanisms could account for the effects of hostility on CHD. For example, hostile persons not only display heightened physiological reactivity to interpersonal stressors, but also experience greater exposure to such stressors at home and work (Smith et al., 1988; 1990). This exposure to stress could reflect the impact of the hostile person's behavior on friends, family members and colleagues (Smith, 1995). That is, hostile persons may engender conflict and undermine otherwise beneficial social support, through their suspicious and cynical thoughts and antagonistic behavior. Further, although the association between hostility and subsequent CHD is generally significant when health behaviors are controlled (Miller et al., 1996), hostile persons do display a variety of unhealthy habits (e.g., smoking, lower activity levels, a less healthy diet; Siegler, 1994). In at least one study these health behaviors accounted for (i.e., mediated) the association between hostility and subsequent health (Everson et al., 1997). Hence, greater exposure and reactivity to stress, reduced physiologic benefit from social support (Lepore, 1995), and an unhealthy lifestyle may all contribute to the health effects of hostility.

Hostility might not be the only unhealthy component of the type A pattern. In analyses of behavioral ratings of type A components, hostility and social dominance emerge as separate characteristics, with the latter characterized by vigorous speech and a tendency to "cut off" or "talk over" the interviewer. Further, hostility and dominance are significantly and independently related to future CHD and early death (Houston et al., 1992, 1997). Other prospective studies using self-reports of social dominance have found that this personality trait predicts CHD (Siegman et al., 2000; Whiteman, et al., 1997). In a non-human primate model, socially dominant male macaques are vulnerable to the development of CAD in response to chronic social stress (Kaplan and Manuck, 1998). This vulnerability to stress-induced atherosclerosis can be prevented through the administration of β-blocking agents, which dampen sympathetic nervous system stimulation of the heart rate, suggesting that recurrent activation of the "fight or flight" response in stressed, dominant male animals underlies their susceptibility to CAD. In humans, efforts to influence or control others evoke heightened cardiovascular reactivity (Smith et al., 1989, 1997, 2000). Hence, as in hostility, social dominance may increase the risk of future CHD through psychophysiological mechanisms, in this case the physiological "cost" of recurring effortful attempts to maintain status and exert social control.

Chronic negative affect is another risk factor for the development of CHD and for recurrent events following MI (Rozanski et al., 1999). Among initially healthy persons, symptoms of anxiety and depression predict CHD incidence (Anda et al., 1993; Barefoot and Schroll, 1996; Ford et al., 1998; Kawachi et al., 1994). Among patients with clinically apparent CHD, symptoms of anxiety and depression predict recurrent coronary events and earlier death (Ahern et al., 1990; Barefoot et al., 1996; 2000; Frasure-Smith et al., 1995; Moser and Dracup, 1996), as do clinically diagnosed depressive disorders (Carney et al., 1988; Frasure-Smith et al., 1993; for a review, see Januzzi et al., 2000). Some studies have not reported significant effects (e.g., Herrmann et al., 2000; Mayou et al., 2000), but overall depression and anxiety appear to confer increased risk for both the initial development and a more negative course of CHD (Kubzanski and Kawachi, 2000). Related constructs, such as exhaustion (e.g., Appels et al., 2000), pessimism (Helgeson and Fritz, 1999; Scheier et al., 1999) and hopelessness (Everson et al., 1996, 1997b) also predict the development and course of CHD.

Several mechanisms could underlie these effects. Anxiety and depression have been associated with both heightened sympathetic and decreased parasympathetic responses to stress (Berntson et al., 1998; Stein et al., 2000; Watkins et al., 1998). These mechanisms could foster the development of CAD and the precipitation of CHD events (Kop, 1999; Rozanski et al., 1999). Ambulatory studies indicate that the experience of sad and depressed moods can evoke silent ischemia in CHD patients (Gullette et al., 1997). Chronic negative affect is also associated with increased exposure to stressful life experiences (Daley et al., 1997; Potthoff et al., 1995), at least partly because depressed persons engender conflict and undermine support (Joiner and Coyne, 1999). Anxiety and depression are also associated with poor adherence to medical regimens (DiMatteo et al., 2000; Carney et al., 1995; Ziegelstein et al., 2000).

Adaptation to Coronary Heart Disease and Related Care

Coronary patients experience many important negative emotional and behavioral changes (Swenson and Clinch, 2000). Predictors of individual differences in the severity of these effects can identify high-risk patients at need of additional assistance and suggest specific targets for intervention (Smith and Nicassio, 1995). During the crisis of acute coronary events, the longer course of cardiac rehabilitation, and the indefinite period of living with CHD, emotional adaptation is a central concern. After the cardiac crisis, when patients have stabilized, the return to prior levels of vocational, social, sexual, and recreational functioning becomes a primary goal, as does adherence to prescribed medical regimens and lifestyle changes.

Adjustment During Coronary Crises

The psychological aspects of coronary emergencies (e.g., acute MI) begin before the patient is hospitalized. After noticing symptoms many patients do not decide that they are ill for several minutes or even hours. Reaching the decision that they are sufficiently ill as to require medical attention requires still more time (Matthews et al., 1983). Such delays increase the likelihood of MI, as well as cardiac arrest, under circumstances in which expert resuscitation is unavailable. Hence, for high-risk persons and their families a knowledge of coronary emergencies and training in appropriate responses can save lives.

Once an ongoing cardiac event is confirmed, the medical task at hand is to stabilize the heart rhythm and pumping effectiveness, and minimize damage to the heart muscle. During this period patients are often highly distressed, both physically and emotionally, yet emotional distress is often followed by denial or minimization of the gravity of the situation (Cassem and Hacket, 1973). Denial can have positive effects on medical status, because it can reduce otherwise destabilizing levels of physiological arousal (Levenson et al., 1989; Levine et al., 1987), but despite these beneficial initial effects denial can confer a more negative long-term prognosis (Havik and Maeland, 1988; Levine et al., 1987), perhaps because it reflects limited capacity for adaptive coping or undermines adherence to lifestyle changes.

Diagnostic angiography, PCTA, and CABG are quite stressful. Brief psychological interventions can facilitate adjustment during hospitalization in the coronary care unit (CCU), angiography, and CABG. These interventions include brief supportive counseling, in which the patient's typical coping responses are rehearsed, relaxation therapy, a videotaped presentation of procedural information, and simple emotional support. Delivered in the CCU, such interventions have been found to produce more rapid medical stabilization (Gruen, 1975). Delivered prior to angiography, such interventions have been found to reduce distress (Kendall et al., 1979). Delivered prior to CABG, these brief interventions can reduce emotional distress and physical discomfort (Anderson, 1987; Leserman et al., 1989), the likelihood of complications such as postoperative hypertension and delirium (Anderson, 1987; Smith and Dimsdale, 1989), and the length of hospitalization (Mahler and Kulick, 1998). Reductions in emotional distress may reduce physical discomfort and length of hospital stay, partly by promoting wound healing (Keicolt-Glaser et al., 1998) or by improving self-efficacy regarding postoperative behaviors (e.g., deep breathing; Mahler and Kulick, 1998).

Several factors predict short-term adjustment during cardiac hospitalization. Emotional support from family members is associated with reduced distress and a more rapid recovery (Kulick and Mahler, 1993), as is the use of information provided by patients with similar experiences (Thoits et al., 2000). Dispositional optimism is associated with better adjustment and more rapid recovery following PCTA and CABG (Fitzgerald et al., 1993; Helgeson, 1999; King et al., 1998; Scheier et al., 1999). In addition to effects on prognosis, anxiety and depression are associated with poor emotional recovery and a more limited return to prior levels of functioning following MI (Mayou et al., 2000). Hence, brief interventions may be particularly useful for socially isolated, pessimistic and distressed patients. Coronary crises are distressing for the patient, and for family members. During hospitalizations for MI, PCTA and CABG, the adjustment of key family members should be assessed (Delon, 1996), not only for their own sake but also because distressed family members might be less effective in providing support.

Long-Term Adjustment of CHD Patients

After the coronary crisis, most CHD patients return to levels of emotional adjustment and functional activity that at least approach their prior levels. Given the economic toll of CHD, patients' return to employment is a major concern. Most patients who were employed prior to MI or CABG return to work within 6 months, although it may take longer and be less complete than is medically necessary. Predictors of delayed and incomplete return to work include more severe disease, increasing age, less education, blue-collar occupational status, continuing emotional distress (Dimsdale et al., 1982; Hlatky et al., 1986; Mark et al., 1992), and patients' expectations (Bar-on and Cristal, 1987; Ewart et al., 1983; Maeland and Havik, 1987; Petrie et al., 1996). Similar factors predict return to work following PCTA (Fitzgerald et al., 1989).

Physical activity also generally returns to prior levels fairly rapidly. However, anxiety and depression are associated with lower levels of activity for many months after MI or CABG (Mayou et al., 2000; Sullivan et al., 1997). Social functioning, marital and family adjustment, and levels of sexual activity also generally return to prior levels within a few months, although a sizable minority of patients display continuing impairments in these domains of health-related quality of life (Swenson and Clinch, 2000). Despite the good recovery of most patients, when these aspects of long-term adaptation are combined with vocational functioning, physical symptoms, and emotional adjustment, CHD patients suffer as much or more impairment in health-related quality of life as do patients with other serious chronic diseases (Stewart et al., 1989). Hence, improved quality of life is a key goal for rehabilitation (Duits et al., 1997; Oldridge, 1997). Some elements of quality of life (e.g., emotional adjustment, physical activity) can impact physical prognosis, and therefore take on added significance.

Behavioral and Psychological Treatments as Adjuncts to Usual Care

The psychosocial risk factors for the development and course of CHD comprise a menu for adjunctive psychosocial interventions. Although reduced likelihood of cardiac recurrence and improved survival are key intervention goals, reducing the psychosocial impact of CHD is also important. Interventions designed to improve the often problematic levels of adherence to the typical medication regimen in the management of CHD patients (see table 5.1) are often overlooked as adjunctive psychosocial treatments. Lipid-lowering drugs, β-blockers, and other classes of medication have been found to reduce recurrence and improve survival. Yet adherence is often problematic and additional interventions should be considered (Burke et al., 1997).

Exercise in Cardiac Rehabilitation

Regular aerobic exercise is a cornerstone of rehabilitation following MI, PCTA, and CABG, and a standard component of the medical management of patients with stable angina and those who have diagnosed CHD but no prior history of events (e.g., MI, CABG; Balady et al., 1994). Such programs involve supervised exercise for a number of months, with gradual increases in independent exercise. Some studies of exercise in CHD do not find benefits, but quantitative summaries find significant reductions in recurrent coronary events and reduced cardiac mortality (O'Connor et al., 1989; Oldridge et al., 1988). These benefits, in terms of years of life saved, are produced at a cost that compares quite favorably to thombolytic therapies, CABG, and cholesterol-lowering medications (Ades et al., 1997; Bondestam et al., 1995), although the cost-effectiveness is less than that associated with smoking cessation treatments in CHD. Exercise programs can improve coronary risk factors, including hypertension (Blumenthal et al., 2000), and can promote increased functional activity levels in CHD patients (Ades et al., 1999) and reduce depression (Blumenthal et al., 1999; Kugler et al., 1994).

Not all appropriate patients are urged by their cardiologists to participate in such programs. Of those referred, not all attend even initially, and many of those who do attend drop out much too early. Hence, strategies for increasing participation in formal rehabilitation, as well as longer-term maintenance of medically appropriate regular exercise, are valuable additions to cardiac care (Miller et al., 1997). Recently, less restrictive alternatives to highly structured and closely supervised traditional rehabilitation programs have been developed and found to be safe and effective (Carlson et al., 2000; Dunn et al., 1999), yet this aspect of patient management continues to pose a major challenge in research and clinical care.

Smoking Cessation

Smoking cessation following MI reduces the risk of recurrent coronary events and coronary death as much as or more than any aspect of patient care, and similar effects are observed following CABG and PCTA (Hasadi et al., 1997; Voors et al., 1996; Wilson et al., 2000). Despite these compelling benefits, many smokers who suffer an MI do not attempt to quit and those who do typically relapse. Although interventions for smoking cessation are far from optimally effective, this mature body of intervention research has produced sound guidelines for graded interventions, ranging from strong advice from healthcare professionals to involved behavioral programs with pharmacologic components (Fiore et al., 1997).

Simple, low-cost interventions can improve smoking cessation rates among CHD patients. Importantly, for some of these interventions positive effects are maintained over long-term follow-ups. For example, a 30-minute inpatient counseling session delivered to patients with documented CAD, combined with follow-up phone calls, was found to produce significant initial reductions in smoking which were maintained for several years (Rosal et al., 1998). Hence, graded strategies consisting of strong physician advice, inpatient counseling, and follow-up contacts for several months following a cardiac event or diagnosis should be implemented for most smokers with CHD (DeBusk et al., 1994; Taylor et al., 1996). More involved small group or individual multicomponent programs with behavioral and pharmacological elements can be used with smokers for whom the initial treatment is not successful.

Stress Management and the Modification of Coronary-Prone Behavior

Two lines of epidemiological and clinical research converge to suggest that stress management and related psychosocial interventions would be useful additions to the medical management of CHD patients. First, psychosocial risk factors (e.g., anger and hostility) are reliably associated with subsequent CHD, and physiological stress responses are implicated as mechanisms underlying this effect. Second, among patients with CAD, experimentally manipulated stressors can induce transient ischemia assessed in the laboratory, and naturally occurring stress and negative emotions evoke ischemia assessed via Holter monitoring during daily activities (Rozanski et al., 1999). As noted previously, Friedman and colleagues (1986) tested this basic premise in a large controlled trial of group therapy intended to reduce type A behavior. The group treatment included training in relaxation and other stress management techniques, training in the identification and self-monitoring of type A behavior, rehearsal of alternative behaviors to be used in provoking situations, and cognitive restructuring of the beliefs underlying type A behavior. They found that this structured group therapy not only reduced levels of type A behavior among patients with a previous MI, but, compared to a cardiac counseling comparison group, the treatment reduced recurrent cardiac events overall and reduced cardiac mortality among patients with less severe initial MIs (Friedman et al., 1986; Powell and Thoresen, 1988). This trial provides clear evidence of the clinical relevance of research on psychosocial risk factors, as well as the feasibility and benefits of related interventions.

Over the past two decades, other controlled trials of stress-management and related techniques have been reported, with varying outcomes (Linden et al., 1996). In a recent quantitative review of controlled studies of such interventions compared to standard care in CHD, these adjunctive treatments reduced cardiac recurrences by over 40% (Dusseldorp et al., 1999). Interventions producing a significant reduction in psychological distress were generally responsible for these effects on recurrent events and mortality. Hence, the variable results of prior trials could be accounted for by their effectiveness in altering the proximal target of emotional adjustment; only interventions that reduce the intervening mechanism of stress and emotional maladjustment have a reliable effect on coronary prognoses. Given the relatively low cost of these psychosocial interventions, future cost-effectiveness studies may provide even more support for expanding cardiac care into this domain (Linden, 2000).

The association of depression with risk of recurrence and reduced survival among CHD patients has prompted controlled trials of related interventions. Although current pharmacological treatments for depression can safely be used in CHD (e.g., Strik et al., 2000; Tabrizi et al., 1996), their effects on prognosis has not been determined. The results of ongoing trials will be available soon (Shapiro et al., 1999). Similarly, a multisite controlled trial of psychological interventions (i.e., cognitive therapy) for depression in CHD is currently nearing completion (ENRICHD: The ENRICHD investigators, 2000). As noted above, some evidence suggests that the exercise component of cardiac rehabilitation has a beneficial effect on depressive symptoms (Kugler et al., 1994; Milani et al., 1996), although the role of reduced depression in the effects of exercise on cardiac prognosis is not known. Interventions for emotional distress could also reduce the increased healthcare expenditures associated with comorbid depression and CHD (Allison et al., 1995; Frasure-Smith et al., 2000).

Multicomponent Interventions

One of the most dramatic demonstrations of the potential value of behavioral interventions in CHD involves the impact of a multicomponent program on the underlying disease process. In controlled trials of a program of regular exercise, a very low-fat diet, stress management, and group support, Ornish and colleagues have demonstrated that this comprehensive and aggressive modification of behavioral risk factors can produce a reduction in angiographically assessed CAD severity (Gould et al., 1992; Ornish et al., 1990) and improved blood flow to the myocardium that are sustained over several years (Gould et al., 1995). The multiple and extensive demands of this approach raise concerns about its usefulness in general clinical practice (Billings, 2000). However, it does demonstrate the potential value of behavioral risk factor modification in the management of CHD.

Implications and Future Directions

When combined with the general biopsychosocial model (Engel, 1977), a review of psychosocial aspects of CHD suggests the outlines of an integrated approach to the assessment and management of these patients (Smith and Nicassio, 1995). Table 5.3 presents issues to be considered in assessment. In addition to a clear understanding of the pathophysiology, medical assessment, and management of CHD, clinical health psychologists should begin their assessments with a complete description of the specific patient's medical condition.

Table 5.3 Outline for psychosocial assessment of coronary heart disease

The illness
- Extent and location of coronary artery disease
- History and location of previous myocardial infarction
- Pumping effectiveness (left ventricular ejection fraction)
- Diagnosed arrhythmias
- Risk factors (see table 5.2)
- Previous and planned diagnostic procedures
- Prior, current, and planned medical/surgical management

The patient
- DSM-IV Axis I conditions
- Personality characteristics and coping style
- Knowledge and conceptualization of illness and treatment
- Educational and vocational status
- Impact of illness on subjective distress, social functioning, activity level, and self-care

The social and cultural context
- Quality of marital and family relationships
- Use and effectiveness of social support
- Family members' conceptualizations of disease
- Risk factor status of family members
- Training in CPR and emergency care
- Patient–physician relationship and interactions
- Patient and family cultural background

The healthcare system
- Medical organization, setting, culture
- Insurance coverage for risk factor modification
- Geographical, social, psychological barriers to care
- Disability benefits and funding for vocational retraining

Aspects of the individual patient's functioning and social context should also be assessed, including their and their family members' understanding of the disease and its treatment, and the quality of the patient's communication and relationship with physicians. These are important influences on adherence and functional activity levels. Finally, various aspects of the healthcare and health insurance systems are important influences on the patient's participation in treatment and the degree of functional activity, especially access to supervised exercise facilities and the availability of support for vocational retraining.

Ideally – but certainly not typically – psychosocial assessment is an integral part of patient care. Once psychosocial issues are identified as requiring intervention, treatment plans should be developed and implemented in an active, multidisciplinary team approach. Coordinated comprehensive care with prioritized intervention efforts can help patients avoid becoming overwhelmed and confused by multiple demands and conflicting advice. A prioritized list would include (in decreasing importance): adherence to medication regimens;

smoking cessation (if relevant); regular exercise training; sensible diet; stress management; and additional interventions for depression and anger (with psychopharmacological consultation if needed). Psychoeducational interventions for behavioral risk reduction and stress management can reduce the risk of recurrence (Dusseldorp et al., 1999; Sebregts et al., 2000), but maintenance of behavior change requires particular attention.

Psychosocial management of CHD has a firm and growing foundation in research. Widespread adoption of the psychosocial approach could reduce the economic and human burden of CHD, yet this approach is largely comprised of individual and small group-based interventions delivered late in the natural history of CHD, thereby limiting their impact. Hence, behavioral approaches to risk reduction and the prevention of CAD could have a far greater impact, especially comprehensive risk factor modification using individual, family, institutional (e.g., school and work site-based), community, and public health interventions (Kaplan, 2000; Smith and Leon, 1992). Yet, even with dramatic increases in the number and effectiveness of prevention efforts, hundreds of thousands of people would still develop CHD each year in the United States. Hence, psychosocial assessment and management of CHD will remain important for many years.

The psychosocial aspects of CHD vary as a function of gender, socioeconomic status, and ethnicity, suggesting the importance of diversity. Women have a lower lifetime risk of CHD, and their age at onset is on average several years later than for men. Yet women have a worse prognosis following MI and CABG (Mosca et al., 1997). Women's roles may make it difficult to reduce work demands during convalescence and to participate sufficiently in the behavioral risk factor reduction (Abbey and Stewart, 2000). Further, there are sex differences in several psychosocial risk factors for CHD and the underlying psychophysiological mechanisms (Shumaker and Smith, 1995; Smith et al., 1998). Contributions to and the impacts of cardiovascular disease also vary as a function of ethnicity and socioeconomic status (Anderson, 1989; Anderson and Armstead, 1995; Dries et al., 1999; Williams et al., 1992). Some of these effects may involve medical decision making. That is, similar clinical presentations for men versus women, or white versus ethnic minority patients, can prompt different decisions by physicians about tests and procedures (e.g., Schulman et al., 1999). Variations in risk factors, underlying mechanisms, prognoses, and approaches to management related to sex, ethnicity, and socioeconomic status require much additional research and considerable clinical sensitivity. Ultimately, psychosocial interventions with ethnic minority and economically disadvantaged populations must be tested directly (Castillo-Richmond et al., 2000).

Each of the psychosocial issues in CHD described above can involve personal relationships. In some cases (e.g., social isolation), personal relationships are the critical concern. Risk reduction efforts – such as smoking cessation, changes in diet, increases in activity level – are heavily influenced by risk factor status and the level of supportive encouragement of immediate family members. Stress can provoke ischemia, and stressful relationships are common. Further, the stress of acute coronary crises is felt not only by patients, but also by spouses and other family members. Hence, clinical assessment and management of CHD can be usefully extended to include the spouse (Rankin-Esquer et al., 2000). Interventions for psychosocial risk factors developed elsewhere – such as marital approaches to depression (Beach, 2001) – should be considered in clinical practice and studied in future research.

Advances in medical technology create new opportunities for research on the psychosocial aspects of CHD and new issues. New approaches to the treatment of CHD (e.g., PCTA with stent implantation) raise questions about the psychosocial predictors of prognosis in new clinical groups. Medical imaging technologies, such as CT scans of early CAD, create opportunities to test the effects of psychosocial risk factors on stages of disease that heretofore have been unexamined (Iribarren et al., 2000). Similarly, imaging technologies permit tests of the effects of psychosocial risk factors on myocardial ischemia (Rozanski, 1998), and more definitive research on the precipitants of coronary events. Finally, new technologies provide sensitive evaluations of psychosocial interventions. Cardiac imaging techniques can document the effects of lifestyle interventions on CAD (Gould et al., 1992, 1995), and Holter monitoring has demonstrated that stress management reduces ischemia during daily activities (Blumenthal et al., 1997). Once clinical interventions have been found to alter these more frequent and sensitive outcomes, larger trials can assess the less frequent but more compelling outcome of recurrent events.

In his early descriptions of angina pectoris, Osler (1910) suggested that it was found among "not the neurotic, delicate person . . . but the robust, vigorous in mind and body, the keen and ambitious man, the indicator of whose engine is always at full speed ahead" (p. 810). Although recent findings differ somewhat from his description, decades of research have supported Osler's general assertion that stress and other psychosocial issues are involved in many aspects of CHD. Future research and increased utilization of existing knowledge in clinical care have the potential to reduce the medical, economic, and human burden of this disease.

References

Abbey, S. E. and Stewart, D. E. (2000). Gender and psychosomatic aspects of ischemic heart disease. *Journal of Psychosomatic Research*, 48, 417–423.

Ades, P. A., Maloney, A., Savage, P. and Carhart, R. L. (1999). Determinants of physical functioning in coronary patients. *Archives of Internal Medicine*, 159, 2357–2360.

Ades, P. A., Pashkow, F. J., and Nestor, J. R. (1997). Cost-effectiveness of cardiac rehabilitation after myocardial infarction. *Journal of Cardiopulmonary Rehabilitation*, 17, 222–231.

Adler, N., and Matthews, K. (1994). Health psychology: Why do some people get sick and some stay well? *Annual Review of Psychology*, 45, 229–259.

Ahern, D. K., Gorkin, L., Anderson, J. L., Tierney, C., Hallstrom, A., Ewart, C., Capone, R. J., Schron, E., Kornfeld, D., Herd, J. A., Richardson, D. W., and Follick, M. J. (1990). Biobehavioral variables and mortality or cardiac arrest in the Cardiac Arrythmia Pilot Study (CAPS). *American Journal of Cardiology*, 66, 59–62.

Allan, R., and Scheidt, S. (Eds.). (1996). *Heart and Mind: The Practice of Cardiac Psychology*. Washington, DC: American Psychological Association.

Allison, T. G., Williams, D. E., Miller, T. D., Patten, C. A., Bailey, K. R., Squires, R. W., and Gau, G. T. (1995). Medical and economic costs of psychologic distress in patients with coronary artery disease. *Mayo Clinic Proceedings*, 70, 734–742.

American Heart Association. (2001). *2001 Heart and Stroke Statistical Update*. Dallas, TX: American Heart Association.

Anderson, E. A. (1987). Preoperative preparation for cardiac surgery facilitates recovery, reduces psychological distress, and reduces the incidence of acute postoperative hypertension. *Journal of Consulting and Clinical Psychology*, 42, 223–232.

Anderson, N. B. (1989). Racial differences in stress-induced cardiovascular reactivity and hypertension: Current status and substantive issues. *Psychological Bulletin*, 105, 89–105.

Andersen, N. B., and Armstead, C. A. (1995). Toward understanding the association of socioeconomic status and health: A new challenge for the biopsychosocial approach. *Psychosomatic Medicine*, 57, 213–225.

Appels, A., Golombeck, B., Gorgels, A., de Vreede, J., and van Breukelen, G. (2000). Behavioral risk factors of sudden cardiac arrest. *Journal of Psychosomatic Research*, 48, 463–469.

Baker, B., and Newman, D. (Eds.). (2000). Special issue: Cardiology. *Journal of Psychosomatic Medicine*, 48, 313.

Balady, G. J., Fletcher, B. J., Froelicher, E. S., Hartley, L. H., Krauss, R. M., and Oberman, A. (1994). *Cardiac Rehabilitation Programs: A Statement for Healthcare Professionals from the American Heart Association*. Dallas, TX: American Heart Association.

Barefoot, J. C., Brummett, B. H., Helms, M. J., Mark, D. B., Siegler, I. C., and Williams, R. B. (2000). Depressive symptoms and survival of patients with coronary artery disease. *Psychosomatic Medicine*, 62, 790–795.

Barefoot, J. C., Helms, M. S., Mark, D. B., Blumenthal, J. A., Califf, R. M., Haney, T. L., O'Connor, C. M., Siegler, I. C., and Williams, R. B. (1996). Depression and long term mortality risk in patients with coronary artery disease. *American Journal of Cardiology*, 78, 613–617.

Barefoot, J. C., and Lipkus, I. M. (1994). The assessment of anger and hostility. In A. W. Siegman and T. W. Smith (Eds.), *Anger, Hostility, and the Heart* (pp. 43–66). Hillsdale, NJ: Lawrence Erlbaum Associates.

Barefoot, J. C., and Schroll, M. (1996). Symptoms of depression, acute myocardial infarction, and total mortality in a community sample. *Circulation*, 93, 1976–1980.

Bar-on, D., and Cristal, N. (1987). Causal attributions of patients, their spouses and physicians, and the rehabilitation of the patients after their first myocardial infarction. *Journal of Cardiopulmonary Rehabilitation*, 7, 285–298.

Benotsch, E. G., Christensen, A. J., and McKelvey, L. (1997). Hostility, social support and ambulatory cardiovascular activity. *Journal of Behavioral Medicine*, 20, 163–176.

Berkman, L. F. (1995). The role of social relations in health promotion. *Psychosomatic Medicine*, 57, 245–254.

Berntson, G. G., Sarter, M., and Cacioppo, J. T. (1998). Anxiety and cardiovascular reactivity: The basal forebrain cholinergic link. *Behavioral Brain Research*, 94, 225–248.

Billings, J. H. (2000). Maintenance of behavior change in cardiorespiratory risk reduction: A clinical perspective from the Ornish program for reversing coronary heart disease. *Health Psychology*, 19, 70–75.

Blumenthal, J. A., Babyak, M. A., Moore, K. A., Craighead, W. E., Herman, S., Khatri, P., Waugh, R., Napolitano, M. A., Forman, L. M., Appelbaum, M., Doraiswamy, M., and Krishnan, K. R. (1999). Effects of exercise training on older patients with major depression. *Archives of Internal Medicine*, 159, 2349–2356.

Blumenthal, J. A., Jiang, W., Babyak, M. A., Krantz, D. S., Frid, D., Coleman, R., Waugh, R., Hanson, M., Appelbaum, M., O'Connor, C., and Morris, J. (1997). Stress management and exercise training in cardiac patients with myocardial ischemia. *Archives of Internal Medicine*, 157, 2213–2223.

Blumenthal, J. A., Sherwood, A., Gullette, E. C. D., Babyak, M., Waugh, R., and Georgiades, A. (2000). Exercise and weight loss reduce blood pressure in men and women with mild hypertension: Effects on cardiovascular, metabolic, and hemo-dynamic functioning. *Archives of Internal Medicine*, 160, 1947–1958.

Bondestam, E., Breikks, A., and Hartford, M. (1995). Effects of early rehabilitation on consumption of medical care during the first year after acute myocardial infarction in patients > 65 years of age. *American Journal of Cardiology*, 75, 767–771.

Burke, L. E., Dunbar-Jacob, J. M., and Hill, M. N. (1997). Compliance with cardiovascular disease prevention strategies: A review of the research. *Annals of Behavioral Medicine*, 19, 239–263.

Campeau, L., Hunninghake, D. B., Knatterud, G. L., White, C. W., Domanski, M., and Forman, S. A. (1999). Aggressive cholesterol lowering delays saphenous vein graft artherosclerosis in women, the elderly, and patients with associated risk factors. *Circulation*, 99, 3241–3247.

Carlson, J. J., Johnson, J. A., Franklin, B. A., and Vanderlaan, R. L. (2000). Program participation, exercise adherence, cardiovascular outcomes, and program cost of traditional versus modified cardiac rehabilitation. *American Journal of Cardiology*, 86, 17–23.

Carney, R. M., Freedland, K., Rich, M., and Jaffe, A. S. (1995). Depression as a risk factor for cardiac events in established coronary heart disease: A review of possible mechanisms. *Annals of Behavioral Medicine*, 17, 142–149.

Carney, R. M., Rich, M. W., and Freedland, K. E. (1988). Major depressive disorder predicts cardiac events in patients with coronary artery disease. *Psychosomatic Medicine*, 50, 627–633.

Cassem, N. H., and Hackett, T. P. (1973). Psychological rehabilitation of myocardial infarction patients in the acute phase. *Heart and Lung*, 2, 382–388.

Castillo-Richmond, A., Schneider, R. H., Alexander, C. N., Cook, R., Myers, H., and Nidich, S. (2000). Effects of stress reduction on carotid atherosclerosis in hypertensive African Americans. *Stroke*, 31, 568–573.

Cohen, S., Kaplan, J. R., and Manuck, S. B. (1994). Social support and coronary heart disease: Underlying psychological and biological mechanisms. In S. A. Schumaker and S. M. Czajkowski (Eds.), *Social Support and Cardiovascular Disease* (pp. 195–222). New York: Plenum.

Cooper, T., Detre, T., and Weiss, S. M. (1981). Coronary-prone behavior and coronary heart disease: A critical review. *Circulation*, 63, 1199–1215.

Daley, S. E., Hammen, C., Burge, D., Davila, J., Paley, B., Linberg, N., and Herzberg, D. S. (1997). Predictors of the generation of episodic stress: A longitudinal study of late adolescent women. *Journal of Abnormal Psychology*, 106, 251–259.

Daviglus, M. L., Liu, K., Greenland, P., Dyer, A. R., Garside, D. B., Manheim, L., Lowe, L. P., Rodin, M., Lubitz, J., and Stamler, J. (1998). Benefit of a favorable cardiovascular risk-factor profile in middle age with respect to medicare costs. *New England Journal of Medicine*, 339, 1122–1129.

DeBusk, R. F., Houston Miller, N., Superko, H. R., Dennis, C. A., Thomas, R. J., Lew, H. T., Berger, W. E., Heller, R. S., Rompf, J., Gee, D., Kraemer, H. C., Bandura, A., Ghandour, G., Clark, M., Shah, R. V., Fisher, L., and Taylor, C. B. (1994). Case-management system for coronary risk factor modification after acute myocardial infarction. *Annals of Internal Medicine*, 120, 721–729.

Deedwania, P. C. (1995). Clinical perspectives on primary and secondary prevention of coronary atherosclerosis. *Medical Clinics of North America*, 79, 973–998.

De Leon, C. F. M., Kop, W. J., de Swart, H. B., Far, F. W., and Appels, P. W. M. (1996). Psychosocial characteristics and recurrent events after percutaneous transluminal coronary angioplasty. *American Journal of Cardiology*, 77, 252–255.

Delon, M. (1996). The patient in the CCU waiting room: In-hospital treatment of the cardiac spouse. In R. Allan and S. Scheidt (Eds.), *Heart and Mind: The Practice of Cardiac Psychology* (pp. 421–432). Washington DC: American Psychological Association.

DiMatteo, M. R., Lepper, H. S., and Croghan, T. W. (2000). Depression is a risk factor for noncompliance with medical treatment: Meta-analysis of the effects of anxiety and depression on patient adherence. *Archives of Internal Medicine*, 160, 2101–2107.

Dimsdale, J. E., Hackett, T. P., Hutter, A. M., and Block, P. C. (1982). The association of clinical, psychosocial, and angiographic variables with work status in patients with coronary artery disease. *Journal of Psychosomatic Research*, 26, 215–221.

Dries, D. L., Exner, D. V., Gersh, B. J., Cooper, H. A., Carson, P. E., and Domanski, M. J. (1999). Racial differences in the outcome of left ventricular dysfunction. *New England Journal of Medicine*, 340, 609–616.

Duits, A. A., Boeke, S., Taams, M. A., Passchier, J., and Erdman, R. A. M. (1997). Prediction of quality of life after coronary artery bypass graft surgery: A review and evaluation of multiple, recent studies. *Psychosomatic Medicine*, 59, 257–268.

Dunn, A. L., Marcus, B. H. Kampert, J. B., Garcia, M. E., Kohl III, H. W., and Blair, S. N. (1999). Comparison of lifestyle and structured interventions to increase physical activity and cardiorespiratory fitness: A randomized trial. *Journal of the American Medical Association*, 281, 327–334.

Dusseldorp, E., van Elderen, T., Maes, S., Meulman, J., and Kraaij, V. (1999). A meta-analysis of psychoeducational programs for coronary heart disease patients. *Health Psychology*, 18, 506–519.

The ENRICHD investigators (2000). Enhancing recovery in coronary heart disease patients (ENRICHD): Study design and methods. *American Heart Journal*, 139, 1–9.

Engel, G. L. (1977). The need for a new medical model: A challenge for biomedicine. *Science*, 196, 129–136.

Everson, S. A., Goldberg, D. E., Kaplan, G. A., Cohen, R. D., Pukkala, E., Tuomilehto, J., and Salonen, S. T. (1996). Hopelessness and risk of mortality and incidence of myocardial infarction and cancer. *Psychosomatic Medicine*, 58, 113–121.

Everson, S. A., Kaplan, G. A., Goldberg, D. E., Salonen, R., and Salonen, J. T. (1997a). Hopelessness and 4-year progression of carotid atherosclerosis. *Arteriosclerosis, Thrombosis, and Vascular Biology*, 17, 1490–1495.

Everson, S. A., Kauhanen, J., Kaplan, G., Goldberg, D., Julkunen, J., Tuomilehto, J., and Salonen, J. T. (1997b). Hostility and increased risk of mortality and myocardial infarction: The mediating role of behavioral risk factors. *American Journal of Epidemiology*, 146, 142–152.

Ewart, C. K., Taylor, C. B., Reese, L. B., DeBusk, R. F. (1983). Effects of early postmyocardial infarction exercise testing on self-perception and subsequent physical activity. *American Journal of Cardiology*, 51, 1076–1080.

Fiore, M. C., Jorenby, D. E., and Baker, T. B. (1997). Smoking cessation: Principles and practice based upon the AHCPR Guideline, 1996. *Annals of Behavioral Medicine*, 19, 213–219.

Fitzgerald, S. T., Becker, D. M., Celentano, D. D., Swank, R., and Brinker, J. (1989). Return to work after percutaneous transluminal coronary angioplasty. *American Journal of Cardiology*, 64, 1108–1112.

Fitzgerald, T. E., Tennen, H., Affleck, G., and Pransky, G. S. (1993). The relative importance of dispositional optimism and control appraisals in quality of life after coronary artery bypass surgery. *Journal of Behavioral Medicine*, 16, 25–43.

Ford, D. E., Mead, L. A., Chang, P. P., Cooper-Patrick, L., Wang, N., and Klag, M. J. (1998). Depression is a risk factor for coronary artery disease in men. *Archives of Internal Medicine*, 158, 1422–1426.

Frasure-Smith, N., Lesperance, F., Gravel, G., Masson, A., Juneau, M., and Talajic, M. (2000). Depression and health-care costs during the first year following myocardial infarction. *Journal of Psychosomatic Research*, 48, 471–478.

Frasure-Smith, N., Lesperance, F., and Talajic, M. (1993). Depression following myocardial infarction. *Journal of the American Medical Association*, 270, 1819–1825.

Frasure-Smith, N., Lesperance, F., and Talajic, M. (1995). The impact of negative emotions on prognosis following myocardial infarction: Is it more than depression? *Health Psychology*, 14, 388–398.

Friedman, M., and Rosenman, R. H. (1959). Association of a specific overt behavior pattern with increases in blood cholesterol, blood clotting time, incidence of arcus senilis and clinical coronary artery disease. *Journal of the American Medical Association*, 169, 1286–1296.

Friedman, M., Thoreson, C. E., Gill, J. J., Ulmer, D., Powell, L. H., Price, V. A., Brown, B., Thompson, L., Rabin, D. D., Brall, W. S., Bourg, E., Levy, R., and Dixon, T. (1986). Alteration of Type-A behavior and its effects on cardiac recurrences in post-myocardial infarction patients: Summary results of the Recurrent Coronary Prevention Project. *American Heart Journal*, 112, 653–665.

Gabbay, F. H., Krantz, D. S., Kop, W., Hedges, S., Klein, J., Gottdiener, J., and Rozanski, A. (1996). Triggers of myocardial ischemia during daily life in patients with coronary artery disease: Physical and mental activities, anger, and smoking. *Journal of the American College of Cardiology*, 27, 585–592.

Gersh, B. J. (1994). Efficacy of percutaneous transluminal coronary angioplasty (PTCA) in coronary artery disease: Why we need clinical trials. In E. J. Topol (Ed.), *Textbook of Interventional Cardiology* (2nd ed., pp. 251–273). Philadelphia, PA: W. B. Saunders.

Goodman, M., Quigley, J., Moran, G., Meilman, H., and Sherman, M. (1996). Hostility predicts resentosis after percutaneous transluminal coronary angioplasty. *Mayo Clinic Proceedings*, 71, 729–734.

Gould, K. L., Ornish, D., Kirkeeide, R., Brown, S., Stuart, Y., and Buchi, M. (1992). Improved stenosis geometry by quantitative coronary arteriography after vigorous risk factor modification. *American Journal of Cardiology*, 69, 845–853.

Gould, K. L., Ornish, D., Scherwitz, L., Brown, S., Edens, R. P., Hess, M. J., Mullani, N., Bolomey, L., Dobbs, F., Armstrong, W. T., Merritt, T., Ports, T., Sparler, S., and Billings, J. (1995). Changes in myocardial perfusion abnormalities by position emission tomography after long-term, intense risk factor modification. *Journal of the American Medical Association*, 274, 894–901.

Gruen, W. (1975). Effects of brief psychotherapy during the hospitalization period on the recovery process in heart attacks. *Journal of Consulting and Clinical Psychology*, 42, 223–232.

Gullette, E., Blumenthal, J., and Babyak, M. (1997). Mental stress triggers myocardial ischemia during daily life. *Journal of the American Medical Association*, 277, 1521–1526.

Guyll, M., and Contrada, R. J. (1998). Trait hostility and ambulatory cardiovascular activity: Responses to social interaction. *Health Psychology*, 17, 30–39.

Hasadi, D., Garratt, K. N., Grill, D. E., Lerman, A., and Holmes, D. R., Jr. (1997). Effect of smoking status on the long-term outcome after successful percutaneous coronary revascularization. *New England Journal of Medicine*, 336, 755–761.

Havik, O. E., and Maeland, J. G. (1988). Verbal denial and outcome in myocardial infarction patients. *Journal of Psychosomatic Research*, 32, 145–157.

Helgeson, V. S. (1999). Applicability of cognitive–adaptation theory to predicting adjustment ot heart disease after coronary angioplasty. *Health Psychology*, 18, 561–569.

Helgeson, V. S., and Fritz, H. L. (1999). Cognitive adaptation as a predictor of new coronary events after percutaneous transluminal coronary angioplasty. *Psychosomatic Medicine*, 61, 488–495.

Helmers, K. F., Krantz, D. S., Howell, R., Klein, J., Bairey, N., and Rozanski, A. (1993). Hostility and myocardial ischemia in coronary artery disease patients: Evaluation by gender and ischemic index. *Psychosomatic Medicine*, 50, 29–36.

Herrmann, C., Brand-Driehorst, S., Buss, U., and Ruger, U. (2000). Effects of anxiety and depression on 5-year mortality in 5057 patients referred for exercise testing. *Journal of Psychosomatic Research*, 48, 455–462.

Hlatky, M. A., Haney, T., and Barefoot, J. C. (1986). Medical, psychological, and social correlates of work disability among men with coronary artery disease. *American Journal of Cardiology*, 58, 911–915.

Houston, B. K. (1988). Cardiovascular and neuroendocrine reactivity, global Type A, and components of Type A behavior. In B. K. Houston and C. R. Snyder (Eds.), *Type A Behavior Pattern: Research, Theory, and Intervention* (pp. 212–253). New York: Wiley.

Houston, B. K. (1994). Anger, hostility, and psychophysiological reactivity. In A. W. Siegman and T. W. Smith (Eds.), *Anger, Hostility, and the Heart* (pp. 97–115). Hillsdale, NJ: Lawrence Erlbaum Associates.

Houston, B. K., Babyak, M. A., Chesney, M. A., Black, G., and Ragland, D. R. (1997). Social dominance and 22-year all-cause mortality in men. *Psychosomatic Medicine*, 59, 5–12.

Houston, B. K., Chesney, M. A., Black, G. W., Cates, D. S., and Hecker, M. L. (1992). Behavioral clusters and coronary heart disease risk. *Psychosomatic Medicine*, 54, 447–461.

Hunink, M. G. M., Goldman, L., Tosteson, A. N. A., Mittleman, M. A., Goldman, P. A., Williams, L. W., Tsevat, J., and Weinstein, M. C. (1997). The recent decline in mortality from coronary heart disease, 1980–1990. *Journal of the American Medical Association*, 277, 535–542.

Iribarren, C., Sidney, S., Bild, D. E., Liu, K., Markovitz, J. H., Roseman, J. M., and Matthews, K. (2000). Association of hostility with coronary artery calcification in young adults: The CARDIA study. *Journal of the American Medical Association*, 283, 2546–2551.

Ironson, G., Taylor, C. B., Boltwood, M., Bartzokis, T., Dennis, C., Chesney, M., Spitzer, S., and Segall, G. M. (1992). Effects of anger on left ventricular ejection fraction in coronary disease. *American Journal of Cardiology*, 70, 281–285.

Irvine, J., Baker, B., Smith, J., Jandciu, S., Paquette, M., Cairns, J., Connolly, S., Roberts, R., Gent, M., and Dorian, P. (1999). Poor adherence to placebo or amiodarone therapy predicts mortality: results from the CAMIAT Study. *Psychosomatic Medicine*, 61, 566–575.

Januzzi, J. L., Stern, T. A., Pasternak, R., and DeSanctis, R. W. (2000). The influence of anxiety and depression on outcomes of patients with coronary artery disease. *Archives of Internal Medicine*, 160, 1913–1921.

Joiner, T., and Coyne, J. C. (1999). *The Interactional Nature of Depression: Advances in Interpersonal Approaches*. Washington, D.C.: American Psychological Association.

Julkunen, J., Salonen, R., Kaplan, G. A., Chesney, M. A., Salonen, J. T. (1994). Hostility and the progression of carotid atherosclerosis. *Psychosomatic Medicine*, 56, 29–36.

Kamarck, T. W., Peterman, A. H., and Raynor, D. A. (1998). The effects of the social environment on stress-related cardiovascular activation: Current findings, prospects, and implications. *Annals of Behavioral Medicine*, 20, 247–256.

Kaplan, J. R., and Manuck, S. B. (1998). Monkeys, aggression, and the pathobiology of atherosclerosis. *Aggressive Behavior*, 24, 323–334.

Kaplan, R. M. (2000). Two pathways to prevention. *American Psychologist*, 55, 382–396.

Kawachi, I., Sparrow, D., Spiro, A., Vokonas, P., and Weiss, S. T. (1996). A prospective study of anger and coronary heart disease. The Normative Aging Study. *Circulation*, 94, 2090–2095.

Kendall, P. C., Williams, L., Pechacek, T. F., Graham, L. E., Shisslak, C., and Herzoff, N. (1979). Cognitive–behavioral and patient education interventions in cardiac catheterization procedures: The Palo Alto Medical Psychology Project. *Journal of Consulting and Clinical Psychology*, 47, 49–58.

Kiecolt-Glaser, J. K., Page, G. G., Marucha, P. T., MacCallum, R. C., and Glaser, R. (1998). Psychological influences on surgical recovery: Perspectives from psychoneuroimmunology. *American Psychologist*, 53, 1209–1218.

King, K. B., Rowe, M. A., Kimble, L. P., Zerwic, J. J. (1998). Optimism, coping, and long-term recovery from coronary artery surgery in women. *Research Nursing Health*, 21, 15–26.

Kop, W. J. (1999). Chronic and acute psychological risk factors for clinical manifestations of coronary artery disease. *Psychosomatic Medicine*, 61, 476–487.

Krantz, D. S., Hedges, S. M., Gabbay, F. H., Klein, J., Falconer, J. J., Merz, C. N., Gottdiener, J. S., Lutz, H., Rozanski, A. (1994). Triggers of angina and ST-segment depression in ambulatory patients with coronary artery disease: Evidence for an uncoupling of angina and ischemia. *American Heart Journal*, 128, 703–712.

Kubzansky, L. D., and Kawachi, I. (2000). Going to the heart of the matter: Do negative emotions cause coronary heart disease? *Journal of Psychosomatic Research*, 48, 323–337.

Kugler, J., Seelbach, H., Krueskemper, G. M. (1994). Effects of rehabilitation exercise programmes on anxiety and depression in coronary patients: A meta-analysis. *British Journal of Clinical Psychology*, 33, 401–410.

Kulik, J. A., and Mahler, H. I. M. (1989). Social support and recovery from surgery. *Health Psychology*, 8, 221–238.

Kulik, J. A., and Mahler, H. I. (1989). Social support and recovery from surgery. *Health Psychology*, 8, 221–228.

Kulik, J. A., and Mahler, H. I. (1993). Emotional support as a moderator of adjustment and compliance after coronary artery bypass surgery: A longitudinal study. *Journal of Behavioral Medicine*, 16, 45–63.

Kuulasmaa, K., Tunstall-Pedoe, H., Dobson, A., Fortmann, S., Sans, S., Tolonen, H., Evans, A., Ferrario, M., and Tuomilehto, J. (2000). Estimation of contribution of changes in classic risk factors to trends in coronary-event rates across the WHO MONICA Project populations. *Lancet*, 355, 675–687.

Leon, G. R., Finn, S. E., Murray, D., and Bailey, J. M. (1988). The inability to predict cardiovascular disease from hostility scores or MMPI items related to Type A behavior. *Journal of Consulting and Clinical Psychology*, 56, 597–600.

Lepore, S. J. (1995). Cynicism, social support, and cardiovascular reactivity. *Health Psychology*, 14, 210–216.

Lepore, S. J. (1998). Problems and prospects for the social support–reactivity hypothesis. *Annals of Behavioral Medicine*, 20, 257–269.

Leserman, J., Stuart, E. M., Mamish, M. E., and Benson, H. (1989). The efficacy of the relaxation response in preparing for cardiac surgery. *Behavioral Medicine*, 2, 111–117.

Levenson, J. L., Kay, R., Monteperrante, J., and Herman, M. V. (1984). Denial predicts favorable outcome in unstable angina pectoris. *Psychosomatic Medicine*, 46, 25–32.

Levenson, J. L., Mishra, A., Hamer, R. M., and Hastillo, A. (1989). Denial and medical outcome in unstable angina. *Psychosomatic Medicine*, 51, 27–35.

Levine, J., Warrenburg, S., Kerns, R., Schwartz, G., Delaney, R., Fontana, A., Gradman, A., Smith, S., Allen, S., and Cascione, R. (1987). The role of denial in recovery from coronary heart disease. *Psychosomatic Medicine*, 49, 109–117.

Linden, W. (2000) Psychological treatments in cardiac rehabilitation: review of rationales and outcomes. *Journal of Psychosomatic Research*, 48, 443–454.

Linden, W., Stossel, C., and Maurice, J. (1996). Psychosocial interventions for patients with coronary artery disease: A meta-analysis. *Archives of Internal Medicine*, 156, 745–752.

Lloyd-Jones, D. M., Larson, M. G., Beiser, A., and Levy, D. (1999). Lifetime risk of developing coronary heart disease. *Lancet*, 353, 89–92.

Maeland, J. G., and Havik, O. E. (1987). Psychological predictors for return to work after a myocardial infarction. *Journal of Psychosomatic Research*, 31, 471–481.

Mahler, H. I., and Kulik, J. (1998). Effects of preparatory videotapes on self-efficacy beliefs and recovery from coronary bypass surgery. *Annals of Behavioral Medicine*, 20, 39–46.

Mark, D. B., Lam, L. C., Lee, K. L., Clapp-Channing, N. E., Williams, R. B., Pryor, D. B., Califf, R. M., and Hlatky, M. A. (1992). Identification of patients with coronary disease at high risk for loss of employment. A prospective validation study. *Circulation*, 86, 1485–1494.

Maruta, T., Hamburgen, M. E., Jennings, C. A., Offord, K. P., Colligan, R. C., Frye, R. L., Malinchoc, M. (1993). Keeping hostility in perspective: Coronary heart disease and the Hostility Scale on the Minnesota Multiphasic Personality Inventory. *Mayo Clinic Proceedings*, 68, 109–114.

Matthews, K. A., Owens, J. F., Kuller, L. H., Sutton-Tyrrell, K., and Jansen-McWilliams, L. (1998). Are hostility and anxiety associated with cartoid atherosclerosis in healthy post-menopausal women? *Psychosomatic Medicine*, 60, 633–638.

Matthews, K. A., Siegel, J. M., Kuller, L. H., Thompson, M., and Varat, M. (1983). Determinants of decisions to seek medical treatment by patients with acute myocardial infarction symptoms. *Journal of Personality and Social Psychology*, 44, 1144–1156.

Mayou, R. A., Gill, D., Thompson, D. R., Day, A., Hicks, N., and Volmink, J. (2000). Depression and anxiety as predictors of outcome after myocardial infarction. *Psychosomatic Medicine*, 62, 212–219.

McGill, H. C., McMahan, C. A., Zieske, A. W., Tracy, R. E., Malcom, G. T., Herderick, E. E. and Strong, J. P. (2000). Association of coronary heart disease risk factors with microscopic qualities of coronary atherosclerosis in youth. *Circulation*, 102, 374–379.

Milani, R. V., Lavie, C. J., and Cassidy, M. (1996). Effects of cardiac rehabilitation and exercise training programs on depression in patients after major coronary events. *American Heart Journal*, 12, 726–732.

Miller, T. D., Balady, G. J., and Fletcher, G. F. (1997). Exercise and its role in the prevention and rehabilitation of cardiovascular disease. *Annals of Behavioral Medicine*, 19, 220–229.

Miller, T. Q., Smith, T. W., Turner, C. W., Guijarro, M. L., and Hallet, A. J. (1996). Meta-analytic review of research on hostility and physical health. *Psychological Bulletin*, 119, 322–348.

Miller, T. Q., Turner, C. W., Tindale, R. S., Posavac, E. J., and Dugoni, B. L. (1991). Reasons for the trend toward null findings in research on Type-A behavior. *Psychological Bulletin*, 110, 469–485.

Mittleman, M. A., Maclure, M., Sherwood, J. B., Mulry, R. P., Tofler, G. H., Jacobs, S. C., Friedman, R., Benson, H., and Muller, J. E., for the Determinants of Myocardial Infarction Onset Study Investigators. (1995). Triggering of acute myocardial infarction onset by episodes of anger. *Circulation*, 92, 1720–1725.

Mosca, L., Manson, J. E., Sutherland, S. E., Langer, R. D., Manolio, T., and Barrett-Connor, E. (1997). Cardiovascular disease in women: A statement for healthcare professionals from the American Heart Association. *Circulation*, 96, 2468–2482.

Moser, D. K., and Dracup, K. (1996). Is anxiety early after myocardial infarction associated with subsequent ischemic and arrhythmic events? *Psychosomatic Medicine*, 58, 395–401.

O'Connor, G. T., Buring, J .E., Yusuf, S., Goldhaber, S. Z., Olmstead, E. M., Paffenbarger, R. S., Jr., and Hennekens, C. H. (1989). An overview of randomized trials of rehabilitation with exercise after myocardial infarction. *Circulation*, 80, 234–244.

Oldridge, N. B. (1997). Outcome assessment in cardiac rehabilitation. Health-related quality of life and economic evaluation. *Journal of Cardiopulmonary Rehabilitation*, 17, 179–194.

Oldridge, N. B., Guyatt, G. H., Fisher, M. E., and Rimm, A. A. (1988). Cardiac rehabilitation after myocardial infarction. Combined experience of randomized clinical trials. *Journal of the American Medical Association*, 260, 945–950.

Ornish, D., Brown, S. E., Scherwitz, L. W., Billings, J. H., Armstrong, W. T., Ports, T. A., Melanahan, S. M., Kirkeeide, R. L., Brand, R. J., and Gould, K. L. (1990). Can lifestyle changes reverse coronary heart disease? *Lancet*, 336, 129–133.

Osler, W. (1910). The Lumelin Lectures on angina pectoris. *Lancet*, 1, 839–844.

Pearson, T. A., and Feinberg, W. (1997). Behavioral issues in the efficacy versus effectiveness of pharmacologic agents in the prevention of cardiovascular disease. *Annals of Behavioral Medicine*, 19, 230–238.

Petrie, K. J., Weinman, J., Sharpe, N., and Buckley, J. (1996). Role of patients' view of their illness in predicting return to work and functioning after myocardial infarction: Longitudinal study. *British Medical Journal*, 312, 1191–1194.

Pope, M. K., and Smith, T. W. (1991). Cortisol excretion in high and low cynically hostile men. *Psychosomatic Medicine*, 53, 386–392.

Potthoff, J. G., Holahan, C. J., and Joiner, T. E. (1995). Reassurance seeking, stress generation, and depressive symptoms: An integrative model. *Journal of Personality and Social Psychology*, 68, 664–670.

Powell, L. H., and Thoresen, C. E. (1988). Effects of Type-A behavioral counseling and severity of prior acute myocardial infarction on survival. *American Journal of Cardiology*, 62, 1159–1163.

Pronk, N. P., Goodman, M. J., O'Connor, P. J., and Martinson, B. C. (1999). Relationship between modifiable health risks and short-term health care charges. *Journal of the American Medical Association*, 282, 2235–2239.

Ragland, D. R., and Brand, R. J. (1988). Type A behavior and mortality from coronary heart disease. *New England Journal of Medicine*, 318, 65–69.

Rankin-Esquer, L. A., Deeter, A., and Taylor, C. B. (2000). Coronary heart disease and couples. In K. B. Schmaling and T. G. Sher (Eds.), *The Psychology of Couples and Illness: Theory, Research, and Practice* (pp. 43–70). Washington, DC: American Psychological Association.

Rosal, M. C., Ockene, J. K., Ma, Y., Herbert, J. R., Ockene, I. S., and Meriam, P. (1998). Coronary artery smoking intervention study (CASIS): 5-year follow-up. *Health Psychology*, 17, 476–478.

Rozanski, A. (1998). Laboratory techniques for assessing the presence and magnitude of mental stress-induced myocardial ischemia in patients with coronary artery disease. In D. S. Krantz and A. Baum (Eds.), *Technology and Methods in Behavioral Medicine* (pp. 47–67). Mahwah, NJ: Lawrence Erlbaum.

Rozanski, A., Blumenthal, J. A., and Kaplan, J. (1999). Impact of psychological factors on the pathogenesis of cardiovascular disease and implications for therapy. *Circulation*, 99, 2192–2217.

Scheidt, S. (1996). A whirlwind tour of cardiology for the mental health professional. In R. Allan and S. Scheidt (Eds.), *Heart and Mind: The Practice of Cardiac Psychology* (pp. 15–67). Washington, D.C.: American Psychological Association.

Scheier, M. F., Matthews, K. A., Owens, J. F., Schulz, R., Bridges, M. W., Magovern, G. J., and Carver, C. S. (1999). Optimism and rehospitalization after coronary artery bypass graft surgery. *Archives of Internal Medicine*, 159, 829–833.

Schulman, K. A., Berlin, J. A., Harless, W., Kerner, J., Sistrunk, S., Gersh, B. J., Dube, R., Taleghani, C., Burke, J. E., Williams, S., Eisenberg, J. M., and Escarce, J. J.

(1999). The effect of race and sex on physician's recommendations for cardiac catheterization. *New England Journal of Medicine*, 340, 618–626.

Sebregts, E. H. W. J., Falger, P. R. J., and Bar, F. W. H. M. (2000). Risk factor modification through nonpharmacological interventions in patients with coronary heart disease. *Journal of Psychosomatic Research*, 48, 425–441.

Shapiro, P. A., Lesperance, F., Frasure-Smith, N., O'Connor, C. M., Baker, B., Jiang, J. W., Dorian, P., Harrison, W., and Glassman, A. H. (1999). An open-label preliminary trial of sertraline for treatment of major depression after acute myocardial infarction (the SADHAT Trail). *American Heart Journal*, 137, 1100–1106.

Shekelle, R. B., Gale, M., and Norusis, M. (1985). Type A score (Jenkins Activity Survey) and risk of recurrent coronary heart disease in the Aspirin Myocardial Infarction Study. *American Journal of Cardiology*, 56, 221–225.

Shepherd, J., Cobbe, S. M., Ford, I., Isles, C. G., Lorimer, A. R., Macfarlane, P. W., McKillop, J. H., and Packard, C. J., for the West of Scotland Coronary Prevention Study Group. (1995). Prevention of coronary heart disease with pravastatin in men with hypercholesterolemia. *New England Journal of Medicine*, 333, 1301–1307.

Shumaker, S. A., and Smith, T. R. (1995). Women and coronary heart disease: A psychological perspective. In A. L. Stanton and S. J. Gallant (Eds.), *The Psychology of Women's Health: Progress and Challenges in Research and Application* (pp. 25–49). Washington, DC: American Psychological Association.

Siegler, I. C. (1994). Hostility and risk: Demographic and lifestyle variables. In A. W. Siegman and T. W. Smith (Eds.), *Anger, Hostility, and the Heart* (pp. 199–214). Hillsdale, NJ: Lawrence Erlbaum Associates.

Siegman, A. W., Kubzansky, L. D., Kawachi, I., Boyle, S., Vokonas, P. S., and Sparrow, D. (2000). A prospective study of dominance and coronary heart disease in the normative aging study. *American Journal of Cardiology*, 86, 145–149.

Smith, L. W., and Dimsdale, J. E. (1989). Postcardiotomy delirium: Conclusions after 25 years? *American Journal of Psychiatry*, 146, 452–458.

Smith, T. W. (1992). Hostility and health: Current status of a psychosomatic hypothesis. *Health Psychology*, 11, 139–150.

Smith, T. W. (1994). Concepts and methods in the study of anger, hostility, and health. In A. W. Siegman and T. W. Smith (Eds.), *Anger, Hostility, and the Heart* (pp. 23–42). Hillsdale, NJ: Lawrence Erlbaum Associates.

Smith, T. W. (1995). Assessment and modification of coronary-prone behavior: A transactional view of the person in social context. In A. J. Goreczny (Ed.), *Handbook of Health and Rehabilitation Psychology* (pp. 197–217). New York: Plenum.

Smith, T. W., Allred, K. D., Morrison, C. A., and Carlson, S. D. (1989). Cardiovascular reactivity and interpersonal influence: Active coping in a social context. *Journal of Personality and Social Psychology*, 56, 209–218.

Smith, T. W., and Gallo, L. C. (1999). Hostility and cardiovascular reactivity during marital interaction. *Psychosomatic Medicine*, 61, 436–445.

Smith, T. W., and Gallo, L. C. (2001). Personality traits as risk factors for physical illness. In A. Baum, T. Revenson, and J. Singer (Eds.), *Handbook of Health Psychology* (pp. 139–172). Hillsdale, NJ: Lawrence Erlbaum.

Smith, T. W., Gallo, L. C., Ngu, L., Goble, L., and Stark, K. A. (1998). Agency, communion, and cardiovascular reactivity during marital interaction. *Health Psychology*, 17, 537–545.

Smith, T. W., and Leon, A. S. (1992). *Coronary Heart Disease: A Behavioral Perspective*. Champaign-Urbana, IL: Research Press.

Smith, T. W., Nealey, J. B., Kircher, J. C., and Limon, J. P. (1997). Social determinants of cardiovascular reactivity: Effects of incentive to exert influence and evaluative threat. *Psychophysiology, 34*, 65–73.

Smith, T. W., and Nicassio, P. (1995). Psychosocial practice in chronic medical illness: Clinical application of the biopsychosocial model. In P. C. Nicassio and T. W. Smith (Eds.), *Managing Chronic Illness: A Biopsychosocial Perspective* (pp. 1–32). Washington, DC: American Psychological Association.

Smith, T. W., Pope, M. K., Sanders, J. D., Allred, K. D., and O'Keefe, J. L. (1988). Cynical hostility at home and work: Psychosocial vulnerability across domains. *Journal of Research in Personality, 22*, 525–548.

Smith, T. W., and Ruiz, J. M. (1999). Methodological issues in adult health psychology. In P. C. Kendall, J. N., Butcher, and G. N. Holmbeck (Eds.), *Handbook of Research Methods in Clinical Psychology* (2nd ed., pp. 499–536). New York: Wiley.

Smith, T. W., Ruiz, J. M., and Uchino, B. N. (2000). Vigilance, active coping, and cardiovascular reactivity during social interaction in young men. *Health Psychology, 19*, 382–392.

Smith, T. W., Sanders, J. D., and Alexander, J. F. (1990). What does the Cook and Medley Hostility Scale measure: Affect, behavior, and attributions in the marital context. *Journal of Personality and Social Psychology, 58*, 699–708.

Stamler, J., Stamler, R., Neaton, J. D., Wentworth, D., Daviglus, M. L., Garside, D., Dyer, A. R., Liu, K., and Greenland, P. (1999). Low risk-factor profile and long-term cardiovascular and noncardiovascular mortality and life expectancy: Findings for 5 large cohorts of young adult and middle-aged men and women. *Journal of the American Medical Association, 282*, 2012–2018.

Stary, H. C., Chandler, A. B., Dinsmore, R. E., Fuster, V., Glagov, S., Insull, Jr., W., Rosenfeld, M. E., Schwartz, C. J., Wagner, W. D., and Wissler, R. W. (1995). A definition of advanced types of atherosclerotic lesions and a histological classification of atherosclerosis. *Circulation, 92*, 1355–1374.

Stary, H. C., Chandler, A. B., Glagov, S., Guyton, J. R., Insull, Jr., W., Rosenfeld, M. E., Schaffer, S. A., Schwartz, C. J., Wagner, W. D., and Wissler, R. W. (1994). A definition of initial, fatty streak, and intermediate lesions of atherosclerosis. *Circulation, 89*, 2462–2478.

Stein, P. K., Carney, R. M., Freedland, K. E., Skala, J. A., Jaffe, A. S., and Kleiger, R. E. (2000). Severe depression is associated with markedly reduced heart rate variability in patients with stable coronary heart disease. *Journal of Psychosomatic Research, 48*, 493–500.

Stewart, A. L., Greenfield, S., Hays, R. D., Wells, K., Rogers, W. H., Berry, S. D., McGlynn, E. A., and Ware, J. (1989). Functional status and wellbeing of patients with chronic conditions. Results from the Medical Outcomes Study. *Journal of the American Medical Association, 262*, 907–913.

Strik, J. J. M. H., Hong, A., Lousberg, R, Lousberg, A. H., Cheriex, E. C., and Tuynman-Qua, H. G. (2000). Efficacy and safety of fluoxetine in the treatment of patients with major depression after first myocardial infarction: Findings from a double-blind, placebo-controlled trial. *Psychosomatic Medicine, 62*, 783–789.

Strong, J. P., Malcom, G. T., McMahan, C. A., Tracy, R. E., Newman, W. P., Herderick, E. E., Cornhill, J. F., and the Pathobiological Determinants of Atherosclerosis in Youth Research Group. (1999). Prevalence and extent of atherosclerosis in adolescents and young adults: Implications for prevention from the pathobiological determinants of atherosclerosis in youth study. *Journal of the American Medical Association, 281*, 727–735.

Suarez, E. C., Kuhn, C. M., Schanberg, S. M., Williams, R. B., and Zimmermann, E. A. (1998). Neuroendocrine, cardiovascular, and emotional responses of hostile men: The role of interpersonal challenge. *Psychosomatic Medicine, 60*, 78–88.

Sullivan, M. D., LaCroiz, A. Z., Baum, C., Grothaus, L. C., and Katon, W. J. (1997). Functional status in coronary artery disease: A one-year prospective study of the role of anxiety and depression. *American Journal of Medicine*, 103, 348–356.

Swenson, J. R. and Clinch, J. J. (2000). Assessment of quality of life in patients with cardiac disease: the role of psychosomatic medicine. *Journal of Psychosomatic Research*, 48, 405–415.

Tabrizi, K., Littman, A., Williams, R. B., and Scheidt, S. (1996). Psychopharmacology and cardiac disease. In R. Allan and S. Scheidt (Eds.), *Heart and Mind* (pp. 397–419). Washington D.C.: American Psychological Association.

Taylor, C. B., Houston Miller, N., Herman, S., Smith, P. M., Sobel, D., Fisher, L., and DeBusk, R. F. (1996). A nurse-managed smoking cessation program for hospitalized smokers. *American Journal of Public Health*, 86, 1561–1569.

Thoits, P. A., Harvey, M. R., Hohman, A. A., and Fletcher, B. (2000). Similar-other support for men undergoing coronary artery bypass surgery. *Health Psychology*, 19, 264–273.

Topol, E. J. and Serruys, P. (1998). Frontiers in interventional cardiology. *Circulation*, 98, 1802–1820.

Tunstall-Pedoe, H., Vanuzzo, D., Hobbs, M., Mahonen, M., Cepaitis, Z., Kuulasmaa, K., and Keil, U. (2000). Estimation of contribution of changes in coronary care to improving survival, event rates, and coronary heart disease mortality across the WHO MONICA Project populations. *Lancet*, 355, 688–700.

Uchino, B. N., Cacioppo, J. T., and Kiccolt-Glaser, J. K. (1996). The relationship between social support and physiological processes: A review with emphasis on underlying mechanisms and implications for health. *Psychological Bulletin*, 119, 488–531.

Voors, A. A., van Brussel, B. L., Plokker, H. W. T., Ernst, S. M. P. G., Ernst, N. M., and Koomen, E. M. (1996). Smoking and cardiac events after venous coronary bypass surgery. *Circulation*, 93, 42–47.

Wannamethee, S. G., Shaper, A. G., Walker, M., and Ebrahim, S. (1998). Lifestyle and 15-year survival free of heart attack, stroke and diabetes in middle-aged British men. *Archives in Internal Medicine*, 158, 2433–2440.

Watkins, L. L., Grossman, P., Krishnan, R., and Sherwood, A. (1998). Anxiety and vagal control of heart rate. *Psychosomatic Medicine*, 60, 498–502.

Whiteman, M. C., Deary, I. J., Lee, A. J., and Fowkes, F. G. R. (1997). Submissiveness and protection from coronary heart disease in the general population: Edinburgh Artery Study. *Lancet*, 350, 541–545.

Williams, J. E., Paton, C. C., Siegler, I. C., Eigenbrodt, M. L., Nieto, F. J., and Tyroler, H. A. (2000). Anger proneness predicts coronary heart disease risk: Prospective analysis from the Atherosclerosis Risk in Communities (ARIC) study. *Circulation*, 101, 2034–2039.

Williams, R. B., Barefoot, J. C., and Califf, R. M. (1992). Prognostic importance of social and economic resources among medically treated patients with angiographically documented coronary artery disease. *Journal of the American Medical Association*, 267, 520–152.

Wilson, K., Gibson, N., Willan, A., and Cook, D. (2000). Effect of smoking cessation on mortality after myocardial infarction. *Archives of Internal Medicine*, 160, 939–944.

Ziegelstein, R. C., Fauerbach, J. A., Stevens, S. S., Romanelli, J., Richter, D. P., and Bush, D. E. (2000). Patients with depression are less likely to follow recommendations to reduce cardiac risk during recovery from a myocardial infarction. *Archives of Internal Medicine*, 160, 1818.

CHAPTER 6

Cancer

Barbara L. Andersen and Sharla Wells

Ohio State University

Introduction

If we focus on the numbers, they are staggering. Each year in the US over 1.2 million individuals are diagnosed and another half million people – one person every 80 seconds – die from cancer (Greenlee et al., 2000). The increase in cancer incidence and mortality in recent years appears to be related to advances in early detection as well as the aging of the population. The most common diagnosis for women is breast cancer and for men prostate cancer, each accounting for about 30% of the new cases per year. However, lung cancer is the number one killer, accounting for 25% of cancer-related mortality in women and 31% in men. Cancer is the leading cause of death for individuals aged 45–64 (National Vital Statistics Reports; Murphy, 2000) and affects the health status of millions of cancer survivors.

Research on the psychological, social, and behavioral aspects of oncology began in the early 1950s, but the knowledge base has significantly expanded in the last 20 years, with research into cancer prevention and control. We have learned from two decades of descriptive research that the burdens of cancer can be multiple, heavy, and chronic. In addition, the stability of many cancer mortality rates, particularly those with the highest incidence, such as breast, prostate, lung, and colorectal, makes it imperative that new, innovative steps be taken to enhance quality of life and improve survival. The biobehavioral model of cancer stress and disease course (Andersen et al., 1994; see figure 6.1) guides our discussion. This model specifies the psychological, behavioral, and biologic pathways by which cancer outcomes might be influenced. Also, we expand on the contribution of social factors, as they can affect each component of the model. Consistent with the focus of this

This effort was supported by funds from the following: National Institute of Mental Health (RO1 MH51487), the Dana Foundation, the Walther Cancer Institute, and the American Cancer Society Ann and Herbert Siegel Postdoctoral Fellowship (PF-01-017-01-PBP).

Correspondence concerning this chapter should be directed to Barbara L. Andersen, Ph.D. Department of Psychology, 202 Townshend Hall, The Ohio State University, Columbus, Ohio 43210-1222.

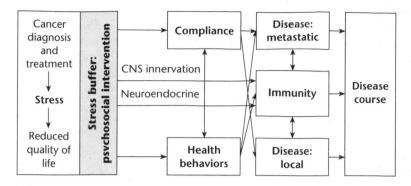

Figure 6.1   A biobehavioral model of the psychological, behavioral, and biologic pathways from cancer stressors to disease course. (CNS = Central Nervous System). From Andersen, B. A., Kiecolt-Glaser, J. K., and Glaser, R. (1994). A biobehavioral model of cancer stress and disease course. *American Psychologist*, 49, 1–16. Reprinted with permission. Copyright © 1994 American Psychological Association. All rights reserved.

volume, we extend our discussion to the revisiting of the cancer stressor – the diagnosis of recurrent disease.

A Biobehavioral Model of Cancer Stress and Disease Course

Psychological Pathways: Stress and Lowered Quality of Life

The biobehavioral model suggests that both acute and chronic stress can contribute to emotional distress, life disruptions, and, in turn, a stable, lower quality of life for cancer patients (see figure 6.1). Severe, acute stress occurs at the time of cancer diagnosis (Andersen et al., 1989a,b; Epping-Jordan et al., 1999; Maunsell et al., 1992). Data suggest that the combination of prior life stressors and limited social support resources relate to lower quality of life, including mood disturbance and stress-related symptoms. Individuals who experienced noncancer stressors – death of loved ones, other illnesses, work difficulties, or financial problems – have an added burden and these additional stressors are important in subsequent adjustment. Andrykowski and Cordova (1998) have found that women recently completing treatment who had experienced more precancer traumatic stressors and lower levels of support reported more post-traumatic stress symptoms. Related data have demonstrated higher mood disturbance (i.e., anxiety, depression, anger) for patients with greater life stress and fewer social ties (Koopman et al., 1998).

Many studies of social factors have focused on the benefits of social support for cancer patients; however, the earliest empirical efforts pointed to the difficulties faced by patients when support was attempted by friends, family members, and acquaintances (Gates, 1980; Peters-Golden, 1982; Wortman and Dunkel-Schetter, 1979). These studies brought to light the inexperience and, at times, the awkwardness of the responses of loved ones to the needs of cancer patients. For example, Peters-Golden (1982) noted that support offered to breast cancer patients was limited in its focus on the woman's response to breast loss, rather than her predominant concerns about other treatment effects, or fears of recurrence. Alternatively, other people responded to the cancer patient with "unrelenting optimism," and thus prevented patients' adequate expression of fears and concerns (Peters-Golden, 1982; Wortman and Dunkel-Schetter, 1979).

Indeed, ineffective support attempts and aversive support have been associated with poorer psychological responses. Even support that is well intended – but not necessary or desired – has been related to increased negative affect, lowered self-esteem, decreased feelings of mastery, and greater existential difficulties (Revenson et al., 1983). Especially for women, aversive "support" such as criticism, callousness or disrespect, demanding behavior, and other difficult behaviors by healthcare professionals, friends, and family is a useful predictor of post-traumatic stress symptoms (Hampton-Rucklos and Fromback, 2000).

Some sequelae of cancer treatments have the potential to impact social support and intimate relationships, and thereby heighten emotional distress and reduce quality of life (Ey et al., 1998; Ganz et al., 1996; Gluhoski et al., 1997; Hagedoorn et al., 2000; Spencer et al., 1999), particularly for women with breast or gynecologic cancer. For these women, the extent of the cancer treatment and the symptomatology portend lower levels of sexual activity and responsiveness (Andersen et al., 1997; Yurek et al., 2000).

It is also clear that after lengthy, difficult treatments have ended, individuals may still report disruptions in major life areas and, for some, chronic stress (Cordova et al., 1995). Many cancer survivors report continuing problems with emotional distress, fatigue, reduced energy levels, and loss of stamina (Andrykowski et al., 1997). Individuals without intimate relationships may experience new stressors, such as pessimism about future relationships, concerns about disclosing the illness to dating partners, and reticence to engage in sexual activity (Gluhoski et al., 1997). Finally, a cancer diagnosis can also result in subsequent financial difficulties, jeopardize insurance coverage, and narrow employment options, as one-fifth of cancer survivors report these chronic, stressful difficulties (Hewitt et al., 1999). Thus, stress and lowered quality of life conspire to produce a difficult trajectory on the road to cancer survivorship (Gotay and Muraoka, 1998; Green et al., 2000).

Behavioral pathways: Health behaviors and compliance

The biobehavioral model suggests important heath behavior sequelae (see arrow from stress/lowered QoL to health behaviors in figure 6.1). There are many manifestations of negative health behaviors. Individuals who are depressed and/or anxious are more likely to self-medicate with alcohol and other drugs, and, in addition, alcohol abuse can potentiate distress (Grunberg and Baum, 1985). Distressed individuals often have appetite disturbances or dietary changes, such as eating less often, or eating meals of lower nutritional value (Grunberg and Straub, 1992). If eating habits are changed because of cancer treatments (e.g. food restriction with nausea, or taste aversions from chemotherapy; Broeckel et al., 2000; Jacobsen et al., 1995), vulnerability may be heightened (Wellisch et al., 1989). Other data suggest that breast cancer patients who have received adjuvant chemotherapy are at risk for weight gain (Camoriano et al., 1990). Distressed individuals may report sleep disturbances, such as early-morning awakening or insomnia (Lacks and Morin, 1992). Cigarette smoking and caffeine use, which often increase during periods of stress (Miller et al., 1999), can intensify the physiologic effects of psychosocial stress, such as increasing catecholamine release (Grunberg et al., 1988). In contrast, individuals who are stressed may abandon positive health behaviors, such as regular physical exercise.

The model suggests that health behaviors, in turn, affect immunity (see arrow in figure 6.1). Negative health behaviors have, in general, an adverse, downregulating effect on immunity. The covariations of immunity and sleep difficulties (Cover and Irwin, 1994; Savard et al., 1999), alcohol intake (Szabo, 1999; Watson et al., 1994), smoking (Jung and Irwin, 1999; McAllister-Sistilli et al., 1998), and drug use (Friedman et al., 1991) have each been reported. Moreover, many problematic health behaviors coalesce to produce additional, detrimental consequences. For example, alcohol abuse has direct, negative effects on immunity (Irwin and Miller, 2000), as well as indirect effects via alterations in nutrition (i.e., poor eating habits; Chandra and Newberne, 1977). Poor nutrition is also associated with a variety of immunological impairments (Chandra, 1999; LeSourd, 1997).

Alternatively, if negative health behaviors can be reduced or eliminated and/or positive health behaviors increased, immunity may be enhanced (or at least rebound to basal levels). Even a month-long abstinence from smoking has been found to reduce cortisol levels and increase natural killer (NK) cell cytotoxity (Meliska et al., 1995). Nutritional improvements can enhance immune responses, reduce rates of infection, and improve mortality (Galban et al., 2000). Also, there is evidence that physical activity may have positive consequences for both the immune (Nieman and Pedersen, 1999; Woods et al., 1999) and the endocrine systems (Smith and Weidemann, 1990). The available data suggest that a program of physical exercise following cancer diagnosis can reduce stress, enhance quality of life, and improve physical and functional responses, including greater muscle strength and reduced nausea/ vomiting and pain symptoms, and result in more favorable hematological indices (e.g. lower neutropenia following stem cell transplantation; see Courneya and Friedenreich, 1999).

Additionally, the biobehavioral model suggests that health behaviors are related to disease progression (see arrow from health behaviors to disease: metastatic in figure 6.1). Data suggest that obesity at diagnosis, increased fat intake, and weight gain may be related to recurrence and poorer survival in breast cancer patients (Holm et al., 1993; Saxe et al., 1999; Willet, 1999; Zhang et al., 1995). Clinical trials of dietary interventions for breast cancer patients were advocated (Wynder et al., 1997) and multicenter trials are in progress (WINS; Chlebowski et al., 1993). Smaller trials have indicated that fat intake can be significantly reduced and/or fiber intake increased (Nordevang et al., 1992; Pierce et al., 1997). Further, second-generation trials incorporating regular physical exercise to reduce and maintain weight change have been advocated (Stoll, 1996). Taken together, these data suggest that health behaviors relevant to nutrition, fat/fiber balance, and energy expenditure may be relevant to disease progression.

A second behavioral factor is treatment compliance, as psychological and behavioral variables (e.g., depression, confusion regarding medications) are correlates of low rates of compliance (see arrow from stress/QoL to compliance and arrow from compliance to local/metastatic disease in figure 6.1; Lebovits et al., 1990; McDonough et al., 1996). The impact of noncompliance on disease progression may vary depending on the topology of noncompliant behaviors. Refusal or noncompliance with radiation therapy, for example, would adversely impact local control, although if radiation fields included the regional lymph nodes, for example, distant control would also be compromised. Studies are available regarding compliance with therapies aimed at systemic control of the disease, such as chemotherapy. The literature suggests that noncompliance rates may range from 8% (Taylor et al., 1984) to 23–25% (Berger et al., 1988; Richardson et al., 1987). This is very important, as dosage reductions can compromise survival. Budman et al. (1998) reported that women receiving high or moderate dose intensity had a 77–79% 5-year survival rate versus only 66% for women receiving a low dose intensity of the same chemotherapy (i.e., cyclophosphamide, doxorubicin, and 5-FU) for stage II breast cancer.

Despite their relevance, social factors have not been studied in relation to compliance in adults (Given and Given, 1989; Spiegel, 1997), but data on relevant health behaviors prior to diagnosis suggests that they may well be important. In a study of Los Angeles County residents, Berkanovic (1982) found that individuals' decision to seek treatment for cancerrelevant symptoms such as fever, nausea, masses, and fatigue was most influenced by social network factors and personal health beliefs about symptoms. Specifically, individuals who discussed cancer-relevant symptoms with friends and family and who were encouraged to seek treatment were then, in turn, more likely to seek medical care.

The biobehavioral model also specifies that the processes governing compliance and health behavior interact (see double-headed arrow between compliance and health behaviors in figure 6.1). That is, those who are compliant may expect better health outcomes and, as well, engage in dietary, exercise, sleep or other behaviors indicative of "good health." Personality may provide one basis for such synergy (see Friedman et al., 1995, for data relating mortality to conscientiousness), but social influences may also contribute (Allen et al., 1998; Black et al., 1990; Umberson, 1992). Changes in health behaviors and/or compliance have been offered as *post hoc* explanations for some of the most notable intervention findings, including survival (Spiegel et al., 1989). However, health behaviors and compliance have been understudied in psychological intervention studies in cancer (Andersen, 1992; Andersen and Golden-Kreutz, in press) despite their importance.

Biological Pathways: Endocrine and Immune

Stress triggers important biological effects involving the autonomic, endocrine, and immune systems (see arrows from stress to immunity in figure 6.1). Stress may be routed to the immune system by the central nervous system (CNS) via activation of the sympathetic nervous system (e.g., Felten et al., 1987), or through neuroendocrine–immune pathways (i.e., the release of steroid hormones, glucocorticoids). The endocrine axes include the hypo-thalamopituitary–thyroid (HPT) axis and the hypothalamicgrowth hormone axis, although it is the hypothalamopituitary–adrenal (HPA) axis that has received the greatest empirical attention in the human stress literature. There are few neuroendocrine studies of cancer patients, but data suggest that such patients may exhibit dysregulation of the HPA axis that is similar to that observed in depressed patients without cancer (i.e., hypersecretion of ACTH and cortisol, and adrenal and pituitary hypertrophy; Evans et al., 1986; Joffe et al., 1986; McDaniel et al., 1995). Also, hormones released under stress (e.g., catecholamines, cortisol, prolactin, and growth hormone) have been implicated in immune modulation (see Maier et al., 1994 for a discussion; Rabin et al., 1989; Sabharwal et al., 1992). Lymphocytes, monocytes/macrophages, and granulocytes possess receptors for neurotransmitters that are capable of immune regulation (Felten, 1991). Epinephrine and norepinephrine, for example, regulate lymphocyte levels that can, in turn, alter immune responses such as cellular migration, lymphocyte proliferation, antibody secretion, and cell lysis (Madden and Livnat, 1991). *In vitro* work has shown that the addition of catecholamines to human whole blood produced a suppression of interleukin-12 (IL-12) production, yet an increase in IL-10 production (Elenkov et al., 1996). This cytokine shift (i.e. suppression of IL-12 yet enhancement of IL-10) causes a T-helper (Th) cell shift from Th1 cells involved with cell-mediated inflammatory reactions to Th2 cells that produce cytokines promoting humoral responses, such as encouraging antibody production. Thus, a stress-related, lower Th1 response might, for example, increase susceptibility to infectious pathogens requiring a cellular response (Clerici et al., 1997). Also, Th1 responses may be more important to antitumor immune responses (e.g. Brunda et al., 1993).

Experimental data on stress and immunity in cancer patients has been slow to accumulate. In an early study by Levy and colleagues (Levy et al., 1990), NK (natural killer) cell activity was predicted by the perception of high-quality emotional support from the partners of breast cancer patients, perceived support from the patient's physician, and prognostic and treatment variables (estrogen receptor status, type of treatment). More recent data come from Andersen and colleagues (Andersen et al., 1998) illustrating the downregulating effects of stress on measures of NK and T-cell responses. Experimental data were first provided by Fawzy and colleagues (1990a,b). Specifically, 80 stage I or II melanoma patients were randomized to no intervention or to a structured short-term (10 sessions) group support intervention. Significant psychological and coping outcomes for the intervention subjects were evident by 6 months post treatment, as well as significant increases in NK cell numbers and interferon-α (IFN-α)-augmented NK cell activity. The correlational data indicated that NK cell cytotoxic activity increased with concomitant reductions in anxiety (-0.37) and depression (-0.33).

In the intervening years there have been few studies and, collectively, they illustrate the difficulties inherent in intervention research with cancer patients and the added challenge of including biologic measures. Null findings were reported with one quasi-experimental (Lekander et al., 1997) and six experimental intervention studies (Cruess et al., 2000; Elsesser et al., 1994; Gruber et al., 1993; Larson et al., 2000; Richardson et al., 1997; Van der Pompe et al., 1997). Small sample sizes (n from 13 to 47) and high attrition (e.g., 26% in van der Pompe, 1997; 46% in Larson et al., 2000) were problematic.

Disease course

Psychological interventions can reduce stress and benefit quality of life (Andersen, 1992; Andersen and Golden-Kreutz, in press; Meyer and Mark, 1995; Sheard and Maguire, 1999), and there is suggestive evidence linking psychological interventions to disease course (see arrow from stress and psychological intervention to disease course, figure 6.1). Four early intervention studies reported disease outcomes, but none had been designed to test disease end-points (Sampson in *Oncology News*, 1997). The most comprehensive was the study by Fawzy et al. (1990a,b) described above. After a 6-year follow-up they reported differences in survival, with 29% of controls but only 9% of experimental subjects dying (Fawzy et al., 1993). *Post hoc* analyses indicated that the survivors had reported significant reductions in affective distress, increases in active behavioral coping, and increases in CD16 NK cells and IFN-α NK cell activity from baseline to the 6-month follow-up. Those who died did not show this pattern, i.e., no QoL improvement or immune enhancement. Richardson and colleagues (Richardson et al., 1990) provided an intervention that significantly enhanced compliance with chemotherapy and clinic visits for 94 patients with hematological malignancies; follow-up indicated improved survival for the intervention patients.

Two studies provided data from patients with a poor prognosis. Spiegel and colleagues (Spiegel and Bloom, 1983; Spiegel et al., 1981) randomized 86 women to a supportive–expressive therapy intervention or control group. Ten years later Spiegel et al. (1989) reported a striking survival time difference: 18.9 months for the control subjects and 36.6 months for the intervention subjects. However, reanalysis of the data suggests that the control group may have had more progressive disease, with more bony ($P = 0.07$) and lung metastases ($P = 0.09$) and receipt of more radical treatment (i.e., adrenalectomy, $P = 0.08$; Kogon et al., 1997). In addition, Linn et al. (1982) offered a supportive, death and dying intervention to 120 male cancer patients (46% had lung cancer) and found no survival advantage despite favorable QoL outcomes.

Since these early efforts, other intervention studies have reported survival data, but selective study samples, high rates of attrition, and weak/nonexistent intervention effects weaken their findings. Three quasi-experimental studies included breast (Gellert et al., 1993; Shrock et al., 1999), prostate (Shrock et al., 1999), or a mixed disease site sample (DeVries et al., 1997); all studies reported null effects. Of the experimental studies, two accrued women with recurrent breast cancer (Cunningham et al., 1999; Edelman et al., 1999) and the third a heterogeneous sample (Ilnyckyj et al., 1994). These studies also reported null effects.

Cancer as a Chronic Illness: Recurrence

Cancer patients face difficult circumstances throughout their illness, but the shock of learning the disease has recurred can, for some, be devastating. For others, it appears to be just one more challenge, similar to previous ones, e.g., undergoing surgery, receiving chemotherapy or radiation, or, for many, some lengthy combination of treatments. Although biobehavioral research is advancing our knowledge of the cancer experience, our understanding of the psychological and behavioral aspects of recurrence needs to be greater. Indeed, although the absolute numbers of new diagnoses per year are staggering, over half a million will die of their disease, with the majority having faced recurrence in the process (Greenlee et al., 2000).

In contrast to the scholarly and empirical understandings of the initial cancer experience (e.g., Rowland and Holland, 1989), there are few studies of the psychological aspects of cancer recurrence, and none that have included biologic variables for simultaneous analysis. Quasi-experimental designs have included single group reports of patients at or near the time of their diagnosis (Cella et al., 1990; Classen et al., 1996; Jenkins et al., 1991; Koopman et al., 1998; Mahon and Casperson, 1997; Rummans et al., 1998; Schultz et al., 1995), although other studies have used convenience samples at various points in time following the diagnosis of recurrence (Newsom et al., 1996; Steptoe et al., 1991). The majority of studies include samples which are heterogeneous in terms of their original diagnosis or the nature of the recurrence, although a few have focused on breast cancer patients only (i.e., Classen et al., 1996; see also Jenkins et al., 1991; Koopman et al., 1998) or breast and gynecologic cancer patients (Rummans et al., 1998). To our knowledge, there have only been two cross-sectional studies that have included a comparison group, one comparing patients who received an initial versus a recurrent diagnosis (Munkres et al., 1992) and the other comparing recurrent patients with those who were disease free on follow-up (Kullmer et al., 1999).

The majority of these reports are clinically focused and describe emotional sequelae and other difficulties (e.g., Lynch, 1991; Plumb and Holland, 1977). A variety of data indicate that the most salient emotions that occur with an initial or recurrent cancer diagnosis, are fear/anxiety and depression (e.g., Derogatis et al., 1983). Whereas anxiety responses are common for individuals diagnosed with a medical condition and facing treatment (Cassem, 1990), the depressive responses may be more unique to those conditions for which the threat to life is tangible and the prognosis guarded or poor. Indeed, the notion of "existential plight" (Weisman and Worden, 1976) – a term used to characterize the emotional trauma that comes with the initial diagnosis of cancer – appears relevant to recurrence as well, as individuals once again fear for their present circumstances (including symptoms and treatments) and worry about the future.

The limited data available on the experience of recurrence suggests that the majority of patients find recurrence to be more distressing than the initial diagnosis (Cella et al., 1990; Mahon et al., 1990), although a small number (20–30 percent) believe the recurrence diagnosis is less stressful (Mahon et al., 1990; Weisman and Worden, 1976). Others have reported at least 45 percent of their sample to be anxious or depressed at the time of local recurrence diagnosis (Jenkins et al., 1991). More recent findings indicate that partners or spouses may also be more distressed by a diagnosis of recurrence than by the initial cancer diagnosis (Morse and Fife, 1998), and that partners may be even more distressed than the patient by recurrence (Given and Given, 1992).

Patients with a greater number of concurrent stressors, particularly financial difficulties, appear to have an elevated risk of emotional distress during recurrence (Schultz et al., 1995; Weisman and Worden, 1986). Younger patients and those who are more surprised by or not anticipating the diagnosis might also experience more distress (Cella et al., 1990; Northouse et al., 1995; Weisman and Worden, 1986). The degree of physical symptoms, pain, and discomfort are especially important in predicting psychological adjustment during recurrence, with more symptoms or greater pain and discomfort indicating poorer adjustment (Bull et al., 1999; Northouse et al., 1995; Rummans et al., 1998; Schultz et al., 1995). Although these patients may indeed experience increased pain (Portenoy and LeSage, 1999) and problems with appetite (e.g., anorexia and cachexia; Body et al., 1997), it is also plausible that patients with recurrence might be more sensitive to or distressed by their symptoms, attributing more prognostic significance to these experiences.

Recurrence has also been associated with increased hopelessness and greater attention to existential concerns (Cella et al., 1990; Weisman and Worden, 1986). In turn, this surge in hopelessness and decline in optimism has been associated with adjustment difficulties and attenuated wellbeing (Northouse et al., 1995; Schulz et al., 1995). Patients have also reported worries about burdening their family (Cella et al., 1990), reductions in family support (Mahon et al., 1990), and more frequent family arguments (Mahon and Casperson, 1995). Several studies note the essential role of the partner or spouse in supporting the patient through this difficult experience, but these studies also suggest the reluctance of couples to discuss the recurrence and other existential concerns (Chekyrn, 1984; Mahon and Casperson, 1995; Wilber, 1988).

It remains unclear whether these psychosocial adjustment issues impact the survival of recurrent cancer. A few early studies found that mood was a significant predictor of survival (Derogatis et al., 1979; Levy et al., 1988), whereas others have reported that psychosocial considerations did not predict survival (Weisman and Worden, 1986). However, these studies applied different measures and did not include biologic variables for simultaneous analysis, thereby limiting our understanding of the processes by which psychological variables might impact survival. Other areas in need of further study include marital adjustment, communication, and sexual difficulties, the biobehavioral responses of patients and other family members following recurrence diagnosis, as well as areas of positive adjustment and coping with a cancer recurrence.

Summary

A biobehavioral perspective of cancer provides insight into the psychological, behavioral, and biologic pathways by which cancer outcomes might be influenced. In addition to important quality of life benefits that can be achieved with psychological interventions, research considers whether interventions might influence biologic responses and, perhaps, disease outcomes. Can this be achieved? The need for experimental data remains critical. Moreover, studies must be designed to answer these difficult questions and rigorous methodology must be employed, including methodologic consideration of prognostic factors, the provision of an effective stress-reducing/quality of life-enhancing intervention, and psychological/behavioral efforts to enhance compliance and initiate protective health behaviors.

Our need for an empirical understanding of recurrence as an acute and chronic stressor is important and pressing. The research literature is in the earliest of stages, and has been dominated by retrospective reports. Despite being of clinical import, single-group retrospective studies are, of course, confounded by the difficulties of recall bias, convenience samples, lack of repeated measures, and the absence of comparison groups, among others. A longitudinal study of recurrence is needed. Consideration of cancer recurrence as a chronic illness phenomenon may represent the next challenge for biobehavioral cancer researchers.

Clinical Implications of the Biobehavioral Model

Researchers have estimated that 20–44 percent of cancer patients meet the criteria for a formal psychiatric disorder during the diagnostic/treatment period. The most common diagnosis is adjustment disorder, but major depressive and anxiety disorders occur as well (Derogatis et al., 1983; Dobkin and Morrow, 1986; Irvine et al., 1991). For many, the stress of cancer diagnosis and treatment will abate with time, although recent work suggests that clinical disorders may persist, with some adjustment disorders evolving into anxiety disorders, dysthymia, or major depression at follow-up (Grassi and Rosti, 1996). This scenario highlights the importance of identifying early in the treatment process individuals at greatest risk for psychological distress. Here we discuss risk factors and describe how the biobehavioral model can be used to select interventions for cancer patients who vary in their level of psychological risk.

Risk Factors for Psychological/Behavioral Morbidity

During the past two decades researchers have identified several demographic, medical, and psychosocial factors useful in predicting psychological distress for individuals with a cancer diagnosis. These can be used to identify individuals with the greatest need for preventive or rehabilitative psychological or behavioral medicine services. Demographic factors identified in the current literature include age and socioeconomic status, with those who are younger than 60 or who have a lower socioeconomic status reporting greater psychological distress (Bloom and Kessler, 1994; Dean, 1987; Pinder et al., 1993; Vinokur et al., 1989, 1990). Medical factors associated with poorer psychological adjustment include a greater frequency of postoperative symptoms or side-effects of adjuvant treatment (Razavi et al., 1993; Ward et al., 1992; Weijmar Schultz et al., 1992; Woods and Earp, 1978), more physical impairment (Taylor et al., 1985; Vinokur et al., 1990), and comorbidity of chronic illnesses (Stewart et al., 1989). Cancer stage appears to predict psychological distress only to the extent that stage relates to greater physical complaints or extent of treatment (Edgar et al., 1992; Pinder, et al., 1993). Cancer recurrence is also associated with heightened levels of distress, comparable to or beyond that experienced upon initial diagnosis (Jenkins et al., 1991; Mahon et al., 1990; Morse and Fife, 1998).

An individual's psychological and support status at the time of diagnosis and treatment can also be useful in predicting consequent psychological disruption. A history of psychiatric disorder, particularly depression, places an individual at increased risk beyond the base rate for depression in a healthy population (Maunsell et al., 1992; Plumb and Holland, 1981). Conversely, an individual's optimism, sense of control, and a higher ratio of problem-focused to emotion-focused coping might portend less psychological distress (Carver et al., 1993; Stanton and Snider, 1993; Taylor et al., 1984). Finally, it might be worth assessing the individual's degree of perceived or received support from his or her family or spouse, as opposed to merely assessing marital status, as limited functional support and negative interactions have also been associated with psychological distress in cancer populations (Bloom et al., 1978; Butler et al., 1999; Manne, 1999).

These factors can thus be used to identify individuals at low, moderate, and high risk of developing heightened psychological distress during or following the course of cancer treatment. An individual at low risk might have adequate financial resources and support from friends and family, may experience few postoperative medical symptoms, and not require adjuvant treatment, have no comorbid physical or psychiatric illness, but experience difficulty adapting to the crisis of cancer diagnosis and surgical treatment. An individual at moderate risk may have more extensive disease, require both surgery and adjuvant treatment, and experience greater functional impairment accompanied by moderate psychological vulnerability (i.e., less optimism, greater use of avoidance, or prior psychiatric diagnosis). Those at greatest risk may be diagnosed with advanced or recurrent disease, have a significant degree of surgical sequelae and physical impairment, and very limited fiscal and psychosocial resources. These are merely examples demonstrating how demographic, medical, and psychosocial factors can covary to put an individual at low, moderate, or high risk for the development of psychological adjustment difficulties.

Clinical Interventions Based on the Biobehavioral Model

The biobehavioral model (Andersen et al., 1994) provides an alternative and more comprehensive approach to cancer patient assessment and intervention than other approaches focused solely on emotional adjustment. In addition to emotional foci of treatment, the biobehavioral approach includes educational, stress management, cognitive, communication and support, sexuality, and behavioral health components. These strategies can be used to assist an individual effectively throughout the entire process of cancer adjustment, including the stressful diagnostic period, coping with surgery and adjuvant treatment, enhancing relationships with treatment providers, improving quality of life as a cancer survivor, and taking steps to minimize the potential for recurrence. Thus, the biobehavioral model provides an array of interventions and helps to clarify the behavioral medicine specialist's role in the multidisciplinary setting.

Education

Education/informational components have been shown to be effective in psychological interventions for cancer patients (Helgesen et al., 1999; McArdle et al., 1996). It is difficult for behavioral scientists to be fully versed in the technical and medical aspects of cancer diagnosis and treatment, but didactic materials are often available free from federal and state cancer organizations. Familiarity with community resources can also be beneficial. Finally, assisting the patient to clarify questions and otherwise improve communication with treatment providers can be invaluable in helping them meet their own informational and educational needs.

Stress Management

Many techniques can be used to reduce patient stress, but we have found three to be particularly effective. First, patients can be provided with information to assist in conceptualizing the stress process and to understand how stress can affect physical and psychological wellbeing. For example, Gatchel et al.'s (1989) model of stress as a psychophysiological process can be useful in identifying potential consequences of acute and chronic stress. Lazarus and Folkman's (1984) stress, appraisal, and coping model can also be used to demonstrate that stress is a process that can be interrupted through alterations in appraisal or coping. Second, teaching patients a repertoire of coping strategies can be important. Patients can be taught to identify less effective strategies (i.e., denial and avoidance) and to replace them with more active, problem-focused approaches to coping (i.e., seeking support and information, positive appraisal, acceptance). These skills can be role played, learned, and potentially generalized to noncancer stressor circumstances. Finally, patients can reduce overall tension and anxiety with progressive muscle relaxation (Bernstein et al., 2000). Relaxation methods can also aid in reducing the side-effects of chemotherapy (see Burish and Tope, 1992 for a review). Patients can be provided with audiotapes for use in the clinic or at home.

Cognitive Strategies

Two cognitive components can be used to help the patient to identify stressors and manage the specific stressful aspects of living with cancer. With a specific stressor in mind, cognitive restructuring or the A (Activating Events)–B (Beliefs/automatic thoughts)–C (Consequences – feelings and behaviors) model can be used to help the patient understand and identify beliefs/cognitions that contribute to his or her negative feelings, thoughts, and behaviors (Ellis and Harper, 1975). Problem-solving techniques can also be used to find solutions for specific cancer-related (e.g., fatigue) and noncancer-related problems (e.g., time management). This method consists of five stages: a) understanding the principles of problem solving; b) defining target problems; c) generating problem solutions; d) decision making or choosing a solution; and e) verifying the solution or trying one strategy, evaluating its effectiveness, and modifying the strategy, if necessary (Goldfried and Davison, 1994; Hawton and Kirk, 1989).

Communication and Support

Three primary intervention components can be used to assist the cancer patient to enhance his or her social skills and support. First, support groups can be used to facilitate social comparison processes, whereby members learn that many of their reactions are normal and shared by others (see Taylor's conceptualization of adjustment to threatening events; Taylor et al., 1984). Second, a concentric circle model (with the patient at the center) can be used to map out the support available in the patient's social network (e.g., co-workers and friends, physicians, parents/in-laws and siblings, children, and spouse or partner). This can then be used to identify sources of satisfaction and clarify areas of difficulty within the individual's network. The third component involves teaching assertive communication skills to help patients to express their thoughts, feelings, and needs in a manner that facilitates support from and effective communication with members of their social network, including the medical treatment team. Communication training includes: a) making one's message specific and clear; b) using direct communication; c) owning one's message (i.e., use of "I" and "my" statements); and, d) eliciting feedback (Jakubowski-Spector, 1973).

Sexuality

The cancer experience can create or exacerbate sexual problems and, further, can alter the patient's body image or sense of bodily integrity. Women with negative sexual self-schemas may be particularly vulnerable to these effects (Andersen et al., 1997; Yurek et al., 2000). Several interventions can be used to facilitate sexual adjustment. First, didactic components can be used to review bodily changes associated with surgery and adjuvant treatment. The potential effects of these treatments on the sexual response cycle can then be reviewed in an attempt to assess specific responses (e.g. desire, arousal, plateau, orgasm) that might be disrupted. The contexts for sexual activity can be broadened by consideration of the optimal timing of sexual activity given the patient's current health status, expanding the behavioral repertoire (e.g., sexual activities in lieu of intercourse, alternative intercourse positions), and using strategies to facilitate desire (e.g., fantasy, erotic materials). Enhancing sexual communication is also important, including discovering the partner's sexuality concerns and understanding the patient's needs and concerns. For patients without partners, one can discuss strategies for sharing information about cancer and treatments to a prospective partner. More specific interventions may be needed to treat dyspareunia, vaginismus, erectile dysfunction, or orgasmic disorder, and may require referral to a clinician trained in sex therapy techniques (see Andersen and Elliott, 1994 for a discussion of assessment of the sexual concerns of female cancer survivors).

Behavioral Health

Lifestyle factors such as tobacco use, dietary habits, and alcohol consumption account for an estimated 68 percent of all cancer deaths in the United States (Heath and Fontham, 2001). Despite the potential survival benefits of many health-protective (e.g., appointment adherence and medication compliance) and health-promoting behaviors (e.g., smoking cessation, exercise, dietary alterations), these behaviors are rarely incorporated by behavioral medicine professionals into cancer interventions. This is not an inconsequential oversight, given the role that these lifestyle factors might play in disease-free survival versus recurrence for specific cancer sites (Davidow et al., 1996; Demark-Whahnefried et al., 1997; Oh et al., 2000; Stoll, 1996).

Dietary interventions designed to decrease fat intake and increase fiber consumption show promising results on both self-report and biochemical indices of behavior change (Chlebowski et al., 1993; Pierce, et al., 1997). Current National Cancer Institute guidelines recommend a dietary fat intake less than or equal to 25 percent of energy intake, and dietary fiber of 20–30 g/day from fruits, vegetables, and grains. Exercise programs including bicycles or treadmills have also demonstrated some benefit for cancer patients (i.e., attenuation of pain and fatigue, reduced anxiety and depression, and prevention of weight gain); however, the majority of these studies have been completed with breast cancer patients and may not generalize to other cancer populations. Finally, interventions designed to eliminate smoking among cancer patients are less conclusive. Although a greater number of cancer patients remain abstinent 5–6 weeks from cessation than in the general population (60–75% versus 25%), it is not yet clear if this can be attributed to motivation owing to the cancer diagnosis, or to the smoking intervention. Pinto et al. (2000) provide an excellent review of the published health behavior interventions completed with cancer patients during the last two decades.

Tailoring Biobehavioral Intervention to Patient Needs

Most individuals will not experience clinically significant problems in coping with cancer diagnosis and treatment. In fact, many will report positive changes as a result of the experience (Petrie et al., 1999). Risk assessment can be used to identify those at greatest risk for developing cancer-related psychological sequelae. Risk assessment in combination with an awareness of the specific stressors at each phase (i.e., diagnosis, surgery, adjuvant treatment, survivorship) can assist clinicians to more effectively target cancer interventions. A blending of techniques such as education, emotional support, and stress management/relaxation might be most useful for individuals at low risk who are experiencing difficulty coping with diagnosis and/or surgical intervention. However, more intensive interventions incorporating communication and support enhancement, behavioral pain management, and cognitive/decision-making strategies might be more useful for those experiencing advanced cancer or recurrent disease. Broadening the spectrum to include stress management, cognitive, communication, sexual, and behavioral health interventions can enhance patient self-efficacy and invite generalization beyond cancer stressors. Although cancer research is far from understanding which interventions are most effective for each individual at a particular phase of survivorship, the biobehavioral model widens the scope of intervention, thus permitting the fit of treatment to the individual rather than fitting the individual to one mode of intervention.

References

Allen, J., Sorensen, G., Stoddard, A., Colditz, G., and Peterson, K. (1998). Intention to have a mammogram in the future among women who have underused mammography in the past. *Health Education and Behavior*, 25, 474–488.

Andersen, B. L. (1992). Psychological interventions for cancer patients to enhance the quality of life. *Journal of Consulting and Clinical Psychology*, 60, 552–568.

Andersen, B. L., Anderson, B., and deProsse, C. (1989a). Controlled prospective longitudinal study of women with cancer: I. Sexual functioning outcomes. *Journal of Consulting and Clinical Psychology*, 57, 683–691.

Andersen, B. L., Anderson, B., and deProsse, C. (1989b). Controlled prospective longitudinal study of women with cancer: II. Psychological outcomes. *Journal of Consulting and Clinical Psychology*, 57, 692–697.

Andersen, B. L. and Elliott, M. L. (1994). Female cancer survivors: Appreciating their sexual concerns. *Canadian Journal of Human Sexuality*, 3, 107–122.

Andersen, B. A., Farrar, W. B., Golden-Kreutz, D., Kutz, L. A., MacCallum, R., Courtney, M. E., and Glaser, R. (1998). Stress and immune responses after surgical treatment for regional breast cancer. *Journal of the National Cancer Institute*, 90, 30–36.

Andersen, B. L., and Golden-Kreutz, D. (in press). Biobehavioral outcomes following psychological interventions for cancer patients. *Journal of Consulting and Clinical Psychology*.

Andersen, B. A., Kiecolt-Glaser, J. K., and Glaser, R. (1994). A biobehavioral model of cancer stress and disease course. *American Psychologist*, 49, 1–16.

Andersen, B. L., Woods, X. A., and Copeland, L. J. (1997). Sexual self-schema and sexual morbidity among gynecologic cancer survivors. *Journal of Consulting and Clinical Psychology*, 65, 221–229.

Andrykowski, M. A., Carpenter, J. S., Greiner, C. B., Altmaier, E. M., Burish, T. G., Antin, J. H., Gingrich, R., Cordova, M. J., and Henslee-Downey, P. J. (1997). Energy level and sleep quality following bone marrow transplantation. *Bone Marrow Transplantation*, 20, 669–679.

Andrykowski, M. A., and Cordova, M. J. (1998). Factors associated with PTSD symptoms following treatment for breast cancer: Test of the Andersen model. *Journal of Traumatic Stress*, 11, 189–203.

Bernstein, D. A., Borkovec, T. D., and Hazlett-Stevens, H. (2000). *New Directions in Progressive Relaxation Training: A Guidebook for Helping Professionals.* Westport, CT: Praeger Publishers/Greenwood Publishing Group, Inc.

Berger, D., Braverman, A., Sohn, C. K., and Morrow, M. (1988). Patient compliance with aggressive multimodal therapy in locally advanced breast cancer. *Cancer*, 61, 1453–1456.

Berkanovic, E. (1982). Seeking care for cancer relevant symptoms. *Journal of Chronic Diseases*, 35, 727–734.

Black, D. R., Gleser, L. J., and Kooyers, K. J. (1990). A meta-analytic evaluation of couples weight-loss programs. *Health Psychology*, 9, 330–347.

Bloom, J. R., Ross, R. D., and Burnell, G. (1978). The effect of social support on patient adjustment after breast cancer. *Patient Counseling and Health Education*, 1, 50–59.

Bloom, J. R. and Kessler, L. (1994). Risk and timing of counseling and support interventions for younger women with breast cancer. *Journal of the National Cancer Institute Monographs*, 16, 199–206.

Body, J. J., Lossignol, D., and Ronson, A. (1997). The concept of rehabilitation of cancer patients. *Current Opinion in Oncology*, 9, 332–340.

Broeckel, J. A., Jacobsen, P. B., and Hann, D. M. (2000). Quality of life after adjuvant chemotheapy for breast cancer. *Breast Cancer Research and Treatment*, 62, 141–150.

Brunda, M. J., Luistro, L., Warrier, R. R., Wright, R. B., Hubbard, B. R., Murphy, M., Wolf, S. F., and Gately, M. K. (1993). Antitumor and antimetastatic activity of inteleukin 12 against murine tumors. *Journal of Experimental Medicine*, 178, 1223–1230.

Budman, D. R., Berry, D. A., Cirrincione, C. T., Henderson, I. C., Wood, W. C., Weiss, R. B., Ferree, C. R., Muss, H. B., Green, M. R., Norton, L., and Frei III, E. (1998). Dose and dose intensity as determinants of outcome in the adjuvant treatment of breast cancer. *Journal of the National Cancer Insitute*, 90, 1205–1211.

Bull, A. A., Meyerowitz, B. E., Hart, S., Mosconi, P., Apolone, G., and Liberati, A. (1999). Quality of life in women with recurrent breast cancer. *Breast Cancer Research and Treatment*, 54, 47–57.

Burish, T. G., and Tope, D. M. (1992). Psychological techniques for controlling the adverse side effects of cancer chemotherapy: Findings from a decade of research. *Journal of Pain and Symptom Management*, 7, 287–301.

Butler, L. D., Cooper, C., Classen, C., and Spiegel, D. (1999). Traumatic stress, life events, and emotional support in women with metastatic breast cancer: Cancer-related traumatic stress symptoms associated with past and current stressors. *Health Psychology*, 18, 555–560.

Camoriano, J. K., Loprinizi, C. L., Ingle, J. N., Therneau, T. M., Krook, J. E., and Veeder, M. H. (1990). Weight change in women treated with adjuvant therapy or observed following mastectomy for node-positive breast cancer. *Journal of Clinical Oncology*, 8, 1327–1334.

Carver, C. S., Pozo, C., Harris, S. D., Noriega, V., Scheier, M. F., Robinson, D. S., Katchman, A. S., Moffat, F. L., and Clark, K. C. (1993). How coping mediates the effect of optimism on distress: A study of women with early stage breast cancer. *Journal of Personality and Social Psychology*, 65, 375–390.

Cassem, E. H. (1990). Depression and anxiety secondary to medical illness. *Psychiatric Clinics of North America*, 13, 597–612.

Cella, D. F., Mahon, S. M., and Donovan, M. I. (1990). Cancer recurrence as a traumatic event. *Journal of Behavioral Medicine*, 16, 15–22.

Chandra, R. K. (1999). Nutrition and immunology: From the clinic to cellular biology and back again. *Proceedings of the Nutrition Society*, 58, 681–683.

Chandra, R. K., and Newberne, P. M. (1977). *Nutrition, Immunity, and Infection: Mechanisms of Interactions*. New York, NY: Plenum Press.

Chekryn, J. (1984). Cancer recurrence: Personal meaning, communication, and marital adjustment. *Cancer Nursing*, 7, 491–498.

Chlebowski, R. T., Blackburn, G. L., Buzzard, I. M., Rose, D. P., Manno, Khandedar, J. D., et al. (1993). Feasibility of using dietary fat intake reduction in postmenopausal women with resected breast cancer. *Proceedings of the American Society of Clinical Oncology*, 12, 473–474.

Classen, C., Koopman, C., Angell, K., and Spiegel, D. (1996). Coping styles associated with psychological adjustment to advanced breast cancer. *Health Psychology*, 15, 434–437.

Clerici, M., Merola, M., Ferrario, E., Trabattoni, D., Villa, M. L., Stefanon, B., Venzon, D. J., Shearer, G. M., DePalo, G., and Clerici, E. (1997). Cytokine production patterns in cervical intraepithelial neoplasia: Association with human papillomavirus infection. *Journal of the National Cancer Institute*, 89, 245–250.

Cordova, M. J., Andrykowski, M. A., Kenady, D. E., McGrath, P. C., Sloan, D. A., and Redd, W. L. (1995). Frequency and correlates of PTSD-like symptoms following treatment for breast cancer. *Journal of Consulting and Clinical Psychology*, 63, 981–986.

Courneya, K. S., and Friedenreich, C. M. (1999). Physical exercise and quality of life following cancer diagnosis: A literature review. *Annals of Behavioral Medicine*, 21, 171–179.

Cover, H., and Irwin, M. (1994). Immunity and depression: Insomnia, retardation, and reduction of natural killer cell activity. *Journal of Behavioral Medicine*, 17, 217–223.

Cruess, D. G., Antoni, M. H., McGregor, B. A., Kilbourn, K. M., Boyers, A. E., Alferi, S. M., Carver, C. S., and Kumar, M. (2000). Cognitive–behavioral stress management reduces serum cortisol by enhancing benefit finding among women being treated for early stage breast cancer. *Psychosomatic Medicine*, 62, 304–308.

Cunningham, A. J., Edmonds, C. V. I., and Williams, D. (1999). Delivering a very brief psychoeducational program to cancer patients and family members in a large group format. *Psycho-Oncology*, 8, 177–182.

Davidow, A. L., Neugat, A. I., Jacobson, J. S., Ahsan, H., Garbowski, G. C., Forde, K. A., Treat, M. R., and Waye, J. D. (1996). Recurrent adenomatous polyps and body mass index. *Cancer Epidemiology, Biomarkers, and Prevention*, 5, 313–315.

Dean, C. (1987). Psychiatric morbidity following mastectomy: Preoperative predictors and types of illness. *Journal of Psychosomatic Research*, 31, 385–392.

Demark-Wahnefried, W., Rimer, B. K., and Winer, E. P. (1997). Weight gain in women diagnosed with breast cancer. *Journal of the American Dietetic Association*, 97, 519–526.

Derogatis, L., Abeloff, M., and Melisaratos, N. (1979). Psychological coping mechanisms and survival time in metastatic breast cancer. *Journal of the American Medical Association*, 242, 1504–1509.

Derogatis, L. R., Morrow, G. R., Fetting, J., Penman, D., Piasetsky, S., Schmale, A. M., Henrichs, M., and Carnicke, C. L. Jr. (1983). The prevalence of psychiatric disorders among cancer patients. *Journal of the American Medical Association*, 249, 751–757.

DeVries, M. J., Schilder, J., Mulder, C., Vrancken, A. M. E., Remie, M. E., and Garssen, B. (1997). Phase II study of psychotherapeutic intervention in advanced cancer. *Psycho-Oncology*, 6, 129–137.

Dobkin, P. L., and Morrow, G. R. (1986). Long-term side effects in patients who have been treated successfully for cancer. *Journal of Psychosocial Oncology*, 3, 23–51.

Edelman, S., Lemon, J., Bell, D. R., and Kidman, A. D. (1999). Effects of group CBT on the survival time of patients with metastatic breast cancer. *Psycho-Oncology*, 8, 474–481.

Edgar, L., Rosberger, Z., and Nowlis, D. (1992). Coping with cancer during the first year after diagnosis: Assessment and intervention. *Cancer*, 69, 817–828.

Elenkov, I. J., Papanicolaou, D. A., Wilder, R. L., and Chrousos, G. P. (1996). Modulatory effects of glucocorticoids and catecholamines on human interleukin-12 and interleukin-10 production: Clinical implications. *Proceedings of the Association of American Physicians*, 108, 374–381.

Ellis, A., and Harper, R. A. (1975). *A New Guide to Rational Living*. New York: Prentice Hall.

Elsesser, K., van Berkel, M., Sartory, G., Biermann-Gocke, W., and Ohl, S. (1994). The effects of anxiety management training on psychological variables and immune parameters in cancer patients: A pilot study. *Behavioural and Cognitive Psychotherapy*, 22, 13–23.

Epping-Jordan, J. E., Compas, B. E., Osowiecki, D. M., Oppedisano, G., Gerhardt, C., Primo, K., and Krag, D. N. (1999). Psychological adjustment in breast cancer: Processes of emotional distress. *Health Psychology*, 18, 315–326.

Evans, D. L., McCartney, C. F., Nemeroff, C. B., Raft, D., Quade, D., Golden, R. M., Haggerty, J. J., Jr., Holmes, V., Simon, J. S., Droba, M., et al. (1986). Depression in women treated for gynecological cancer: Clinical and neuroendocrine assessment. *American Journal of Psychiatry*, 143, 447–452.

Ey, S., Compas, B. E., Epping-Jordan, J. E., and Worsham, N. (1998). Stress responses and psychological adjustment in patients with cancer and their spouses. *Journal of Psychosocial Oncology*, 16, 59–77.

Fawzy, F. I., Cousins, N., Fawzy, N. W., Kemeny, M. E., et al. (1990a). A structured psychiatric intervention for cancer patients. I. Changes over time in methods of coping and affective disturbance. *Archives of General Psychiatry*, 47, 720–725.

Fawzy, F. I., Kemeny, M. E., Fawzy, N. W., Elashoff, R., et al. (1990b). A structured psychiatric intervention for cancer patients. II. Changes over time in immunological measures. *Archives of General Psychiatry*, 47, 729–735.

Fawzy, F. I., Fawzy, N. W., Hyun, C. S. Elashoff, R., Guthrie, D., Fahey, J. L., and Morton, D. L. (1993). Malignant melanoma: Effects of a structured psychiatric intervention, coping, affective state, and immune parameters on recurrence and survival six years later. *Archives of General Psychiatry*, 50, 681–689.

Felten, D. L. (1991). Neurotransmitter signaling of cells of the immune system: Important progress, major gaps. *Brain, Behavior and Immunity*, 5, 2–8.

Felten, D. L., Ackerman, K. D., Wiegand, S. J., and Felten, S. Y. (1987). Noradrenergic sympathetic innervation of the spleen: I. Nerve fibers associate with lymphocyctes and macrophages in specific compartments of the splenic white pulp. *Journal of Neuroscience Research*, 18, 28–36.

Friedman, H., Klein, T., and Specter, S. (1991). Immunosuppression by marijuana and components. In R. Ader and D. L. Felten, *Psychoneuroimmunology* (2nd ed.). San Diego, CA: Academic Press, Inc.

Galban, C., Montejo, J. C., Mesejo, A., Celaya, S., Sanchez-Segura, J. M., Farre, M., and Bryg, D. J. (2000). An immune-enhancing enteral diet reduces mortality rate and episodes of bacteremia in septic intensive care unit patients. *Critical Care Medicine*, 28, 643–648.

Ganz, P. A., Coscarelli, A., Fred, C., Kahn, B., Polinsky, M. L., and Petersen, L. (1996). Breast cancer survivors: Psychosocial concerns and quality of life. *Breast Cancer Research and Treatment*, 38, 183–199.

Gatchel, R. J., and Barnes, D. (1989). *Physiological Self-Control and Emotion. Handbook of Social Psychophysiology.* (pp. 121–138) New York: John Wiley and Sons.

Gates, C. C. (1980). Husbands of mastectomy patients. *Patient Counseling and Health Education*, First Quarter, 38–41.

Gellert, G. A., Maxwell, R. M., and Siegel, B. S. (1993). Survival of breast cancer patients receiving adjunctive psychosocial support therapy: A 10 year follow-up study. *Journal of Clinical Oncology*, 11, 66–69.

Given, B. A., and Given, C. W. (1989). Compliance among patients with cancer. *Oncology Nursing Forum*, 16, 97–103.

Given, B., and Given, C. W. (1992). Patient and family caregiver reaction to new and recurrent breast cancer. *Journal of the American Medical Association*, 47, 201–206.

Gluhoski, V. L., Siegel, K., and Gorey, E. (1997). Unique stressors experienced by unmarried women with breast cancer. *Journal of Psychosocial Oncology*, 15, 173–183.

Goldfried, M. R., and Davison, G. C. (1994). *Clinical Behavior Therapy*. New York: John Wiley and Sons.

Gotay, C. C., and Muraoka, M. Y. (1998). Quality of life in long-term survivors of adult-onset cancers. *Journal of the National Cancer Institute*, 90, 656–67.

Grassi, L., and Rosti, G. (1996). Psychosocial morbidity and adjustment to illness among long-term cancer survivors: A six-year follow-up study. *Psychosomatics*, 37, 523–532.

Green, B. L., Krupnick, J. L., Rowland, J. H., Epstein, S. A., Stockton, P., Spertus, I., and Stern, N. (2000). Trauma history as a predictor of psychologic symptoms in women with breast cancer. *Journal of Clinical Oncology*, 18, 1084–1093.

Greenlee, R. T., Murray, T., Bolden, S., and Wingo, P. A. (2000). Cancer statistics, 2000. *Ca-A Cancer Journal for Clinicians*, 50, 7–33.

Gruber, B. L., Hersh, S. P., Hall, N. R., Waletzky, L. R., et al. (1993). Immunological responses of breast cancer patients to behavioral interventions. *Biofeedback and Self-Regulation*, 18, 1–22.

Grunberg, N. E., and Baum, A. (1985). Biological commonalities of stress and substance abuse. In S. Shiffman and T. A. Wills (Eds.), *Coping and Substance Use* (pp. 25–62). New York: Academic Press.

Grunberg, N. E., Popp, K. A., Bowden, D. J., Nespor, S. M., Winders, S. E., and Eury, S. E. (1988). Effects of chronic nicotine administration on insulin, glucose, epinephrine, and norepinephrine. *Life Sciences*, 42, 161–170.

Grunberg, N. E., and Straub, R. O. (1992). The role of gender and taste class in the effects of stress on eating. *Health Psychology*, 11, 97–100.

Hagedoorn, M., Kuijer, R. G., Buunk, B. P., DeJohng, G. M., Wobbes, T., and Sanderman, R. (2000). Marital satisfaction in patients with cancer: Does support from intimate partners benefit those who need it the most? *Health Psychology*, 19, 274–282.

Hampton-Rucklos, M., and Frombach, I. (2000). Women's experience of traumatic stress in cancer treatment. *Health Care for Women International*, 21, 67–76.

Hawton, K., and Kirk, J. (1989). Problem solving. In K. Hawton and P. M. Salkovskis et al., *Cognitive Behavior Therapy for Psychiatric Problems: A Practical Guide* (pp. 406–426). New York: Oxford University Press.

Heath, C. W., and Fontham, E. T. H. (2001). Cancer etiology. In R. E. Lenhard, R. T. Osteem, and T. Tansler (Eds.), *American Cancer Society's Clinical Oncology* (pp. 37–54). Atlanta: American Cancer Society.

Helgeson, V., Cohen, S., Schulz, R., and Yasko, J. (1999). Education and peer discussion group interventions and adjustment to breast cancer. *Archives of General Psychiatry*, 56, 340–347.

Hewitt, M., Breen, N., and Devesa, S. (1999). Cancer prevalence and survivorship issues: Analyses of the 1992 National Health Interview Survey. *Journal of the National Cancer Insitute*, 91, 1480–1486.

Holm, L. E., Nordevang, E., Hjalmar, M. L., Lidbrink, E., Callmer, E., and Nilsson, B. (1993). Treatment failure and dietary habits in women with breast cancer. *Journal of the National Cancer Institute*, 85, 32–36.

Ilnyckyj, A., Farber, M., Cheang, J., and Weinerman, B. H. (1994). A randomized controlled trial of psychotherapeutic intervention in cancer patients. *Annals of the Royal College of Physicians and Surgeons of Canada*, 27, 93–96.

Irvine, D., Brown, B., Crooks, D., Roberts, J., and Browne, G. (1991). Psychosocial adjustment in women with breast cancer. *Cancer*, 67, 1097–1117.

Irwin, M., and Miller, C. (2000). Decreased natural killer cell responses and altered interleukin-6 and interleukin-10 production in alcoholism: An interaction between alcohol dependence and African-American ethnicity. *Alcoholism – Clinical and Experimental Research*, 24, 560–569.

Jacobsen, P. B., Bovberg, D. H., Schwartz, M. D., Hudis, C. A., Gilewski, T. A., and Norton, L. (1995). Conditioned emotional distress in women receiving chemotherapy for breast cancer. *Journal of Consulting and Clinical Psychology*, 63, 108–114.

Jakubowski-Spector, P. (1973). Facilitating the growth of women through assertive training. *Counseling Psychologist*, 4, 75–86.

Jenkins, P. L., May, V. E., and Hughes, L. E. (1991). Psychological morbidity associated with local recurrence of breast cancer. *International Journal of Psychiatry in Medicine*, 21, 149–55.

Joffe, R. T., Rubinow, D. R., Denicoff, K. D., Maher, M., and Sindelar, W. F. (1986). Depression and carcinoma of the pancreas. *General Hospital Psychiatry*, 8, 241–245.

Jung, W., and Irwin, M. (1999). Reduction of natural killer cytotoxic activity in major depression: Interaction between depression and cigarette smoking. *Psychosomatic Medicine*, 61, 263–270.

Kogon, M. M., Biswas, A., Pearl, D., Carlson, R. W., and Spiegal, D. (1997). Effects of medical and psychotherapeutic treatment on the survival of women with metastatic breast carcinoma. *Cancer*, 80, 225–230.

Koopman, C., Hermanson, K., Diamond, S., Angell, K., and Spiegel, D. (1998). Social support, life stress, pain and emotional adjustment to advanced breast cancer. *Psycho-Oncology*, 7, 101–111.

Kullmer, U., Stenger, K., Milch, W. Zygmunt, M., Sachsse, S., and Munstedt, K. (1999). Self-concept, body image, and use of unconventional therapies in patients with gynaecological malignancies in the state of complete remission and recurrence. *European Journal of Obstetrics, Gynecology, and Reproductive Biology*, 82, 101–106.

Lacks, P., and Morin, C. M. (1992). Recent advances in the assessment and treatment of insomnia. *Journal of Consulting and Clinical Psychology*, 60, 586–594.

Larson, M. R., Duberstein, P. R., Talbot, N. L., Caldwell, C., and Moynihan, J. A. (2000). A presurgical psychosocial intervention for breast cancer patients: Psychological distress and the immune response. *Journal of Psychosomatic Research*, 48, 187–194.

Lazarus, R. S., and Folkman, S. (1984). *Stress, Appraisal, and Coping*. New York: Springer Publishing Company.

Lebovits, A. H., Strain, J. J., Schleifer, S. J., Tanaka, J. S., Bhardwaj, S., and Messe, M. R. (1990). Patient noncompliance with self-administered chemotherapy. *Cancer,* 65, 17–22.

Lekander, M., Furst, C. J., Rotstein, S., Hursti, T. J., and Fredrikson, M. (1997). Immune effects of relaxation during chemotherapy for ovarian cancer. *Psychotherapy and Psychosomatics,* 66, 185–191.

LeSourd, B. M. (1997). Nutrition and immunity in the elderly: Modification of immune responses with nutritional treatments. *American Journal of Clinical Nutrition,* 66, 478s–484s.

Levy, S. M., Herberman, R. B., Whiteside, T., Sanzo, K., Lee, J., and Kirkwood, J. (1990). Perceived social support and tumor estrogen/progesterone receptor status as predictors of natural killer cell activity in breast cancer patients. *Psychosomatic Medicine,* 52, 73–85.

Levy, S. M., Lee, J., Bagley, C., and Lippman, M. (1988). Survival hazards analysis in first recurrent breast cancer patients: Seven-year follow-up. *Psychosomatic Medicine,* 50, 520–528.

Linn, M. W., Linn, B. S., and Harris, R. (1982). Effects of counseling for late stage cancer patients. *Cancer,* 49, 1048–1055.

Lynch, H. T., Watson, P., Conway, T. A., and Lynch, J. F. (1991). Monitoring high risk women: Psychological aspects. In A. B. Stoll (Ed.), *Developments in Oncology Series: Approaches to Breast Cancer Prevention* (vol. 62). Dordrecht, Netherlands: Kluwer Academic Publishers.

Madden, K. S., and Livnat, S. (1991). Catecholamine action and immunologic reactivity. In R. Ader, D. L. Felten, and N. Cohen (eds.), *Psychoneuroimmunology* (2nd ed., pp. 283–310). San Diego, CA: Academic Press, Inc.

Maier, S. F., Wakins, L. R., and Fleshner, M. (1994). Psychoneuroimmunology: The interface between behavior, brain, and immunity. *American Psychologist,* 49, 1004–1017.

Mahon, S. M., and Casperson, D. S. (1995). Psychosocial concerns associated with recurrent cancer. *Cancer Practice,* 3, 372–380.

Mahon, S. M., and Casperson, D. M. (1997). Exploring the psychosocial meaning of recurrent cancer: A descriptive study. *Cancer Nursing,* 20, 178–186.

Mahon, S. M., Cella, D. F., and Donovan, M. I. (1990). Psychosocial adjustment to recurrent cancer. *Oncology Nursing Forum,* 17, 47–54.

Manne, S. L. (1999). Intrusive thoughts and psychological distress among cancer patients: The role of spouse avoidance and criticism. *Journal of Consulting and Clinical Psychology,* 67, 539–546.

Maunsell, E., Brisson, J., and Deschenes, L. (1992). Psychological distress after initial treatment of breast cancer. *Cancer,* 70, 120–125.

McAllister-Sistilli, C. G., Caggiula, A. R., Knopf, S., Rose, C. A., Miller, A. L., and Donny, E. C. (1998). The effects of nicotine on the immune system. *Psychoneuroendocrinology,* 23, 175–187.

McArdle, J. M., George, W. D., McArdle, C. S., Smith, D. C., Moodie, A. R., Hughson, A. V., Murray, G. D. (1996). Psychological support for patients undergoing breast cancer surgery: A randomized study. *British Medical Journal (Clinical Research Edition),* 312, 813–816.

McDaniel, J. S., Musselman, D. L., Porter, M. R., Reed, D. A., and Nemeroff, C. B. (1995). Depression in patients with cancer: Diagnosis, biology, and treatment. *Archives of General Psychiatry,* 52, 89–99.

McDonough, E. J., Boyd, J. H., Varvares, M. A., and Maves, M. D. (1996). Relationship between psychological status and compliance in a sample of patients treated for cancer of the head and neck. *Head and Neck,* 18, 269–276.

Meliska, C. J., Stunkard, M. E., Gilbert, D. G., Jensen, R. A., and Martinko, J. M. (1995). Immune function in cigarette smokers who quit smoking for 31 days. *Journal of Allergy and Clinical Immunology*, 95, 901–910.

Meyer, T. J., and Mark, M. M. (1995). Effects of psychosocial interventions with adult cancer patients: A meta-analysis of randomized experiments. *Health Psychology*, 14, 101–108.

Miller, G. E., Cohen, S., and Herbert, T. (1999). Pathways linking major depression and immunity in ambulatory female patients. *Psychosomatic Medicine*, 61, 850–860.

Morse, S. R., and Fife, B. (1998). Coping with a partner's cancer: Adjustment at four stages of illness trajectory. *Oncology Nursing Forum*, 25, 751–760.

Munkres, A., Oberst, M. T., and Hughes, S. H. (1992). Appraisal of illness, symptom distress, self-care burden, and mood states in patients receiving chemotherapy for initial and recurrent cancer. *Oncology Nursing Forum*, 19, 1201–1209.

Murphy, S. L. (2000). Deaths: Final data for 1998. *National Vital Statistics Reports*, 48, 2.

Newsom, J. T., Knapp, J. E., and Schultz, R. (1996). Longitudinal analysis of specific domains of internal control and depressive symptoms in patients with recurrent cancer. *Health Psychology*, 15, 323–31.

Nieman, D. C., and Pedersen, B. K. (1999). Exercise and immune function: Recent developments. *Sports Medicine*, 27, 73–80.

Nordevang, E., Callmer, E., Marmur, A., and Holm, L. E. (1992). Dietary intervention in breast cancer patients: Effects on food choice. *European Journal of Clinical Nutrition*, 46, 387–396.

Northouse, L. L., Laten, D., and Reddy, P. (1995). Adjustment of women and their husbands to recurrent breast cancer. *Research in Nursing and Health*, 18, 515–524.

Northouse, L. L., Dorris, G., and Charron-Moore, C. (1995). Factors affecting couples' adjustment to recurrent breast cancer. *Social Science Medicine*, 41, 69–76.

Oh, W. K., Manola, J., Renshaw, A. A., Brodkin, D., Loughlin, K. R., Richie, J. P., Shapiro, C. L., and Kantoff, P. W. (2000). Smoking and alcohol use may be risk factors for poorer outcome in patients with clear cell renal carcinoma. *Urology*, 55, 31–35.

Peters-Golden, H. (1982). Breast cancer: Varied perceptions of social support in the illness experience. *Social Science and Medicine*, 16, 483–491.

Petrie, K. J., Buick, D. L., Weinman, J., and Booth, R. J. (1999). Positive effects of illness reported by myocardial infarction and breast cancer patients. *Journal of Psychosomatic Research*, 47, 537–543.

Pierce, J. P., Faeber, S., Wright, F. A., Newman, V., Flatt, S. W., Kealey, S., Rock, C. L., Hryniuk, W., and Greenberg, E. R. (1997). Feasibility of a randomized trial of a high-vegetable diet to prevent breast cancer recurrence. *Nutrition and Cancer*, 28, 282–288.

Pinder, K. L., Ramirez, A. J., Black, M. E., Richardson, M. A., Gregory, W. M., and Rubins, I. D. (1993). Psychiatric disorder with patients with advanced breast cancer: Prevalence and associated factors. *European Journal of Cancer*, 29, 524–527.

Pinto, B. M., Eakin, E., and Maruyama, N. C. (2000). Health behavior changes after a cancer diagnosis: What do we know and where do we go from here? *Annals of Behavioral Medicine*, 22, 38–52.

Plumb, M., and Holland, J. (1977). Comparative studies of psychological function in patients with advanced cancer: I. Self-reported depressive symptoms. *Psychosomatic Medicine*, 39, 264–276.

Plumb, M., and Holland, J. (1981). Comparative studies of psychological function in patients with advanced cancer: II. Interviewer-rated current and past psychological symptoms. *Psychosomatic Medicine*, 43, 243–254.

Portenoy, R. K. and Lesage, P. (1999). Management of cancer pain. *Lancet*, 365, 1695–1700.

Rabin, B. S., Cohen, S., Ganguli, R., Lysle, D. T., and Cunnick, J. E. (1989). Bidirectional interaction between the central nervous system and the immune system. *Critical Reviews in Immunology*, 9, 279–312.

Razavi, D., Delvaux, N., Farvacques, C., De Brier, F., Van Heer, C., Kaufman, L., Derde, M. F., Beauduin, M., and Piccart, M. (1993). Prevention of adjustment disorders and anticipatory nausea secondary to adjuvant chemotherapy: A double-blind, placebo-controlled study assessing the usefulness of alprazolam. *Journal of Clinical Oncology*, 11, 1384–1390.

Revenson, T. A., Wollman, C. A., and Felton, B. J. (1983). Social supports as stress buffers for adult cancer patients. *Psychosomatic Medicine*, 45, 321–331.

Richardson, J. L., Marks, G., Anderson Johnson, C., Graham, J. W., et al. (1987). Path model of multidimensional compliance with cancer therapy. *Health Psychology*, 6, 183–207.

Richardson, M. A., Post-White, J., Grimm, E. A., Moye, L. A., Singletary, S. E., and Justice, B. (1997). Coping, life attitudes, and immune responses to imagery and group support after breast cancer treatment. *Alternative Therapies*, 3, 62–70.

Richardson, J. L., Zarnegar, Z., Bisno, B., and Levine, A. (1990). Psychosocial status at initiation of cancer treatment and survival. *Journal of Psychosomatic Research*, 34, 189–201.

Rowland, J. H., and Holland, J. C. (1989). *Handbook of Psycho Oncology: Psychological Care of the Patient with Cancer*. New York: Oxford University Press.

Rummans, T. A., Frost, M., Suman, V. J., Taylor, M., Novotny, P., Gendron, T., Johnson, R., Hartmann, L., Dose, A. M., and Evans, R. W. (1998). Quality of life and pain in patients with recurrent breast and gynecologic cancer. *Psychosomatics*, 39, 437–45.

Sabharwal, P. J., Glaser, R., Lafuse, W., Liu, Q., Arkins, S., Koojiman, R., Lutz, L., Kelly, K. W., and Malarky, W. B. (1992). Prolactin synthesis and secretion by human peripheral blood mononuclear cells: An autocrine growth factor for lymphoproliferation. *Proceedings of the National Academy of Science*, 89, 7713–7716.

Sampson, W. L. (1997). Studies of counselings' impact on survival challenged: AAAS meeting. *Oncology News*, 6.

Savard, J., Miller, S. M., Mills, M., O'Leary, A., Harding, H., Douglas, S. D., Mangan, C. E., Belch, R., and Winokur, A. (1999). Association between subjective sleep quality and depression on immunocompetence in low-income women at risk for cervical cancer. *Psychosomatic Medicine*, 61, 496–507.

Saxe, G. A., Rock, C. L., Wicha, M. S., and Schottenfeld, D. (1999). Diet and risk for breast cancer recurrence and survival. *Breast Cancer Research and Treatment*, 53, 241–253.

Schultz, R., Williamson, G. M., Knapp, J. E., Bookwala, J., Lave, J., and Fello, M. (1995). The psychological, social, and economic impact of illness among patients with recurrent cancer. *Journal of Psychosocial Oncology*, 13, 21–45.

Sheard, T., and Maguire, P. (1999). The effect of psychological interventions on anxiety and depression in cancer patients: results of two meta-analyses. *British Journal of Cancer*, 80, 1770–1780.

Shrock, D., Palmer, R. F., and Taylor, B. (1999). Effects of a psychosocial intervention on survival among patients with stage I breast and prostate cancer: A matched case–control study. *Alternative Therapies and Health Medicine*, 5, 49–55.

Smith, J. A., and Weidemann, M. J. (1990). The exercise and immunity paradox: A neuroendocrine/cytokine hypothesis. *Medical Science Research*, 18, 749–753.

Spencer, S. M., Lehman, J. M., Wynings, C., Arena, P., Carver, C. S., Antoni, M. H., Derhagopian, R. P., and Ironson, G. (1999). Concerns about breast cancer and relations to psychosocial well-being in a multiethnic sample of early stage patients. *Health Psychology*, 18, 159–168.

Spiegel, D. (1997). Psychosocial aspects of breast cancer treatment. *Seminars in Oncology*, 24, SI, 36–47.

Spiegel, D., and Bloom, J. R. (1983). Group therapy and hypnosis reduce metastatic breast carcinoma pain. *Psychosomatic Medicine*, 45, 333–339.

Spiegel, D., Bloom, J. R., and Yalom, I. (1981). Group support for patients with metastatic cancer: A randomized outcome study. *Archives of General Psychiatry*, 38, 527–533.

Spiegel, D., Bloom, J. R., Kraemer, H. C., and Gottheil, E. (1989). Effect of psychosocial treatment on survival of patients with metastatic breast cancer. *Lancet*, 2, 888–901.

Stanton, A. L., and Snider, P. R. (1993). Coping with a breast cancer diagnosis: A prospective study. *Health Psychology*, 12, 16–23.

Steptoe, A., Sutcliffe, I., Bryony, A., and Coombes, C. (1991). Satisfaction with communication, medical knowledge, and coping style in patients with metastatic cancer. *Social Science and Medicine*, 32, 627–632.

Stewart, A. L., Greenfield, S., Hays, R. D., Wells, K., Rogers, W. H., Berry, S. D, McGlynn, E. A., and Ware, J. E., Jr. (1989). Functional status and well-being of patients with chronic conditions: Results from the Medical Outcomes Study. *Journal of the American Medical Association*, 262, 907–913.

Stoll, B. A. (1996). Diet and exercise regiments to improve breast carcinoma prognosis. *Cancer*, 78, 2465–2470.

Szabo, G. (1999). Consequences of alcohol consumption on host defense. *Alcohol and Alcoholism*, 34, 830–841.

Taylor, S. E., Lichtman, R. R., and Wood, J. V. (1984). Attributions, beliefs, and adjustment to breast cancer. *Journal of Personality and Social Psychology*, 46, 489–502.

Taylor, S. E., Lichtman, R. R., Wood, J. V., Bluming, A. Z., Dosik, G. M., Leibowitz, R. L. (1985). Illness-related and treatment-related factors in psychological adjustment to breast cancer. *Cancer*, 55, 2506–2513.

Umberson, D. (1992). Gender, marital status and the social control of health behavior. *Social Science and Medicine*, 34, 907–917.

van der Pompe, G., Duivenvoorden, H. J., Antoni, M. H., Visser, A., and Heijnen, C. J. (1997). Effectiveness of a short-term group psychotherapy program on endocrine and immune function in breast cancer patients: An exploratory study. *Journal of Psychosomatic Research*, 42, 453–466.

Vinokur, A. D., Threatt, B. A., Caplan, R. D., and Zimmerman, B. L. (1989). Physical and psychosocial functioning and adjustment to breast cancer: Long-term follow-up of a screening population. *Cancer*, 63, 394–405.

Vinokur, A. D., Threatt, B. A., Vinokur-Kaplan, D., and Satariano, W. A. (1990). The process of recovery from breast cancer for younger and older patients: Changes during the first year. *Cancer*, 65, 1242–1254.

Ward, S. E., Viergutz, G., Tormey, D., DeMuth, J., and Paulen, A. (1992). Patients' reactions to completion of adjuvant breast cancer therapy. *Nursing Research*, 41, 362–366.

Watson, R., Borgs, P., Witte, M., and McCluskey, R. S. (1994). Alcohol, immunomodulation, and disease. *Alcohol and Alcoholism*, 29, 131–139.

Weijmar Schultz, W. C. M., Van De Wiel, H. B. M., Hahn, D. E. E., and van Driel, M. F. (1992). Sexuality and cancer in women. *Annual Review of Sex Research*, 3, 151–200.

Weisman, A. D., and Worden, J. W. (1986). The emotional impact of recurrent cancer. *Journal of Psychosocial Oncology*, 3, 5–17.

Wellisch, D. K., Wolcott, D., Pasnau, R., Fawzy, F., and Landsverk, J. (1989). An evaluation of the psychosocial problems of the homebound cancer patient: Relationship of patient adjustment to family problems. *Journal of Psychosocial Research*, 7, 55–76.

Wilber, T. K. (1988). Attitudes and cancer: What kind of help really helps? *Journal of Transpersonal Psychology*, 20, 49–59.

Willett, W. C. (1999). Goals for nutrition in the year 2000. *CA-A Cancer Journal for Clinicians*, 49, 331–352.

Wortman, C. B., and Dunkel-Schetter, C. (1979). Interpersonal relationships and cancer: A theoretical analysis. *Journal of Social Issues*, 35, 120–155.

Woods, J. A., Davis, J. M., Smith, J. A., and Nieman, D. C. (1999). Exercise and cellular innate immune function. *Medicine and Science in Sports and Exercise*, 31, 57–66.

Woods, N. F., and Earp, J. A. (1978). Women with cured breast cancer: A study of mastectomy patients in North Carolina. *Nursing Research*, 27, 279–285.

Wynder, E. L., Cohen, L. A., Muscat, J. E., Winters, B., Dwyer, J. T., and Blackburn, G. (1997). Breast cancer: Weighting the evidence for promoting role of dietary fat. *Journal of the National Cancer Institute*, 89, 766–775.

Yurek, D., Farrar, W., and Andersen, B. L. (2000). Breast cancer surgery: Comparing surgical groups and determining individual differences in post operative sexuality and body change stress. *Journal of Consulting and Clinical Psychology*, 68, 697–709.

Zhang, S. M., Folsom, A. R., Sellers, T. A., Kushi, L., Potter, J. D. (1995). Better breast-cancer survival for postmenopausal women who are less overweight and eat less fat – The Iowa Womens' Health Study. *Cancer*, 76, 275–283.

CHAPTER 7

Diabetes

Linda Gonder-Frederick, Daniel J. Cox, and William L. Clarke

University of Virginia

Introduction

Diabetes mellitus is one of the largest healthcare problems in the US in terms of prevalence, cost, and the physical and psychological burden it places on individuals living with the illness. Diabetes is also one of the most challenging of the chronic diseases from a psychosocial and behavioral perspective (Cox and Gonder-Frederick, 1992). There is no cure, diagnosis can occur at any stage of life, and, after diagnosis, daily treatment is required for the remainder of the lifespan, which may or may not successfully prevent the development of serious long-term complications, such as cardiovascular and kidney disease. The management regimen can be enormously complex and relies almost solely on the intensive, daily efforts of patients and their families to monitor blood glucose (BG) levels and then carefully balance medication, food intake, and physical activity to try to keep glucose controlled. It is difficult to think of any other chronic illness that demands an equivalent level of constant self-monitoring and self-regulation and, not surprisingly, there is a keen interest in identifying psychobehavioral factors that influence diabetes management and outcome.

Diabetes is a multisystem endocrinological disorder characterized by abnormal metabolism of glucose as well as fat and protein. Diagnosis is defined by the presence of hyperglycemia, or abnormally high glucose levels in the bloodstream (see table 7.1). Over the past 40 years the prevalence of diabetes has increased dramatically in the US and worldwide, and by 1998 there were 10.5 million diagnosed cases and an estimated 10 million remaining undiagnosed. In the US, one of every 6–7 healthcare dollars is spent on the treatment of diabetes and its complications (Clark, 1998). The worldwide increase in diabetes is associated with a number of factors, including the growing epidemic of obesity, sedentary lifestyles, and increased longevity. Approximately 90 percent of patients have type 2 diabetes (T2DM, formerly called noninsulin-dependent diabetes), which is strongly associated with obesity and age. In the

Table 7.1 Diagnostic criteria for diabetes

Any BG level > 200 mg/dl	Presence of diabetic symptoms (frequent urination, thirst, wt loss)
Fasting BG level > 126 mg/dl	With or without symptoms
Postprandial BG Level > 200 mg/dl 2 hrs after 75 g of carbohydrate	With or without symptoms

Source: National Diabetes Data Group, 1995

US, 11 percent of people age 65 and older and 6 percent of those 45–65 years old have diabetes, whereas only 1.5 percent of those aged 18–44 are diagnosed (Harris, 1998). Women and men are equally affected, but prevalence varies greatly among racial/ethnic groups. African-Americans have a twofold increase in risk for T2DM compared to Caucasians, whereas Hispanics and Native Americans have a 2.5 and 5 times greater risk, respectively (Haffner, 1998). In contrast, type 1 diabetes (T1DM, formerly called insulin-dependent diabetes) is more common in Caucasians in both the US and Europe, and is the most common chronic illness of childhood in the US (National Diabetes Data Group, 1995). The onset of either type involves both genetic and environmental factors; however, genetic risk is higher for type 2, where more than two-thirds of cases have a first- or second-degree relative with the illness. Other risk factors for T2DM include obesity (80 percent are obese), especially the distribution of body fat (hip to waist circumference ratio), and impaired glucose tolerance (Haffner, 1998; Vinicor, 1998). T1DM is an autoimmune disease involving a gene that makes individuals vulnerable to immune-mediated destruction of the pancreatic β cells, which produce insulin (Dahlquist, 1999). The primary cause of this autoimmune response is virus exposure.

Until recently, it was believed that the onset of T1DM was almost always prior to adulthood, whereas T2DM typically presented after middle age. However, the number of children diagnosed with T2DM has increased greatly over the past decade and is reaching epidemic proportion in the US and other countries (American Diabetes Association, 2000). This disturbing trend is related to the coinciding increase in childhood obesity and sedentary lifestyles. Although 85 percent of children diagnosed are overweight, there is also a strong genetic component, with up to 80 percent of those affected having at least one parent with T2DM. Because T2DM can remain asymptomatic for long periods of time, there is growing concern that many children with the disease are undiagnosed, making them vulnerable to the early development of long-term complications associated with chronic hyperglycemia.

Biological Bases and Pathophysiology

The pathophysiology of all types of diabetes involves abnormalities in the production and/or utilization of insulin, the pancreatic hormone required for most body cells to metabolize glucose. In the nondiabetic body, insulin secretion is autoregulated via a negative feedback system that balances available metabolic fuel and metabolic needs. In T1DM, destruction of the β cells renders the pancreas unable to produce adequate amounts of insulin and, because it cannot be utilized, glucose accumulates in the bloodstream, resulting in hyperglycemia. In an attempt to provide the body with metabolic fuel, fat breakdown occurs and a byproduct of this process is the buildup of ketones. At high levels, ketones are toxic and can lead to diabetic ketoacidosis (DKA), or diabetic coma. Symptoms of T1DM include weight loss, fat breakdown and inability to metabolize nutrients, and polyuria and polydipsia, caused by osmotic diuresis as the kidneys attempt to rid the bloodstream of excess glucose. Because the β cells are incapable of producing adequate insulin, the only way to promote BG utilization and reduce hyperglycemia is exogenous insulin, which must be delivered via subcutaneous injections because stomach enzymes destroy insulin. Without insulin injections, T1DM is fatal.

T2DM is caused by both insulin resistance and defective insulin secretion (Haffner, 1998). The body's initial response to insulin resistance is hyperinsulinemia as the β cells attempt to compensate by increasing production. Eventually, however, the cells are damaged or destroyed by overwork and become unable to produce adequate insulin. In other cases, defective insulin secretion causes T2DM without prior insulin resistance. There is evidence that the etiology of T2DM differs in obese individuals, who tend to be insulin resistant, and the nonobese, who tend to show deficient insulin production (Haffner et al., 1995). T2DM can be treated by diet and exercise, oral medications, or insulin. However, fewer than 10 percent of cases are successfully managed with diet and exercise alone. Oral medications vary in their pharmokinetic action to combat hyperglycemia. One major class increases the release of insulin, whereas other drugs increase insulin sensitivity or inhibit pancreatic and intestinal enzymes that facilitate carbohydrate digestion and glucose absorption.

Gestational diabetes affects 25–50/1,000 pregnancies, typically onsets during the third trimester, and occurs when the pancreas is unable to match the increased insulin requirements of pregnancy (Coustan, 1995). Although glucose metabolism usually normalizes after delivery, approximately 70 percent of these women later develop chronic T2DM. Gestational diabetes is most often managed with medication, but insulin may be used to avoid fetal risks, which include organ malformation and macrosomia. The onset of gestational diabetes presents unique psychobehavioral challenges, as pregnant women must quickly learn and adapt to a rigorous treatment regimen to lower glucose levels before damage to the fetus occurs.

Both T1DM and T2DM are associated with long-term complications that can have devastating health effects. Because T1DM is detected relatively quickly, long-term complications are not typically present at diagnosis. In T2DM, which may remain undetected for years, complications are present in 20–25 percent of patients by the time of diagnosis (Gill, 1992). The types of complications are the same in both types of diabetes and are caused by the damaging effects of chronic hyperglycemia on microvascular and macrovascular systems, as well as changes in blood lipids. The most common serious complications include retinopathy, nephropathy, neuropathy, and cardiovascular disease (see Harris, 1998 for a review). Retinopathy is the leading cause of blindness in adults in the US and affects nearly all people with diabetes, with 60 percent showing proliferative retinopathy 20 years after diagnosis. Diabetes is also the leading cause of end-stage renal disease, as well as nontraumatic lower limb amputations. Cardiovascular disease is the cause of death in 60 percent of men with diabetes. The mortality rate for all types of cardiovascular diseases is 2.5 times higher in men with diabetes, even after adjusting for other risk factors, including blood pressure, cholesterol, obesity, and smoking. Finally, diabetes is the leading cause of physiological erectile dysfunction with no loss of sex drive, affecting 35–59 percent of all male patients (Nofzinger, 1997). Although research on sexual dysfunction in females is inconclusive, there is some evidence that diabetic neuropathy may affect sexual drive (Spector, Leiblum, and Carey, 1993).

Management of Diabetes

The major goal of diabetes treatment is to keep BG levels as close to a normal range as possible through the use of medication, BG monitoring (BGM), diet, and exercise. The 1993 results of the Diabetes Control and Complications Trial (DCCT) radically altered both the standards for diabetes management and the behavioral demands on patients (DCCT Research Group, 1993). This NIH-funded trial followed 1,441 T1DM patients for an average of 6.5 years, with subjects being randomly assigned to an intensive insulin and treatment regimen designed to produce near-normal glycemia, or to conventional therapy. The DCCT results provided definitive evidence that tighter metabolic control could delay or prevent the onset of microvascular complications in T1DM, including retinopathy and renal disease. Subsequent major trials have replicated these findings in both T1DM (Ohkubo et al., 1995; Reichard et al., 1993) and T2DM (Turner et al., 1996). The "gold standard" measure of metabolic control is glycosylated hemoglobin (HbA1c), an estimate of the degree of chronic hyperglycemia over the past 6–8 weeks.

Although normalization of diabetic BG levels is technically possible, in reality only a small minority of patients are able to achieve this goal. Even in the DCCT, where frequent contact and support were provided by an interdisciplinary healthcare team, *only 5 percent of subjects maintained normal HbA1c levels* (DCCT Research Group, 1995). From a psychobehavioral perspective, the primary problem in achieving tight diabetes control lies in the characteristics of the regimen itself. The likelihood of following a prescribed regimen is largely determined by its complexity, demand, and duration. Thus, it is not that surprising that many patients have difficulty performing multiple self-care behaviors several times each day, 7 days a week, 52 weeks a year. Intensive insulin regimens involve three or more injections per day (before each meal, and perhaps at bedtime), or the use of an insulin infusion pump worn continuously. Ideally, patients on intensive regimens test their BG before each meal and at bedtime, and adjust insulin dose, food intake, and physical activity accordingly. BGM is also recommended when patients feel symptoms, plan to exercise, or are physically ill (e.g., viruses). It is not unusual for patients attempting tight control to self-test six or more times per day.

In spite of evidence showing that tight control is equally important in T2DM, only a minority of these patients follow an intensive insulin regimen. Typically, insulin therapy for T2DM involves only one or two injections per day; however, the dose needed to control hyperglycemia can be quite high owing to insulin resistance, and injections are often supplemented by oral medications.

Although intensive therapy improves metabolic control, it also increases the risk of hypoglycemic episodes threefold or more (DCCT Research Group, 1997). Hypoglycemia is the most common acute complication of diabetes, occurring when there is too much insulin in the body relative to recent food intake and metabolic demand, and causing BG to drop precipitously. Hypoglycemia can develop quite quickly, within minutes, and requires immediate treatment with fast-acting carbohydrates (e.g., fruit juice). Fortunately, hypoglycemic episodes are typically accompanied by warning symptoms. Some of these (trembling, sweating) reflect counterregulatory hormonal responses to low BG, such as epinephrine release, which causes the liver to release stored glucose. Other symptoms are caused by the decreased amount of glucose available to brain cells (neuroglycopenia) and subsequent deterioration in cognitive–motor function (mental confusion, slurred speech, incoordination). The threshold and magnitude of symptoms varies greatly across individuals, and a significant subgroup has reduced hypoglycemic awareness, characterized by a decrease or delay in symptoms (Clarke et al., 1995). When symptoms are not detected before neuroglycopenia occurs, patients may be unable to recognize their hypoglycemia or self-treat effectively, thereby increasing the chance of a severe episode, characterized by stupor, unconsciousness, or seizure (Gonder-Frederick, 1998; Gonder-Frederick et al., 1997a). Although the estimated frequency of severe hypoglycemia varies across studies (Clarke et al., 1996; Gonder-Frederick et al., 1997a), it is clear that a minority of patients experience recurrent episodes, resulting in frequent emergency treatment and an increased risk of accidents and physical injury (e.g., falls, automobile accidents). Nocturnal episodes appear to be a significant cause of death in patients under 40 years of age, accounting for 10 percent of these cases (Sovik and Thordarson, 1999).

Given the serious – potentially life-threatening – consequences of hypoglycemia, some patients experience significant levels of worry and anxiety about the occurrence of episodes. Several studies have investigated the psychological construct "fear of hypoglycemia," using the Hypoglycemia Fear Survey (Irvine et al., 1994). Fear of hypoglycemia (FOH) following traumatic episodes can contribute to treatment behaviors that maintain BG levels in a higher, "safer" range, leading to poor control (Cox et al., 1990). FOH is higher in patients who have a history of severe hypoglycemia and unconsciousness/seizure, but also in those with high levels of trait anxiety, who are prone to increased levels of general worry (Polonsky et al., 1992). FOH is also prevalent in family members, including parents of T1DM children and spouses of T1DM partners, who exhibit even higher levels of fear than patients with diabetes (Clarke et al., 1998; Gonder-Frederick et al., 1997b,c).

For both T1DM and T2DM, the goals of diet therapy are the same: 1) to maintain near-normal BG, 2) to maintain normal lipid levels, 3) to keep caloric intake at a level adequate for growth or maintaining acceptable weight, and 4) to prevent acute and chronic complications (Schlundt et al., 1996). The American Diabetes Association's (ADA) most recent guidelines recommended an individualized, patient-centered approach designed to integrate diet therapy into a patient's lifestyle, culture, and ethnicity (American Diabetes Association, 1996). This reflects the general failure of traditional treatment approaches prescribing highly structured diets and significant restriction of certain foods (e.g., sucrose-containing sweets). From a psychobehavioral perspective, the failure of this approach is no surprise given that achieving long-term changes in eating habits and food choices is one of the most difficult lifestyle alterations for most people. In contemporary diabetes management there is no specific "diabetes diet"; rather, what is considered a "healthy" diet for all Americans is typically prescribed (e.g., 30 percent of calories from fat and < 10 percent from saturated fats, 12–20 percent of calories from protein, and 50–60 percent of calories from carbohydrates). Like many in the general population, however, many people with diabetes find it difficult to follow these guidelines.

Although the goals of dietary therapy are the same, regimens can differ greatly for patients with T1DM and T2DM. Because 80 percent of patients with T2DM are obese, diet recommendations often target weight loss, with reduced fat/calorie consumption and a plan for increased physical activity. In both T1DM and T2DM, some method of "quantifying" food intake is important, such as counting calorie/fat intake to facilitate weight loss, or using the exchange system to estimate intake of different nutrients. In T1DM there is a growing trend to use carbohydrate counting (number of grams) to achieve better control of postprandial BG levels, especially in patients attempting intensive therapies. In its simplest form, carbohydrate counting is used to keep food intake more consistent from day to day, making it easier to estimate insulin requirements. A more advanced use of this technique allows patients to adjust their insulin dose on the basis of planned carbohydrate consumption.

Clearly, there is a tremendous demand placed on patients who try to follow meticulously the numerous and varied self-care behaviors required for successful diabetes management. Dr. Richard Rubin, a psychologist and diabetes educator, has written that his teenaged son with T1DM estimates that he "has to think about" his illness and self-care "every 15 minutes" throughout the day (Rubin, 2000). One writer with T1DM recently calculated that the average amount of time she devotes to diabetes management is nearly 3 hours per day (Fena-Kurlovich, 2000)!

Self-Treatment of Diabetes: A Psychobehavioral Approach

Obviously, diabetes management is not easily integrated into traditional, compliance-based medical models in which physicians prescribe a specific regimen that patients follow. In contrast, treatment of diabetes depends almost completely on patient motivation and ability to engage in active decision-making and multiple, daily self-regulatory behaviors on a consistent basis. In this psychobehavioral process, the patient is responsible for the day-to-day treatment of their illness, whereas healthcare professionals play an advisory role. For this reason, experts in diabetes education (Anderson et al., 2000a; Feste and Anderson, 1995) have concluded that diabetes management is best viewed from a "patient empowerment" perspective that aims to enable individuals to make informed choices and gain the skills/resources to execute those choices. Given the inherent difficulty of the diabetes regimen, factors that enhance or interfere with patient self-care have been of considerable interest in behavioral medicine research. However, the complexity of diabetes treatment presents researchers with numerous challenges. Glasgow and his colleagues (Glasgow and Eakin, 1998) have emphasized that self-care is influenced by diverse multilevel factors, including intrapersonal, social, environmental, and institutional variables. In addition, the discrete behaviors that comprise self-treatment must be studied independently, as individual patients vary in the quality of their self-care across the different aspects of the regimen (Glasgow and Eakin, 1996). Few patients engage in consistently "good or bad" self-treatment in all areas of diabetes management. Other caveats regarding "adherence" research have been elucidated before, including measurement issues (e.g., the tendency to view glycosylated hemoglobin values as a measure of behavior, problems with self-report data) as well as the lack of a "gold standard" regimen for all patients.

Rates of Adherence

Precise rates of adequate/inadequate self-care are extremely difficult to assess, and a recent meta-analysis (Robiner and Keel, 1997) showed that adherence rates to the four key elements of treatment (medication, BGM, diet and exercise) vary greatly across studies. However, there is a tendency for adherence to insulin/medication regimens to be higher, which is logical, as failure to take medication, especially insulin injections, may be life-threatening. One limitation of much of this research is that global measures are typically assessed (e.g., number of injections taken per day) whereas other critical, but more subtle, aspects of self-medication are rarely investigated, such as the frequency and accuracy of insulin adjustments. Estimated rates of adherence in BGM also vary (Robiner and Keel, 1997). For BGM to improve glucose control, self-testing must be performed often enough to yield useful data, and used as a guide for adjusting other treatment behaviors (e.g., insulin, food intake). In a large survey, only 39 percent of patients performed BGM two or more times per day (Harris et al., 1993), and a prospective study of parents and their T1DM children showed that BGM results were almost always used in a "reactive" manner (e.g., to treat hypoglycemia) and very rarely used proactively to avoid future BG extremes (Wysocki et al., 1992). Another study found that only 29 percent of so-called "adherent" adult patients used BGM results to adjust insulin doses (Ziegher et al., 1993). There are many environmental barriers to BGM, including time, inconvenience, and cost. There are also psychological barriers. BGM can be a constant reminder of diabetes, and provoke feelings of failure, anxiety, and hopelessness when readings reflect poor control (Wysocki, 1994).

Diet recommendations are the most difficult for patients to follow. For T1DM patients, monitoring and maintaining consistency in food intake can be burdensome, as well as having to eat, even when not hungry, to avoid hypoglycemia. For T2DM patients, caloric restrictions to promote weight loss are the major burden. A decade ago, very low-calorie diets seemed to hold promise for the treatment of obesity, but experience showed that the risk of relapse after returning to a solid diet was nearly 100 percent. Current pharmacological interventions, which target appetite suppression and decreased fat absorption, appear to be effective only when the goal is very modest weight loss. However, studies (Wing et al., 1987) have demonstrated that even modest weight loss (10 percent of body weight) can produce long-term improvements in BG control, although long-term contact and support with patients is still needed for weight loss to be maintained. The general ineffectiveness of most weight loss programs has led some to conclude that more extreme measures, such as weight reduction surgery, should be considered the "treatment of choice" for many obese patients with T2DM (Pories et al., 1995).

Intrapersonal Factors that Influence Self-Care

Much of the research into intrapersonal factors affecting diabetes management has been guided by health belief and self-efficacy models and, in general, studies have supported both theoretical concepts. Health belief models (HBM) predict that levels of self-care are determined by the extent to which individuals believe that 1) their diabetes is serious, 2) they are vulnerable to negative consequences, and 3) the perceived benefits of engaging in treatment behaviors outweigh the perceived costs (Becker, 1985). The self-efficacy model expands the HBM and additionally predicts that self-care will be related to the degree to which individuals believe 1) that they are capable of executing the needed behaviors, and 2) that their actions will influence outcome (O'Leary, 1985). A recent meta-analysis (Robiner and Keel, 1997) concluded that health beliefs do have a significant impact on self-care, which in turn significantly influences glycemic control. In fact, health beliefs can account for up to half of the variance in regimen adherence and 20 percent of the variance in metabolic control (Brownlee-Duffeck et al., 1987). More recent research has investigated the impact of *irrational* health beliefs, finding that a greater tendency to engage in health-related cognitive distortions is associated with poorer diabetes control, independent of other personality factors and comorbidity (Christensen et al., 1999). Self-efficacy is also predictive across the different aspects of the diabetes regimen in both adolescents and adults (McCaul et al., 1987; Robiner and Keel, 1997), even after controlling for past levels of self-care (Kavanagh et al., 1993).

Other intrapersonal variables that influence self-care include psychological stress and psychopathology. Both daily stressors and stressful life events appear to relate to metabolic control, although this relationship is idiosyncratic and not all individuals are glycemically "stress-sensitive" (Aikens et al., 1992; Gonder-Frederick et al., 1990; Lloyd et al., 1999; Stenstrom et al., 1993). Although it is assumed that stress affects BG control through both neuroendocrine responses (e.g., epinephrine) and disruptive effects on self-care (e.g., eating more or less), the data have not strongly confirmed that self-treatment deteriorates when individuals experience more stress. In contrast, clinical depression, which is highly prevalent in patients with diabetes, has a clearer negative impact on self-management and glucose control (Lustman et al., 1986). Another area of recent investigation is the prevalence and impact of needle phobias on adherence to BGM and insulin injections (Snoek et al., 1997; Zambanini and Feher, 1997). Of special concern in young women with diabetes is the presence of eating disorders, which are significantly more prevalent than in nondiabetic populations, perhaps because of the preoccupation with food required by diabetes management, as well as concerns about weight gain secondary to insulin use (Hall, 1997). The coexistence of eating disorders and diabetes is associated with a high incidence and early onset of serious complications (Steel et al., 1987) and has been called "a deadly combination" (Hillard and Hillard, 1984). One issue unique to diabetes is that patients can manipulate their insulin dose to control weight. It is not uncommon for young females with T1DM to compensate for binge eating with insulin underdosing, which reduces the body's ability to metabolize carbohydrates but also induces hyperglycemia and worsens diabetes control (Polonsky et al., 1994; Steel et al., 1987).

Age and developmental factors also mediate self-treatment, and influence the impact of health beliefs in adolescent and older individuals. In adolescents (Skinner and Hampson, 1999), beliefs about long-term consequences (e.g., avoiding future complications) have less impact than beliefs about short-term consequences (controlling daily BG). Perceived costs of self-care behaviors are also important to younger people, whereas in older patients the perceived benefits of treatment have more impact (Brownlee-Duffeck et al., 1987; Zrebiec, 1996). The impact of developmental factors on diabetes management has been studied most intensively in adolescents, who typically show a significant deterioration in metabolic control that is caused by both physiological and behavioral processes. During puberty, insulin resistance increases and there is more variation in insulin requirements throughout the day (Amiel et al., 1986; Rubin et al., 1989). There is also a decline in self-care (Jacobson et al., 1986), and the incidence of DKA peaks during adolescence owing to missed insulin injections (Ellemann et al., 1984). Given that adolescents with diabetes are faced with the same enormous developmental tasks as any other individual in this age group, it is not surprising that consistent and rigorous self-treatment suffers.

The stage of life that perhaps demands the most intensive effort from patients is pregnancy. Maintenance of near-normal BG levels during pregnancy (especially in the first trimester) decreases the frequency of spontaneous abortions and congenital abnormalities caused by maternal hyperglycemia (DCCT Research Group, 1999). Unfortunately, there has been little research into the degree to which women with diabetes successfully achieve such tight control, or the psychobehavioral burdens of following the intense regimen. Because good control is critical, efforts have been made to persuade women who are attempting to conceive to normalize BG prior to pregnancy, but these have met with little success (Snoek, 2000).

Social and Environmental Factors

In children with T1DM, much research has focused on the impact of family characteristics on diabetes management. In young children, parents are responsible for executing almost all of the tasks involved in treatment, which can be a source of considerable emotional stress, especially for mothers (Anderson and Brackett, 2000; Kovacs et al., 1985a). Key characteristics that predict diabetes management and metabolic control include the level of conflict, stress, and cohesion in the family system (Hanson et al., 1995; Jacobson et al., 1994a; Kovacs et al., 1989; Miller-Johnson et al., 1994). Family environments with less conflict and more cohesion at the time of diagnosis experience fewer episodes of DKA and severe hypoglycemia in children, and less deterioration in control over time (Herskowitz et al., 1995). Another critical factor is the division of responsibility for diabetes care between parents and children. Families vary greatly in how treatment responsibilities are divided, and there is growing consensus that giving children and adolescents premature independence over self-care leads to a negative outcome (Anderson et al., 1997 Anderson and Brackett, 2000; Wysocki et al., 1992b). When given too much responsibility, pediatric patients make more mistakes in treatment, are less adherent, and are in poorer control than those whose parents remain more involved (Anderson et al., 1997).

Peer as well as family relationships are important in adolescents (Skinner et al., 2000), although this area has not received the empirical attention it deserves (Glasgow and Anderson, 1995a). One study found that more than half of newly diagnosed adolescents did not discuss their diabetes with their friends, and more than a third believed that their friends would like them more if they did not have diabetes. T1DM adolescents also report feeling "different" and less socially acceptable than their peers (Follansbee, 1989). The impact of social relationships on diabetes management in adults has received virtually no empirical attention. However, there is evidence that negative marital interactions are associated with poorer dietary adherence (Schafer et al., 1986). In one study, Hispanic men were in better metabolic control than Hispanic women, presumably because men's meals are more often prepared by their wives, suggesting that gender and gender-related family roles may mediate the effects of marital factors (Mercado and Vargas, 1989).

Sociodemographic variables are other important risk factors for poor diabetes management and metabolic control. African-American youths are in poorer glycemic control than Caucasians (Auslander et al., 1997), which may be partly due to an increased number of single-parent homes, where only one parent, usually the mother, must bear the burden of being entirely responsible for the child's diabetes management (Overstreet et al., 1995) and where financial resources are often more limited. Lower socioeconomic status is a risk factor for both poor metabolic control and recurrent hospitalizations (Auslander et al., 1990, 1993; Kovacs et al., 1995).

Adjustment and Coping

Although initial diagnosis of diabetes is almost always a life-altering event and requires enormous adjustment on the part of the patient and family, it is important to recognize that coping with diabetes is a lifelong process. Following the initial diagnosis and adjustment, patients are repeatedly required to make psychological and behavioral adaptations in response to the challenges presented by diabetes, such as changes in medical status, new developments in diabetes treatment, acute complications (e.g., hypoglycemia), onset of complications, and "diabetes burnout" over time (Polonsky, 1999). Clearly the ability to cope successfully and maintain an acceptable quality of life while living with diabetes varies greatly across individuals, and depends on a plethora of intrapersonal, social, and environmental factors. In addition, the issues with which individuals and their families are confronted vary greatly across different patient subgroups and time. It is impossible to compare the challenges faced by the mother of a 2-year-old toddler with T1DM who refuses to eat with those facing an elderly patient with T2DM already dealing with other health problems. Ideally, research would investigate the multifactorial process of adjustment and coping across time within discrete patient populations. Unfortunately, such studies are rare because of the cost and effort required for intensive, longitudinal investigations.

A notable exception is the work of Kovacs and her colleagues, who followed children with T1DM and their parents longitudinally, beginning 2–3 weeks after initial diagnosis, for an average of almost 9 years (Kovacs et al., 1990a, 1995). After the initial diagnosis, mild subclinical psychological symptoms (e.g., anxiety and depression) occurred in most children and 36 percent met criteria for psychiatric diagnosis (Kovacs et al., 1985b). Over the next 6 months these initial problems resolved in the majority, suggesting that most children adapt successfully to diabetes relatively quickly (Kovacs et al., 1986). A similar pattern was observed in parents, with mild symptoms occurring after initial diagnosis, especially in mothers, and resolution of emotional disturbance over the next 6 months in the majority (Kovacs et al., 1985a). However, adjustment problems can emerge again 2–3 years following diagnosis for both children and mothers, and children report more difficulty managing their diabetes as the duration increases (Grey et al., 1995; Kovacs et al., 1990a,b). By 9 years after diagnosis, at an average age of 20, almost half of the patients in Kovacs' study had experienced at least one episode of psychiatric disorder, and the probability of subsequent problems was higher in those who had experienced difficulties following diagnosis.

This prevalence rate is significantly elevated compared to the general population (Kovacs et al., 1996), supporting previous evidence of a higher risk for psychiatric morbidity in older adolescents with T1DM (Blanz et al., 1993). Major depression was the most common psychiatric disorder, with 27.5 percent of subjects experiencing at least one episode by the 10th year after diagnosis. Depression is also common in adults with both T1DM and T2DM, having a prevalence rate three times higher than the general US population (Lustman et al., 1997a). Although it is unclear whether this risk is higher than in other chronic diseases, the course of depression appears to be more severe in diabetes, with relapse rates over the 5 years following initial episodes ranging from 79 to 83 percent (Lustman et al., 1997a,b). Increased risk of recurrence also occurs in youths with diabetes, along with a protracted period of recovery (Kovacs et al., 1997a,b).

Depression often remains undiagnosed in patients with diabetes, probably because of the overlap in symptoms caused by the two conditions (Lustman and Harper, 1987). The etiology of depression in diabetes is complex, involving physiological, genetic and psychological factors. There is some overlap between the metabolic and hormonal abnormalities associated with both disorders (Gavard et al., 1993), including the presence of hypercortisolism. Depression can also occur secondary to the stress of coping with diabetes, as well as the decreased quality of life secondary to complications. Although the number and severity of complications are related to depression (Jacobson et al., 1985; Littlefield et al., 1990; Peyrot and Rubin, 1997), the causal direction of this association is unclear. Although poor glycemic control and complications can certainly have a negative impact on psychiatric status, depression also has detrimental effects on self-care, which can lead to poor control (Lustman et al., 1997a; Robinson et al., 1988).

Although it is not as well documented as depression, there is evidence of increased anxiety disorders in diabetic populations, and the prevalence of both generalized anxiety disorder and phobias appears to be higher than in the general population (Lustman et al., 1986; Popkin et al., 1988). In a recent study of more than 600 patients, symptoms of anxiety and depression were reported at an equivalent rate (Peyrot and Rubin, 1997), with no differences between T1DM and T2DM.

In addition to psychiatric disturbance, researchers have assessed quality of life (QOL) as a marker of psychosocial and behavioral adjustment, using both general and diabetes-specific instruments (Jacobson, 1997; Jacobson and The DCCT Research Group, 1994b, 1995). Adults with diabetes generally report decreased QOL compared to healthy individuals (Jacobson, 1997; Jacobson et al., 1994b); however, perceived health and wellbeing are strongly related to complications (Jacobson et al., 1994b), and it has been argued that QOL is not lower in patients who are healthy (Wikblad et al., 1996). Independent of complications, current or past psychiatric history is associated with decreased QOL (Jacobson et al., 1997a). Other studies have found that adults with diabetes live alone and remain childless more frequently than the general population, and engage in fewer social activities (Gafvels et al., 1993). The burden of diabetes management may also have a negative impact. Whereas T1DM patients report poorer QOL than those with T2DM, and some studies found that T1DM patients in extremely tight control report a deterioration in QOL (Wikblad et al., 1991), the DCCT found no decrease in the intensive regimen group (Jacobson et al., 1996). In addition, a British study of intensive therapy in T2DM also found that QOL is not lowered by intensive treatment, but rather by the presence of complications (UK Prospective Diabetes Study Group, 1999).

The impact of diabetes on QOL in pediatric populations has not received as much scientific attention. In these patients, poor control is not consistently related to poorer QOL *per se*, but rather to depression, anxiety, lower socio-economic status, single-parent family situations, low self-esteem and peer problems (Delamater, 2000; La Greca et al., 1995). In a 10-year follow-up study of pediatric patients, self-esteem remained lower in young adults with T1DM than in nondiabetic subjects, suggesting that childhood diabetes can have a pervasive and persistent impact on psychological wellbeing (Jacobson et al., 1997b).

Psychosocial adjustment has also been measured with instruments designed to quantify diabetes-related stress and distress (see Bradley, 1994 for a review of diabetes-specific psychobehavioral instruments.) For example, the Problem Areas in Diabetes Survey (PAID), measures the extent to which diabetes-related worries and dissatisfaction with support are problematic, and suggests that the majority of patients report at least one area of significant concern (Polonsky et al., 1995). The most common sources of distress are worry about complications, guilt or anxiety when "off track" with treatment, and fear caused by having/living with diabetes. Diabetes-specific distress is clinically relevant, and PAID scores are significantly associated with adherence and complications, and account for almost 10 percent of the variance in glycemic control. The ATT39 is a measure of the extent to which patients have successfully "integrated" diabetes into their lifestyle and self-concept in a healthy manner (Welch et al., 1994). High scores indicate that a person has accepted diabetes, is comfortable with others knowing about their condition, and feels well adjusted to the illness and regimen. Low scores indicate that a person continues to feel resentful, embarrassed, helpless, isolated, and poorly adjusted to diabetes. Although the ATT39 does not consistently predict glycemic control, it is sensitive to changes in attitudes following psychoeducational interventions.

An important but relatively neglected area of research is coping and emotional distress in family members of adult patients. Two studies have investigated the impact of severe hypoglycemia on spouses of T1DM patients who have recurrent episodes, finding high levels of anxiety about hypoglycemia, sleep disturbances due to worry about nocturnal episodes, and increased diabetes-related conflict (Gonder-Frederick et al., 1997b; Stahl et al., 1998).

Neuropsychological Impact of Diabetes

There is substantial evidence that both *severe hypoglycemia* and *chronic hyperglycemia* secondary to diabetes can have lasting detrimental effects on neuropsychological function, although the underlying physiological mechanisms are not well understood (Ryan, 1997). Although researchers have emphasized that observed deterioration is *not* necessarily clinically significant (i.e., performance typically remains within normal ranges), this is obviously an area of concern for patients and families. The risk and type of detrimental effects varies as a function of age. In children and adolescents the effect of severe hypoglycemia on the developing nervous system has received the most attention. There appears to be a "fundamental decrease in information processing efficiency" in children with early onset T1DM (< 5 years old), with significant decrements in visuospatial, psychomotor, and attentional skills (Hagen et al., 1990; Rovet et al., 1988; Ryan, 1997). One study found clinically significant impairment in 29 percent of early-onset children (Ryan et al., 1985a). Because severe hypoglycemia is more common in very young children and the developing brain is assumed to be more vulnerable to neural insult, current treatment recommendations *discourage* attempts to achieve very tight control in this age group.

Severe hypoglycemia may also cause neurological damage in children with later onset, and EEG abnormalities are twice as likely when children have had previous episodes (Soltesz and Acsadi, 1989). Prospective studies show a relationship between severe hypoglycemia and performance deficits, including visuospatial skills, numerical skills, and attention (Golden et al., 1989; Rovet et al., 1991). However, some detriments may not be organic in nature. In children with later-onset T1DM, more frequent school absences predict poorer verbal and achievement scores (Kovacs et al., 1992; Ryan et al., 1984 1985b). Another speculation is that the decreased psychomotor efficiency in children may reflect an acquired personality or response style secondary to the demands of T1DM management, such as increased cautiousness and attention to detail (Ryan, 1997).

The effects of chronic or severe *hyperglycemia* on brain function has not received as much scientific attention, but there is some evidence of a detrimental impact. In a prospective study of newly diagnosed children deficits in verbal skills were associated with poorer glycemic control, whereas deficits in visuomotor integration were associated with DKA (Rovet et al., 1991). There is also evidence that chronic hyperglycemia can cause neurological damage in young and middle-aged adults. Adults with T1DM show slower brainstem auditory evoked potentials and more abnormalities in MRI scans (Araki et al., 1994; Jacobson et al., 2000; Nakamura et al., 1991), with one study finding abnormal MRI results in 69 percent of patients. Poor control has also been associated with mild impairments in memory and learning performance (Lichty and Connell, 1988; Franceschi et al., 1984). A study of a large number of adults with T1DM onset prior to age 17 (Ryan et al., 1992) found poorer attention, psychomotor efficiency, and spatial information processing compared to nondiabetic controls. The best predictor of impairment was the presence of peripheral neuropathy, leading Ryan to postulate that chronic hyperglycemia leads to a "central neuropathy." Elderly patients with T2DM show similar deficits in learning and memory that are related to metabolic control in some studies (Perlmuter et al., 1984; Reaven et al., 1990) but not in others (Mooradian et al., 1988). However, there is evidence that improving diabetes control can enhance learning and memory (Gradman et al., 1993).

Also controversial is the effect of severe hypoglycemia on the adult brain. In adults with T1DM, those with a history of severe hypoglycemia have shown deficits in psychomotor speed and visuospatial skills (Wredling et al., 1990). To control for the possible effects of childhood hypoglycemia, studies (Deary et al., 1992) have tested adults diagnosed after age 19, finding that not only do those with a history of severe hypoglycemia show more intellectual decline, but that the frequency of episodes relates to performance (Deary et al., 1993). Consequently, one concern is the possibility that intensive regimens, which increase the frequency of severe hypoglycemia, may contribute to neural damage. Large-scale studies of adults have not found that intensive therapy increases impairments (DCCT Research Group, 1996; Reichard et al., 1991). However, a recent prospective study of children found that those on intensive therapy showed more deficits in spatial and pattern recognition than those on conventional regimens (Hershey et al., 1999).

Psychobehavioral Interventions in Diabetes

In spite of the over 20-year history of psychobehavioral research in diabetes, the task of developing, testing, and implementing clinically useful, cost-effective interventions has not advanced as much as might have been expected. Although numerous studies have investigated potential psychobehavioral interventions, the usefulness of these findings has often been limited by methodological problems, including testing small samples of convenience rather than larger, population-based samples; unsophisticated or inadequate measures of clinical outcomes; use of cross-sectional designs rather than longitudinal studies; and failure to perform large-scale clinical trials to demonstrate efficacy and cost-effectiveness (Glasgow and Anderson, 1995; Rubin and Peyrot, 1992). Lack of a sound theoretical framework has also been problematic. The need for theoretically based interventions was highlighted by a recent meta-analysis showing that such treatments were significantly more effective than atheoretical interventions (Hampson et al., 2000). In addition, intervention research has not focused equivalently on different subpopulations of patients. Although there have been many intervention studies in adolescent patients and their families, virtually none have focused on families with very young T1DM children. In adults, T1DM has received far more attention than T2DM, where most research has addressed the need for weight loss. Finally, only a handful of studies have addressed the need for specific interventions aimed at specific problems, such as treatment during predictable times of crisis, e.g., just after diagnosis, or following the development of complications.

In spite of these problems, there is substantive evidence for the effectiveness of psychobehavioral interventions, especially in two major areas: improving coping skills and enhancing self-care. Coping skills training (CST) has positive results for both adolescents and adults with T1DM (Grey et al., 1998, 2000; Rubin et al., 1993; Zettler et al., 1995). For example, after CST was added to an intensive outpatient education program, improvements in self-treatment, metabolic control, and emotional status were maintained for 1 year (Rubin et al., 1989). However, the impact on lifestyle changes (diet and exercise) was minimal (Rubin et al., 1991). In addition, behavioral family therapy, designed to improve communication and problem-solving skills, can effectively decrease family conflict in adolescent T1DM (Wysocki et al., 2000). Interventions designed to increase self-efficacy also appear promising (Delamater et al., 1990), as well as those designed to increase patient empowerment (Anderson et al., 1995).

There is a growing interest in adapting cognitive–behavioral therapy (CBT) for use in diabetic populations. For example, CBT effectively treats depression in T2DM patients (Lustman et al., 1998). Current research in the Netherlands is testing brief group CBT that addresses diabetes-specific issues, including diabetes-related stress, anxiety about complications, and relationship problems (van der Ven et al., 2000). Preliminary data indicate a reduction in distress and improved wellbeing and metabolic control. Cognitive–analytic therapy, a close relative of CBT, appears to be effective for patients with poorly controlled T1DM when it addresses the psychosocial difficulties that underlie problems in self-treatment, with 9-month follow-up showing a decrease in interpersonal problems and improved glycemic control.

Other efforts to improve self-management have employed behavioral modification techniques, such as reinforcement and goal-setting in adolescents (Delamater et al., 1991; Skinner et al., 2000), but larger trials are needed. One intervention that has been extensively tested is blood glucose awareness training (BGAT), a structured program incorporating behavioral and cognitive strategies to improve self-treatment and decision making in adults with T1DM (Gonder-Frederick et al., 2000). BGAT focuses on specific self-regulatory processes and is designed to improve the ability to: 1) recognize hypo- and hyperglycemic symptoms; 2) avoid BG extremes due to self-treatment behaviors; 3) make appropriate self-treatment decisions; and 4) change attitudes that interfere with diabetes management. BGAT has wide-ranging, positive effects on psychosocial status, ability to recognize symptoms, and decision making, and also reduces hypo- and hyperglycemia as well as automobile violations and accidents. The benefits of BGAT are long-lasting, with follow-up studies up to several years after intervention (Cox et al., 1994, 2001) and the training manual has now been translated into Dutch, German, Bulgarian, and Japanese.[1]

Recent research has addressed the need for user-friendly and cost-effective interventions that can be implemented on a broad scale by developing

[1] Preparation of this manuscript was supported by grants from the National Institute of Child Health and Development (P01 HD33989) and the National Institute of Arthritis and Musculoskeletal and Skin Diseases (R01 AR 44724) awarded to the first author and the National Institutes of Health/Shannon Director's Award (R55 AR44230) awarded to the second Author.

"medical office-based interventions." Even minimal office-based interventions (e.g., providing patients with ongoing contact, reminders, and phone calls) appear to be effective (Cox et al., 1994, 2001; Litzelman et al., 1993; Weinberger et al., 1995), but these strategies are rarely systematically employed. Several researchers have demonstrated that it is possible to provide more sophisticated interventions in conjunction with medical appointments. For example, one study (Anderson et al., 1989) treated parents and adolescents in separate groups for five sessions designed to improve problem-solving skills and increase the use of BGM, and at 18-month follow-up the adolescents had improved metabolic control and self-tested more frequently when exercising. A subsequent study (Anderson et al., 1999) tested a "teamwork" family intervention that emphasized the importance of adolescent–parent sharing of diabetes management responsibilities and provided conflict resolution training. At 12-month follow-up parents had maintained their involvement in their children's diabetes care and family conflict was reduced.

In adults, an early study demonstrated the potential of a "patient activation" intervention delivered just prior to seeing physicians (Greenfield et al., 1988), in which patients reviewed their charts, prepared questions, and practiced communication skills. Subsequent improvements were found in metabolic control, quality of life, and work attendance. Glasgow (Glasgow and Eakin, 2000), a proponent of medical office-based and other pragmatic interventions, and his colleagues have developed a computerized assessment program to improve T2DM dietary management. When patients arrive for medical appointments they complete an assessment that identifies personal diet goals, as well as potential barriers to achieving these goals. They then briefly review this information with a diabetes educator. Follow-up studies show that improvements in diet and serum cholesterol are maintained for at least 1 year (Glasgow et al., 1995, 1997).

Even when effective psychobehavioral interventions are available, practitioners are confronted by numerous problems, not the least of which are reimbursement issues. Although problems with adjustment and coping are common in diabetes, many patients do not meet the criteria for psychiatric diagnosis, making it difficult for mental healthcare practitioners to receive insurance payment for services. For this reason, interventions that can be delivered by other healthcare professionals, such as diabetes educators and nurses, may become more prevalent in the future, although this introduces the need for appropriate training and supervision. An alternative approach that bypasses some of these difficulties is the development of structured, self-learning computerized training programs, such as the current effort to translate BGAT for implementation via the Internet.

Summary and Future Directions

Over the past two decades the involvement of psychologists and behavioral scientists has had a profound impact on medicine's theoretical and treatment approaches to diabetes. However, the full potential contribution of behavioral medicine is far from being recognized. With the DCCT and similar studies showing the importance of tight metabolic control for the delay and/or progression of serious long-term complications, there is an increased pressure on our field to understand more comprehensively the multiple, complex, interacting factors that determine patient/family ability to manage diabetes effectively, from both an emotional and a behavioral perspective. In addition, the DCCT results have placed enormously increased pressure on patients to become even more diligent in their daily regimens, as well as increased anxiety about complications when they fail to maintain ideal control. Behavioral scientists have only begun to delve into the ramifications of these changes; for example, conversations with patients who are highly anxious about complications suggest that many of them "overreact" to high BG readings and tend to "over-insulinize" in response, leading to an increased frequency of hypoglycemia.

It might be argued that the influence of psychobehavioral factors is likely to become less critical in the future as new technological advances in diabetes treatment emerge, such as devices that provide continuous BG monitoring which are in current development. From behavioral medicine's perspective, however, such technology is more likely to simply present its own set of issues and problems to address. For example, these devices will still require daily calibration, and only improve metabolic control to the extent that more frequent BG feedback is used to make better decisions about the adjustment of other relevant behaviors (e.g., insulin and food). In addition, one must wonder what the psychological impact will be of wearing a constant reminder of diabetes, especially given the fact that only a minority of patients are willing to wear diabetes identification tags. As long as it is they who bear the burden of managing and dealing with the numerous challenges their illness presents, it seems highly unlikely that "human factors" can be eliminated from diabetes treatment and clinical outcome.

References

Aikens, J. E., Wallander, J. L., Bell, D. S., and Cole, J. A. (1992). Daily stress variability, learned resourcefulness, regimen adherence, and metabolic control in type I diabetes mellitus: Evaluation of a path model. *Journal of Consulting and Clinical Psychology*, 60, 113–118.

American Diabetes Association. (1996). Nutrition recommendations and principles for people with diabetes mellitus. *Diabetes Care*, Suppl 1, S16–S19.

American Diabetes Association. (2000). Type 2 diabetes in children and adolescents. *Diabetes Care*, 23, 381–389.

Amiel, S. A., Sherwin, R. S., Simonson, D. C., Lauritano, A. A., and Tamborlane,W. V. (1986). Impaired insulin action in puberty. A contributing factor to poor glycemic control in adolescents with diabetes. *New England Journal of Medicine*, 315, 215–219.

Anderson, B., Ho, J., Brackett, J., Finkelstein, D., and Laffel, L. (1997). Parental involvement in diabetes management tasks: Relationships to blood glucose monitoring adherence and metabolic control in young adolescents with insulin-dependent diabetes mellitus. *Journal of Pediatrics*, 130, 257–265.

Anderson, B. J., and Brackett, J. (2000). Diabetes during childhood. In F. J. Snoek and C. Skinner (Eds.), *Psychology in Diabetes Care* (pp. 1–24). London: John Wiley and Sons, Ltd.

Anderson, B. J., Brackett, J., Ho, J., and Laffel, L. M. (1999). An office-based intervention to maintain parent–adolescent teamwork in diabetes management. Impact on parent involvement, family conflict, and subsequent glycemic control. *Diabetes Care*, 22, 713–721.

Anderson, B. J., Wolf, F. M., Burkhart, M. T., Cornell, R. G., and Bacon, G. E. (1989). Effects of peer-group intervention on metabolic control of adolescents with IDDM. Randomized outpatient study. *Diabetes Care*, 12, 179–183.

Anderson, R., Funnell, M. M., Carlson, A., Saleh-Statin, N., Cradock, S., and Skinner, T. C. (2000a). Facilitating self-care through empowerment. In F. J. Snoek and T. C. Skinner (Eds.), *Psychology in Diabetes Care* (pp. 69–98). Chichester: John Wiley and Sons.

Anderson, R. M., Funnell, M. M., Butler, P. M., Arnold, M. S., Fitzgerald, J. T., and Feste, C. C. (1995). Patient empowerment. Results of a randomized controlled trial. *Diabetes Care*, 18, 943–949.

Araki, Y., Nomura, M., Tanaka, H., Yamamoto, H., Yamamoto, T., Tsukaguchi, I., and Nakamura, H. (1994). MRI of the brain in diabetes mellitus. *Neuroradiology*, 36, 101–103.

Auslander, W. F., Anderson, B. J., Bubb, J., Jung, K. C., and Santiago, J. V. (1990). Risk factors to health in diabetic children: A prospective study from diagnosis. *Health in Social Work*, 15, 133–142.

Auslander, W. F., Bubb, J., Rogge, M., and Santiago, J. V. (1993). Family stress and resources: Potential areas of intervention in children recently diagnosed with diabetes. *Health in Social Work*, 18, 101–113. [Published erratum appears in *Health in Social Work*, 1993, 18, 194.]

Auslander, W. F., Thompson, S., Dreitzer, D., White, N. H., and Santiago, J. V. (1997). Disparity in glycemic control and adherence between African-American and Caucasian youths with diabetes. Family and community contexts. *Diabetes Care*, 20, 1569–1575.

Becker, M. H. (1985). Patient adherence to prescribed therapies. *Medical Care*, 23, 539–555.

Blanz, B. J., Rensch-Riemann, B. S., Fritz-Sigmund, D. I., and Schmidt, M. H. (1993). IDDM is a risk factor for adolescent psychiatric disorders. *Diabetes Care*, 16, 1579–1587.

Bradley, C. (1994) *Handbook of Psychology and Diabetes*. Amsterdam: Harwood Academic Publishers.

Brownlee-Duffeck, M., Peterson, L., Simonds, J. F., Goldstein, D., Kilo, C., and Hoette, S. (1987). The role of health beliefs in the regimen adherence and metabolic control of adolescents and adults with diabetes mellitus. *Journal of Consulting Clinical Psychology*, 55, 139–144.

Christensen, A. J., Moran, P. J., and Wiebe, J. S. (1999). Assessment of irrational health beliefs: Relation to health practices and medical regimen adherence. *Health Psychology*, 18, 169–176.

Clark, C. M., Jr. (1998). Reducing the burden of diabetes. The National Diabetes Education Program. *Diabetes Care*, 21, C30–C31.

Clarke, W. L., Cox, D. J., Gonder-Frederick, L. A., Julian, D., Schlundt, D., and Polonsky, W. (1995). Reduced awareness of hypoglycemia in adults with IDDM. A prospective study of hypoglycemic frequency and associated symptoms. *Diabetes Care*, 18, 517–522.

Clarke, W. L., Gonder-Frederick, L. A., and Cox, D. J. (1996). The frequency of severe hypoglycaemia in children with insulin-dependent diabetes mellitus. *Hormone Research*, 45(Suppl 1), 48–52.

Clarke, W. L., Gonder-Frederick, L. A., Snyder, A. L., and Cox, D. J. (1998). Maternal fear of hypoglycemia in their children with insulin dependent diabetes mellitus. *Journal of Pediatric Endocrinology and Metabolism*, 11(Suppl 1), 189–194.

Coustan, D. R. (1995). Gestational Diabetes. In anonymous, *Diabetes in America* (pp. 703–718). Bethesda, MD: National Institutes of Health.

Cox, D. J., and Gonder-Frederick, L. A. (1992). Major developments in behavioral diabetes research. *Journal of Consulting and Clinical Psychology*, 60, 628–638.

Cox, D. J., Gonder-Frederick, L. A., Antoun, B., Clarke, W. L., and Cryer, P. (1990). Psychobehavioral metabolic parameters of severe hypoglycemic episodes [letter]. *Diabetes Care*, 13, 458–459.

Cox, D. J., Gonder-Frederick, L. A., Julian, D. M., and Clarke, W. L. (1994). Long-term follow-up evaluation of blood glucose awareness training. *Diabetes Care*, 17, 1–5.

Cox, D. J., Gonder-Frederick, L. A., Polonsky, W. H., Schlundt, D. G., Julian, D. M., Kovatchev, B. P., and Clarke, W. L. (2001). Blood glucose awareness training (BGAT-II: Long-term benefits). *Diabetes Care*, 24, 637–642.

Dahlquist, G. G. (1999). Primary and secondary prevention strategies of pre-type 1 diabetes. Potentials and pitfalls. *Diabetes Care*, 22(Suppl 2), B4–B6.

DCCT Research Group. (1993). The effect of intensive treatment of diabetes on the development and progression of long-term complications in insulin-dependent diabetes mellitus. The Diabetes Control and Complications Trial Research Group. *New England Journal of Medicine*, 329, 977–986.

DCCT Research Group. (1995). The relationship of glycemic exposure (HbA1c) to the risk of development and progression of retinopathy in the diabetes control and complications trial. *Diabetes*, 44, 968–983.

DCCT Research Group. (1996). Effects of intensive diabetes therapy on neuropsychological function in adults in the diabetes control and complications trial. *Annals of Internal Medicine*, 124, 379–388.

DCCT Research Group. (1997). Hypoglycemia in the diabetes control and complications trial. The Diabetes Control and Complications Trial Research Group. *Diabetes*, 46, 271–286.

DCCT Research Group. (1999). Pregnancy outcomes in the diabetes control and complications trial. *American Journal of Obstetrics and Gynecology*, 174, 1343–1353.

Deary, I. J., Crawford, J. R., Hepburn, D. A., Langan, S. J., Blackmore, L. M., and Frier, B. M. (1993). Severe hypoglycemia and intelligence in adult patients with insulin-treated diabetes. *Diabetes*, 42, 341–344.

Deary, I. J., Langan, S. J., and Graham, K. S. (1992). Recurrent severe hypoglycemia, intelligence, and speed of information processing. *Intelligence*, 19, 337–359.

Delamater, A. M. (2000). Quality of life in youths with diabetes. *Diabetes Spectrum*, 13, 42–47.

Delamater, A. M., Albrecht, D. R., Postellon, D. C., and Gutai, J. P. (1991). Racial differences in metabolic control of children and adolescents with type I diabetes mellitus. *Diabetes Care*, 14, 20–25.

Delamater, A. M., Bubb, J., Davis, S. G., Smith, J. A., Schmidt, L. E., White, N. H., and Santrage, J. (1990). Randomized perspective study at self-management training with newly diagnosed diabetic children. *Diabetic Care*, 13, 492–498.

Ellemann, K., Soerensen, J. N., Pedersen, L., Edsberg, B., and Andersen, O. O. (1984). Epidemiology and treatment of diabetic ketoacidosis in a community population. *Diabetes Care*, 7, 528–532.

Fena-Kurlovich, C. (2000). The time and expenses of being a type 1 diabetic in good control. *Diabetes Interview*, 9, 30–31.

Feste, C. C., and Anderson, R. M. (1995). Empowerment: a winning model for diabetes care. *Patient Education Counseling*, 26, 139–144.

Follansbee, D. S. (1989). Assuming responsibility for diabetes management: What age? What price? *Diabetes Education*, 15, 347–353.

Franceschi, M., Cecchetto, R., Minicucci, F., Smizne, S., Baio, G., and Canal, N. (1984). Cognitive processes in insulin-dependent diabetes. *Diabetes Care*, 7, 228–231.

Gafvels, C., Lithner, F., and Borjeson, B. (1993). Living with diabetes: relationship to gender, duration and complications. A survey in northern Sweden. *Diabetic Medicine*, 10, 768–773.

Gavard, J. A., Lustman, P. J., and Clouse, R. E. (1993). Prevalence of depression in adults with diabetes. An epidemiological evaluation. *Diabetes Care*, 16, 1167–1178.

Gill, G. V. (1992). Non-insulin-dependent diabetes mellitus. In J. C. Pickup and G. Williams (Eds.), *Textbook of Diabetes*. Oxford: Blackwell Scientific Publications.

Glasgow, R. E., and Anderson, B. J. (1995). Future directions for research on pediatric chronic disease management: Lessons from diabetes. *Journal of Pediatric Psychology*, 20, 389–402.

Glasgow, R. E., and Eakin, E. G. (1996). Dealing with diabetes self-management. In B. J. Anderson and R. R. Rubin (Eds.), *Practical Psychology for Diabetes Clinicians* (pp. 53–62). Alexandria, VA: American Diabetes Association.

Glasgow, R. E., and Eakin, E. G. (1998). Issues in diabetes self-management. In S. A. Shumaker, E. B. Schron, J. K. Ockene, and W. L. McBee (Eds.), *The Handbook Of Health Behavior Change* (pp. 435–461). New York: Springer.

Glasgow, R. E., and Eakin, E. G. (2000). Medical office-based interventions. In F. J. Snoek and T. C. Skinner (Eds.), *Psychology in Diabetes Care* (pp. 141–168). Chichester: John Wiley and Sons.

Glasgow, R. E., La Chance, P. A., Toobert, D. J., Brown, J., Hampson, S. E., and Riddle, M. C. (1997). Long-term effects and costs of brief behavioural dietary intervention for patients with diabetes delivered from the medical office. *Patient Education Counseling*, 32, 175–184.

Glasgow, R. E., Toobert, D. J., Hampson, S. E., and Noell, J. W. (1995). A brief office-based intervention to facilitate diabetes dietary self-management. *Health Education Research*, 10, 467–478.

Golden, M. P., Ingersoll, G. M., Brack, C. J., Russell, B. A., Wright, J. C., and Huberty, T. J. (1989). Longitudinal relationship of asymptomatic hypoglycemia to cognitive function in IDDM. *Diabetes Care*, 12, 89–93.

Gonder-Frederick, L. A. (1998). Hypoglycemia. In anonymous, *A Core Curriculum for Diabetes Education*. Chicago, IL: American Association of Diabetes Educators.

Gonder-Frederick, L. A., Carter, W. R., Cox, D. J., and Clarke, W. L. (1990). Environmental stress and blood glucose change in insulin-dependent diabetes mellitus. *Health Psychology*, 9, 503–515.

Gonder-Frederick, L. A., Clarke, W. L., and Cox, D. J. (1997). The emotional, social, and behavioral implications of insulin-induced hypoglycemia. *Seminars in Clinical Neuropsychiatry*, 2, 57–65.

Gonder-Frederick, L. A., Cox, D. J., Clarke, W. L., and Julian, D. M. (2000). Blood Glucose Awareness Training. In F. Snoek and C. Skinner (Eds.), *Psychology in Diabetes Care* (pp. 169–206). London: John Wiley and Sons.

Gonder-Frederick, L. A., Cox, D. J., Kovatchev, B., Julian, D., and Clarke, W. (1997b). The psychosocial impact of severe hypoglycemic episodes on spouses of patients with IDDM. *Diabetes Care*, 20, 1543–1546.

Gonder-Frederick, L. A., Cox, D. J., Kovatchev, B., Schlundt, D., and Clarke, W. (1997a). A biopsychobehavioral model of risk of severe hypoglycemia. *Diabetes Care*, 20, 661–669.

Gradman, T. J., Laws, A., Thompson, L. W., and Reaven, G. M. (1993). Verbal learning and/or memory improves with glycemic control in older subjects with non-insulin-dependent diabetes mellitus. *Journal of the American Geriatric Society*, 41, 1305–1312.

Greenfield, S., Kaplan, S. H., Ware, J. E., Jr., Yano, E. M., and Frank, H. J. (1988). Patients' participation in medical care: Effects on blood sugar control and quality of life in diabetes. *Journal of General Internal Medicine*, 3, 448–457.

Grey, M., Boland, E. A., Davidson, M., Li, J., and Tamborlane, W. V. (2000). Coping skills training for youth with diabetes mellitus has long-lasting effects on metabolic control and quality of life. *Journal of Pediatrics*, 137, 107–113.

Grey, M., Boland, E. A., Davidson, M., Yu, C., Sullivan-Bolyai, S., and Tamborlane, W. V. (1998). Short-term effects of coping skills training as adjunct to intensive therapy in adolescents. *Diabetes Care*, 21, 902–908.

Grey, M., Cameron, M. E., Lipman, T. H., and Thurber, F. W. (1995). Psychosocial status of children with diabetes in the first 2 years after diagnosis. *Diabetes Care*, 18, 1330–1336.

Haffner, S. M. (1998). Epidemiology of type 2 diabetes: risk factors. *Diabetes Care*, 21(Suppl 3), C3–C6.

Haffner, S. M., Miettinen, H., Gaskill, S. P., and Stern, M. P. (1995). Decreased insulin secretion and increased insulin resistance are independently related to the 7-year risk of NIDDM in Mexican-Americans. *Diabetes*, 44, 1386–1391.

Hagen, J. W., Barclay, C. R., Anderson, B. J., Feeman, D. J., Segal, S. S., Bacon, G., and Goldstein, G. W. (1990). Intellective functioning and strategy use in children with insulin-dependent diabetes mellitus. *Child Development*, 61, 1714–1727.

Hall, R. C. (1997). Bulimia nervosa and diabetes mellitus: A dangerous interplay producing accelerated complications. *Seminars in Clinical Neuropsychiatry*, 2, 24–30.

Hampson, S. E., Skinner, T. C., Hart, J., Storey, L., Gage, H., Foxcroft, D., Kimber, A., Cradock, S., and McEvilly, E. A. (2000). Behavioral interventions for adolescents with type 1 diabetes: How effective are they? *Diabetes Care*, 23, 1416–1422.

Hanson, C. L., De Guire, M. J., Schinkel, A. M., and Kolterman, O. G. (1995). Empirical validation for a family-centered model of care. *Diabetes Care*, 18, 1347–1356.

Harris, M. I. (1998). Diabetes in America: Epidemiology and scope of the problem. *Diabetes Care*, 21(Suppl 3), C11–C14.

Harris, M. I., Cowie, C. C., and Howie, L. J. (1993). Self-monitoring of blood glucose by adults with diabetes in the United States population. *Diabetes Care*, 16, 1116–1123.

Hershey, T., Bhargava, N., Sadler, M., White, N. H., and Craft, S. (1999). Conventional versus intensive diabetes therapy in children with type 1 diabetes: Effects on memory and motor speed. *Diabetes Care*, 22, 1318–1324.

Herskowitz, D. R., Jacobson, A. M., Cole, C., Hauser, S. T., Wolfsdorf, J. I., Willett, J. B., Milley, J. E., and Wertlieb, D. (1995). Psychosocial predictors of acute complications of diabetes in youth. *Diabetic Medicine*, 12, 612–618.

Hillard, J. R., and Hillard, P. J. (1984). Bulimia, anorexia nervosa, and diabetes. Deadly combinations. *Psychiatric Clinics of North America*, 7, 367–379.

Irvine, A. A., Cox, D. J., and Gonder-Frederick, L. A. (1994). The fear of hypoglycemia scale. In C. Bradley (Ed.), *Handbook of Psychology and Diabetes* (pp. 133–155). Amsterdam: Harwood Academic Publishers.

Jacobson, A. M. (1997). Quality of life in patients with diabetes mellitus. *Seminars in Clinical Neuropsychiatry*, 2, 82–93.

Jacobson, A. M., Cleary, P., and Baker ,L. (1996). The effect of intensive treatment of diabetes on the quality of life outcomes in the diabetes control and complications trial. *Diabetes Care*, 11, 725–732.

Jacobson, A. M., de Groot, M., and Samson, J. A. (1997a). The effects of psychiatric disorders and symptoms on quality of life in patients with type I and type II diabetes mellitus. *Quality of Life Research*, 6, 11–20.

Jacobson, A. M., Hauser, S. T., Lavori, P., Willett, J. B., Cole, C. F., Wolfsdorf, J. I., Dumont, R. H., and Wertlieb, D. (1994a). Family environment and glycemic control: A four-year prospective study of children and adolescents with insulin-dependent diabetes mellitus. *Psychosomatic Medicine*, 56, 401–409.

Jacobson, A. M., Hauser, S. T., Wertlieb, D., Wolfsdorf, J. I., Orleans, J., and Vieyra, M. (1986). Psychological adjustment of children with recently diagnosed diabetes mellitus. *Diabetes Care*, 9, 323–329.

Jacobson, A. M., Hauser, S. T., Willett, J. B., Wolfsdorf, J. I., Dvorak, R., Herman, L., and de Groot, M. (1997b). Psychological adjustment to IDDM: 10-year follow-up of an onset cohort of child and adolescent patients. *Diabetes Care*, 20, 811–818.

Jacobson, A. M., Rand, L. I., and Hauser, S. T. (1985). Psychologic stress and glycemic control: a comparison of patients with and without proliferative diabetic retinopathy. *Psychosomatic Medicine*, 47, 372–381.

Jacobson, A. M., and The DCCT Research Group. (1994b). The diabetes quality of life measure. In C. Bradley (Ed.), *Handbook of Psychology and Diabetes* (pp. 65–88). Amsterdam: Harwood Academic Publishers.

Jacobson, A. M., Weinger, K., Hill, T. C., Parker, J. A., Suojanen, J. N., Jimerson, D. C., and Soroko, D. J. (2000). Brain functioning, cognition and psychiatric disorders in patients with type 1 diabetes. *American Diabetes Association, 2000* (Conference), P-537.

Kavanagh, D. J., Gooley, S., and Wilson, P. H. (1993). Prediction of adherence and control in diabetes. *Journal of Behavioral Medicine*, 16, 509–522.

Kovacs, M., Brent, D., Steinberg, T. F., Paulauskas, S., and Reid, J. (1986). Children's self-reports of psychologic adjustment and coping strategies during first year of insulin-dependent diabetes mellitus. *Diabetes Care*, 9, 472–479.

Kovacs, M., Charron-Prochownik, D., and Obrosky, D. S. (1995). A longitudinal study of biomedical and psychosocial predictors of multiple hospitalizations among young people with insulin-dependent diabetes mellitus. *Diabetic Medicine*, 12, 142–148.

Kovacs, M., Feinberg, T. L., Paulauskas, S., Finkelstein, R., Pollock, M., and Crouse-Novak, M. (1985b). Initial coping responses and psychosocial characteristics of children with insulin-dependent diabetes mellitus. *Journal of Pediatrics*, 106, 827–834.

Kovacs, M., Finkelstein, R., Feinberg, T. L., Crouse-Novak, M., Paulauskas, S., and Pollock, M. (1985a). Initial psychologic responses of parents to the diagnosis of insulin-dependent diabetes mellitus in their children. *Diabetes Care*, 8, 568–575.

Kovacs, M., Goldston, D., and Morrow, L. (1992). Intellectual development and academic performance of children with insulin-dependent diabetes mellitus. *Developmental Psychology*, 28, 676–684.

Kovacs, M., Goldston, D., Obrosky, D. S., and Bonar, L. K. (1997b). Psychiatric disorders in youths with IDDM: Rates and risk factors. *Diabetes Care*, 20, 36–44.

Kovacs, M., Iyengar, S., Goldston, D., Obrosky, D. S., Stewart, J., and Marsh, J. (1990b). Psychological functioning among mothers of children with insulin-dependent diabetes mellitus: A longitudinal study. *Journal of Consulting Clinical Psychology*, 58, 189–195.

Kovacs, M., Iyengar, S., Goldston, D., Stewart, J., Obrosky, D. S., and Marsh, J. (1990a). Psychological functioning of children with insulin-dependent diabetes mellitus: A longitudinal study. *Journal of Pediatric Psychology*, 15, 619–632.

Kovacs, M., Kass, R. E., Schnell, T. M., Goldston, D., and Marsh, J. (1989). Family functioning and metabolic control of school-aged children with IDDM. *Diabetes Care*, 12, 409–414.

Kovacs, M., Mukerji, P., Iyengar, S., and Drash, A. (1996). Psychiatric disorder and metabolic control among youths with IDDM. A longitudinal study. *Diabetes Care*, 19, 318–323.

Kovacs, M., Obrosky, D. S., Goldston, D., and Drash, A. (1997a). Major depressive disorder in youths with IDDM. A controlled prospective study of course and outcome. *Diabetes Care*, 20, 45–51.

La Greca, A. M., Auslander, W. F., Greco, P., Spetter, D., Fisher, E. B., Jr., and Santiago, J. V. (1995). I get by with a little help from my family and friends: adolescents' support for diabetes care. *Journal of Pediatric Psychology*, 20, 449–476.

Lichty, W., and Connell, C. (1988). Cognitive functioning of diabetics versus nondiabetics. *American Psychological Association, August 1988* (96th Annual Meeting).

Littlefield, C. H., Rodin, G. M., Murray, M. A., and Craven, J. L. (1990). Influence of functional impairment and social support on depressive symptoms in persons with diabetes. *Health Psychology*, 9, 737–749.

Litzelman, D. K., Slemenda, C. W., Langefeld, C. D., Hays, L. M., Welch, M. A., Bild, D. E., Ford, E. S., and Vinicor, F. (1993). Reduction of lower extremity clinical abnormalities in patients with non-insulin-dependent diabetes mellitus. A randomized, controlled trial. *Annals of Internal Medicine*, 119, 36–41.

Lloyd, C. E., Dyer, P. H., Lancashire, R. J., Harris, T., Daniels, J. E., and Barnett, A. H. (1999). Association between stress and glycemic control in adults with type 1 (insulin-dependent) diabetes. *Diabetes Care*, 22, 1278–1283.

Lustman, P. J., Griffith, L. S., and Clouse, R. E. (1997a). Depression in adults with diabetes. *Seminars in Clinical Neuropsychiatry*, 2, 15–23.

Lustman, P. J., Griffith, L. S., Clouse, R. E., and Cryer, P .E. (1986). Psychiatric illness in diabetes mellitus. Relationship to symptoms and glucose control. *Journal of Nervous and Mental Diseases*, 174, 736–742.

Lustman, P. J., Griffith, L. S., Clouse, R. E., Freedland, K. E., Eisen, S. A., Rubin, E. H., Carney, R. M., and McGill, J. B. (1997b). Effects of nortriptyline on depression and glycemic control in diabetes: Results of a double-blind, placebo-controlled trial. *Psychosomatic Medicine*, 59, 241–250.

Lustman, P. J., Griffith, L. S., Freedland, K. E., Kissel, S. S., and Clouse, R. E. (1998). Cognitive behavior therapy for depression in type 2 diabetes mellitus. A randomized, controlled trial. *Annals of Internal Medicine*, 129, 613–621.

Lustman, P. J., and Harper, G. W. (1987). Nonpsychiatric physicians' identification and treatment of depression in patients with diabetes. *Comprehensive Psychiatry*, 28, 22–27.

McCaul, K. D., Glasgow, R. E., and Schafer, L. C. (1987). Diabetes regimen behaviors. Predicting adherence. *Medical Care*, 25, 868–881.

Mercado, F. J., and Vargas, P. N. (1989). Disease and the family: Differences in metabolic control of diabetes mellitus between men and women. *Women's Health*, 15, 111–121.

Miller-Johnson, S., Emery, R. E., Marvin, R. S., Clarke, W., Lovinger, R., and Martin, M. (1994). Parent–child relationships and the management of insulin-dependent diabetes mellitus. *Journal of Consulting and Clinical Psychology*, 62, 603–610.

Mooradian, A., Perryman, K., and Fitten, J. (1988). Cortical function in elderly non-insulin dependent diabetic patients. *Archives of Internal Medicine*, 148, 2369–2372.

Nakamura, Y., Takahashi, M., Kitaguti, M., Imaoka, H., Kono, N., and Tarui, S. (1991). Abnormal brainstem evoked potentials in diabetes mellitus. Evoked potential testings and magnetic resonance imaging. *Electromyographic Clinical Neurophysiology*, 31, 243–249.

National Diabetes Data Group. (1995). *Diabetes in America* (2nd ed.). Bethesda, MD: National Institutes of Health.

Nofzinger, E. A. (1997). Sexual dysfunction in patients with diabetes mellitus: The role of a "central" neuropathy. *Seminars in Clinical Neuropsychiatry*, 2, 31–39.

O'Leary, A. (1985). Self-efficacy and health. *Behavioral Research Therapy*, 23, 437–451.

Ohkubo, Y., Kishikawa, H., Araki, E., Miyata, T., Isami, S., Motoyoshi, S., Kojima, Y., Furuyoshi, N., and Shichiri, M. (1995). Intensive insulin therapy prevents the progression of diabetic microvascular complications in Japanese patients with non-insulin-dependent diabetes mellitus: A randomized prospective 6-year study. *Diabetes Research and Clinical Practice*, 28, 103–117.

Overstreet S., Goins, J., Chen, R. S., Holmes, C. S., Greer, T., Dunlap, W. P., and Frentz, J. (1995). Family environment and the interrelation of family structure, child behavior, and metabolic control for children with diabetes. *Journal of Pediatric Psychology*, 20, 435–447.

Perlmuter, L. C., Hakami, M. K., Hodgson-Harrington, C., Ginsberg, J., Katz, J., Singer, D. E., and Nathan, D. M. (1984). Decreased cognitive function in aging non-insulin-dependent diabetic patients. *American Journal of Medicine*, 77, 1043–1048.

Peyrot, M., and Rubin, R. R. (1997). Levels and risks of depression and anxiety symptomatology among diabetic adults. *Diabetes Care*, 20, 585–590.

Polonsky, W. H. (1999). *Diabetes Burnout*. Alexandria, VA: American Diabetes Association.

Polonsky, W. H., Anderson, B. J., Lohrer, P. A., Aponte, J. E., Jacobson, A. M., and Cole, C. F. (1994). Insulin omission in women with IDDM. *Diabetes Care*, 17, 1178–1185.

Polonsky, W. H., Anderson, B. J., Lohrer, P. A., Welch, G., Jacobson, A. M., Aponte, J. E., and Schwartz, C. E. (1995). Assessment of diabetes-related distress. *Diabetes Care*, 18, 754–760.

Polonsky, W. H., Davis, C. L., Jacobson, A. M., and Anderson, B. J. (1992). Correlates of hypoglycemic fear in type I and type II diabetes mellitus. *Health Psychology*, 11, 199–202.

Popkin, M. K., Callies, A. L., Lentz, R. D., Colon, E. A., and Sutherland, D. E. (1988). Prevalence of major depression, simple phobia, and other psychiatric disorders in patients with long-standing type I diabetes mellitus. *Archives of General Psychiatry*, 45, 64–68.

Pories, W. J., Swanson, M. S., MacDonald, K. G., Long, S. B., Morris, P. G., Brown, B. M., Barakat, H. A., deRamon, R. A., Israel, G., and Dolezal, J. M. (1995). Who would have thought it? An operation proves to be the most effective therapy for adult-onset diabetes mellitus. *Annals of Surgery*, 222, 339–350.

Reaven, G. M., Thompson, L. W., Nahum, D., and Haskins, E. (1990). Relationship between hyperglycemia and cognitive function in older NIDDM patients. *Diabetes Care*, 13, 16–21.

Reichard, P., Berglund, A., Britz, A., Levander, S., and Rosenqvist, U. (1991). Hypoglycaemic episodes during intensified insulin treatment: Increased frequency but no effect on cognitive function. *Journal of Internal Medicine*, 229, 9–16.

Reichard, P., Nilsson, B. Y., and Rosenqvist, U. (1993). The effect of long-term intensified insulin treatment on the development of microvascular complications of diabetes mellitus. *New England Journal of Medicine*, 329, 304–309.

Robiner, W., and Keel, P. K. (1997). Self-care behaviors and adherence in diabetes mellitus. *Seminars in Clinical Neuropsychiatry*, 2, 40–56.

Robinson, N., Fuller, J. H., and Edmeades, S. P. (1988). Depression and diabetes. *Diabetic Medicine*, 5, 268–274.

Rovet, J., Czuchta, D., and Ehrlich, R. (1991). Neuropsychological sequelae of diabetes in childhood: A three year prospective study [Abstract]. *Diabetes*, 40, 430A.

Rovet, J., Ehrlich, R., and Hoppe, M. (1988). Specific intellectual deficits associated with the early onset of insulin-dependent diabetes mellitus in children. *Child Development*, 59, 226.

Rubin, R. R. (2000). Diabetes and quality of life. *Diabetes Spectrum*, 13, 21–23.

Rubin, R. R., and Peyrot, M. (1992). Psychosocial problems and interventions in diabetes. A review of the literature. *Diabetes Care*, 15, 1640–1657.

Rubin, R. R., Peyrot, M., and Saudek, C. D. (1989). Effect of diabetes education on self-care, metabolic control, and emotional well-being. *Diabetes Care*, 12, 673–679.

Rubin, R. R., Peyrot, M., and Saudek, C. D. (1991). Differential effect of diabetes education on self-regulation and life-style behaviors. *Diabetes Care*, 14, 335–338.

Rubin, R. R., Peyrot, M., and Saudek, C. D. (1993). The effect of a diabetes education program incorporating coping skills training on emotional well-being and diabetes self-efficacy. *Diabetes Educator*, 19, 210–214.

Ryan, C., Longstreet, C., and Morrow, L. (1985b). The effects of diabetes mellitus on the school attendance and school achievement of adolescents. *Child Care Health and Development*, 11, 229–240.

Ryan, C., Vega, A., and Drash, A. (1985a). Cognitive deficits in adolescents who developed diabetes early in life. *Pediatrics*, 75, 921–927.

Ryan, C., Vega, A., Longstreet, C., and Drash, A. (1984). Neuropsychological changes in adolescents with insulin-dependent diabetes. *Journal of Consulting Clinical Psychology*, 52, 335–342.

Ryan, C. M. (1997). Effects of diabetes mellitus on neuropsychological functioning: A lifespan perspective. *Seminars in Clinical Neuropsychiatry*, 2, 4–14.

Ryan, C. M., Williams, T. M., Orchard, T. J., and Finegold, D. N. (1992). Psychomotor slowing is associated with distal symmetrical polyneuropathy in adults with diabetes mellitus. *Diabetes*, 4, 107–113.

Schafer, L. C., McCaul, K. D., and Glasgow, R. E. (1986). Supportive and nonsupportive family behaviors: relationships to adherence and metabolic control in persons with type I diabetes. *Diabetes Care*, 9, 179–185.

Schlundt, D. G., Rea, M., Hodge, M., Flannery, M. E., Kline, S., Meek, J., Kinzer, C., and Pichert, J. W. (1996). Assessing and overcoming situational obstacles to dietary adherence in adolescents with IDDM. *Journal of Adolescent Health*, 19, 282–288.

Skinner, T. C., and Hampson, S. E. (1999). Personal models of diabetes in adolescents: a longitudinal study [Abstract]. *Diabetic Medicine*, 16, P82.

Skinner, T. C., John, M., and Hampson, S. E. (2000). Social support and personal models of diabetes as predictors of self-care and well-being: A longitudinal study of adolescents with diabetes. *Journal of Pediatric Psychology*, 25, 257–267.

Snoek, F. J. (2000). Diabetes and pregnancy. In F. J. Snoek and T. C. Skinner (Eds.), *Psychology in Diabetes Care* (pp. 61–68). Chichester: John Wiley and Sons.

Snoek, F. J., Mollema, E. D., Heine, R. J., Bouter, L. M., and van der Ploeg, H. M. (1997). Development and validation of the diabetes fear of injecting and self-testing questionnaire (D-FISQ): First findings. *Diabetic Medicine*, 14, 871–876.

Soltesz, G., and Acsadi, G. (1989). Association between diabetes, severe hypoglycaemia, and electroencephalographic abnormalities. *Archives of Disease in Childhood*, 64, 992–996.

Sovik, O., and Thordarson, H. (1999). Dead-in-bed syndrome in young diabetic patients. *Diabetes Care*, 22(Suppl 2), B40–B42. [Published erratum appears in *Diabetes Care*, 1999, 8, 1389.]

Spector, I. P., Leiblum, S. R., and Carey, M. P. (1993). Diabetes and female sexual dysfunction: A critical review. *Annals of Behavioral Medicine*, 15, 257–264.

Stahl, M., Berger, W., Schaechinger, H., and Cox, D. J. (1998). Spouse's worries concerning diabetic partner's possible hypoglycaemia [letter]. *Diabetic Medicine*, 15, 619–620.

Steel, J. M., Young, R. J., Lloyd, G. G., and Clarke, B. F. (1987). Clinically apparent eating disorders in young diabetic women: associations with painful neuropathy and other complications. *British Medical Journal*, 294, 859–862.

Stenstrom, U., Wikby, A., Hornquist, J. O., and Andersson, P. O. (1993). Recent life events, gender, and the control of diabetes mellitus. *General Hospital Psychiatry*, 15, 82–88.

Turner, R., Cull, C., and Holman, R. (1996). United Kingdom prospective diabetes study 17: A 9-year update of a randomized, controlled trial on the effect of improved metabolic control on complications in non-insulin-dependent diabetes mellitus. *Annals of Internal Medicine*, 124, 136–145.

UK Prospective Diabetes Study Group. (1999). Quality of life in type 2 diabetic patients is affected by complications but not by intensive policies to improve blood glucose or blood pressure control (UKPDS 37). *Diabetes Care*, 22, 1125–1136.

van der Ven, N. C. W., Chatrou, M., and Snoek, F. J. (2000). Cognitive–behavioral group training. In F. J. Snoek and T. C. Skinner (Eds.), *Psychology in Diabetes Care* (pp. 207–234). Chichester: John Wiley and Sons.

Vinicor, F. (1998). The public health burden of diabetes and the reality of limits. *Diabetes Care*, 21(Suppl 3), C15–C18.

Weinberger, M., Kirkman, M. S., Samsa, G. P., Shortliffe, E. A., Landsman, P. B., Cowper, P. A., Simel, D. L., and Feussner, J. R. (1995). A nurse-coordinated intervention for primary care patients with non-insulin-dependent diabetes mellitus: Impact on glycemic control and health-related quality of life. *Journal of General Internal Medicine*, 10, 59–66.

Welch, G., Dunn, S. M., and Beeney, L. J. (1994). The ATT39: A measure of psychological adjustment to diabetes. In C. Bradley (Ed.), *Handbook of Psychology and Diabetes* (pp. 223–246). Amsterdam: Harwood Academic Publishers.

Wikblad, K., Leksell, J., and Wibell, L. (1996). Health-related quality of life in relation to metabolic control and late complications in patients with insulin dependent diabetes mellitus. *Quality of Life Research*, 5, 123–130.

Wikblad, K., Montin, K., and Wibell, L. (1991). Metabolic control, residual insulin secretion and self-care behaviours in a defined group of patients with type 1 diabetes. *Uppsala Journal of Medical Science*, 96, 47–61.

Wing, R. R., Koeske, R., Epstein, L. H., Nowalk, M. P., Gooding, W., and Becker, D. (1987). Long-term effects of modest weight loss in type II diabetic patients. *Archives of Internal Medicine*, 147, 1749–1753.

Wredling, R., Levander, S., Adamson, U., and Lins, P. E. (1990). Permanent neuropsychological impairment after recurrent episodes of severe hypoglycaemia in man. *Diabetologia*, 33, 152–157.

Wysocki, T. (1994). The psychological context of SMBG. *Diabetes Spectrum*, 7, 266–270.

Wysocki, T., Harris, M. A., Greco, P., Bubb, J., Danda, C. E., Harvey, L. M., McDonell, K., Taylor, A., and White, N. H. (2000). Randomized, controlled trial of behavior therapy for families of adolescents with insulin-dependent diabetes mellitus. *Journal of Pediatric Psycholology*, 25, 23–33.

Wysocki, T., Hough, B. S., Ward, K. M., Allen, A. A., and Murgai, N. (1992a). Use of blood glucose data by families of children and adolescents with IDDM. *Diabetes Care*, 15, 1041–1044.

Wysocki, T., Hough, B. S., Ward, K. M., and Green, L. B. (1992b). Diabetes mellitus in the transition to adulthood: Adjustment, self-care, and health status. *Journal of Developmental Behavior and Pediatrics*, 13, 194–201.

Zambanini, A., and Feher, M. D. (1997). Needle phobia in type 1 diabetes mellitus. *Diabetic Medicine*, 14, 321–323.

Zettler, A., Duran, G., Waadt, S., Herschbach, P., and Strian, F. (1995). Coping with fear of long-term complications in diabetes mellitus: a model clinical program. *Psychotherapy and Psychosomatics*, 64, 178–184.

Ziegher, O., Kolopp, M., Louis, J., Musse, J. P., Patris, A., Debry, G., and Drouin, P. (1993). Self-monitoring of blood glucose and insulin dose alteration in type 1 diabetes mellitus. *Diabetes Research and Clinical Practice*, 21, 51–59.

Zrebiec, J. (1996). Caring for elderly patients with diabetes. In B. J. Anderson and R. R. Rubin (Eds.), *Practical Psychology* (pp. 35–42). Alexandria, VA: American Diabetes Association.

CHAPTER 8

Chronic Pain

Dennis C. Turk and Akiko Okifuji

University of Washington

Introduction

Pain is a common reason for seeking medical care. In most instances, pain is an adaptive warning of the potential for bodily harm. This signal helps to prevent further injury and under normal circumstances it is fundamental to the preservation of bodily integrity. However, pain reflects more than tissue damage. We all know of instances where two people with what appear to be equivalent amounts of tissue damage report widely different levels of pain and distress. This observation underlies the important distinction between pain and nociception.

Nociception is a physiological process by which sensory information is activated in specialized nerve endings that convey information about tissue damage or the potential of such damage to the central nervous system (CNS). Pain is an integrated perceptual process. The International Association for the Study of Pain recognizes the complexity and subjective nature of pain, defining it as "an unpleasant *sensory and emotional experience* normally associated with tissue damage or described in terms of such damage" (Merskey, 1986, emphasis added).

Beyond the definition of pain, it is important to distinguish among different types of pain – acute, chronic, and acute–recurrent. *Acute pain* persists for relatively brief periods – minutes, hours, or days – and is usually associated with tissue pathology. When pain exceeds the expected period of healing or is associated with a progressive disease, it is no longer viewed as being acute but now has become chronic. *Chronic pain* can last months and even many years. There may be only a limited relationship between pain and identifiable tissue pathology. *Acute–recurrent* pain has features in common with both acute and chronic pain. The difference between acute–recurrent and chronic pain lies in the fact that in chronic pain the sufferer usually experiences some level of pain at all times. In contrast, in acute–recurrent pain acute episodes of pain

Correspondence concerning this chapter should be addressed to: Dennis C. Turk, Ph.D., Department of Anesthesiology, Box 356540, University of Washington, Seattle, Washington 98195.

recur and alternate with pain-free intervals (e.g., migraine). Thus, although an episode may only last for a few hours, episodes recur over extended periods of time.

In the case of chronic and acute–recurrent pain the adaptive function of pain is not clear. In these cases pain continues after tissue pathology has resolved, or in the absence of tissue pathology. For example, among the majority of people who report backache, headaches, and fibromyalgia there is no identifiable pathology underlying the symptom (e.g., Deyo, 1986), nor are there any medical or surgical treatments that can permanently alleviate the pain.

People with chronic pain are often compelled to modify all aspects of their lives – familial, social, vocational. Not surprisingly, emotional disturbances are prevalent among pain sufferers (Sullivan and Turk, 2001) and their significant others. Loss of gainful employment is common, and as a result, chronic pain can be quite costly owing to disability cost, reduced productivity, and healthcare expenditures.

In this chapter we provide an overview of the current understanding of chronic and acute–recurrent pain. We describe common conceptualizations of pain that are based on single, causal factors, and suggest that each is incomplete. We then describe efforts to integrate a range of factors contributing to the experience of pain – multidimensional perspectives. Finally, we argue that many of the problems in understanding and successfully treating people with chronic pain syndromes result from a tendency to treat patients as if they were a homogeneous group. We describe results demonstrating that different sets of factors influence the variable responses to common treatments. We emphasize a dual-diagnostic approach and the potential benefits of matching treatment to patient characteristics.

Conceptualizations of Chronic Pain

There are two contrasting conceptualization models. Unidimensional models focus on single causes of the symptoms reported, whereas multidimensional models incorporate a range of factors that influence people's reports of pain.

Biomedical Model of Chronic Pain

The traditional biomedical or somatic view of pain is reductionist: it assumes that every report of pain is directly associated with a specific physical cause. As a consequence, the extent of pain should be proportional to the amount of detectable tissue damage. Physicians may spend inordinate amounts of time attempting to establish the specific link between tissue damage and the pain complaint. The expectation is that once the physical cause has been identified, appropriate treatment will follow. Treatment focuses on eliminating the putative cause(s) of the pain pharmacologically, or by disrupting the pain pathways surgically or by the injection of anesthetics.

There are several perplexing features of pain that do not fit neatly within the traditional biomedical model. As noted, a particular conundrum is that pain may be reported even in the absence of pathological processes. Conversely, diagnostic imaging studies using computed tomography (CT) scans and magnetic resonance imaging (MRI) have consistently noted the presence of significant pathology in up to 35 percent of *asymptomatic* people (e.g., Jensen et al., 1994). Thus, there may be reports of pain in the absence of identifiable pathology, and pathology in the absence of pain. Furthermore, the same medical or surgical intervention performed to correct identical pathological "causes" of pain and performed in the same manner may lead to disparate results.

Psychogenic Model of Chronic Pain

As is frequently the case in medicine, when physical explanations prove inadequate to explain symptoms, or when the results of treatment are inconsistent, psychological etiological alternatives are proposed. This is particularly the case when the pain reported is deemed to be "disproportionate," as determined by each clinician based on his or her subjective opinion, to an objectively determined pathological process. Alternatively, if the complaint is recalcitrant to "appropriate" treatment that should eliminate or alleviate the pain, it is assumed that psychological factors are involved. The psychogenic view is posed as an alternative to a somatogenic model. From this perspective, if pain occurs in the absence of, or is disproportionate to, objective physical pathology, then the pain must have a psychological etiology, hence "psychogenic."

Assessment based on the psychogenic perspective attempts to identify personality factors or psychopathological tendencies that initiate and maintain pain. Once identified, treatment is geared toward helping the patient gain insight into the maladaptive psychological factors. The assumption is that once patients become aware of these psychological causes of symptoms they will be able to develop better methods for dealing with their problems and the pain will remit. Unfortunately, to date, insight has not been shown to be effective in reducing symptoms in the majority of patients with chronic pain.

Motivational Model

The motivational conceptualization is an alternative to the psychogenic model. From this perspective, reports of pain, in the absence or in excess of physical pathology, are attributed to the desire of the patient to obtain some benefit, such as financial compensation. In contrast to the psychogenic model, in the motivational model the assumption is that patients *consciously* attempt to acquire a desirable outcome. Thus, pain in the absence of pathological process is regarded as fraudulent.

Assessment of patients from the motivational model focuses on identifying discrepancies between what patients report they are capable of doing and what they can actually do. Discrepancies between what patients say about their pain and disability, and performance on more objective assessment of physical functioning, are taken as evidence of exaggeration or fabrication of symptoms, and are used to label patients as symptom magnifiers or malin-gerers. Surveillance is also used as an assessment method, again looking for discrepancies between the patient's complaints and objective performance. A patient who indicates that he cannot lift weights over 5 lb might be videotaped lifting groceries. The ability to lift groceries is taken as an indication that the patient is capable of lifting. Thus the report of the inability to lift, in the light of the observation of lifting, is viewed as evidence of fabrication.

The treatment from the motivational perspective is simple: denial of disability claims. The assumption is that this will lead to prompt resolution of symptoms. Although this view is prevalent, especially among third-party payers, there is little evidence of dramatic resolution of pain following denial of disability.

The biomedical, psychogenic, and motivational views are unidimensional – the report of pain is ascribed to *either* physical *or* psychological factors, rather than being dualistic, i.e. either somatogenic or psychogenic. In the majority of cases biomedical factors appear to instigate the initial report of pain. Over time, however, psychosocial and behavioral factors may serve to maintain and exacerbate the level of pain, influence adjustment, and contribute to excessive disability. Following from this view, pain that persists over time should not be viewed as solely physical or solely psychological: the experience of pain is maintained by an interdependent set of biomedical, psychosocial, and behavioral factors.

Psychology of Pain

For the person experiencing persistent pain, there is a continuing quest for relief that remains elusive. Feelings of frustration, demoralization, and depres-sion, compromise the quality of all aspects of their lives. People with chronic pain confront not only the stress of pain but also a cascade of problems (e.g., financial, familial). Moreover, the experience of "medical limbo" (i.e., the presence of a painful condition that eludes diagnosis and which carries the stigma of either psychiatric causation or malingering) is itself the source of significant stress.

Pain sufferers frequently resort to the use of ineffective coping strategies, such as inactivity, medication, or alcohol to reduce emotional distress and pain. They also absolve themselves of personal responsibility for managing their pain and, instead, rely on family and healthcare providers.

Consider the following scenario. A back pain sufferer becomes inactive, leading to preoccupation with his or her body, and these cognitive–attentional changes increase the likelihood of detecting pain and amplifying distress. This person may be fearful of pain or reinjury. Thus he or she restricts activities that build flexibility, endurance, and strength. Hurt is viewed as being synonym-ous with harm, and if an activity produces an increase in pain the chronic pain sufferer terminates the activity and avoids similar activities in the future. Deactivation is common. Chronic pain sufferers characteristically develop negat-ive expectations about their own ability to control their pain or their lives. Negative expectations lead to feelings of frustration and demoralization.

Table 8.1 Classical conditioning: example with pain-physical therapy (PT) association From L. Twomey, R. Taylor (Eds), *Physical Therapy for Back Pain*, 3rd edition (2000), pp. 357–360.

Step 1: Natural consequence of pain – fear

PAIN ⇨ FEAR

Step 2: Pairing

PT SESSION
| ⇨ FEAR
PAIN

Step 3: Conditioned fear

PT ⇨ FEAR

In the case of chronic pain and acute–recurrent pain, healthcare providers need to take into consideration not only the physical cause of pain but also the patient's mood, fears, expectancies, coping resources and efforts, and the responses of significant others. Regardless of whether there is an identifiable physical basis for the reported pain, psychosocial and behavioral factors will influence the nature, severity, and persistence of pain and disability (cf. Gatchel and Turk, 1999). They will also affect patients' responses to therapeutic recommendations.

Behavioral Factors

We all attempt to escape from pain, and subsequently avoid, modify, or cope with pain. There are three principles of learning that help explain the acquisition of adaptive as well as dysfunctional behaviors associated with pain – classical conditioning, operant conditioning, and social learning.

Classical Conditioning

Once an acute pain problem persists, fear of physical activities becomes conditioned, resulting in avoidance of activity. Avoidance of pain is a powerful rationale for reduction of activity (Vlaeyan et al., 1995). Although it may be useful to reduce movement in the acute stage, limitation of activities can be maintained not only by pain but also by anticipatory fear. Table 8.1 illustrates how classical conditioning may play an important role in limiting the rehabilitation of people with chronic pain.

In persistent pain, many activities that are neutral or pleasurable may elicit or exacerbate pain, are thus experienced as aversive, and are avoided. Over time, more and more activities may be expected to exacerbate pain and will be avoided. Fear of pain may become associated with an expanding number of situations and behaviors (i.e., generalization). Anticipatory fear and anxiety also elicit physiological reactivity, which may aggravate pain. Thus, psychological factors may directly affect nociceptive stimulation and need not be viewed as simply reactions to pain.

Insofar as activity–avoidance succeeds in preventing pain aggravation, the conviction that patients should remain inactive will be difficult to modify. In contrast, repeatedly engaging in behavior that produces less pain than was predicted (corrective feedback) will be followed by a reduction in anticipatory fear. These adjustments will be increasingly followed by avoidance behavior, even to the elimination of all inappropriate avoidance.

Operant Conditioning

The effects of environmental factors in shaping the experience of pain sufferers were acknowledged in the early part of the 20th century. A new era in thinking about pain began with the work of Fordyce (1976). The main focus of operant learning is modification of the frequency of a given behavior. If the consequence of the given behavior is rewarding, the likelihood of its occurrence increases; if the consequence is aversive, the likelihood of its occurrence decreases.

Behaviors indicative of pain, such as limping and moaning, are called "pain behaviors." When someone is exposed to a stimulus that causes tissue damage, the immediate behavior is withdrawal in an attempt to escape from noxious sensations. Such behaviors are adaptive and appropriate. According to Fordyce (1976), these behaviors are responsive to the principles of *operant conditioning*. For example, behaviors such as the avoidance of activity and help-seeking may effectively prevent or withdraw aversive results (i.e., pain) initially. This negative reinforcement increases the likelihood that such behaviors will recur. The operant view proposes that environmental contingencies may reinforce pain behaviors during the acute stage. Although such behavior is appropriate and adaptive initially, once the behavioral pattern is established through associative learning, the behavior becomes controlled by external reinforcement. In chronic pain, therefore, pain behavior may indicate a learned pattern of responding to the environment, rather than the adaptive pattern of protecting the body from injury.

As we noted, pain behaviors may be positively reinforced directly, for example by attention from a spouse. The principles of learning suggest that behaviors that are positively reinforced will be emitted more frequently. Pain behaviors may also be maintained by the escape from noxious stimulation by the use of drugs or rest, or the avoidance of undesirable activities such as work. In addition "well behaviors" (e.g., activity, working) may not be positively reinforced, and the more rewarding pain behaviors may therefore be maintained and well behaviors extinguished.

We can consider an example to illustrate the role of operant conditioning. When a back pain sufferer's pain flares up, she may lie down and hold her back. Her husband observes her behavior and infers that she is experiencing pain. He may offer to rub her back. This response may positively reward the woman and her pain behavior (i.e., lying down) may be repeated even in the absence of pain. In other words, the woman's pain behaviors are being maintained by the learned consequences of a desirable outcome.

Table 8.2 Operant maintenance of pain behavior in chronic low back pain
From L. Twomey, R. Taylor (Eds), *Physical Therapy for Back Pain*, 3rd edition (2000),
pp. 357–360. Reprinted with permission; Copyright 2000 Churchill Livingstone. All rights
reserved.

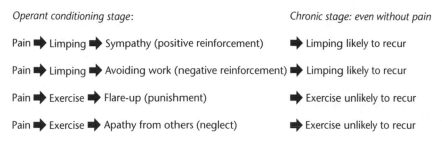

Operant conditioning stage:	*Chronic stage: even without pain*
Pain ➡ Limping ➡ Sympathy (positive reinforcement)	➡ Limping likely to recur
Pain ➡ Limping ➡ Avoiding work (negative reinforcement)	➡ Limping likely to recur
Pain ➡ Exercise ➡ Flare-up (punishment)	➡ Exercise unlikely to recur
Pain ➡ Exercise ➡ Apathy from others (neglect)	➡ Exercise unlikely to recur

Another powerful way in which her husband reinforces her pain behaviors is by permitting her to avoid undesirable activities. When observing his wife lying on the floor, the husband may suggest that they cancel the evening plans with his brother, an activity that she may have preferred to avoid anyway. In this situation, her husband providing her with extra attention and comfort and the opportunity to avoid an undesirable social obligation reward her pain reports and behaviors.

Pain sufferers do not consciously communicate pain to obtain attention or avoid undesirable activities: it is more likely to be the result of a gradual process of behavior shaping that neither the patient nor the significant other recognizes. Thus a person's response to life stressors, as well as how others respond to the pain sufferer, can influence the experience of pain but are not the cause.

Healthcare professionals may also reinforce pain behavior by their responses. The physician who prescribes medication on the patient's complaint may be reinforcing the report of pain (Turk and Okifuji, 1997). That is, patients learn that their behavior elicits a response from the physician, and if the response provides relief the patient may learn to report pain in order to obtain the desired outcome. This is the case when pain medication is prescribed on a "take as needed" (PRN) basis. The patient must indicate that the pain has increased in order to take the medication. If the medication provides relief, then the attention to and self-rating of pain may be maintained by the anticipated outcome of relief.

The combination of reinforced pain behaviors and neglected well behaviors is common in chronic pain (see table 8.2). The operant learning paradigm does not uncover the etiology of pain but focuses on the maintenance of pain behaviors and deficiency in well behaviors.

It is important not to make the mistake of viewing pain behaviors as being synonymous with *malingering*. Malingering involves the patient *consciously and deliberately* faking a symptom such as pain for some gain, usually financial. In the case of pain behaviors there is no suggestion of conscious deception, but rather the unintended performance of pain behaviors resulting from environmental reinforcement contingencies. People are typically not aware that these behaviors are being displayed, nor are they consciously motivated to obtain a positive reinforcement from such behaviors. Contrary to the beliefs of many third-party payers, there is little support for the contention that outright faking of pain for financial gain is prevalent.

Assessment, from the operant perspective, focuses on identifying the antecedents and consequences (reinforcements) of pain behaviors. Operant technique focuses on the elimination of pain behaviors by withdrawing attention and increasing well behaviors by positive reinforcement. The operant view has generated what has proven to be an effective treatment for selected samples of chronic pain patients.

Social Learning

Social learning has received some attention in acute pain and in the development and maintenance of persistent pain. The observation of others in pain is an event that captivates attention. The acquisition of pain behaviors may result from "observational" learning and "modeling" processes. People can acquire responses that were not previously in their repertoire by observing others. The culturally acquired interpretation of symptoms determines how people deal with illness. There is evidence of the role of social learning from controlled laboratory pain studies, and from observations of patients' behaviors in naturalistic and clinical settings.

Physiological responses to pain stimuli may be conditioned during observation of others in pain. For example, children of chronic pain patients may choose more pain-related responses during stressful times than do children with healthy or diabetic parents. These children tend to exhibit greater illness behaviors (e.g., complaining, days absent, visits to school nurse) than children of healthy parents (Richard, 1988). Expectancies and actual behavioral responses to nociceptive stimulation are based, at least partially, on prior social learning history. This may contribute to the marked variability in response to objectively similar physical pathology.

Affective Factors

Pain is ultimately a private experience described in terms of sensory and affective properties (Merskey, 1986). Anxiety and depression have received the greatest amount of attention in chronic pain patients; however, anger has recently received considerable interest as an important emotion in pain patients.

Depression and Anxiety

From 40 to 50 percent of chronic pain patients suffer from depression (Romano and Turner, 1985). In the majority of cases depression appears to reflect patients' reactions to their plight, although some have suggested that chronic pain is a form of "masked depression." It is not surprising that a large number of chronic pain patients are depressed. It is interesting to ponder the other side of the coin. Given the nature of the symptom and the problems created by chronic pain, why is it that all such patients are *not* depressed? We (Okifuji et al., 2000; Turk et al., 1995) examined this question and determined that patients' appraisals of the effects of the pain on their lives, and of their ability to exert any control over the pain and their lives, mediated the pain–depression relationship. That is, those patients who believed that they could continue to function despite their pain, and that they could maintain some control despite their pain, did not become depressed.

Anger

Anger has been widely observed in individuals with chronic pain (Schwartz et al., 1991). Pilowsky and Spence (1976) reported an incidence of "bottled-up anger" in 53 percent of chronic pain patients. Internalized or self-directed anger is common (Kerns et al., 1994; Okifuji et al., 1999) and seems to be related to pain intensity, perceived interference, and reported frequency of pain behaviors. Summers et al. (1991) examined patients with spinal cord injuries and found that anger and hostility were powerful predictors of pain severity. Even though many chronic pain patients present an image of themselves as even-tempered, in one study, 88 percent of the patients treated acknowledged their feelings of anger when these were explicitly sought (Corbishley et al., 1990).

Frustrations related to persistence of symptoms, limited information on etiology, and repeated treatment failures, along with anger toward employers, the insurance, the healthcare system, family members, and themselves, all contribute to the general dysphoric mood of these patients. The effects of anger and frustration on exacerbation of pain and treatment acceptance have not received much attention. It would be reasonable to expect that the presence of anger may serve as a complicating factor, increasing autonomic arousal and blocking motivation and the acceptance of treatments oriented toward rehabilitation and disability management rather than cure, which are often the only treatments available for chronic pain (Fernandez and Turk, 1995).

It is important to be aware of the influence of negative mood in chronic pain patients because it is likely to affect treatment motivation and compliance with treatment recommendations. For example, the patient who is anxious may fear engaging in what they perceive as physically demanding activities; patients who are depressed and who feel helpless may have little initiative to comply; and patients who are angry with the healthcare system are not likely to be motivated to respond to recommendations from yet another healthcare professional.

Cognitive Factors

A great deal of research has been directed toward identifying cognitive factors that contribute to pain and disability. These studies have consistently demonstrated that patients' attitudes, beliefs, and expectancies about their plight, themselves, their coping resources, and the healthcare system affect reports of pain, activity, disability, and response to treatment.

Beliefs About Pain

People respond to medical conditions based partly on their subjective ideas about illness and their symptoms. Healthcare providers working with chronic pain patients are aware that those having similar pain histories and reports of pain may differ greatly in their beliefs about their pain. Behavior and emotions are influenced by interpretations of events, rather than solely by objective characteristics of the event itself. Thus pain, when interpreted as signifying ongoing tissue damage or a progressive disease, is likely to produce considerably more suffering and emotional distress than if it is viewed as being the result of a stable problem that is expected to improve.

People build elaborate views of their physical state, and these views provide the basis for action plans and coping. Beliefs about the meaning of pain and one's ability to function despite discomfort are important aspects of expectations about pain. For example, a belief that one has a very serious condition, that disability is a necessary aspect of pain, that activity is dangerous, and that pain is an acceptable excuse for neglecting responsibilities will likely result in more disability (Turk et al., 1996b). Similarly, if patients believe they have a serious condition that is quite fragile and a high risk for reinjury, they may fear engaging in physical activities. Through a process of stimulus generalization patients may avoid more and more activities, thus becoming more disabled.

Consider the case of a man who wakes up one morning with backache. Very different responses would occur if he attributed the backache to muscular strain from overdoing it when playing tennis the previous day, rather than interpreting the pain as signaling a herniated disc and his friend had a similar problem that required surgery and whose postoperative recovery was poor. If the interpretation was that the back pain was related to overexercise, there might be little emotional arousal and he might take some over-the-counter analgesics, a hot shower, and take it easy for a few days. On the other hand, interpretation of the back pain as indicating a herniated disc would likely generate significant worry and might result in a call to an orthopedist. Thus, although the amount of nociceptive input in both cases may be equivalent, the emotional and behavioral responses would vary.

Certain beliefs may lead to maladaptive coping, increased suffering, and greater disability. Patients who believe their pain is likely to persist may be passive in their coping efforts and fail to make use of self-management strategies. Those who consider their pain to be an unexplainable mystery may negatively evaluate their own abilities to control it, and are less likely to rate their coping strategies as effective.

Chronic pain patients demonstrate poor behavioral persistence in physical tasks. Their performance may be independent of physical exertion, but rather be related to *previous* pain associated with the task. Patients appear to have a negative view of their abilities and expect increased pain if they perform physical exercises. Thus the rationale for avoiding exercise is not the *presence* of pain itself, but the *learned expectation* of heightened pain and accompanying physical arousal that might exacerbate pain, thereby reinforcing patients' beliefs about the pervasiveness of their disability. If patients view disability as a necessary and appropriate reaction to their pain, and think that activity is dangerous, and that pain is an acceptable excuse for neglecting their responsibilities, they are likely to experience greater disability. Patients' negative perceptions of their capabilities for physical performance form a vicious circle, with the failure to perform activities reinforcing the perception of helplessness and incapacity.

Once beliefs and expectations about a disease are formed, they become stable and resistant to change. Patients tend to avoid experiences that could invalidate their beliefs and which guide their behavior in accordance with those beliefs, even in situations where the belief is no longer valid or helpful. Consequently, they do not receive corrective feedback. For example, a chronic pain patient who is out of condition may experience some muscular soreness following activity. Although the soreness does not imply further tissue damage, it nevertheless confirms the belief that he should avoid the activity, so perpetuating the vicious circle. Similarly, beliefs about pain appear to be important in understanding response to treatment, adherence to self-management activities, and disability. When rehabilitation is successful there appears to be an important cognitive shift from beliefs about helplessness and passivity to resourcefulness and an ability to function regardless of pain.

Clearly, it appears essential for patients with chronic pain to develop adaptive beliefs about the relationships between impairment, pain, suffering, and disability, and to de-emphasize the role of pain in their regulation of functioning. In fact, results from numerous outcome studies (cf. Flor et al., 1992) have shown that changes in pain level do not parallel changes in other variables of interest, including activity level, medication use, return to work, rated ability to cope with pain, and the pursuit of further treatment.

Self-Efficacy

A self-efficacy expectation is defined as a personal conviction that one can successfully execute a course of action (perform required behaviors) to produce a desired outcome in a given situation. Self-efficacy has been shown to be a major mediator of therapeutic change. Given sufficient motivation to engage in a behavior, it is a person's self-efficacy beliefs that determine the choice of activities that he or she will initiate, the amount of effort that will be expended, and how long the person will persist in the face of obstacles and aversive experiences. Efficacy judgments are based on four sources of information regarding one's capabilities, listed in descending order of effects; 1) past performance at the task or similar tasks; 2) the performance accomplishments of others who are perceived to be similar to oneself; 3) verbal persuasion by others, and 4) perception of physiological arousal, which is in turn determined partly by prior efficacy estimation.

Encouraging patients to undertake tasks that are attainable, raising the level of difficulty, and subsequently approaching the desired level of performance, can foster a sense of mastery. In a quota-based physical therapy system, the initial goal is set below baseline performance in order to increase mastery. It is important to remember that coping behaviors are influenced by the person's beliefs that the demands of a situation do not exceed their coping resources. For example, Council et al. (1988) asked patients to rate their self-efficacy as well as their expectation of pain related to performance during movement tasks. Patients' performance levels were highly related to their self-efficacy expectations, which in turn appeared to be determined by their expectations regarding the levels of pain that would be experienced.

Catastrophic Thinking

Catastrophizing – experiencing extremely negative thoughts about one's plight and interpreting even minor problems as catastrophes – appears to be a particularly potent way of thinking that influences pain and disability. Several lines of research indicate that catastrophizing and adaptive coping strategies are important in determining reactions to pain. People who spontaneously used more catastrophizing thoughts reported more pain than those who did not. We (Turk et al., 1983) concluded that "what appears to distinguish low from high pain tolerant individuals is their cognitive processing, catastrophizing thoughts and feelings that precede, accompany, and follow aversive stimulation. . . ." (p. 197).

Coping

Self-regulation of pain and its effects depends on the person's specific ways of dealing with pain, adjusting to pain, and reducing or minimizing pain and the distress caused by it – in other words, their coping strategies. Coping can be assessed in terms of overt and covert behaviors. Overt, behavioral coping strategies include rest, medication, and relaxation. Covert coping strategies include various means of distracting oneself from pain, reassuring oneself that the pain will diminish, and problem solving. Coping strategies are thought to act to alter both the perception of pain and one's ability to manage or tolerate pain and to continue everyday activities.

Investigators report that active coping strategies (efforts to function and maintain activity in spite of pain, or to distract oneself from or ignore pain) are associated with adaptive functioning, and passive coping strategies (depending on others for help in pain control and restricted activities) are related to greater pain and depression. However, beyond this there is no evidence to support the greater effectiveness of any one active coping strategy over any other (Fernandez and Turk, 1989). It seems more likely that different strategies will be more effective than others for some people at some times, but not necessarily for all people all of the time.

An integrative model of chronic and acute–recurrent pain needs to incorporate the mutual interrelationships between physical, psychosocial, and behavioral factors and the changes that occur among these over time. A model that focuses on only one of these sets of factors will inevitably be incomplete.

Integrative Models

Based on our discussion of the psychological factors that have been implicated as playing a role in pain, we now consider how these factors can be integrated within comprehensive models of pain. The two most widely discussed multi-dimensional models are the gate control theory and the biopsychosocial model. These models are not competing but are actually complementary.

Gate Control Theory

The first attempt to develop an integrative model designed to address the problems created by unidimensional models and to integrate physiological and psychological factors was the gate control theory (GCT) proposed by Melzack and Wall (1965). Perhaps the most important contribution of the GCT is the way it changed thinking about pain perception. In this model, three systems are postulated as being related to the processing of nociceptive stimulation: sensory–discriminative, motivational–affective, and cognitive–evaluative, all thought to contribute to the subjective experience of pain. Thus, the GCT specifically includes psychological factors as an integral aspect of the pain experience. It emphasizes CNS mechanisms and provides a physiological basis for the role of psychological factors in chronic pain.

Melzack and Wall (1965) postulated further that the spinal gating mechanism is influenced not only by peripheral afferent activity, but also by efferent neural impulses that descend from the brain. From the GCT perspective the experience of pain is an ongoing sequence of activities, largely reflexive in nature at the outset, but modifiable even in the earliest stages by a variety of excitatory and inhibitory influences, and by the integration of ascending and descending nervous system activity. The process results in overt expressions communicating pain, and strategies by the person to terminate the pain. In addition, considerable potential for shaping of the pain experience is implied because the GCT invokes continuous interaction of multiple systems (sensory–physiological, affect, cognition).

The GCT describes the integration of peripheral stimuli with affect and cognition, in the perception of pain. This model contradicts the notion that pain is either somatic or psychogenic, and instead postulates that both factors have either potentiating or moderating effects on pain perception. In this model, for example, pain is not understood to be the result of depression or vice versa, but rather the two are seen as evolving simultaneously.

The GCT's emphasis on the modulation of inputs in the dorsal horns and the dynamic role of the brain in pain processes and perception resulted in the integration of psychological variables such as past experience, attention, and other cognitive activities into current research and therapy on pain. Prior to this formulation, psychological processes were largely dismissed as reactions to pain. This new model suggested that cutting nerves and pathways was inadequate because a host of other factors modulated the input. Perhaps the major contribution of the GCT was that it highlighted the CNS as an essential component in pain processes and perception.

The GCT provides a powerful summary of the phenomena observed in the spinal cord and brain, and has the capacity to explain many of the most mysterious and puzzling problems encountered in the clinic. This theory has had enormous heuristic value in stimulating further research in the basic science of pain mechanisms, as well as in spurring the development and use of new clinical treatments (e.g., neural stimulation techniques, pharmacological advances, interventions targeting modification of attentional and perceptual processes involved in the pain experience). After the GCT, no one could try to explain pain exclusively in terms of peripheral factors.

Biopsychosocial Model of Chronic Pain

Although the GCT provides a conceptual basis for the role of psychological factors in pain, it does not address the nature of the interaction in depth. Unlike the unidimensional biomedical perspective, which focuses on etiological and pathophysiological explanations for chronic pain, or the psychogenic view, which suggests pain to be a physical manifestation of psychological difficulties, the biopsychosocial view provides an integrated model that incorporates purely mechanical and physiologic processes as well as psychological and social contextual variables that may cause and perpetuate chronic pain. In contrast to the biomedical model's emphasis on the disease process, the biopsychosocial model views illness as a dynamic and reciprocal interaction between biological, psychological, and sociocultural variables that shapes the person's response to pain (Turk, 1996; Turk and Flor, 1999). The biological substrate of a disease is known to affect psychological factors (e.g., mood) and the social context within which the person exists (e.g., interpersonal relationships).

Our biopsychosocial model presumes some form of physical pathology, or at least physical changes in the muscles, joints, or nerves that generate nociceptive input to the brain. Perception involves the interpretation of nociceptive input and identifies the type of pain (i.e., sharp, burning, punishing). Appraisal involves the meaning that is attributed to the pain, and influences subsequent behaviors. The person may choose to ignore the pain and continue working, walking, socializing, and engaging in previous levels of activity, or may choose to leave work, refrain from all activity, and assume the sick role. In turn, this interpersonal role is shaped by responses from significant others that may promote either the healthy and active response or the sick role. The biopsychosocial model has been instrumental in the development of cognitive–behavioral treatment approaches for chronic pain.

Cognitive–Behavioral Model for the Treatment of Chronic Pain

The cognitive–behavioral (C–B) model has become the most commonly accepted and clinically useful conceptualization of chronic pain because it appears to have heuristic value in explaining the experience of and response to chronic pain. The C–B perspective suggests that behaviors and emotions are influenced by interpretations of events, rather than solely by the objective characteristics of an event itself. Rather than focusing on the contribution of cognitive and emotional factors to the perception of a set of symptoms in a static fashion, or exclusively on behavioral responses and environmental reinforcement contingencies, emphasis is placed on the ongoing reciprocal relationships between physical, cognitive, affective, social, and behavioral factors.

The C–B model incorporates many of the psychological variables described above, namely, anticipation, avoidance, and contingencies of reinforcement, but suggests that cognitive factors, and in particular expectations, are of central importance. The model asserts that conditioned reactions are largely self-activated on the basis of learned expectations, rather than automatically evoked. The critical factor for the C–B model, therefore, is not that events occur together in time, but that people learn to predict them and to summon appropriate reactions. It is the patient's processing of information that results in anticipatory anxiety and avoidance behaviors. According to the C–B model, it is patients' perspectives based on their idiosyncratic attitudes, beliefs, and unique representations that filter and interact reciprocally with emotional factors, social influences, behavioral responses, and sensory phenomena. Moreover, patients' behaviors elicit responses from significant others that can reinforce both adaptive and maladaptive modes of thinking, feeling, and behaving. Thus a reciprocal and synergistic model is proposed.

Assumptions of Cognitive–Behavioral Treatment

There are five central assumptions that characterize the C–B perspective. The first is that all people are active processors of information rather than passive reactors to environmental contingencies. People attempt to make sense of the stimuli from the external environment by filtering information through organizing attitudes derived from their prior learning histories, and by general strategies that guide the processing of information. People's responses (overt as well as covert) are based on these appraisals and subsequent expectations, and are not totally dependent on the actual consequences of their behaviors (i.e., positive and negative reinforcements and punishments). From this perspective, the *anticipated* consequences are as important in guiding behavior as are the actual consequences.

A second assumption is that thoughts (for example, appraisals, attributions, expectations) can elicit or modulate affect and physiological arousal, both of which may serve as impetuses for behavior. Conversely, affect, physiology, and behavior can instigate or influence one's thinking processes. Thus the causal priority depends on where in the cycle one chooses to begin. Causal priority may be less of a concern than the view of an interactive process that extends over time with the interaction of thoughts, feelings, physiological activity, and behavior.

Unlike the more behavioral models, which emphasize the influence of the environment on behavior, the C–B perspective focuses on the reciprocal effects of the person on the environment, as well as the influence of environment on behavior. The third assumption of the C–B perspective, therefore, is that behavior is reciprocally determined by both the environment and the individual. People not only passively respond to their environment, but also elicit environmental responses by their behavior. In a very real sense, people create their environments. The patient who becomes aware of a physical event (symptoms) and decides that the symptoms require attention from a healthcare provider initiates a set of circumstances different from those initiated by the individual with the same symptoms who chooses to self-medicate.

A fourth assumption is that if people have learned maladaptive ways of thinking, feeling, and responding, then successful interventions designed to alter behavior should focus on these, and not on one to the exclusion of the others. There is no expectation that changing only thoughts, or feelings, or behaviors will necessarily result in changes in the others.

The final assumption of the C–B perspective is that, in the same way as people are instrumental in the development and maintenance of maladaptive thoughts, feelings, and behaviors, they can become active agents of change to these modes of responding. Patients with chronic pain, no matter how severe, despite their common beliefs to the contrary, are not helpless pawns of fate. They can and should become instrumental in learning and carrying out more effective modes of responding to their environment and their plight.

From the C–B model, people with pain are viewed as having negative expectations about their own ability to control certain motor skills without pain. Moreover, pain patients tend to believe that their ability to exert any control over their pain is limited. Such negative, maladaptive appraisals about the situation and personal efficacy may reinforce the experience of demoralization, inactivity, and overreaction to nociceptive stimulation. These cognitive appraisals and expectations are postulated as having an effect on behavior leading to reduced efforts and activity, which may contribute to increased psychological distress (helplessness) and subsequent physical limitations. If one accepts that pain is a complex, subjective phenomenon that is experienced uniquely by each person, then knowledge about idiosyncratic beliefs, appraisals, and coping repertoires becomes critical for optimal treatment planning and for accurately evaluating treatment outcome.

Biomedical factors that may have initiated the original report of pain play less of a diminishing role in disability over time, although secondary problems associated with deconditioning may exacerbate and maintain the problem. Inactivity leads to increased focus on and preoccupation with the body and pain, and these cognitive–attentional changes increase the likelihood of misinterpreting symptoms, overemphasizing symptoms, and of perceiving oneself as being disabled. Reduction of activity, fear of reinjury, pain, loss of compensation, and an environment that, perhaps, unwittingly supports the *pain-patient role*, can impede the alleviation of pain, successful rehabilitation, reduction of disability, and improvement in adjustment. As has been noted, cognitive factors may not only affect the patient's behavior and indirectly their pain, but may actually have a direct effect on physiological factors believed to be associated with the experience of pain.

Patients' beliefs, appraisals, and expectations about pain, their ability to cope, social supports, their disorder, the medicolegal system, and their employers are all important because they may facilitate or disrupt the patient's sense of control. These factors also influence patients' investment in treatment, acceptance of responsibility, perceptions of disability, adherence to treatment recommendations, support from significant others, expectations for treatment, and acceptance of treatment rationale.

Interpretations affect how patients display symptoms to significant others, including healthcare providers. Overt communication of pain and suffering will enlist responses that may reinforce the pain behaviors and impressions about the seriousness and severity of the pain. That is, complaints of pain may lead a physician to prescribe potent medications, order additional diagnostic tests, and in some cases perform surgery (Turk and Okifuji, 1997). Family members may express sympathy, excuse the patient from their usual responsibilities, and encourage passivity, thereby further fostering physical deconditioning (Turk et al., 1992). Here we can see how the C–B perspective integrates the operant emphasis on external reinforcement and respondent view of learned avoidance with information processing.

The C–B perspective on pain management focuses on providing the patient with techniques to gain a sense of control over the effects of pain on his or her life, as well as actually modifying the affective, behavioral, cognitive, and sensory facets of the experience. Behavioral experiences help to show patients that they are capable of more than they assumed, thereby increasing their sense of personal competence. Techniques (e.g., self-monitoring to identify relationships between thoughts, mood, and behavior; distraction using imagery; and problem solving) help to place affective, behavioral, cognitive, and sensory responses under the patient's control.

The assumption is that behavioral changes will be maintained long term only if the patient has learned to attribute success to his or her own efforts. There are suggestions that these treatments can result in changes of beliefs about pain, coping style, and reported pain severity, as well as direct behavior changes. Further treatment that results in increases in perceived control over pain and decreased catastrophizing also are associated with reductions in pain severity ratings and functional disability.

From the C–B perspective, assessment and treatment of the patient with persistent pain requires a broader strategy than those based on dichotomous models. Furthermore, the phenomenology of each person's experience and expectations makes this approach somewhat more versatile in addressing the patient's needs. Investigators have begun to realize that treatments for chronic pain have neglected individual differences among patients, thereby compromising the efficacy of various treatment approaches.

Homogeneity vs. Heterogeneity of Pain Populations

There are a number of chronic pain syndromes, such as low back pain, fibromyalgia syndrome (FMS), and temporomandibular disorders (TMD) that are very prevalent but for which the diagnostic criteria are quite vague. These syndromes create a great deal of distress and disability, yet despite their prevalence, the etiology and pathophysiology are elusive. No pathophysiological mechanisms have been identified – but not for lack of trying.

Our limited understanding of causal mechanisms has not interfered with attempts to treat patients with these diagnoses with a diversity of interventions. The results appear consistent: about one-third of patients derive some benefit from each treatment, no matter how varied.

Prescribing treatment based on diagnoses is logical when there is a known etiology, but this approach has no basis when the cause(s) is unknown. When there is no consensus regarding what treatment should be prescribed the choice becomes empiric, delivered on a trial-and-error basis. This may help explain why so many treatments have been tried but with such discouraging outcomes.

Available data suggest that greater attention should be paid to identifying the characteristics of patients who improve and those who do not. Treatment should be prescribed only for those who are likely to derive significant benefit. The ability to identify the characteristics of patients who do not benefit from specific treatment should facilitate the development of innovative treatment approaches tailored to the needs of those who do not benefit from existing programs. The development of individualized treatments matched to patient characteristics should improve outcome and reduce costs.

Identification of Subgroups of Patients

In order to counter the pain-patient homogeneity assumption and the use of group means, several investigators have suggested the need to identify subgroups of patients based on specific characteristics. Attempts have been made to do this within broad diagnostic classifications based on physical signs and symptoms (e.g., Dworkin and LeResche, 1992). A number of studies have also focused on empirically identifying patient subgroups based on psychological characteristics and psychopathology. Investigators have assumed that important patient differences will be associated with psychological distress and personality features (e.g., Minnesota Multiphasic Personality Inventory (MMPI): Bradley et al., 1978; Symptom Checklist – 90R: Jamison et al., 1988). Although patient subgroups have been identified, few attempts have been made to evaluate the differential efficacy of treatments customized specifically to patient characteristics. The studies reported have used retrospective methods, rather than looking prospectively at differential responses to the same treatment.

On the basis of retrospective studies, McGill et al. (1983) and Moore et al. (1986) have speculated that different patients may benefit from different components of a comprehensive multidisciplinary program. That is, because the usual pain clinic treatment is not individualized, differential effects could be washed out as each patient finds some aspect of the program to be helpful. For example, McGill et al. suggested that subgroups distinguished by elevations on the MMPI neurotic triad scales might best respond to a treatment program of respondent conditioning and antidepressant medication, whereas subgroups with elevations on the relatively psychotic, as well as neurotic, scales would benefit from an individualized reinforcement program and antipsychotic medication. Furthermore, they speculate that those patients who produce MMPI scale scores within one standard deviation of the mean "would be most likely to respond to traditional management, or to an operant program designed to identify and reinforce positive coping styles" (p. 91).

In considering the failure to find subgroups predictive of treatment success, Guck et al. (1988) offer the alternative proposal, that despite clear initial differences on the MMPI, all patients received comparable benefits from the same components of the program. That is, the treatment has nonspecific effects. Perhaps an equally plausible interpretation of the results is that subgroups based on general personality characteristics are not useful for identifying a specific response to treatment. At this point, each of these explanations must be viewed as only suggestive, as only a handful of studies have directly examined the speculations.

The delineation of homogeneous subgroups of pain patients would provide a framework for the development of specific, optimal treatment regimens for specific subgroups, when treatment can be matched to assessment or relevant variable areas (a) that are reasonably distinct and not consistently correlated; (b) when valid measures of these response classes are available; and (c) when treatments that affect these response classes are available.

Up to this point, the attempts to identify subgroups of chronic pain patients reviewed have focused on single factors such as symptoms, demographics, psychopathology, idiosyncratic thinking patterns, and behavioral expression. Outcomes, however, are likely to be determined by the interactive effects of multiple factors, as single factors may not account for a statistically significant or clinically meaningful proportion of the variance. Several studies that included measures of both physical and psychological functioning have reported interactive effects of biopsychosocial factors on the outcome of pain patients (Frymoyer et al., 1985; Reesor and Craig, 1988).

Empirically Derived Classification of Pain Patients

Using the West Haven–Yale Multidimensional Pain Inventory (MPI; Kerns et al., 1985), we (Turk and Rudy, 1988) were able to group patients within three relatively homogeneous sets. The MPI consists of a set of empirically derived scales designed to assess chronic pain patients' (a) reports of pain severity and suffering; (b) perceptions of how pain interferes with their lives, including interference with family and marital functioning, work, and social and recreational activities; (c) dissatisfaction with present levels of functioning in family, marriage, work, and social life; (d) appraisals of support received from significant others; (e) perceived life control, incorporating perceived ability to solve problems and feelings of personal mastery and competence; (f) affective distress, including depressed mood, irritability, and tension; and (g) activity levels.

Table 8.3 Percentage distributions of the MPI profiles in various pain disorders (*n*)

MPI profiles	FMS (91)	CLBP (200)	H (245)	TMD (200)
DYS	26	62	44	46
ID	39	18	26	22
AC	35	20	30	32

We (Turk and Rudy, 1988) performed cluster analyses on a heterogeneous sample of chronic pain patients' responses on the MPI scales. Three distinct profiles were identified: (1) "dysfunctional (DYS)," i.e., patients who perceived the severity of their pain to be high, reported that pain interfered with much of their lives, reported a higher degree of psychological distress due to pain, and reported low levels of activity; (2) "interpersonally distressed (ID)," i.e., patients with a common perception that significant others were not very supportive of their pain problems; and (3) "adaptive copers (AC)," i.e., patients who reported high levels of social support, relatively low levels of pain and perceived interference, and relatively high levels of activity. This classification system has been replicated in several studies conducted in Finland (Talo et al., 1992), the Netherlands (Lousberg et al., 1997), and in a large, multicentered study in the United States (Jamison et al., 1994).

Robustness of the MPI Profiling

We (Turk et al., 1996a; Turk and Rudy, 1990) examined the generalizability of the MPI taxonomy with different pain syndromes, specifically, chronic low back pain (CLBP), head pain (H), FMS, and temporomandibular disorders (TMD) (see table 8.3). A higher percentage of CLBP patients were classified as DYS than in the other three patient samples; a greater percentage of TMD, H, and FMS patients than CLBP patients were classified as AC; and no between-group differences were observed for the ID, but the FMS patients did contain a higher percentage of ID patients than the other three groups. All four syndrome groups, however, were represented in each of the subgroups. Thus, it is possible that TMD, H, FMS, and CLBP patients who are classified within the same subgroup may be psychologically more similar to each other than patients with the same diagnosis but who are classified within different subgroups.

We also found (Turk et al., 1998b) similar subgroups in a sample of patients with both metastatic and regional/localized cancer. Although there may be variability in the mean scale scores of the MPI, all three profiles are present in each diagnostic group – those with pain associated with metastatic disease, and those with different cancer-related chronic pain syndromes.

The results suggest that although different physical diagnostic groups may require common biomedical treatment targeting the pathophysiologic mechanisms underlying each disorder, they may also benefit from specific psychosocial interventions tailored to their psychosocial–behavioral characteristics (MPI-based profiles).

Treatment Responses by Psychosocial Subgroups: Illustration Treatment for TMD

Based upon the previous findings of three subgroups of TMD patients described, we (Turk et al., 1993) developed a treatment program specifically tailored to the clinical needs of the DYS patients. TMD patients classified as DYS were randomly assigned to one of two treatment conditions: 1) inter-occlusal appliance (IA), biofeedback-assisted relaxation (BF), and supportive counseling (IA+BF+SC); and 2) IA+BF treatment plus cognitive therapy (CT) for depression (IA+BF+CF). Both groups received six weekly treatment sessions, followed by post-treatment and 6-month follow-up evaluations. Analyses of indices measuring physical, psychosocial, and behavioral changes indicated that both groups displayed significant improvements at the follow-up. Compared to the IA+BF+SC patients, IA+BF+CT patients displayed significantly greater changes, particularly in pain and depression. These results suggest that DYS patients demonstrated and maintained significant improvement on physical, psychosocial, and behavioral measures following treatment that targets problems uniquely related to the DYS profile. Including a specific component tailored to the DYS patients added incrementally to the outcome.

Overall, the treatment may have been effective, but only for a subset of patients. These findings support the clinical utility of the psychosocial–behavioral classification system, and suggest that individualizing treatments based upon patients' adaptation to pain may improve treatment efficacy. Additionally, these findings have important methodological implications. That is, combining heterogeneous samples without statistically controlling for subgroup differences may result in nonsignificant findings (Rudy et al., 1995).

Treatment Responses by Psychosocial Subgroup: Treatment for FMS

We also tested the differential treatment response by MPI profiles to the treatment program for FMS. The program consisted of six half-day sessions, spaced over 4 weeks. Each session included medical (education, medication management), physical (aerobic and stretching exercise), occupational (pacing, body mechanics), and psychological (pain and stress management) components (Turk et al., 1998a). Overall, the patients in the DYS group improved in most areas, whereas the ID patients, who reported levels of pain and disability comparable to those of the DYS group, failed to respond to the treatment. There was little change in the AC patients, possibly because of a floor effect. The results further support the need for different treatments targeting characteristics of subgroups, and that suggest that psychosocial characteristics of FMS patients are important predictors of treatment responses and may be used to customize treatment. For example, whereas the ID patients may require additional treatment components addressing clinical needs specific to this group (e.g., interpersonal skills), some components of the standard interdisciplinary treatment may not be essential for the AC patients.

Potential of Customizing Treatment

The results of the studies reviewed above support the presence of different subgroups of pain patients. Consequently, treating them all the same – *patient uniformity myth* – may dilute the ability to demonstrate treatment efficacy. That is, specific interventions may have their greatest utility with particular subgroups of patients. Combining heterogeneous samples in treatment outcome studies without statistically controlling for subgroup differences (e.g., by blocking) may result in nonsignificant or only modest therapeutic gains.

Moreover, failure to customize the treatments might lead to erroneous conclusions regarding treatment efficacy. For example, Moore and Chaney (1985) reported that the addition of spouses to treatment groups did not add to the efficacy of a cognitive–behavioral intervention. However, no effort was made to establish the quality of the marital relationship. We (Flor et al., 1989) reported that operant reinforcement factors were only related to reports of pain and activity levels in those couples for whom the marital relationship was rated as satisfactory or better. Furthermore, we (Turk et al. 1996a; Turk and Rudy, 1988) demonstrated that approximately 25–39 percent of chronic pain patients could be characterized by the perceived lack of support from significant others in their environment. These data raise the question of whether Moore and Chaney would have observed different outcomes had they matched the inclusion of spouses with marital dissatisfaction, or whether different types of spouse involvement, tailored to the patients' marital characteristics, would have led to a different outcome.

Dual-Diagnostic Approach

Several groups (e.g., Dworkin and Le Resche, 1992; Turk, 1990) have proposed the use of a dual-diagnostic approach, whereby two diagnoses – physical and psychosocial–behavioral – are assigned concurrently. Treatment could then be directed toward both simultaneously. A pain patient might have diagnoses on two complementary taxonomies, for example IASP- and MPI-based classifications. The most appropriate treatment for these groups might vary, with different complementary components of treatments addressing the physical diagnosis (IASP) and the psychosocial diagnosis (MPI based).

Adopting the dual-diagnostic approach advocated by us (Turk, 1990) would encourage clinicians as well as researchers to think concurrently in terms of these two different (i.e., biomedical and psychosocial–behavioral) but complementary diagnostic systems. Empirical studies would be needed to evaluate the efficacy of individualized treatments based on the dual-diagnostic approach.

Additional clinical investigations should be conducted to determine the relative utility of different treatments based on the match of treatment to patient characteristics and classification, and to predict which patients are most likely to benefit from what combination of therapeutic modalities. Thus, rather than accepting the pain-patient homogeneity myth, the field might be advanced by asking: "What treatment, by whom, is most effective for [this] individual, with that specific problem, under which set of circumstances?"

Treatments might be provided in a modular fashion, where separate components are woven into an overall treatment regimen based on individual patient characteristics. For example, all back pain patients may require physical therapy and psychological support and encouragement; however, some may need additional modules, such as treatment for depression. The combination of physical therapy and psychological interventions may provide complementary advantages by addressing different symptoms.

It is important to acknowledge that the identification of subgroups, regardless of the method used, does not mean that the resulting classification will incorporate all features of the patients. Subgroups should be viewed as prototypes with significant room for individual variability within the subgroup. Thus, treatments designed to be matched to subgroup characteristics will also need to consider and address unique characteristics of the individual patient. The subgroup customization fits somewhere between the exclusively idiographic approach evaluated by single case treatment designs and the generic "pain-patient homogeneity" approach that has characterized many of the pain treatment outcome studies. At this point, whether treatment tailoring will produce greater effects than providing completely idiographic or generic treatments can only be viewed hypothetically. Until more prospective studies matching treatment to patient characteristics have been conducted, all that can be said is that the matching hypothesis is plausible, albeit intriguing.

Concluding Comments

It has become abundantly clear that no isomorphic relationship exists between tissue damage, nociception, and pain report. Recent multidimensional conceptualizations view pain as a perceptual process resulting from the nociceptive input, which is modulated on a number of different levels in the CNS. In this chapter conceptual models were presented to explain the subjective experience of pain. As was noted, the current state of knowledge suggests that pain must be viewed as a complex phenomenon that incorporates physical, psychosocial, and behavioral factors. Failure to incorporate each of these factors will lead to an incomplete understanding.

The range of psychological variables that have been identified as being of central importance in pain, along with current understanding of the physiological basis of pain, were reviewed. The fact that a significant proportion of chronic pain patients are not successfully treated by current general approaches, and the identification of various subgroups of patients, makes investigation of treatment matching particularly important. The data presented, although preliminary, suggest that there are subgroups of chronic pain patients based on a range of psychosocial and behavioral characteristics and ways of adapting to their chronic disease. Research is needed to identify the necessary and sufficient components of treatment that can be tailored to the psychological, as well as the physiological, characteristics of patients who may have the same diagnosis.

Note

Preparation of this chapter was supported by grants from the National Institute of Child Health and Development (P01 HD33989) and the National Institute of Arthritis and Musculoskeletal and Skin Diseases (R01 AR44724) awarded to the first author and the National Institutes of Health/Shannon Director's Award (RSS AR44230) awarded to the second author.

References

Bradley, L. A., Prokop, C. K., Margolis, R., and Gentry, W. D. (1978). Multivariate analyses of the MMPI profiles of low back pain patients. *Journal of Behavioral Medicine*, 1, 253–272.

Corbishley, M., Hendrickson, R., Beutler L., and Engle, D. (1990). Behavior, affect, and cognition among psychogenic pain patients in group expressive psychotherapy. *Journal of Pain and Symptom Management*, 5, 241–8.

Council, J., Ahern, D., Follick, M., and Kline, C. (1988). Expectancies and functional impairment in chronic low back pain. *Pain*, 33, 323–331.

Deyo, R. A. (1986). Early diagnostic evaluation of low back pain. *Journal of General Internal Medicine*, 1, 328–338.

Dworkin, S. F., and LeResche, L. (1992). Research diagnostic criteria for temporomandibular disorders: Review, criteria, examination and specifications, critique. *Journal of Craniomandibular Disorders*, 6, 301–355.

Fernandez, E., and Turk, D. C. (1989). The utility of cognitive coping strategies for altering pain perception: A meta-analysis. *Pain*, 38, 123–135.

Fernandez, E., and Turk, D. C. (1995). The scope and significance of anger in the experience of chronic pain. *Pain*, 61, 165–175.

Flor, H., Fydrich, T., and Turk, D. C. (1992). Efficacy of multidisciplinary pain treatment centers: A meta-analytic review. *Pain*, 49, 221–230.

Flor, H., Turk, D. C., and Rudy, T. E. (1989). Relationship of pain impact and significant other reinforcement of pain behaviors: The mediating role of gender, marital status and marital satisfaction. *Pain*, 38, 45–50.

Fordyce, W. E. (1976). *Behavioral Methods in Chronic Pain and Illness*. St. Louis: CV Mosby.

Frymoyer, J. W., Rosen, J. C., Clements, J., and Pope, M. H. (1985). Psychologic factors in low back pain disability. *Clinical Orthopedics*, 195, 178–184.

Gatchel, R. J., and Turk, D. C. (Eds.) (1999). *Psychosocial Factors in Pain: Critical Perspectives*. New York: Guilford.

Guck, T. P., Meilman, P. W., Skultety, F. M., and Poloni, L. D. (1988). Pain-patient Minnesota Multiphasic Personality Inventory (MMPI) subgroups: Evaluation of long-term treatment outcome. *Journal of Behavioral Medicine*, 11, 159–169.

Jamison, R. N., Rock, D. L., and Parris, W. C. V. (1988). Empirically derived Symptom Checklist-90 subgroups of chronic pain patients: A cluster analysis. *Journal of Behavioral Medicine*, 11, 147–158.

Jamison, R. N., Rudy, T. E., Penzien, D. B., and Mosley, T. H. (1994). Cognitive–behavioral classifications of chronic pain: Replication and extension of empirically derived patient profiles. *Pain*, 57, 277–292.

Jensen, M., Brant-Zawadzki, M., Obuchowski, N., Modic, M. T., Malkasian, D., and Ross, J. S. (1994). Magnetic resonance imaging of the lumbar spine in people without back pain. *New England Journal of Medicine*, 331, 69–73.

Kerns, R., Rosenberg, R., and Jacob, M. (1994). Anger expression and chronic pain. *Journal of Behavioral Medicine*, 17, 57–67.

Kerns, R. D., Turk, D. C., and Rudy, T. E. (1985). The West Haven–Yale Multidimensional Pain Inventory (WHYMPI). *Pain*, 23, 345–356.

Lousberg, R., Schmidt, A. J., Groenman, N. H., Vendrig, L., and Dijkman-Caes, C. I. (1997). Validating the MPI-DLV using experience sampling data. *Journal of Behavioral Medicine*, 20, 195–206.

McGill, J. C., Lawlis, G. F., Selby, D., Mooney, V., and McCoy, C. E. (1983). The relationship of Minnesota Multiphasic Personality Inventory (MMPI) profile cluster to pain behaviors. *Journal of Behavioral Medicine*, 6, 77–92.

Melzack, R., and Wall, P. (1965). Pain mechanisms: A new theory. *Science*, 150, 971–979.

Merskey, H. (1986). Classification of chronic pain. Descriptions of chronic pain syndromes and definitions. *Pain*, Suppl 4, S1–S225.

Moore, J. E., Armentrout, D. P., Parker, J. C., and Kivlahan, D. R. (1986). Empirically derived pain-patients MMPI subgroups: prediction of treatment outcome. *Journal of Behavioral Medicine*, 9, 51–63.

Moore, J. E., and Chaney, E. F. (1985). Outpatient group treatment of chronic pain: Effects of spouse involvement. *Journal of Consulting and Clinical Psychology*, 53, 326–334.

Okifuji, A., Turk, D. C., and Curran, S. L. (1999). Anger in chronic pain: Investigation of anger targets and intensity. *Journal of Psychosomatic Research*, 61, 771–780.

Okifuji, A., Turk, D. C., and Sherman, J. J. (2000). Evaluation of the relationship between depression and fibromyalgia syndrome: Why aren't all patients depressed? *Journal of Rheumatology*, 27, 212–219.

Pilowsky, I., and Spence, N. (1976). Pain, anger, and illness behaviour. *Journal of Psychosomatic Research*, 20, 411–416.

Richard, K. (1988). The occurrence of maladaptive health-related behaviors and teacher-related conduct problems in children of chronic low back pain patients. *Journal of Behavioral Medicine*, 11, 107–116.

Romano, J. M., and Turner, J. A. (1985). Chronic pain and depression: does the evidence support a relationship? *Psychological Bulletin*, 97, 18–34.

Reesor, K. A., and Craig, K. (1988). Medically incongruent chronic back pain: physical limitations, suffering and ineffective coping. *Pain*, 32, 35–45.

Rudy, T. E., Turk, D. C., Kubinski, J. A., and Zaki, H. S. (1995). Differential treatment responses of TMD patients as a function of psychological characteristics. *Pain*, 61, 103–112.

Rudy, T. E., Turk, D. C., Zaki, H. S., and Curtin, H. D. (1989). An empirical taxometric alternative to traditional classification of temporomandibular disorders. *Pain*, 36, 311–320.

Schwartz, L., Slater, M., Birchler, G., and Atkinson, J. (1991). Depression in spouses of chronic pain patients: The role of patient pain and anger, and marital satisfaction. *Pain*, 44, 61–67.

Summers, J. D., Rapoff, M. A., Varghese, G., Porter, K., and Palmer, R. E. (1991). Psychosocial factors in chronic spinal cord injury. *Pain*, 47, 183–189.

Sullivan, M. D., and Turk, D. C. (2001). Psychiatric disorders and psychogenic pain. In J. D. Loeser, S. N. Butler, C. R. Chapman, and D. C. Turk (Eds.), *Bonica's Management of Pain* (3rd ed., pp. 483–500). Philadelphia: Lippincott, Williams and Wilkins.

Talo, S., Rytokoski, U., and Puukka, P. (1992). Patient classification, a key to evaluate pain treatment: A psychological study in chronic low back pain patients. *Spine*, 17, 998–1011.

Turk, D. C. (1990). Customizing treatments for chronic pain patients: Who, what, and why. *Clinical Journal of Pain*, 6, 255–270.

Turk, D. C. (1996). Biopsychosocial perspective on chronic pain. In R. J. Gatchel and D. C. Turk (Eds.), *Psychological Approaches to Pain Management: A Practitioner's Handbook* (pp. 3–32). New York: Guilford.

Turk, D. C., and Flor, H. (1999). Chronic pain: A biobehavioral perspective. In R. J. Gatchel and D. C. Turk (Eds.), *Psychosocial Factors in Pain* (pp. 18–34). New York: Guilford.

Turk, D. C., Kerns, R. D., and Rosenberg, R. (1992). Effects of marital interaction on chronic pain and disability: Examining the down-side of social support. *Rehabilitation Psychology*, 37, 357–372.

Turk, D. C., Meichenbaum, D., and Genest, M. (1983). *Pain and Behavioral Medicine: A Cognitive–Behavioral Perspective*. New York, Guilford.

Turk, D. C., and Okifuji, A. (1997). What factors affect physicians' decisions to prescribe opioids for chronic non-cancer pain patients? *Clinical Journal of Pain*, 13, 330–336.

Turk, D. C., Okifuji, A., Sinclair, J. D., and Starz, T. W. (1996a). Pain, disability, and physical functioning in subgroups of fibromyalgia patients. *Journal of Rheumatology*, 23, 1255–1262.

Turk, D. C., Okifuji, A., and Scharff, L. (1995). Chronic pain and depression: Role of perceived impact and perceived control in different age cohorts. *Pain*, 61, 93–102.

Turk, D. C., Okifuji, A., Sinclair, J. D., and Starz, T. W. (1998a). Interdisciplinary treatment for fibromyalgia syndrome: Clinical and statistical significance. *Arthritis Care and Research*, 11, 397–404.

Turk, D. C., Okifuji, A., Starz, T. W, and Sinclair, J. D. (1996b). Effects of type of symptom onset on psychological distress and disability in fibromyalgia syndrome patients. *Pain*, 68, 423–430.

Turk, D. C., and Rudy, T. E. (1988). Toward an empirically derived taxonomy of chronic pain patients: integration of psychological assessment data. *Journal of Consulting and Clinical Psychology*, 56, 233–238.

Turk, D. C., and Rudy, T. E. (1990). The robustness of an empirically derived taxonomy of chronic pain patients. *Pain*, 42, 27–35.

Turk, D. C., Sist, T. C., Okifuji, A., Miner, M. F., Florio, G., Harrison, P., Massey, J., Lema, M. L., and Zevon M. A. (1998b). Adaptation to metastatic cancer pain, regional/local cancer pain, and non-cancer pain: Role of psychological and behavioral factors. *Pain*, 74, 247–256.

Turk, D. C., Zaki, H. S., and Rudy, T. E. (1993). Effects of intraoral appliance and biofeedback/stress management alone and in combination in treating pain and depression in TMD patients. *Journal of Prosthetic Dentistry*, 70, 158–164.

Vlaeyan, J. W. S., Kole-Snijders, A. M. J., Boeren, R. G. B., and van Eek, H. (1995). Fear of movement/(re)injury in chronic low back pain and its relation to behavioral performance. *Pain*, 62, 363–372.

CHAPTER 9

HIV and AIDS

Michael H. Antoni

University of Miami

Introduction

The human immunodeficiency virus (HIV) is a retrovirus of the human T-cell leukemia/lymphoma line and is believed to be the primary cause of the acquired immunodeficiency syndrome (AIDS). A diagnosis of AIDS is made when a person shows laboratory-based signs of a severe decline in the number of T-helper/inducer (CD4) cells (< 200 cell/mm^3), or clinical signs consistent with the emergence of opportunistic infections and neoplasias. Prior to the development of the current medication "cocktails" also known as highly active antiretroviral therapy (HAART), including protease inhibitors (PI), even people who were aggressively treated often died within a few years of diagnosis (Lemp et al., 1990). By 1996, however, widespread use of HAART was significantly increasing survival time among infected people and had altered the form of HIV infection to that of a chronic disease. Consequently, many of the aspects of chronic disease management could be applied to HIV/AIDS, and many of these involve behavioral medicine.

Many people with primary HIV infection develop an acute mononucleosis-like syndrome about a month after initial infection (Tindall and Cooper, 1991). A period of clinical latency, lasting for a number of years, follows the initial sequence of primary infection, viral dissemination, development of HIV-specific immunity, and curtailment of extensive viral replication. Importantly, during the clinically latent period one still sees an increasing viral load, depletion of CD4 cells in peripheral blood and associated loss of "immune repertoire," and an increasing proportion of HIV-infected lymphoid cells (Pantaleo et al., 1993). The decline in CD4 cells and related immunologic surveillance functions leaves the infected person susceptible to a number of opportunistic infections and cancers characteristic of AIDS. Some of the more commonly observed infections include *Pneumocystic carinii* pneumonia (PCP), cryptococcal meningitis, toxoplasmosis, and candida esophagitis (Kaplan et al., 1987). Many

Correspondence concerning this chapter should be addressed to: Michael H. Antoni, Ph.D., Department of Psychology, P.O. Box 248185, University of Miami, Coral Gables, FL 33124.

other diseases manifest in HIV-infected persons are caused by ubiquitous herpes viruses (e.g., cytomegalovirus (CMV)-associated retinitis is a major cause of blindness in such patients). HIV-infected persons are also vulnerable to relatively rare cancers, including Kaposi's sarcoma and Burkitt's lymphoma, and, in women, cervical carcinoma. Interestingly, these cancers are believed to be promoted by fairly common viruses as well (e.g., human papillomavirus types are associated with cervical neoplasia and squamous cell cervical carcinoma; Maiman and Fruchter, 1996). In all, HIV-infected persons are extremely vulnerable to a wide range of pathogens normally controlled by the immune system, and, over the course of the infection, may contract a number of life-threatening diseases.

Because there is no cure for AIDS, prevention is the major tool for limiting its spread. *Primary prevention* efforts use many behavioral change techniques aimed at increasing the availability and use of condoms, and changing high-risk substance use (e.g., injection drugs) (Schneiderman et al., 1992). Many of these techniques are those that are commonly employed by behavioral medicine experts working in the area of risk management. *Secondary and tertiary prevention* programs have also been undertaken to slow HIV disease progression in people who have already become infected (e.g., chronic disease management). These also find behavioral medicine specialists in a central role. Because only a relatively small proportion of the people in the United States infected with HIV have AIDS (CDC, 2000), and because of the relatively prolonged period of time between the onset of infection and the development of AIDS – now extended by the widespread use of HAART – there is a clear need to develop treatments to manage HIV spectrum disease and slow disease progression. Much of this chapter will focus on such secondary and tertiary prevention activities.

Behavioral Medicine and HIV Infection

Central to the application of behavioral medicine principles is the idea that managing HIV disease involves addressing psychosocial as well as biomedical issues (Antoni et al., 1990). The anticipation and the impact of HIV antibody test notification, for instance, are highly stressful (Ironson et al., 1990). Feelings of life-threat, doom, and anger are usually encountered, and people need to contemplate making major lifestyle changes (Kaisch and Anton-Culver, 1989). There is a clear need to develop behavioral management techniques to help infected persons cope with the psychosocial aspects of their situation. There is also some evidence that improving psychological adaptation to HIV may have implications for physical health (Ironson et al., 1994). Two areas that have been the focus of much behavioral medicine research in HIV infection and AIDS examine how psychosocial factors such as coping and social resources, as well as certain risk behaviors, might contribute to the ways in which people adjust to having the HIV, and to the actual health course of the infection.

Psychological Adjustment to HIV Infection

Behavioral medicine studies focusing on HIV and AIDS began in the early to mid-1980s, concurrent with the identification of HIV as the putative cause of many AIDS-related conditions that were emerging in clinics and hospitals around the world. Behavioral scientists began studying the effects of psychosocial factors such as stressors and stress management interventions, mostly in HIV-infected gay men. A major thrust for this research was to examine the processes underlying psychological adjustment. HIV infection presents multiple challenges that can create a state of *chronic stress*, which may overwhelm an individual's coping resources, and this can significantly impair their ability to adjust emotionally to ongoing and future demands of the illness. It stands to reason that HIV-infected individuals are among those who might benefit substantially from interventions that teach them to cope with these chronic demands. By learning how stress-reducing psychosocial interventions help such people adapt, adjust, and adhere to various lifestyle changes, behavioral medicine specialists gain insight into ways to facilitate the coping process in people facing this life-threatening condition, as well as other chronic diseases. (For a review see Antoni and Schneiderman, 1998.)

Psychosocial Factors and Disease Course

As with other chronic diseases, HIV infection is characterized by a disorder in one or more bodily systems. Here, symptoms are clinically manifest across long periods of time as a function of the degree of immune system impairment. HIV-infected people in fact become ill from the "complications" of their chronic disease, not from the disease itself. One can compare their illness to that of persons with diabetes mellitus. Just as diabetics who are unable to maintain their blood glucose levels within a certain range may develop kidney disease or suffer heart attacks, HIV-infected people who cannot retain adequate immune system functioning go on to develop the life-threatening infections or cancers that characterize the condition known as AIDS. Dysregulated physiologic processes underlying HIV disease may be exacerbated by stressors (Antoni and Schneiderman, 1998). To the extent that HIV infection increases distress levels (Antoni et al., 1990), which in turn have been shown to influence the immune system (Kiecolt-Glaser et al., 1987), it is plausible that behavioral interventions that decrease distress may beneficially influence immune status and possibly health status in HIV-infected people (Antoni et al., 1990).

Psychosocial factors are hypothesized to relate to the immune system via stress- or distress-induced changes in hormonal regulatory systems (Maier et al., 1994). There are several adrenal hormones – including cortisol and catecholamines (norepinephrine and epinephrine) – known to be altered as a function of an individual's appraisals of and coping responses to stressors (McEwen, 1998). These hormones have also been associated with alterations in immune system functions such as lymphocyte proliferation and natural killer cell cytotoxicity (NKCC) (Antoni and Schneiderman, 1998). Some are also known to be dysregulated in depressed or chronically stressed/distressed individuals (Calabrese et al., 1987) and those reporting other psychological states, such as loneliness and social isolation (Kiecolt-Glaser et al., 1984). Uncontrollable stressors and perceived loss of control (both possibly tied to the appraisal of low self-efficacy), and social losses such as divorce and bereavement, have been related to alterations in some of these immunomodulatory hormones. It has been reasoned that the relationships between these phenomena and immune parameters might be mediated, in part, by hormonal changes that are linked to an individual's appraisals of and coping resources for dealing with environmental challenges (for reviews see Antoni and Schneiderman, 1998).

Psychological Challenges in HIV Infection

Some 15 years ago, a diagnosis of HIV seropositivity was viewed as an acute health crisis by medical professionals and as a death sentence by many infected patients. Because more effective antiretroviral medications are now available, there is a fast-growing population of HIV-infected individuals who are coping with the complex and multiple psychosocial demands of what can be more accurately classified as a chronic life-threatening illness. Although gay and bisexual men comprise a majority of HIV-infected individuals in the United States, an increasingly large percentage are heterosexual male drug users and women (Centers for Disease Control, 2000). Each of these populations faces unique social stigmas and challenges, in addition to the direct physical and financial burdens of the HIV infection. We have reasoned that at the initial onset of HIV-related symptoms these individuals may be overwhelmed and socially isolated, and may use maladaptive coping strategies, possibly resulting in an increased likelihood of depression and distress, and negative health behaviors such as high-risk sexual activities, substance use, and poor adherence to medications – all of these potentially associated with a decline in immunologic status, increased HIV viral load, and hastened disease progression (Antoni and Schneiderman, 1998).

Even for those who use adaptive coping strategies and have adequate resources there still remain *critical stressor events* – the emergence of new symptoms, development of resistance to a successful drug regimen, loss of health insurance benefits, deaths of friends, rejection from family members, etc – that can intensify mood disturbances and other distress reactions on the one hand, and promote negative health behaviors on the other. Psychosocial interventions may be capable of reducing the frequency and severity of these reactions and may, in so doing, improve quality of life, reduce immunologic perturbations, and slow the progression of the infection. Obviously, behavioral medicine researchers and practitioners can make a substantial contribution to chronic disease management in HIV-infected individuals by way of identifying the presence of mood disturbances, maladaptive stressor appraisals and coping strategies, and inadequate social resources, and then designing interventions to address these key components of the adjustment process, and health maintenance. *What are some of the key challenges that HIV-infected persons must deal with and which might be modified by these forms of intervention?*

Managing Mood Changes

HIV-infected persons appear to be at somewhat increased risk for DSM-IV-Axis I affective and adjustment disorders, as well as subclinical distress reactions following the initial news of an HIV-seropositive diagnosis (Rabkin et al., 1996). Although adjustment disorder with depressed mood may be the most common presenting complaint, major depressive disorder and suicidal ideation are a concern (Rabkin et al., 1996). Pharmacologic agents such as imipramine and serotonin reuptake inhibitors have been shown to be safe and effective with HIV-infected persons (Rabkin et al., 1996). Psychosocial interventions that provide support, teach coping strategies and offer the opportunity for mastery experiences may also be beneficial, and may constitute an optimal long-term approach. These efforts are likely to be facilitated within a supportive group environment (Antoni and Schneiderman, 1998).

Support for the psychological benefits of a cognitive–behavioral treatment orientation for HIV-infected individuals comes from research with gay men, showing that the ways in which individuals cope cognitively and behaviorally with HIV-related stressors relate to lower levels of depressive symptoms (Rabkin et al., 1990). Whereas the psychosocial sequelae of HIV infection are reasonably well documented for gay and bisexual men, far less is known about what women experience during the course of this disease. Importantly, more than 20 percent of all new AIDS cases are women (CDC, 2000), and HIV-infected women are disproportionately represented among minority populations, especially blacks (Antoni et al., 1992b). These women suffer the triple stigmas of race, class and gender, prior to the additional burden of HIV seropositivity (Quinn, 1993) and multiple chronic daily stressors (Mays and Cochran, 1988). These stressors include drug and alcohol dependency, financial problems, over-burdened public clinics, lack of transportation, and inaccessibility of child care – all potentially fueling a general feeling of helplessness and powerlessness (Quinn, 1993). They may be compounded by pregnancy and related psycho-social challenges, such as the decision to abort or to continue pregnancy to term, or fears of becoming too ill to provide for offspring (Antoni et al., 1992b). If both mother and child are seropositive, the lack of emotional and financial support could make the situation even worse. Thus the risk for significant emotional problems in populations ranging from middle-class gay men to inner-city mothers with HIV is clear.

Making Lifestyle Changes

Despite reductions in sexual risk behaviors among urban gay men over the past 10 years, a significant number continue to engage in unprotected anal intercourse (Martin, 1989), the sexual activity that carries the highest risk for HIV infection in gay men (Kingsley et al., 1987). One important factor influencing sexual risk-taking behavior is the use of alcohol and drugs during sex

(Martin, 1990). Importantly, depressed people may engage in more high-risk sex, and depressive symptoms may be more likely to occur in HIV-infected men and women who are substance abusers, especially those who are injection drug users (IDUs) (Rabkin et al., 1996). Thus, chronic depressive symptoms, substance abuse, and unprotected sexual behaviors may be highly interrelated and self-perpetuating. Conversely, the adoption and maintenance of reduced sexual risk behaviors is facilitated by perceptions of self-efficacy for safe sex, having alternative coping strategies for dealing with high-risk sexual impulses, and possessing interpersonal skills for negotiating with intimate contacts (Kelly and St Lawrence, 1988). These findings argue strongly for the plausibility of using psychosocial interventions such as CBSM to manage stress and improve mood while helping HIV-infected persons change lifestyle behaviors. The role of ethnic, racial, cultural, and religious factors in influencing sexual behavior patterns is also an important consideration here (Mays and Cochran, 1988); hence sociocultural influences on risk behavior reduction need to be understood when developing interventions. For example, among poor ethnic minority HIV-infected women, the risk of AIDS is only one in a long list of multiple risks that are prevalent in daily existence. Accordingly, behavioral medicine researchers developing psychosocial interventions need to be aware of more immediate survival needs, which, if met, can provide the opportunity for professionals to educate and intervene effectively on other planes.

Dealing with HIV-Related Physical Symptoms

In addition to the life-threatening physical symptoms often associated with AIDS (e.g., pneumonia, Kaposi's sarcoma and cervical cancer), many HIV-infected persons must deal on a daily basis with other physical changes that can greatly disrupt their careers, family roles, and overall quality of life. Some of the more pervasive of these are pain (Jacobsen and Breitbart, in press), sleep disturbances (D. Cruess, in press), and neurological symptoms. Pain is reported to be present in 30–90 percent of HIV-infected persons, and it is clear that the prevalence of pain increases as disease progresses (Jacobsen and Brietbart, in press). The most commonly observed pain-related conditions are: painful sensory peripheral neuropathy, pain related to Kaposi's sarcoma, pharyngeal and abdominal pain, headache pain, arthralgia and myalgia, and painful dermatologic conditions (reviewed in Jacobsen and Breitart, in press). The presence of pain appears to have a profound negative impact on emotional wellbeing, daily functioning, and employment, and is associated with the severity of depressive symptoms and increased risk of suicidal ideation. The use of analgesic medications represents the cornerstone of the multimodal treatment of HIV-related pain. Surprisingly, very little research has tested the efficacy of psychosocial interventions for managing pain in HIV-infected persons, though many assume that the interventions developed for cancer patients may be equally effective for them. Some of these include: patient education, hypnosis, progressive relaxation training, and cognitive–behavioral interventions (for a review see Jacobsen and Breitbart, in press).

Another overlooked sequel of HIV infection that can significantly impair quality of life is sleep disruption. Given the immunologic correlates of sleep disturbance, the effects of psychological treatments for sleep disturbance in HIV-infected persons may have implications for physical health outcomes as well as quality of life improvements. Several cognitive–behavioral techniques can be used by psychologists to improve sleep quality in HIV-infected patients. These include stimulus control, sleep restriction, relaxation training, psychoeducation to improve sleep hygiene, and cognitive restructuring (for extensive review see D. Cruess, in press).

Many HIV-infected persons must cope with ongoing neurocognitive changes, such as mental slowing, cognitive–motor impairments, and difficulties with memory, attention, and other functional areas. All of these can greatly compromise the quality of life of these patients, and may also contribute to poorer psychological adjustment and difficulties with the management of healthcare regimens (e.g., medication adherence). Behavioral medicine practitioners can make a sizeable contribution to the healthcare teams working with these populations. Their knowledge of the ways in which neuropsychological status can be affected by mood states and personality traits; and the effects of various medical treatments (e.g., medication, surgery, anesthesia, chemotherapy, radiation), can be valuable in helping the treatment team make decisions about treatment plans. Health psychologists are also trained to interpret this information in the context of a range of socioeconomic and cultural forces that operate in the patient's life to shape the meaning of illness, recovery, and health.

Changing Cognitive Responses to Stressors

Receiving an HIV+ diagnosis, being diagnosed with one's first HIV-related symptom or with an AIDS-defining event, and learning of the death or AIDS diagnosis of a lover, were rated in one study as the most emotionally distressing events that HIV-infected persons deal with (Rosser et al., 1988). In addition to providing an overt sign of disease progression, physical changes such as skin lesions, muscle wasting, and fungal infections can reduce one's sense of personal control and compromise self-image (Hoffman, 1991). Individuals undergoing such changes may attempt to cope by way of denial and increased substance use, which, as noted previously, may affect mood states such as anxiety and depression, as well as sexual risk behaviors, medication adherence, and physical health.

Mounting research suggests that an HIV-infected person's *appraisal* of stressful events may determine his/her coping responses and emotional state (Lazarus and Folkman, 1984). For instance, HIV+ men with greater irrational beliefs and who used denial and disengagement coping strategies to deal with ongoing symptoms and the threat of AIDS in their lives, showed greater mood disturbance and substance use (Penedo et al., 2001). Therefore, one important goal of psychosocial intervention is to help these individuals change their appraisals and coping responses when dealing with the *losses, threats and challenges* associated with HIV infection. Efforts to make these changes and ultimately build self-efficacy may be most effective early in the course of the psychosocial intervention, and are likely enhanced by constructing a supportive group environment and teaching participants tangible strategies for changing their cognitive (cognitive restructuring), behavioral (coping skills training), and interpersonal (assertiveness and anger management) responses to these events (Antoni, 1997).

Building Social Support Resources

Social resources have been found to buffer the negative physical and psychological effects of major stressful events (Cohen and Wills, 1985). *Buffering effects of social support* have been attributed to increased opportunities for intimacy, integration through shared concerns, reassurance of worth, nurturance, reliable alliance and guidance (cf. Antoni and Schneiderman, 1998) – all potentially facilitating task-oriented thinking and active coping. On the other hand, socially isolated individuals may be more likely to harbor maladaptive stressor appraisals such as catastrophizing, self-blame, and helplessness, and may use denial as a major coping strategy.

A seropositive diagnosis may reduce both the availability and the utilization of social support, which may increase the risk of depression and hopelessness as well as substance use (Ostrow et al., 1989). Similar phenomena may occur in those diagnosed with HIV symptoms or AIDS for the first time (Namir et al., 1989). Issues regarding social support may be quite different for HIV-infected men (Zuckerman and Antoni, 1995) and women (Antoni et al., 1992a). Because many HIV+ women are indigent minority group members who have been marginalized by their social groups, they are left with limited resources to care for themselves or their children (Guinan, 1987). Trying to cope with being ill and the challenges of motherhood concurrently can be overwhelming, and community support efforts may appear to them to be directed primarily to gay men (Mackie, 1993). However, gay men are also at increased risk for social isolation. Given the number of HIV-infected gay men experiencing multiple bereavements (Martin, 1988), coupled with their reported low average support network size (comprised mainly of friends) (Namir et al., 1989), any loss in social support may be especially devastating.

Social support may be viewed as a "coping resource" to the extent that it channels, facilitates, or perpetuates the use of coping strategies with stress-buffering properties. It is important to realize, however, that some forms of social interaction may actually be associated with *increased* levels of psychological distress in HIV-infected persons. Among asymptomatic HIV-infected gay men *increases in social conflict* and dissatisfaction with social support in general predicted greater increases in distress and depression over a 1-year period (Leserman et al., 1995). These social conflicts can include rejection messages from family members, breaking up or declining quality of romantic relationships, and trouble with employers, among others. Interventions that teach interpersonal skills, such as assertiveness training and anger management, may be particularly effective in helping HIV-infected persons express their needs to members of their social network in such a way that support persons can be most effective (Antoni, 1997). Interventions that provide skills for building useful, nonconflicting bonds with others may be particularly important for HIV-infected persons.

Biological, Behavioral and Psychosocial Factors Influencing the Health Course of HIV Infection

For decades, behavioral medicine researchers have been examining associations between the occurrence of stressful life events and alterations in people's resiliency or susceptibility to a wide variety of pathogenic processes underlying chronic diseases such as coronary heart disease, diabetes mellitus, rheumatoid arthritis, and cancer. In addition to studying the impact of stressful events, behavioral medicine researchers over the past two decades have also focused on the role of stress-"moderating" psychosocial variables (e.g., coping strategies and social support) and psychosocial interventions (e.g., stress management) that might reduce the health effects of stressors in medically vulnerable populations. These studies have revealed large variations in the severity of medical symptoms, disease progression, and even survival time in patients being treated for serious medical conditions, with some of this variability being attributable to behavioral and psychosocial factors (Schneiderman et al., 2001).

With the emergence of data from long-term cohort studies in recent years it is now well established that some HIV-infected patients develop symptoms rapidly, whereas others remain symptom free for over a decade. From a secondary prevention standpoint this means that it is important to isolate factors that account for the wide variability in the transit time for the clinical manifestations of HIV infection. New terms such as "Long-term survivors" have been developed to reflect those people who somehow outlive or outpace their prognosis following HIV infection. One grouping consists of "non-progressors with HIV" – persons who are HIV positive yet maintain near normal levels of CD4 numbers. Another grouping consists of those who are "asymptomatic low CD4" – people with very low CD4 counts (<50 cells/mm^3) who remain asymptomatic for extended periods of time. Finally there are those known as "long-term survivors of symptomatic AIDS." Although the sources of individual variability in HIV progression remain largely unknown, a growing body of literature suggests that the key may lie in some combination of biological, behavioral, and psychosocial factors (Ironson et al., 1995b).

Biological Factors and Disease Progression

Some biological factors that influence length of survival include *age* (i.e., younger persons live longer once infected; Lemp et al., 1990; Jacobson et al., 1991), *gender* (i.e., men live longer following a diagnosis of AIDS; Brown, 1989), *ethnicity* (Friedland et al., 1991) *and initial AIDS-related disease manifestation* (having *Pneumocystis carinii* pneumonia (PCP) as the presenting symptomatic criterion for AIDS; Friedland et al., 1991). *Risk group membership* (Detels et al., 1988), and the presence of or a prior history of other concomitant *sexually transmitted diseases* (STDs) also appear important. Prior rate of CD4 decline and body mass index predict the time until the level of CD4 cells in the peripheral blood drops below $200/mm^3$, the point at which symptomatic AIDS often occurs (Hoover et al., 1995). Another major set of biological factors includes coinfection with other latent viruses (e.g., several types of herpes viruses and human papillomaviruses, HPV) and the extent to which they become reactivated (Rosenberg and Fauci, 1991). Because the surveillance mechanisms keeping these infections in check may be influenced by psycho-social factors, behavioral medicine research and practice with HIV-infected persons may provide major health benefits.

Behavioral Factors and Disease Progression

Behavioral factors such as the use of alcohol, tobacco, caffeine, recreational drugs (cocaine, nitrites during sex), unprotected anal intercourse, poor antiretroviral medication adherence, and poor nutrition have also been sug-gested as influencing the rate of HIV disease progression (Chiappelli et al., 1992; Ekstrand and Chesney, in press). For instance, there is growing evid-ence that injection drug use (Seage et al., 1993) and even cigarette smoking (Nieman et al., 1993) may be associated with faster disease progression in HIV-infected people. Interestingly, some of these behavioral factors are associ-ated with alterations in those physiological stress response systems noted previously as mediating stress-immune associations. For instance, nicotine in cigarette smoke is associated with catecholamine discharge (Blaney, 1985), and ethanol consumption is also linked with catecholamine elevations due to blockage of reuptake (Davidson, 1985). Among HIV-infected persons, elevations in catecholamines such as norepinephrine and epinephrine have been asso-ciated with elevated distress and anxiety on the one hand, and with immune decrements on the other (Antoni et al., 2000b).

Nutritional factors and vitamin deficiencies may contribute to immunologic decrements in HIV infection (Baum et al., 1991). There is also evidence for immune effects of sleep deprivation, including decreases in lymphoproliferative responses and diminished granulocyte functioning in healthy persons (Palmblad et al., 1979). A number of studies show that decrements in immune functions such as NKCC, evident in victims of major stressors or traumas, are mediated in part by sleep disruption (Hall et al., 1998; Ironson et al., 1997). As noted previously, sleep disruption occurs at a remarkable rate among HIV-infected individuals, suggesting that behavioral medicine research into interventions for sleep disruption could provide health benefits.

Psychosocial Factors and Disease Progression

Longitudinal studies relating depressive symptoms to rates of immunologic decline and disease progression in HIV-infected persons have produced mixed results (Burack et al., 1993; Lyketsos, Hoover et al., 1993). A meta-analysis found that depressive symptoms, but not stressors, were longitudinally related to symptoms of HIV infection as well as declines in NK and NKCC, yet not with reductions in CD4 cell counts (Zorilla et al., 1996). Leserman et al. (1999) suggest that the negative findings may be explained by the inclusion of studies having short follow-up periods, and those that measured depressive symptoms only at baseline rather than making repeated assessments more proximal to disease changes. In a study of HIV-infected asymptomatic gay men, Leserman et al. (1999) found that more cumulative stressful life events, more cumulative depressive symptoms, and less cumulative social support predicted faster progression to AIDS over a 5–6-year period. Further analyses on this cohort at 7-year follow-up confirmed the findings for stressful life events and lack of social support, but also related faster disease progression to denial coping and elevated serum cortisol (Leserman et al., 2000).

Two studies found that stressful life events were unrelated to CD4 counts or HIV-related symptoms (Kessler et al., 1991; Rabkin et al., 1991), but another found that elevated life events were predictive of decreases in CD4 counts (Goodkin et al., 1992). Focusing on the effects of prevalent unitary stressors in HIV+ persons has produced more consistent results. One relatively common stressful event associated with disease progression in HIV-infected persons is bereavement. Coates et al. (1989a) found that both the number of losses and the accompanying distress levels were significantly related to faster HIV progression during a 2-year follow-up. Similarly, Kemeny and colleagues (1994) found that a group of HIV-infected men whose partners had died had significantly higher serum neopterin levels (a disease progression marker) and lower lymphocyte proliferative responses to phytohemagglutinin (PHA) than a matched group of nonbereaved HIV+ men. Other work has suggested an interaction wherein individuals who display the greatest distress levels during particularly stressful periods may show the poorest health outcomes (Patterson et al., 1996). It is plausible that individuals who use maladaptive stressor appraisals and coping strategies, and who have inadequate social resources, are the most logical candidates for behavioral medicine interventions.

One study providing some insight here examined how the manner in which HIV+ infected individuals "processed" the stress of HIV seropositivity notification predicted their immunologic status during the early period of adjustment to this stressor. Men showing the greatest avoidance increases after diagnosis demonstrated greater anxiety, depression, and confusion 5 weeks later (Lutgendorf et al., 1997a). Those with avoidance increases also displayed lower lymphocyte proliferative responses to pokeweed mitogen and lower NKCC at 5-week follow-up, compared to those whose avoidance scores decreased over the study. These findings suggested that post-notification processing, colored by avoidance, was associated with poorer psychological adjustment and immune system functioning in the weeks after antibody testing among asymptomatic HIV+ men.

Other "stress processing" variables that have been related to immunologic parameters and health changes include denial (Ironson et al., 1994), fatalism (Reed et al., 1994), optimism/pessimism (Byrnes et al., 1998; S. Cruess et al., 2000b), and deriving a sense of meaning from the HIV experience (Bower et al., 1999). Ironson et al. (1994) found that using denial and behavioral disengagement to cope with an HIV+ diagnosis predicted lower CD4 counts at

1-year follow-up, and a greater likelihood of progressing to HIV-related symptoms and AIDS at 2-year follow-up. A more fine-grained analysis found that HIV+ men scoring above the median on post-notification disengagement coping strategies (e.g., denial and behavioral disengagement) had significantly lower concurrently measured T-helper/suppressor (CD4/CD8) cell ratios, T-inducer subset (CD4+CD45RA+) percentage values, and proliferative responses to PHA than subjects scoring below the median on these coping scales. Greater disengagement coping responses also predicted poorer lymphocyte proliferation to PHA at the 1-year follow-up (Antoni et al., 1995a). These coping strategies may be detrimental because of their tendency to induce a state of passivity and disengagement. Goodkin et al. (1992) found that passive coping strategies (including denial and disengagement) were inversely related to long-term CD4 cell count in HIV+ gay men. Solano et al. (1993) also found that denial was associated prospectively with the emergence of symptoms in an HIV-positive sample. Conversely, Mulder et al. (1995ba) found that active confrontational coping with HIV infection was predictive of decreased clinical progression over a 1-year period, after taking into account baseline biomedical and behavioral control variables.

Another series of studies found that fatalistic gay men with a diagnosis of AIDS had a significantly shorter survival time than men scoring low on fatalism (Reed et al., 1994). Men who were both fatalistic and bereaved within the past year had the shortest survival time, the steepest declines in CD4 number and proliferative response to PHA, and a more rapid increase in disease progression markers (Kemeny et al., 1995). A closely related construct – pessimism – has been related to lower NKCC in HIV+ women (Byrnes et al., 1998) and to higher IgG antibody titers to Epstein–Barr virus (EBV) among HIV+ men (S. Cruess et al., 2000a). Finally, one study showed that HIV+ men who derived a greater sense of meaning from the disease showed a better disease course than those who did not develop such meaning (Bower et al., 1998). This is interesting in light of other work showing that a key psychological feature of HIV+ men who become long-term survivors is a sense of meaning and purpose (Ironson et al., 1995). Less is known about the ways in which other cognitive appraisal variables, such as benefit finding and meaning making, different cognitive distortions such as catastrophizing, and self-efficacy might relate to the course of HIV infection.

There is reason to believe that the role of these cognitive appraisal variables in predicting disease outcomes may be quite complex. For instance, whereas Ironson et al. (1994) found that greater use of denial among asymptomatic HIV-infected gay men predicted a greater likelihood of disease progression 2 years later, Reed et al. (1994) found that "realistic acceptance" was a significant predictor of decreased survival time in gay men diagnosed with AIDS. Thus it appears that being at the extreme end of either denial or realistic acceptance might be dysfunctional. One study may shed some light on the notion of a balance between the extremes of denial and acceptance. Mulder et al. (1999) found that greater use of distraction (i.e., focusing on other things to take your mind off HIV/AIDS) predicted a slower rate of decline in CD4 cells, less appearance of syncytium-inducing HIV variants, and less progression to immunologically defined AIDS (<200 CD4 cells/mm^3) over a 7-year period. Ironson et al. (1995b) note that, together, these findings suggest that strategies that predict longevity may involve using some distraction, coupled with staying away from the extremes of either denial or passive acceptance to the point where fatalism and rumination occurs. Psychosocial interventions may be helpful in facilitating such a balance.

There has been an enormous amount of research into the ability of social networks to offer health benefits to a wide variety of populations (House et al., 1988). For instance, it appears that being married is associated with greater survival time among patients who have experienced a myocardial infarction (Williams et al., 1992) or a diagnosis of breast cancer (Neale et al., 1986). Although a growing body of evidence supports the potential benefits of social ties in healthy people and several chronic disease populations (e.g., cancer patients), scientists are just beginning to learn the complexities of examining the health correlates of social support in HIV-infected individuals (Miller and Cole, 1998).

For HIV-infected persons, social support may help define certain stressors as being less overwhelming; provide a chance for them to express their fears, frustrations, and other emotions; offer key information and informational support; and make them feel more connected (Zuckerman and Antoni, 1995). The same mechanisms that provide these psychological benefits from social support may also moderate endocrine and immunologic changes associated with stressful experiences (e.g., Esterling et al., 1996). We hypothesized that HIV-infected people who maintain adequate support networks may have less extreme and protracted biological responses (e.g., immune decrements) to stressors because sympathetic adrenal medullary (SAM) and hypothalamo-pituitary (HPA)-related stress hormone levels (e.g., peripheral catecholamines and cortisol) are better regulated (Antoni et al., 1990). For instance, greater perceived social support was associated with better immune surveillance (reflected in lower IgG antibody titers) of HHV-6 in HIV+ men undergoing the stress of Hurricane Andrew (Dixon et al., in press).

Some work provides preliminary evidence that social support may relate to the rate of HIV disease progression as well. One study found that a larger social network and more perceived informational social support predicted longer survival in men with AIDS (Patterson et al., 1996). In other work, greater availability of social support (Theorell et al., 1995) predicted a slower decline in CD4 counts and longer survival. An HIV-infected person's decision to enlist social support may be a key step in managing the challenges of this chronic disease. However, the decision may encounter significant obstacles. Cole et al. (1995) followed 80 HIV+ gay men for 9 years and found that those who concealed their sexual identity (being at least "half in the closet") had a faster decline in CD4 counts, a shorter time to AIDS diagnosis, and a shorter time to AIDS mortality than those who did not. It is plausible that such concealment may have come at the cost of missed social support opportunities from friends and family. Therefore, social support and decisions to utilize the available support and make new connections may all contribute to the course of HIV disease. Group-based psychosocial interventions that model the value of disclosure and mutual sharing may facilitate increases in and maintenance of social support resources (Antoni, 1997).

It should be noted that in each of the lines of work just reviewed, there is contradictory evidence suggesting that these associations may not generalize across research centers or populations. Subtle methodological differences (psychosocial instruments and their timing, statistical control differences, immune assay differences) can alter results obtained across different laboratories. Work completed to date has largely involved testing the effects of behavioral interventions (e.g., stress management, relaxation, massage, aerobic exercise) on psychological, neuroendocrine and immunologic functioning in HIV-infected men. Although similar studies have begun with women and other groups, the trials were initiated much more recently and the results are some years off. The balance of this chapter will review what we have learned about the effects of such interventions on mental and physical health-related outcomes in HIV-infected men.

Interventions, Adjustment and Health Course in HIV Infection

Psychosocial Interventions with HIV-Infected People

Individual-Based Interventions

There are many issues that can be addressed with individual psychotherapy in HIV-infected individuals, though there are very few published clinical trials testing the efficacy of these approaches in such populations. The earliest point of the therapeutic alliance may actually form when a person decides to be HIV tested. This may come as a result of their awareness or acknowledgement of high-risk behaviors on their own part or by their partner(s) (Remien and Rabkin, in press). It may be this same alliance that facilitates the patient's adjustment to a seropositive diagnosis, including the ability to work through a set of emotional reactions that may be the focus of therapy for an extended period (Remien and Rabkin, in press). Some of these reactions may include fear, guilt, anger, and depression, though not necessarily in that order (Hoffman, 1991). It has been suggested by some that individual counseling may be key during this period, as the infected person may be too overwhelmed to join a support group and too reticent to disclose their serostatus to members of their support network (Remien and Rabkin, in press).

Other therapeutic issues that may be addressed in individual-based interventions with HIV+ persons across the disease spectrum include normalizing emotional experiences; working through the process of disclosing one's HIV status or sexual orientation; making arrangements for healthcare and becoming an active participant with the medical team; making treatment decisions concerning the type and timing of antiretroviral medications; and then maintaining adequate adherence to this medication regimen (Remien and Rabkin, in press). During each of these experiences behavioral medicine practitioners are well placed to assess functional and psychiatric status (including suicidal risk) and needs for pharmacological interventions, and to encourage patients to employ productive coping strategies and maintain a lifestyle that promotes optimal health (Remien and Rabkin, in press). For some patients the individual relationship with their therapist may be a central means of support as they encounter physical health declines following a diagnosis of AIDS, as family and friends may be burned out by that point in time. For patients who are successfully treated with HAART (i.e., able to reach a point of undetectable levels of viral load), the counseling relationship may also help them adjust to the "demands" of having a second chance at a healthy life (e.g., returning to work; Remien and Rabkin, in press). It should also be borne in mind that although individual therapy offers all of the benefits of an intense personal relationship, group-based interventions may also offer some unique benefits.

Group-Based Interventions

Over the past few years a number of relatively small trials have examined the effects of group-based psychosocial interventions on psychosocial and immune parameters in HIV-infected populations, but so far very few of them have completed long enough follow-up periods to document health/disease progression effects clearly. Most of these interventions employ anxiety-reduction techniques such as relaxation, and/or cognitive behavioral techniques such as cognitive restructuring (Ironson et al., in press). Coates et al. (1989b) randomized 64 HIV+ gay men to either an 8-week stress management training intervention or a control group. The intervention included systematic relaxation (with take-home tapes), health behavior education (diet, rest, exercise, drug and alcohol use, smoking), and stress management skills. Men in this group reported significantly fewer sexual partners but revealed no changes in enumerative or functional immune measures. Auerbach et al. (1992) randomized 26 symptomatic seropositive gay men to an 8-week behavioral medicine intervention (thermal biofeedback, guided imagery, and hypnosis), or a wait-list control group. The intervention reduced self-reported symptoms of HIV (fever, fatigue, pain, headache, nausea and insomnia), and increased vigor and hardiness relative to controls, but did not change anxiety, depression, or immune status (CD4 cell counts). The authors speculate that if they had selected a more stressed/distressed sample of patients they might have obtained changes in immune status variables and anxiety and depression measures. A more efficient way to evaluate the effects of these "stress management" interventions might be to test them in the context of measurable recent or ongoing stressful events (e.g., bereavement, diagnosis notification).

Responding to an HIV Seropositive Diagnosis Sixty-five gay men who did not know their HIV serostatus were randomly assigned to either the 10 week CBSM intervention, a 10-week group-based aerobic exercise intervention, or a no-treatment control group. After 5 weeks of participation in one of these groups, blood was drawn for antibody testing and the men received news of their serostatus 72 hours later; approximately one-third proved to be seropositive ($n = 23$). The intervention continued for another 5 weeks and the men were followed through the initial "adjustment" period. Pre-to-post notification (weeks 5–7) men who tested seronegative showed predictable decreases in anxiety and depression, indicating their relief over the news of their status. Over the same period, the HIV+ controls showed significant increases in anxiety and depression whereas the HIV+ CBSM subjects showed no significant changes in anxiety or depression scores (Antoni et al., 1991). The same "buffering" effect was present for the HIV+ men assigned to the aerobic exercise group (LaPerriere et al., 1990). The HIV+ controls also showed slight decrements in lymphocyte proliferative responses to PHA, NKCC and NK cell counts pre-to-post notification (with no change in CD4 counts). In contrast, the HIV+ men in CBSM had significant increases in CD4 and NK cells and smaller increases in PHA responsivity and NKCC, thus showing a "buffering" of the stress-associated immunologic changes (Antoni et al., 1991). Exercise had a similar buffering effect on CD4 and NK cell counts (LaPerriere et al., 1990).

There continued to be immunologic changes over the entire 10-week intervention period. Men assigned to either CBSM or exercise showed significant decreases in antibody titers (reflecting better immunologic control) to EBV and to HHV-6, which moved into the normal range, compared to assessment-only controls, whose antibody titers remained constant over the 10-week intervention period and elevated relative to healthy male laboratory controls (Esterling et al., 1992). During this same period, men in the control group showed significant decrements in perceived social support, whereas those in the CBSM group maintained their social support levels (Friedman et al., 1991). The reductions in EBV antibody titers in the CBSM group appeared to be mediated by this greater social support (Antoni et al., 1996). In particular, greater levels of perceived guidance and reliable alliance from one's social network accounted for the intervention's effects on this index of immune functioning.

A 2-year follow-up of the HIV+ men recruited for these studies examined psychological predictors of disease progression to symptoms and death from AIDS (Ironson et al., 1994). Less distress at diagnosis, decreased HIV-specific denial coping (5 weeks post diagnosis minus pre diagnosis) and better treatment adherence (based on attendance for either CBSM or exercise groups, and frequency of home relaxation practice and stress monitoring homework during the 10 weeks for those in CBSM) all predicted slower disease progression to symptoms and AIDS. Denial coping and treatment adherence remained significant even after controlling for initial disease severity at study entry (CD4 cell number). Furthermore, decreases in denial and a greater frequency of home relaxation practice during the 10-week intervention period predicted higher CD4 cell counts and greater lymphocyte proliferative responses to PHA at 1-year follow-up (Ironson et al., 1994). These findings suggest that those men who attended intervention sessions regularly and dealt with their denial during the intervention period were most likely to show longer-term immune and health benefits.

Coping with the Asymptomatic Stage of HIV Infection Asymptomatic HIV disease is accompanied by many psychosocial challenges, characterized by extreme uncertainty with regard to future health course and available resources. Concerns over declining resources may occur as a function of impaired occupational and social functioning, decreased earning power, high costs of medical care, complex medical treatments, difficulties with self-care, multiple bereavements, and declining social support (Lutgendorf et al., 1994). The effects of CBSM intervention have been examined with gay men who had been diagnosed with HIV infection for at least 6 months but were still symptom free. This required some degree of "tailoring" of the intervention to address the specific challenges of this population. Although their physical functioning had not yet been compromised, knowledge of their positive serostatus had begun to affect these men's interpersonal behaviors and sense of wellbeing (Lutgendorf et al., 1994). Some salient issues included reluctance to terminate relationships, hesitating to have sex with someone who was uninfected for fear of infecting them, deciding to disclose HIV status to family members, and making job and career transitions. The predominant emotional experiences reported by these men included anger, fear, loss, and uncertainty.

The 10-week CBSM intervention developed for these asymptomatic men was specifically adapted to address these concerns (Antoni et al., 1992a). The early part of the intervention maintained its psychoeducational focus, with sessions on HIV and the stress response, cognitive appraisals, refuting and replacing cognitive distortions. The group sessions discussing impending serostatus notification and post-notification concerns were replaced by a session dealing with unfinished issues related to seropositivity notification, and notification of others regarding one's seropositivity. Behavior change, assertiveness, and social support were addressed extensively in these group sessions, especially strategies for eliciting social support. From a sample of 23 men, 11 were randomized to CBSM and 12 to an aerobic exercise program, each lasting 10 weeks. Participants in CBSM significantly reduced their anxiety, depression, anger, fatigue, and confusion levels, as well as increasing feelings of vigor relative to those in the exercise group (Antoni et al., 1992a). They also reported increased use of adaptive coping strategies, active coping, planning and acceptance, and decreases in several maladaptive coping strategies, such as mental disengagement and denial. These men also revealed significant increases in lymphocyte proliferative responses to PHA and NKCC. Although the study lacked a no-treatment control condition, findings suggest that it is possible to adapt CBSM to different challenges across the HIV spectrum, with effects on both psychosocial and immunologic parameters.

Other cognitive–behavioral interventions have produced similar psychosocial changes in asymptomatic HIV-infected men. One group that assigned depressed HIV+ gay men to one of three different treatment conditions found significant reductions in depression, hostility, and somatization in a cognitive–behavioral group as well as in a matched-time social support/emotional expression group, compared to a no-treatment control group, although the cognitive–behavioral group was somewhat more effective at reducing drug use (Kelly et al., 1993). Another study comparing cognitive–behavioral group intervention and existential experiential group intervention in HIV+ gay men found that both groups reduced distress and depressive symptoms compared to a wait-list control condition (Mulder et al., 1994). A specific form of CBSM group intervention (Coping Effectiveness Training, CET; Folkman et al., 1991), when compared with an information group and a wait-list control group, was found to increase self-efficacy and decrease perceived stress and burnout (Chesney et al., 1996). Although none of these interventions produced significant changes in biological or health parameters two teams found that greater intervention-associated distress reductions predicted slower declines in CD4 cell counts over follow-up periods of 1 (Ironson et al., 1994) and 2 years (Mulder et al., 1995). One intervention designed specifically to provide support and coping skills to asymptomatic HIV+ men dealing with bereavement reduced grief (Goodkin et al., 1996) and also reduced plasma cortisol and healthcare visits over a 6-month period (Goodkin et al., 1998). Therefore, some work indicates that group-based psychosocial interventions may be adaptable and successful in helping HIV-infected people deal with different challenges during the early asymptomatic stage of the infection.

Dealing with Emerging Symptoms of HIV Infection A number of very recently published studies have evaluated the effects of group-based CBSM intervention in HIV+ gay men who are dealing with the initial symptoms of the infection, before the onset of AIDS. In one study, those who had mild symptoms (category B of the 1993 CDC definition) were randomly assigned to either a 10-week group-based CBSM intervention or a modified wait-list control group in which they completed a 10-week waiting period before being reassessed and provided with a 1-day CBSM seminar. Compared to men in the control condition, those in the CBSM group showed a significant decrease in depression and anxiety and a significant decrease in antibody titers to herpes simplex virus-type 2 (HSV-2) (Lutgendorf et al., 1997b). Path analyses revealed that the effects of CBSM on HSV-2 antibody reductions appeared to be mediated, in part, by intervention-associated changes in depression (Antoni et al., 1996). The relative contribution of intervention-related changes in coping skills and social support to reductions in dysphoria, anxiety, and distress-related symptoms were also examined over the study period. Those men randomized to CBSM reported significant increases in the use of cognitive coping strategies such as positive reframing and acceptance for dealing with HIV symptoms, as well as revealing increases in total perceived social support provisions (in the domains of guidance, reliable alliance, and attachment) compared to a wait-list control condition (Lutgendorf et al., 1998). Path analyses indicated that changes in social support and cognitive coping strategies appeared to mediate the effects of the CBSM intervention on distress reduction. Follow-up studies in a larger sample of 76 HIV+ men revealed that these CBSM effects on HSV-2 antibody titers are replicated, and are mediated, in part, by increases in social support provision over the intervention period (S. Cruess et al., 2000b).

A number of studies have been conducted by this team to examine neuroendocrine changes occurring during CBSM in HIV-infected persons. Specifically, CBSM has been shown to decrease 24-hour urinary free cortisol (Antoni et al., 2000a) and norepinephrine (NE; Antoni et al., 2000b) and plasma cortisol/DHEA-S ratio (D. Cruess et al., 1999), while increasing plasma testosterone levels (D. Cruess et al., 2000b) over the 10-week intervention period. Interestingly, whereas NE reductions paralleled decreases in anxiety (Antoni et al., 2000b), urinary cortisol and plasma cortisol/DHEA-S decreases paralleled decreases in depressed mood (Antoni et al., 2000a; D. Cruess et al., 1999). These hormonal changes have also been related to immunologic effects of this intervention, in direct support of the PNI model underlying this program of research. For instance, reductions in cortisol/DHEA-S ratio (D. Cruess et al., 1999) partially mediated reductions in HSV-2 antibody titers during the 10-week CBSM intervention period (S. Cruess et al., 2000b). Prior work indicates that cortisol can facilitate the HIV infectivity of immune cells (Markham et al., 1986), whereas DHEA-S may inhibit HIV replication (Yang et al., 1994) and HIV latent virus reactivation (Yang et al., 1993). Therefore, the changes in HSV-2 antibody titers seen in CBSM may be the result of changes in HIV replication and activation that are mediated by cortisol and/or DHEA-S. Recent efforts to examine determinants of individual differences in hormonal changes during the 10-week intervention period have found significant within-session reductions in salivary cortisol that improve progressively over the period, and which are associated with improvements in relaxation skills demonstrated during home practice (D. Cruess et al., 2000b). Changes in NE during CBSM have also been shown to mediate the increases in T-cytotoxic/suppressor cells observed in CBSM participants at one-year follow-up (Antoni et al., 2000b).

Adjusting to the Demands of AIDS To date, most of the published empirical studies evaluating the efficacy of psychosocial interventions with HIV-infected people have focused on gay men in the earlier stages of infection. There is little or no work testing the effects of various interventions with men or women who have progressed to AIDS. We do know that the onset of AIDS may be accompanied by a lessening of psychological distress from the levels experienced by symptomatic (pre-AIDS) HIV-infected men (Tross and Hirsch, 1988). This may reflect a relief from the unpredictability of not knowing if and when the first signs of AIDS may occur.

As individuals progress to develop more serious symptoms, and eventually AIDS, they may undergo a continual process of emotional crises, recycling through the stages that Kubler-Ross (1969) originally noted as comprising the dying process (Lutgendorf et al., 1994). Although it is clear that these individuals are in need of psychosocial services, one must be cautious in applying what has been learned from asymptomatic and early-stage populations. There is a lack of empirical studies evaluating the effectiveness of psychosocial interventions such as CBSM or other approaches, such as expressive–supportive therapy, conducted in a group or individual-based format with patients at this stage of infection. It may be that those with AIDS will find structured CBSM techniques useful, but may also require additional emotional support. For these people a therapeutic plan that combines a group-based stress reduction intervention with individual-based therapy directed toward these existential issues may be very useful. There is recent evidence that a 10-week group-based psychosocial intervention that combines elements of CBSM with expressive–supportive therapy buffers declines in quality of life in women with AIDS (Lechner et al., under review). An optimal therapy plan may also involve pharmacological treatment blended with the psychosocial intervention. One study compared the effect of different forms of individual-based psychosocial interventions, including a combined imipramine plus supportive psychotherapy condition in depressed HIV+ patients (Markowitz et al., 1998). The combined medication plus supportive psychotherapy condition showed significantly greater reductions in depressive symptoms than did cognitive–behavioral or supportive psychotherapy alone. This suggests that although group-based CBSM may be quite effective for HIV-infected persons who need help in coping with the burdens of their illness, a combination regimen may be optimal for those who present with significant comorbid mental health problems.

Conclusions and Future Directions

Given our increasing knowledge of the epidemiological trends in HIV incidence, the clinical manifestations of the infection, and the best medications available for treating the primary infection (HAART) and secondary "opportunistic" infections and cancers, it seems critical that behavioral medicine researchers, practitioners and policy makers keep up with such advances in knowledge when designing new psychosocial interventions. Clearly such contemporary efforts in the US will need to focus on emerging populations, such as minority (Latino and African-American) women (including mothers; Pereira, in press) and substance abusers (DesJarlais et al., in press). This requires, first, conducting focus groups to identify the central clinical issues that each group faces and the optimal treatment format that they are likely to respond to. This may also include developing linguistically translated and culturally appropriate versions of such interventions in order to reach the many monolingual, first-generation infected persons who have migrated to some major urban areas in the country. With regard to ensuring that HIV-infected persons receive optimal medical treatment, behavioral medicine specialists are particularly well equipped to design interventions that facilitate regular diagnostic monitoring, early treatment for newly emerging symptoms, and adequate medication adherence. The contemporary treatment philosophy now views HIV infection as a chronic disease in which patient management is critical. The key to optimal quality of life and disease course may require consistent adherence to a demanding medication schedule in the context of an already stressful daily existence. Psychosocial interventions that provide information, skills and support to patients can facilitate adherence to difficult medication protocols. Documented improvements in immune function following these psychosocial interventions raise the possibility that behavioral medicine interventions can help reconstitute the compromised immune system once treatments such as HAART have contained the virus. Ongoing work in behavioral medicine is currently tackling these secondary and tertiary prevention issues in the emerging populations of HIV-infected persons.

References

Antoni, M. H., Baggett, L., Ironson, G., August, S., LaPerriere, A., Klimas, N., Schneiderman, N., and Fletcher, M. A. (1991). Cognitive behavioral stress management intervention buffers distress responses and immunologic changes following notification of HIV-1 seropositivity. *Journal of Consulting and Clinical Psychology*, 59, 906–915.

Antoni, M. H., Esterling, B., Lutgendorf, S., Fletcher, M. A., and Schneiderman, N. (1995). Psychosocial stressors, herpes virus reactivation and HIV-1 infection. In M. Stein and A. Baum (Eds.), *AIDS and Oncology: Perspectives in Behavioral Medicine* (pp. 135–168). Hillsdale, N.J.: Erlbaum.

Antoni, M. H. (1997). Cognitive behavioral stress management for gay men learning of their HIV-1 antibody test results. In J. Spira (Ed.), *Group Therapy for Patients with Chronic Medical Diseases* (pp. 55–91). New York: Guilford Press.

Antoni, M. H., Cruess, S., Cruess, D., Kumar, M., Lutgendorf, S., Ironson, G., Dettmer, E., Williams, J., Klimas, N., Fletcher, M. A., and Schneiderman, N. (2000a). Cognitive behavioral stress management reduces distress and 24-hour urinary free cortisol among symptomatic HIV-infected gay men. *Annals of Behavioral Medicine*, 22, 1–11.

Antoni, M. H., Cruess, D. G., Cruess, S., Lutgendorf, S., Kumar, M., Ironson, G., Klimas, N., Fletcher, M. A., and Schneiderman, N. (2000b). Cognitive behavioral stress management intervention effects on anxiety, 24-hour urinary catecholamine output, and T-cytotoxic/suppressor cells over time among symptomatic HIV-infected gay men. *Journal of Consulting and Clinical Psychology*, 68, 31–45.

Antoni, M. H., and Schneiderman, N. (1998). HIV/AIDS. In A. Bellack and M. Hersen (Eds), *Comprehensive Clinical Psychology* (pp. 237–275). New York: Elsevier Science.

Antoni, M. H., Goldstein, D., Ironson, G., LaPerriere, A., Fletcher, M. A., and Schneiderman, N. (1995a). Coping responses to HIV-1 serostatus notification predict concurrent and prospective immunologic status. *Clinical Psychology and Psychotherapy*, 2, 234–248.

Antoni, M. H., Ironson, G., Helder, L., Lutgendorf, S., Friedman, A., LaPerriere, A., Fletcher, M. A., and Schneiderman, N. (1992a). *Stress Management Intervention Reduces Social Isolation and Maladaptive Coping Behaviors in Gay Men Adjusting to an HIV-1 Seropositive Diagnosis*. Paper presented at the scientific meeting of the Society of Behavioral Medicine, New York.

Antoni, M. H., Lutgendorf, S., Ironson, G., Fletcher, M. A., and Schneiderman, N. (1996). CBSM intervention effects on social support, coping, depression and immune function in symptomatic HIV-infected men. *Psychosomatic Medicine*, 58, 86. [Abstract]

Antoni, M. H., Schneiderman, N., Fletcher, M. A., Goldstein, D., Ironson, G., and LaPerriere, A. (1990). Psychoneuroimmunology and HIV-1. *Journal of Consulting and Clincal Psychology*, 58, 38–49.

Antoni, M. H., Schneiderman, N., LaPerriere, A., O'Sullivan, M. J., Marks, J., Efantis, J., Skyler, J., and Fletcher, M. A. (1992b). Mothers with AIDS. In P. Ahmed (Ed.), *Living and Dying with AIDS*. NJ: Plenum.

Auerbach, J. E., Oleson, T. D., and Solomon, G. F. (1992). A behavioral medicine intervention as an adjunctive treatment for HIV-related illness. *Psychology and Health*, 6, 325–334.

Axelrod, J., and Reisine, T. (1984). Stress hormones: Their interaction and regulation. *Science*, 224, 452–459.

Baum, M. K., Mantero-Atienza, E., Shor-Posner, G., Fletcher, M. A., Morgan, R., Eisdorfer, C., Sauberlich, H. E., Cornwell, P. E., and Beach, R. S. (1991). Association of vitamin B6 status with parameters of immune function in early HIV-1 infection. *Journal of Acquired Immune Deficiency Syndrome, 4,* 1122–1132.

Blaney, N. (1985). Smoking: Psychophysiological causes and treatment. In N. Schneiderman, and J. Tapp (Eds.), *Behavioral Medicine: The Biopsychosical Approach* (pp. 347–377). NJ: Lawrence Erlbaum.

Bower, J., Kemeny, M., Taylor, S., and Fahey, J. (1998). Cognitive processing, discovery of meaning, CD4 decline, and AIDS-related mortality among bereaved HIV-seropositive men. *Journal of Consulting and Clinical Psychology, 66,* 979–986.

Brown, G. R. (1989). Prospective study of psychiatric morbidity in HIV seropositive women. *Psychosomatic Medicine, 51,* 246–277.

Burack, J. H., Barrett, D. C., Stall, R. D., Chesney, M. A., Ekstrand, M. L., and Coates, T. J. (1993). Depressive symptoms and CD4 lymphocyte decline among HIV-infected men. *Journal of the American Medical Association, 270,* 2567–2573.

Byrnes, D., Antoni, M. H., Goodkin, K., Efantis-Potter, J., Asthana, D., Simon, T., Munjai, J., Ironson, G., and Fletcher, M. A. (1998). Stressful events, pessimism, natural killer cell cytotoxicity and cytotoxic/suppressor T cells in HIV+ black women at risk for cervical cancer. *Psychosomatic Medicine, 60,* 714–722.

Calabrese, J., King, M., and Gold, P. (1987). Alterations in immunocompetence during stress, bereavement, and depression: Focus on neuroendocrine regulation. *American Journal of Psychiatry, 144,* 1123–1134.

Centers for Disease Control (2000). *HIV/AIDS Surveillance Report,* 12(1).

Chesney, M. A., Folkman, S., and Chambers, D. (1996). Coping effectiveness training for men living with HIV: Preliminary findings. *International Journal of STDs and AIDS,* 7(Suppl. 2), 75–82.

Chiapelli, F., Ben-Eliyahu, S., Hanson, L., and Wylie, T. (1992). Modulation of immune surveillance of HIV-related cancers by alcohol and cocaine metabolites. *Alcologia,* 4, 219–227.

Coates, T. J., Stall, R., Ekstrand, M., and Solomon, G. (1989a). *Psychological Predictors as Cofactors for Disease Progression in Men Infected with HIV: The San Francisco Men's Health Study.* Presented at the V International AIDS Conference, Montreal, Canada.

Coates, T., McKusick, L., Stites, D., and Kuno, R. (1989b). Stress management training reduced number of sexual partners but did not improve immune function in men infected with HIV. *American Journal of Public Health, 79,* 885–887.

Cohen, S., and Wills, T. A. (1985). Stress, social support, and the buffering hypothesis. *Psychological Bulletin, 98,* 310–357.

Cole, S., Kemeny, M., Taylor, S., Visscher, B., and Fahey, J. (1995). Accelerated course of HIV infection in gay men who conceal their homosexuality. *Psychosomatic Medicine, 58,* 219–231.

Cruess, D. (in press). Improving sleep quality in patients with chronic illness. In M. Chesney, and M. H. Antoni (Eds), *Health Psychology Innovations: New Target Populations for Prevention and Care.* Washington, D.C.: American Psychological Association.

Cruess, D., Antoni, M. H., Schneiderman, N., Ironson, G., Fletcher, M. A., and Kumar, M. (1999). Cognitive behavioral stress management effects on DHEA-S and serum cortisol in HIV seropositive men. *Psychoneuroendocrinology, 24,* 537–549.

Cruess, D., Antoni, M. H., Schneiderman, N., Ironson, G., McCabe, P., Fernandez, J. B., Cruess, S. E., Klimas, N., and Kumar, M. (2000a). Cognitive–behavioral stress management increases free testosterone and decreases psychological distress in HIV-seropositive men. *Health Psychology, 19,* 12–20.

Cruess, D., Antoni, M. H., Kumar, M., and Schneiderman, N. (2000b). Reductions in salivary cortisol are associated with mood improvement during relaxation training among HIV-1 seropositive men. *Journal of Behavioral Medicine, 23,* 107–122.

Cruess, S., Antoni, M. H., Cruess, D., Fletcher, M. A., Ironson, G., Kumar, M., Lutgendorf, S., Hayes, A., Klimas, N., and Schneiderman, N. (2000a). Reductions in HSV-2 antibody titers after cognitive behavioral stress management and relationships with neuroendocrine function, relaxation skills, and social support in HIV+ gay men. *Psychosomatic Medicine*, 62, 828–837.

Cruess, S., Antoni, M. H., Kilbourn, K., Ironson, G., Klimas, N., Fletcher, M., Baum, A., and Schneiderman, N. (2000b). Optimism, distress and immunologic status in HIV-infected gay men following Hurricane Andrew. *International Journal of Behavioral Medicine*, 7, 160–182.

Davidson, R. (1985). Behavioral medicine and alcoholism. In N. Schneiderman, and J. Tapp (Eds.), *Behavioral Medicine: The Biopsychosocial Approach*. NJ: Lawrence Erlbaum.

Detels, R., English, P. A., Giogi, J. V., Visscher, B. R., Fahey, J. L., Taylor, J. M. G., Dudley, J. P., Nishanian, P., Munoz, A., Phair, J. P., Polk, B. F., and Rinaldo, C. R. (1988). Patterns of CD4+ cell changes after HIV-1 infection indicate the existence of a co-determinant of AIDS. *Journal of the Acquired Immune Deficiency Syndrome*, 1, 390–395.

DesJarlais, D. (in press). Strategies for working with injection drug users: Taking interventions to the streets. In M. Chesney and M. H. Antoni (Eds), *Health Psychology Innovations: New Target Populations for Prevention and Care*. Washington, D.C.: American Psychological Association.

Dixon, D., Kilbourn, K., Cruess, S., Klimas, N., Fletcher, M. A., Ironson, G., Baum, A., Schneiderman, N., and Antoni, M. H. (in press). Social support mediates the relationship between loneliness and human herpesvirus-type 6 (HHV-6) antibody titers in HIV+ gay men following Hurricane Andrew. *Journal of Applied Social Psychology*.

Ekstrand, M., and Chesney, M. (in press). Adhering to complex medication regimens. In M. Chesney and M. H. Antoni (Eds), *Health Psychology Innovations: New Target Populations for Prevention and Care*. Washington, D. C.: American Psychological Association.

Esterling, B., Kiecolt-Glaser, J., and Glaser, R. (1996). Psychosocial modulation of cytokine-induced natural killer cell activity in older adults. *Psychosomatic Medicine*, 58, 264–272.

Esterling, B., Antoni, M., Schneiderman, N., Ironson, G., LaPerriere, A., Klimas, N., and Fletcher, M. A. (1992). Psychosocial modulation of antibody to Epstein–Barr viral capsid antigen and herpes virus type-6 in HIV-1 infected and at-risk gay men. *Psychosomatic Medicine*, 54, 354–371.

Folkman, S., Chesney, M., McKusick, L., Ironson, G., Johnson, D., and Coates, T. J. (1991). Translating coping theory into intervention. In J. Eckenrode (Ed.), *The Social Context of Stress* (pp. 239–260). New York: Plenum.

Friedland, G. H., Saltzman, B., Vileno, J., Freeman, K., Schrager, L. K., and Klein, R. S. (1991). Survival differences in patients with AIDS. *Journal of Acquired Immune Deficiency Syndrome*, 4, 144–153.

Friedman, A., Antoni, M. H., Ironson, G., LaPerriere, A., Schneiderman, N., and Fletcher, M. A. (1991). *Behavioral Interventions, Changes in Perceived Social Support and Depression Following Notification of HIV-1 Seropositivity*. Presented at Society of Behavioral Medicine Annual Meeting, Washington, D.C.

Goodkin, K., Fuchs, I., Feaster, D., Leeka, J., and Dickson-Rishel, D. (1992). Life stressors and coping style are associated with immune measures in HIV-1 infection – a preliminary report. *International Journal of Psychiatry in Medicine*, 22, 155–172.

Goodkin, K., Tuttle, R., Blaney, N. T., Feaster, D., Shapshak, P., Burkhalter, J., Leeds, B., Baldewicz, T., Kumar, M., and Fletcher, M. A. (1996). *A Bereavement Support Group Intervention is Associated with Immunological Changes in HIV-1+ and*

HIV-1-Homosexual Men. Paper presented at the annual meeting of the American Psychosomatic Society, Williamsburg, VA. Abstract in *Psychosomatic Medicine*, 58, 83–84.

Goodkin, K., Feaster, D., Asthana, D., Blaney, N. T., Kumar, M., Baldewicz, T., Tuttle, R., Maher, K., Baum, M. K., Shapshak, P., and Fletcher, M. A. (1998). A bereavement support group intervention is longitudinally associated with salutary effects on the CD4 cell count and number of physician visits. *Clinical and Diagnostic Laboratory Immunology*, 5, 382–391.

Guinan, M. (1987). Women, children and AIDS. *Journal of the American Medical Association*, 42, 186.

Hall, M., Baum, A. Buysse, D. J., Prigerson, H. G., Kupfer, D. J., and Reynolds, C. F. (1998). Sleep as a mediator of the stress–immune relationship. *Psychosomatic Medicine*, 60, 48–51.

Hoffman, M. A. (1991). Counseling the seropositive client: A psychosocial model for assessment and intervention. *Counseling Psychologist*, 19, 467–542.

Hoover, D. R., Rinaldo, C., He, Y., Phair, J., Fahey, J., and Graham, N. M. H. (1995). Long-term survival without clinical AIDS after CD4+ cell counts fall below 200 × 10^6/l. *AIDS*, 9, 145–152.

House, J. S., Landis, K. R., and Umberson, D. (1988). Social relationship and health. *Science*, 241, 540–545.

Ironson, G., Wynings, C., Schneiderman, N., Baum, A., Rodriquez, M., Greenwood, D., Benight, C., Antoni, M. H., LaPerriere, A., Huang, H., Klimas, N., and Fletcher, M. A. (1997). Posttraumatic stress symptoms, intrusive thoughts, loss and immune function after Hurricane Andrew. *Psychosomatic Medicine*, 59, 128–141.

Ironson, G., Antoni, M., and Lutgendorf, S. (1995a). Can psychological interventions affect immunity and survival? Present findings and suggested targets with a focus on cancer and human immunodeficiency virus. *Mind/Body Medicine*, 1, 85–110.

Ironson, G., Solomon, S., Cruess, D., Barroso, J., and Stivers, M. (1995b). Psychosocial factors related to long-term survival with HIV/AIDS. *Clinical Psychology and Psychotherapy*, 2, 249–266.

Ironson, G., Friedman, A., Klimas, N., Antoni, M., Fletcher, M. A., LaPerriere, A., Simoneau, J., and Schneiderman, N. (1994). Distress, denial and low adherence to behavioral interventions predict faster disease progression in gay men infected with human immunodeficiency virus. *International Journal of Behavioral Medicine*, 1, 90–105.

Ironson, G., LaPerriere, A., Antoni, M., Klimas, N., Fletcher, M. A., and Schneiderman, N. (1990). Changes in immunologic and psychological measures as a function of anticipation and reaction to news of HIV-1 antibody status. *Psychosomatic Medicine*, 52, 247–270.

Ironson, G., Antoni, M. H., Schneiderman, N., Chesney, M., O'Cleriheigh, C., Balbin, E., Greenwood, D., Lutgendorf, S., LaPerriere, A., Klimas, N., and Flecther, M. A. (in press). Coping: Interventions for optimal disease management. In M. Chesney and M. H. Antoni (Eds), *Health Psychology Innovations: New Target Populations for Prevention and Care*. Washington, D.C.: American Psychological Association.

Jacobson, M. A., Bacchetti, P., Kolokathis, A., Chiasson, R. E., Szabo, S., Polsky, B., Valainis, G. T., Mildvan, D., Abrams, D., Wilber J., Winger, E., Sacks, H. S., Hendricksen, C., and Moss, A. (1991). Surrogate markers for survival in patients with AIDS and AIDS-related complex treated with ziduvudine. *British Medical Journal*, 302, 73–78.

Jacobsen, P., and Breitbart, W. (in press). Evaluation and management of pain related to HIV infection. In M. Chesney, and M. H. Antoni (Eds), *Health Psychology Innovations:*

New Target Populations for Prevention and Care. Washington, D.C.: American Psychological Association.

Kaisch, K., and Anton-Culver, H. (1989). Psychological and social consequences of HIV exposure: Homosexuals in Southern California. *Psychology and Health*, 3, 63–75.

Kaplan, L. D., Wofsky, C. B., and Volberding, P. A. (1987). Treatment of patients with acquired immunodeficiency syndrome and associated manifestations. *Journal of the American Medical Association*, 257, 1367–1376.

Kelly, J., Murphy, D., Bahr, G., Koob, J., Morgan, M., Kalichman, S., Stevenson, L., Brashfield, T., Bernstein, B., and St. Lawrence, J. (1993). Factors associated with severity of depression and high-risk sexual behavior among persons diagnosed with human immunodeficciency virus (HIV) infection. *Health Psychology*, 12, 215–219.

Kelly, J. A., and St. Lawrence, J. S. (1988). AIDS prevention and treatment: Psychology's role in the health crisis. *Clinical Psychology Review*, 8, 255–284.

Kemeny, M. E., Weiner, H., Duran, R., Taylor, S. E., Visscher, B., and Fahey, J. L. (1995). Immune system changes after the death of a partner in HIV-positive gay men. *Psychosomatic Medicine*, 57, 547–554.

Kemeny, M. E., Weiner, H., Taylor, S. E., Schneider, S., Visscher, B., and Fahey, J. L. (1994). Repeated bereavement, depressed mood, and immune parameters in HIV seropositive and seronegative gay men. *Health Psychology*, 13, 1424.

Kessler, R. C., Foster, C., Joseph, J., Ostrow, D., Wortman, C., Phair, J., and Chmiel, J. (1991). Stressful life events and symptom onset in HIV infection. *American Journal of Psychiatry*, 148, 733–738.

Kiecolt Glaser, J. K., Glaser, R., Shuttleworth, E. C., Dyer, C. S., Ogrocki, P., and Speicher, C. E. (1987). Chronic stress and immunity in family caregivers of Alzheimer's disease victims. *Psychosomatic Medicine*, 49, 523–535.

Kiecolt-Glaser, J., Garner, W., Speicher, C., Penn, G. M., Holiday, J., and Glaser, R. (1984). Psychosocial modifiers of immunocompetence in medical students. *Psychosomatic Medicine*, 46, 7–14.

Kingsley, L., Kaslow, R., Rinaldo, C., Detre, K., Odaka, N., VanRaden, M., Detels, R. Polk, B., Chmiel, J., Kelsey, S., Ostrow, D., and Visscher, B. (1987). Risk factors for sero-conversion to human immunodeficiency virus among male homosexuals. *Lancet*, 1, 345–349.

Kubler-Ross, E. (1969). *On Death and Dying*. New York: Macmillan.

LaPerriere, A., Antoni, M. H., Schneiderman, N., Ironson, G., Klimas, N., Caralis, P., and Fletcher, M. A. (1990). Exercise intervention attenuates emotional distress and natural killer cell decrements following notification of positive serologic status for HIV-1. *Biofeedback and Self-Regulation*, 15, 125–131.

Lazarus, R. S., and Folkman, S. (1984). *Stress Appraisal and Coping*. New York, Springer Publishing Company.

Lechner, S., Antoni, M. H., Lydston, D., LaPerriere, A., Ishii, M., Devieux, J., Ironson, G., Schneiderman, N., Brondolo, E., Tobin, J., and Weiss, S. (under review). Group-based stress management intervention buffers decline in emotional well-being in women with AIDS: The SMART/EST Women's Project.

Lemp, G. F., Payne, S. F., Neal, D., Temelso, T., and Rutherford, G. W. (1990). Survival trends for patients with AIDS. *Journal of the American Medical Association*, 263, 402–406.

Leserman, J., DiSantostefano, R., Perkins, D., Murphy, C., Golden, R., and Evans, D. (1995). Longitudinal study of social support and social conflict as predictors of depression and dysphoria among HIV-positive and HIV-negative gay men. *Depression*, 2, 189–199.

Leserman, J., Jackson, E. D., Petitto, J. M., Golden, R. N., Silva, S. G., Perkins, D. O., Cai, J., Folds, J. D., and Evans, D. L. (1999). Progression to AIDS: The effects of stress, depressive symptoms, and social support. *Psychosomatic Medicine*, 61, 397–406.

Leserman, J., Petitto, J. M., Golden, R. N., Gaynes, B. N., Gu, H., and Perkins, D. O. (2000). The impact of stressful life events, depression, social support, coping and cortisol on progression to AIDS. *American Journal of Psychiatry*, 157, 1221–1228.

Lutgendorf, S., Antoni, M. H., Ironson, G., Klimas, N., Fletcher, M. A., and Schneiderman, N. (1997a). Cognitive processing style, mood and immune function following HIV seropositivity notification. *Cognitive Therapy and Research*, 21, 157–184.

Lutgendorf, S., Antoni, M., Ironson, G., Starr, K., Costello, N., Zuckerman, M., Klimas, N., Fletcher, M. A., and Schneiderman, N. (1998). Changes in cognitive coping skills and social support during cognitive behavioral stress management and distress outcomes among symptomatic HIV positive gay men. *Psychosomatic Medicine*, 60, 204–214.

Lutgendorf, S., Antoni, M., Ironson, G., Klimas, N., Kumar, M., Starr, K., McCabe, P., Cleven, K., Fletcher, M. A., and Schneiderman, N. (1997b). Cognitive behavioral stress management decreases dysphoric mood and herpes simplex virus-type 2 antibody titers in symptomatic HIV-seropositive gay men. *Journal of Consulting and Clinical Psychology*, 65, 31–43.

Lutgendorf, S., Antoni, M. H., Schneiderman, N., Ironson, G., and Fletcher, M. A. (1994). Psychosocial interventions and quality of life changes across the HIV spectrum. In A. Baum, and J. Dimsdale (Eds.), *Perspectives in Behavioral Medicine* (pp. 205–239). NJ: Erlbaum.

Lyketsos, C. G., Hoover, D. R., Guccione, M., Senterfitt, W., Dew, M. A., Wesch, J., VanRaden, M., Treisman, G. J., and Morganstem, H. (1993). Depressive symptoms as predictors of medical outcomes in HIV infection. *Journal of the American Medical Association*, 270, 2563–2567.

Mackie, I. (1993). AIDS, the female patient and the family physician. *Canadian Family Physician*, 39, 1600–1607.

Maier, S. F., Watkins, L. R., and Fleshner, M. (1994). Psychoneuroimmunology: The interface between behavior, brain, and immunity. *American Psychologist*, 49, 1004–1017.

Maiman, M., and Fruchter, R. (1996). Cervical neoplasia and the human immunodeficiency virus. In S. Rubino, and W. Hoskins (Eds.), *Cervical Cancer and Preinvasive Neoplasia* (pp. 405–416). Philadelphia: Lippincott-Raven.

Markham, P., Salahuddin, S., Veren, K., Orndorff, S., and Gallo, R. (1986). Hydrocortisone and some other hormones enhance the expression of HTLV-III. *International Journal of Cancer*, 37, 67–72.

Markowitz, J. C., Kocsis, J. H., Fishman, B., Speilman, L. A., Jacobsberg, L. B., Frances, A. J., Klerman, G. L., and Perry, S. W. (1998). Treatment of depressive symptoms in human immunodeficiency virus-positive patients. *Archives of General Psychiatry*, 55, 452–457.

Martin, D. (1989). Human immunodeficiency virus infection and the gay community: Counseling and clinical issues. *Special Issue: Gay, Lesbian, and Bisexual Issues in Counseling. Journal of Counseling and Development*, 68, 67–72.

Martin, J. (1988). Psychological consequences of AIDS-related bereavement among gay men. *Journal of Consulting and Clinical Psychology*, 56, 856–862.

Martin, J. (1990b). Drug use and unprotected anal intercourse among gay men. *Health Psychology*, 9, 450–465.

Mays, V., and Cochran, S. (1988). Issues in the perception of AIDS risk and risk reduction activities by Black and Hispanic/Latina women. *American Psychologist*, 43, 949–957.

McEwen, B. (1998). Protective and damaging effects of stress mediators. *New England Journal of Medicine*, 338, 171–179.

Miller, G. E., and Cole, S. W. (1998). Social relationships and the progression of human immunodeficiency virus infection: a review of evidence and possible underlying mechanisms. *Annals of Behavioral Medicine*, 20, 181–189.

Mulder, C. L., Emmelkamp, P., Antoni, M. H., Mulder, J., Sandfort, T., and de Vries, M. (1994). Cognitive–behavioral and experiential group psychotherapy for HIV-infected homosexual men: A comparative study. *Psychosomatic Medicine*, 56, 423–431.

Mulder, C., de Vroome, E., van Griensven, G., Antoni, M. H., and Sandfort, T. (1999). Distraction as a predictor of the virological course of HIV-1 infection over a 7-year period in gay men. *Health Psychology*, 18, 107–113.

Mulder, N., Antoni, M. H., Duivenvoorden, H., Kauffman, R., and Goodkin, K. (1995a). Active confrontational coping predicts decreased clinical progression over a one-year period in HIV-infected homosexual men. *Journal of Psychosomatic Research*, 39, 957–965.

Mulder, N., Antoni, M. H., Emmelkamp, P., Veugelers, P., Sandfort, T., van der Vijver, F., and de vries, M. (1995b). Psychosocial group intervention and the rate of decline of immunologc parameters in asymptomatic HIV-infected homosexual men. *Journal of Psychotherapy and Psychosomatics*, 63, 185–192.

Namir, S., Alumbaugh, M. J., Fawzy, F. I., and Wolcott, D. L. (1989). The relationship of social support to physical and psychological aspects of AIDS. *Psychology and Health*, 3, 77–86.

Neale, A., Tilley, B., and Vernon, S. (1986). Marital status, delay in seeking treatment and survival from breast cancer. *Social Science and Medicine*, 23, 305–312.

Nieman, R., Fleming, J., Coker, R., Harris, J, and Mitchell, D. (1993). The effect of cigarette smoking on the development of AIDS in HIV-1-seropositive individuals. *AIDS*, 7, 705–710.

Ostrow, D., Joseph, J., Kessler, R., Soucy, J., Tal, M., Eller, M., Chmiel, J., and Phair, J. (1989). Disclosure of HIV antibody status: Behavioral and mental health correlates. *AIDS Education and Prevention*, 1, 1–11.

Palmblad, J., Petrini, B., Wasserman, J., and Akerstedt, T. (1979). Lymphocyte and granulocyte reactions during sleep deprivation. *Psychosomatic Medicine*, 41, 273–278.

Pantaleo, G., Graziosi, C., and Fauci, A. S. (1993). The immunopathogenesis of human immunodeficiency virus infection. *New England Journal of Medicine*, 328, 327–335.

Patterson, T., Shaw, W, Semple, S., Cherner, M., McCutchan, J., Atkinson, J., Grant, I., and Nannis, E. (1996). Relationship of psychosocial factors to HIV disease progression. *Annals of Behavioral Medicine*, 18, 30–39.

Penedo, F., Antoni, M. H., Schneiderman, N., Ironson, G., Malow. R., Wagner, S., Hurwitz, B., and LaPerriere, A. (2001). Dysfunctional attitudes, coping and psychological distress among HIV-infected gay men. *Cognitive Therapy and Research* 25, 591–606.

Pereira, D. (in press). Interventions for mothers during pregnancy and postpartum: Behavioral and pharmacological approaches to maximize health for mother and child. In M. Chesney and M. H. Antoni (Eds), *Health Psychology Innovations: New Target Populations for Prevention and Care*. Washington, D.C.: American Psychological Association.

Quinn, S. (1993). AIDS and the African American woman. The triple burden of race, class and gender. *Health Education Quarterly*, 20, 305–320.

Rabkin, J. G., Williams, J. B. W., Remien, R. H., Goetz, R. R., Kertzner, R., and Gorman, J. M. (1991). Depression, lymphocyte subsets, and human immunodeficiency virus symptoms on two occasions in HIV-positive homosexual men. *Archives of General Psychiatry*, 48, 111–119.

Rabkin, J., Wagner, G., and Rabkin, R. (1996). Treatment of depression in HIV+ men: Literature review and report of an ongoing study of testosterone replacement therapy. *Annals of Behavioral Medicine*, 18, 24–29.

Rabkin, J., Williams, J., Neugebauer, R., and Goetz, R. (1990). Maintenance of hope in HIV-spectrum homosexual men. *American Journal of Psychiatry*, 147, 1322–1326.

Reed, G. M., Kemeny, M. E., Taylor, S. E., Wang, H. J., and Visscher, B. (1994). Realistic acceptance as a predictor of decreased survival time in gay men with AIDS. *Health Psychology*, 13, 299–307.

Remien, R., and Rabkin, J. G. (in press). Individual therapy with patients across the spectrum of HIV. In M. Chesney, and M. H. Antoni (Eds), *Health Psychology Innovations: New Target Populations for Prevention and Care*. Washington, D.C.: American Psychological Association.

Rosenberg, Z. F., and Fauci, A. S. (1991). Activation of latent HIV infection. *Journal of the national Institutes of Health Research*, 2, 41–45.

Rosser, B., Simon, R., and Michael, W. (1988). Perceived emotional and life change impact of AIDS on homosexual men in two countries. *Psychology and Health*, 2, 301–317.

Schneiderman, N., Antoni, M., Ironson, G., LaPerriere, A., and Fletcher, M. A. (1992). Applied psychosocial science and HIV-1 spectrum disease. *Journal of Applied and Preventive Psychology*, 1, 67–82.

Schneiderman, N., Antoni, M. H., Saab, P., and Ironson, G. (2001). Health psychology: Psychosocial and biobehavioral chronic disease management. *Annual Reviews in Psychology*, 52, 555–580.

Seage, G., Oddleifson, S., Carr, E., Shea, B., Makarewicz-Robert, L., vanBeuzekom, M., and DeMaria, A. (1993). Survival with AIDS in Massachusetts, 1979 to 1989. *American Journal of Public Health*, 83, 72–78.

Solano, L., Costa, M., Salvati, S., Coda, R., Aiuta, F., Mezzaroma, I., and Bertini, M. (1993). Psychosocial factors and clinical evolution in HIV-1 infection: A longitudinal study. *Journal of Psychosomatic Research*, 37, 39–51.

Theorell, T., Blomkvist, V., Jonsson, H., Schulman, S., Berntorp, E., and Stigendal, L. (1995). Social support and the development of immune function in human immunodeficiency virus infection. *Psychosomatic Medicine*, 57, 32–36.

Tindall, B., and Cooper, D. A. (1991). Primary HIV infection: Host responses and intervention strategies. *AIDS*, 5, 1–14.

Tross, S., and Hirsch, D. A. (1988). Psychological distress and neuropsychological complications of HIV infection and AIDS. *American Psychologist*, 43, 929–934.

Williams, R., Barefoot, J., Califf, R., Haney, T., Saunders, W., Pryor, D., Hlatky, M., Siegler, I., and Mark, D. (1992). Prognostic importance of social and economic resources among medically treated patients with angiographically documented coronary artery disease. *Journal of the American Medical Association*, 267, 520–524.

Yang, J. Y., Schwartz, A., and Henderson, E. E. (1994). Inhibition of 3' azido-3' deoxythymidine-resistant HIV-1 infection by dehydroepiandrosterone in vitro. *Biochemical and Biophysical Research Communications*, 201, 1424–1432.

Yang, J. Y., Schwartz, A., and Henderson, E. E. (1993). Inhibition of HIV-1 latency reactivation by dehydroepiandrosterone (DHEA) and an analog of DHEA. *AIDS Research and Human Retroviruses*, 9, 747–754.

Zorrilla, E. P., McKay, J. R., Luborsky, L., and Schmidt, K. (1996). Relation of stressors and depressive symptoms to clinical progression of viral illness. *American Journal of Psychiatry*, 153, 626–635.

Zuckerman, M., and Antoni, M. H. (1995). Social support and its relationship to psychological physical and immune variables in HIV infection. *Clinical Psychology and Psychotherapy*, 2, 210–219.

CHAPTER 10

End-stage Renal Disease

Alan J. Christensen and Katherine Raichle

University of Iowa

Introduction

End-stage renal disease (ESRD) afflicts over 300,000 patients in the United States (USRDS, 2000). ESRD is typically the end-result of a progressive deterioration in kidney function over a period of months or years. In most cases it is a secondary complication of another underlying physical disorder. The most common ESRD etiologies include diabetic nephropathy (approximately 40 percent of all ESRD patients are diabetic) and hypertensive nephrosclerosis (approximately 24 percent of ESRD patients). Whereas the progression of renal failure can sometimes be slowed through the successful management of the contributory disorder (e.g., improved glucose control in the diabetic patient with progressive renal failure), for the large majority of patients the deterioration is irreversible and life threatening. The incidence of ESRD is slightly higher among males than among females, and considerably higher among African-Americans, due largely to the higher rate of hypertension among these individuals.

Only three decades ago, an ESRD diagnosis meant death was imminent. Upon the cessation of renal function, excess fluid, metabolic toxins, and electrolytes rapidly accumulate in blood and bodily tissues. These substances must be removed by alternative means if the ESRD patient is to survive. The introduction in the 1960s of renal dialysis as an effective, life-sustaining treatment for kidney failure brought the hope of long-term survival to hundreds of thousands of individuals afflicted with the disorder. Unfortunately, in the "early years" access to this expensive and scarce treatment was very limited. During this time, treatment allocation decisions were based on an attempt to define the ideal candidates for the intervention (Schupak et al., 1967), and multidisciplinary selection boards were charged with determining what subset

Preparation of this chapter was supported, in part, by National Institutes of Diabetes, Digestive, and Kidney Diseases grant #DK49129 awarded to Alan Christensen.

Correspondence concerning this chapter should be addressed to Alan Christensen, Department of Psychology, 11 Seashore Hall E, The University of Iowa, Iowa City, IA 52242-1407, USA.

of patients in need would be allowed access to the life-sustaining treatment. A significant component of the selection process involved the use of psychiatric and psychosocial criteria, ostensibly to predict which individuals would be the "best" patients or derive the most benefit from treatment (Comty, 1969; Schupak et al., 1967). However, the lack of any empirical basis for making such judgments led to the use of an inconsistent set of criteria, with highly questionable reliability and lacking evidence of predictive validity.

In the mid-1970s the need to restrict access to ESRD treatment began to diminish. The Medicare ESRD entitlement program enacted by the United States Congress in 1973 made all citizens with chronic renal failure eligible for benefits and dramatically improved the availability of this life-preserving treatment. However, as with medical care in general, the costs associated with the Medicare ESRD program have risen exponentially. In 1999 over $11 billion in healthcare benefits were provided by Medicare for the treatment of ESRD patients (USRDS 2000). Rising costs have led to an emerging realization that the costs associated with providing essentially unlimited access to ESRD treatment are becoming prohibitive (Rettig and Levinsky, 1991).

Currently available "renal replacement" treatments for ESRD include renal transplantation and several forms of renal dialysis. In general, the choice of a particular modality is substantially influenced by nonmedical factors, including patient and provider preferences, and judgments about which modality is likely to be associated with the most favorable patient adherence or quality of life (Christensen and Ehlers, in press; Davison, 1996).

The ESRD Treatment Context

There is an important difference in the degree of patient self-management or control over the delivery of the different forms of ESRD treatment. Center hemodialysis is the most common (approximately 62 percent of ESRD patients nationally). The center hemodialysis patient is a relatively passive recipient of a treatment that is carried out in a hospital or clinic. The procedure is typically performed three times a week by nurses or technicians, with each session lasting approximately 4 hours. Hemodialysis involves a vascular connection between the artificial kidney machine and the patient, usually through an arteriovenous fistula placed permanently in the patient's forearm. Nurses or technicians are responsible for directing each step in the initiation, monitoring, and discontinuation of each dialysis session. Little patient participation is required or allowed during treatment.

For a smaller number of patients hemodialysis is carried out at home. Although home and center hemodialysis are essentially analogous from a physiological and mechanical standpoint, home hemodialysis patients have the opportunity to be more actively involved in treatment delivery and direction. Home hemodialysis patients typically are responsible for placing their own arterial and venous needles at the beginning of the session, administering heparin and other necessary medications, and monitoring their blood pressure, as well as various vital functions of the dialysis machine. Moreover, home dialysis patients have considerably less frequent contact with renal care providers, and are able to set and maintain their own dialysis schedules. In contrast to their center hemodialysis counterparts, home patients clearly play a more central and behaviorally involved role in dialysis treatment delivery.

An increasingly common form of ESRD treatment is peritoneal dialysis (approximately 10 percent of ESRD patients nationally). Peritoneal dialysis typically requires the patient to take an even more active role in treatment delivery. In continuous ambulatory peritoneal dialysis (CAPD), the most common form of peritoneal dialysis, a permanent catheter is surgically implanted in the abdomen and a sterile tube is used to connect the catheter to a bag of sterile dialysis solution (dialysate). The bag is elevated to allow the dialysate to flow into the peritoneal cavity. After this procedure is completed the bag is tucked away under the patient's clothing. Over the next 4–8 hours the patient remains ambulatory as blood filters through the peritoneal membrane, leaving toxins and excess fluid behind in the dialysate. After this phase of the procedure is complete, the bag is lowered and the used solution is drained back into the bag, where it is discarded and the dialysate exchange procedure begins again.

In the late 1960s renal transplantation became another viable treatment option for the ESRD patient. Approximately 28 percent of ESRD patients currently have a functioning kidney transplant (USRDS, 2000). Renal grafts come from either a cadaveric (brain-dead) or living (typically a first-degree relative) donor. Although the data are not entirely consistent, a successful renal transplant is generally thought to hold certain advantages in terms of patient quality of life (Christensen et al., 1991, 2000). However, owing to a marked shortage of donor organs, a significant transplant rejection rate, and other potential complications or barriers, renal dialysis remains the prescribed treatment for the large majority of patients. Even patients who eventually receive a renal transplant have typically undergone chronic dialysis for a period of time prior to transplant surgery. For most patients, the renal transplantation experience involves a transition toward greater independence from renal care providers, and the assumption of greater responsibility for the management of their own health. Transplant patients are responsible for the management of their immunosuppressive medication regimen, having regular work done at a laboratory or clinic near their home, monitoring themselves for early signs of organ rejection, and guarding against communicable disease and infection. Direct contact between post-renal transplant patients and care providers is generally much less frequent than the intensive contact between center hemodialysis patients and their care providers.

Despite recent advances in immunosuppressive therapy, activation of the patient's immune system, resulting in organ rejection and potential graft failure, remains an important limitation to the potential benefit of transplantation. Approximately 40 percent of cadaveric renal graft recipients experience a clinically significant acute rejection episode in the first year following transplantation (Johnson et al., 1997). Most acute rejections are successfully reversed, as 10–15 percent of cadaveric transplants actually fail in the first year (USRDS, 2000). Success rates for kidney grafts from living donors are considerably higher than for cadaveric grafts, having a less than a 6 percent failure rate. Living-related donation also offers potential advantages in terms of donor availability. Unfortunately, factors that might influence living-organ donation decisions have been largely ignored by ESRD and organ transplantation researchers.

Major Psychosocial Issues in Renal Failure

From a biomedical, behavioral, and healthcare policy perspective, ESRD is unique among medical conditions. The extreme dependence on artificial means for survival, the substantial behavioral demands placed on the patient, and the tremendous investment of the Medicare system in the treatment of the disease, all have few parallels in healthcare. Despite the uniqueness of the disorder, most of the central clinical issues and problems observed in this population are also seen in other chronic medical conditions. This chapter will focus on four broad issues that we believe each reflect an opportunity for behavioral medicine research and practice to make an important and unique contribution to the care of ESRD patients. These issues include patient nonadherence with the medical treatment regimen; assessing and treating psychological distress and disorder in this population; neuropsychological sequelae in ESRD; and psychosocial and behavioral influences on patient survival.

Nonadherence with the Renal Dialysis and Transplantation Regimens

In addition to undergoing frequent and time-consuming dialysis sessions, patients receiving all forms of ESRD treatment are required to follow a multifaceted behavioral regimen to help ensure the efficacy and safety of the medical intervention. For example, center and home hemodialysis patients face extreme restrictions on the amount of fluid that can be safely consumed, because of the intermittent nature of the fluid clearance accomplished by the typical three-times weekly dialysis regimen. Prolonged fluid overload is associated with congestive heart failure, hypertension, pulmonary edema, and shortened patient survival (Kimmel et al., 2000b; Wolcott et al., 1986). One report suggested that dietary nonadherence was the primary contributing factor to the death of over 50 percent of ESRD patients dying of cardiac-related causes (Plough and Salem, 1992).

Both peritoneal and hemodialysis patients are required to take regular doses of phosphate-binding medication, as well as to reduce their intake of phosphorus-rich foods (e.g., dairy products, meats), owing to the body's inability to excrete phosphorus while undergoing dialysis. Sustained elevations in serum phosphate (P) are associated with a variety of bone-related complications, including renal osteodystrophy, serious decreases in calcium, and subsequent bone demineralization. Serum P levels greater than 6.0 mg/dl are generally considered indicative of problematic adherence. In addition, restriction of potassium-rich foods (e.g., most fruits) is necessary for dialysis patients to maintain safe serum potassium (K) levels. Hyperkalemia (i.e., serum K > 5.5 mEq/l) can result in potentially life-threatening cardiac arrhythmia.

As is the case with other medical populations, identifying a "gold standard" for the evaluation of patient adherence presents a significant challenge to both researchers and clinicians. The most commonly employed adherence criteria in the ESRD research literature involve indirect biochemical or physiologic markers of patient adherence. Although biochemical assessments have the advantage of being relatively unaffected by human judgments, such assessments are potentially confounded by nonbehavioral factors. For example, serum K is known to be influenced by changes in the dialysis prescription, and by a variety of acute medical illnesses. When interpreting serum P levels as an indicator of adherence it is difficult to know whether elevations are due to dietary indiscretions, missed medication, or some combination of factors.

In contrast to the limitations in obtaining valid judgments of adherence to diet and medication regimens, adherence to the fluid-intake restrictions among hemodialysis patients can be quite accurately determined by computing the amount of weight a patient gains between treatment sessions. This is particularly true for patients who have been receiving hemodialysis for an extended period of time and who typically have little or no urine output. The values resulting from this computation (termed "interdialytic weight gain", or IWG) are believed to be a valid reflection of the amount of fluid the ESRD patient ingests between sessions (Manley and Sweeney, 1986). Interdialytic weight gains greater than 2.5 kg are generally considered indicative of problematic adherence.

Some investigations have examined patient compliance with the dialysis treatment schedule itself as an indicator of regimen adherence (Kimmel et al., 1995, 1998a). In these studies, adherence has been defined either as the percentage attendance with the three-times weekly hemodialysis schedule, or as the amount of time a patient actually receives dialysis relative to the amount of dialysis time the physician had prescribed for a given 3–4-hour session. Assessing adherence to the dialysis schedule itself avoids many of the problems inherent in relying on indirect biochemical markers as reflections of behavior. However, missing a dialysis session altogether and prematurely curtailing a given session are relatively rare occurrences. For example, Kimmel et al. (1998a) reported that in a study of 295 patients, on average less than 2 percent of hemodialysis sessions were missed over a 3-month period. Moreover, the shortening of a particular session by a patient may be confounded by many factors, such as symptoms or problems that occur during a session, or simply differences in provider judgments or practice styles.

Despite the severe consequences of nonadherence in this population, studies involving renal dialysis patients have typically observed that between 30 and 60 percent do not adhere to diet, fluid-intake, or medication regimens (Bame et al., 1993; Christensen et al., 1992; Friend et al., 1997a; Moran et al., 1997; Schneider et al., 1991). In general, past reports have indicated that nonadherence is most common for fluid-intake restrictions and somewhat less common for dietary or medication guidelines, although differences in the validity and reliability of the various parameters makes it difficult to compare across different aspects of the regimen.

Nonadherence Following Renal Transplantation

Patients receiving a renal transplant are largely free from the dietary and fluid-intake constraints posed by dialysis treatment. However, transplant patients are required to follow a strict immunosuppressive medication regimen, attend frequent clinic and laboratory appointments, and remain vigilant about physical changes that may signal organ rejection or infection. Patient nonadherence to the immunosuppressive regimen is believed to be an important contributor to renal graft rejection and failure (Armstrong and Weiner, 1981; De Geest et al., 1995; Didlake et al., 1988). As many as 75 percent of renal graft failures in the second year after transplant may be due to nonadherence (Kiley et al., 1993).

Assessing regimen adherence in renal transplant patients has proved even more difficult than among dialysis patients. Blood levels of the most common immunosuppressive medications (e.g., cyclosporin, tacrolimus) are quite unstable over time and are influenced by a number of factors other than medication adherence (e.g., food intake, other medications, acute illness). Thus, reliably determining the rate of nonadherence through the use of biochemical markers is extremely difficult in this population. The large majority of past studies involving transplant patients have simply relied on patient self-reports of adherence behavior (e.g., De Geest et al., 1995; Raiz et al., 1999; Rovelli, et al., 1989; Siegel and Greenstein, 1999). Given the difficulties in assessing adherence in this population, it is not surprising that estimates of nonadherence have varied greatly, ranging from less than 5 percent to as many as 75 percent of patients (De Geest et al., 1995; Didlake et al., 1988; Kiley et al., 1993; Raiz et al., 1999; Rovelli, et al., 1989; Siegel and Greenstein, 1997, 1999; Sketris et al., 1994). One finding that is quite consistent is that problems with post-transplant adherence are particularly high among pediatric patients (Bell, 2000; Blowey et al., 1997; Ettenger et al., 1991).

A promising advance in adherence assessment involves the use of electronic monitoring technologies (Blowey et al., 1997; Diaz-Buxo et al., 1999). Using a medication monitoring device (a "MEMS cap"), Blowey et al., reported that 26 percent of the pediatric renal transplant recipients studied missed three or more consecutive cyclosporin doses over a 2–3-month period. Only half of those who were classified as noncompliant according to electronic dosing records were similarly classified using physician or nurse ratings, or based on blood levels of cyclosporin.

In the renal dialysis population, an electronic device designed to record the degree to which a patient's prescribed home peritoneal dialysis schedule is being followed has recently been introduced (Diaz-Buxo et al., 1999). This "memory card" is inserted into a specially adapted dialysis machine prior to use, and stores a range of parameters related to the dialysis process over a 2-month period. Although increasing use of electronic technologies to track adherence behavior holds considerable promise, all available adherence measures and assessment methodologies are limited in important ways. Given these limitations, we believe it is critical for researchers to use multiple indicators of patient adherence in order to minimize the impact of the limitations or idiosyncrasies of a single methodology (see also Dunbar-Jacob, this volume).

Determinants of Adherence

Demographic Characteristics

The more general research literature involving patient factors as potential predictors of regimen adherence has produced very inconsistent findings (Haynes, 1979; Kaplan and Simon, 1990). Studies of ESRD patient adherence behavior have examined a range of demographic, cognitive, and personality characteristics, with modestly better success than in the adherence literature more broadly. In a number of studies, younger patients exhibited consistently poorer adherence to various aspects of the dialysis and renal transplant regimens than did older patients (Bame, et al., 1993; Boyer et al., 1990; Christensen and Smith, 1995; Cummings et al., 1982; Didlake et al., 1988; Ettenger et al., 1991; Kimmel et al., 1995; Siegel and Greenstein, 1999). Other evidence suggests that males exhibit significantly poorer adherence than females (Boyer et al., 1990; De Geest et al., 1995; Kiley et al., 1993; Morduchowicz et al., 1993). No other consistent patterns involving demographic variables have emerged in the ESRD adherence literature.

Personality Influences on Adherence

Empirical evidence linking personality dispositions to ESRD patient adherence remains limited. In a study of 72 renal dialysis patients, Christensen and Smith (1995) reported that higher conscientiousness scores from the NEO-Five Factor Inventory (Costa and McCrae, 1992) were significantly associated with more favorable medication adherence (i.e., lower serum P values) after controlling for a number of demographic factors. This finding is consistent with theorizing that a diligent, self-disciplined, purposeful style is essential to meeting the self-management demands of the ESRD treatment regimen (Wiebe and Christensen, 1996). However, in two more recent studies, conscientiousness failed to exert a direct effect on fluid-intake or medication adherence (Moran et al., 1997; Wiebe and Christensen, 1997).

Other research suggests that individual differences in trait hostility may have important implications for adherence behavior. Christensen et al. (1997) examined individual differences on the Cook–Medley (1954) hostility (Ho) scale in a sample of 48 hemodialysis patients. Christensen et al. (1997) obtained a significant main effect between higher Ho scale scores and poorer adherence to the phosphorus control regimen. Moderational analyses indicated that the deleterious effect of hostility on adherence was most pronounced among patients possessing the expectation that positive health outcomes are not contingent on the actions or advice of healthcare providers (i.e., low powerful others health locus of control). In other words, the generally mistrustful nature of cynically hostile patients seemed to be most deleterious among those who specifically believed that the actions of their healthcare providers fail to influence health outcomes in a positive way. However, the results failed to generalize across multiple adherence domains. Neither hostility nor patient control expectations were significantly associated with fluid-intake adherence in this study.

A number of studies have examined the association of locus of control expectations with adherence in this population. The results are clearly mixed. Several early studies reported evidence that patients with an internal locus of control exhibit more favorable dialysis regimen adherence (Kaplan De-Nour and Czaczkes, 1972; Oldenburg et al., 1988; Poll and Kaplan De-Nour, 1980). However, other research suggests that internal control expectations are not significantly related to adherence in this population (Brown and Fitzpatrick, 1988; Schneider et al., 1991; Wittenberg et al., 1983). Moreover, a recent study involving a sample of 357 renal transplant patients found an internal health locus of control to be associated with poorer self-reported adherence to immunosupressive medication (Raiz et al., 1999). In this same study the belief that health outcomes are controlled by "powerful others" (i.e., healthcare providers) was associated with more favorable adherence.

Health Beliefs

A number of studies involving ESRD patients have examined components of the health belief model (HBM; Rosenstock, 1966) as predictors of adherence. Poorer adherence has been reported among center hemodialysis patients (Cummings et al., 1982; Horne and Weinman, 1999; Weed-Collins and Hogan, 1989) and renal transplant patients (Kiley et al., 1993) reporting greater perceived barriers (e.g., being away from home for treatment or follow-up, medication costs, medication side-effects) to following the regimen. There is little evidence linking other components of the HBM (e.g., perceived threat, perceived benefits) to adherence among ESRD patients (Hartmann and Becker, 1978; Rosenbaum and Ben-Ari Smira, 1986; Wiebe and Christensen, 1997).

Christensen et al. (1999a) have proposed that irrational health beliefs or health-related cognitive distortions may play a more central role in determining nonadherent behavior than do more conventional conceptualizations of health-related beliefs such as the HBM. For example, patients prone to making overgeneralizations about health-related experiences might be more likely to appraise their physician's recommendation as being unnecessary on the basis of an irrelevant past experience. Consistent with this reasoning, Christensen et al. (1999a) found that higher scores on the newly devised Irrational Health Belief scale were associated with significantly poorer blood glucose control (higher glycosylated hemoglobin values) in a study of 107 type 1 diabetic patients not yet suffering from chronic renal failure.

Other evidence suggests that self-efficacy expectations are related to both fluid-intake and medication adherence among dialysis patients, as well as to medication adherence among transplanted patients (Brady et al., 1997; Christensen et al., 1996; De Geest et al., 1995; Eitel et al., 1998; Rosenbaum and Ben-Ari Smira, 1986; Schneider, et al., 1991). In a study of 40 hemodialysis patients, Eitel and colleagues (1998) reported that adherence-specific self-efficacy expectations significantly predicted future fluid-intake adherence assessed 3 months later. However, self-efficacy failed to predict dietary or medication adherence.

Social and Family Environment Influences on Adherence

Considerable evidence in other chronic illness populations suggests that the availability and perceived quality of social support is an important correlate of regimen adherence (e.g., Sherbourne et al., 1992; Stanton, 1987). Research regarding support and adherence among ESRD patients is limited. Two studies have examined the effects of a supportive family environment on adherence among ESRD patients (Christensen et al., 1992; Davis et al., 1996). In a study involving a sample of 78 center hemodialysis patients, Christensen et al. (1992) reported that those patients reporting a family environment characterized by greater cohesion and expressiveness among members and less intrafamily conflict, exhibited significantly more favorable adherence to fluid-intake restrictions. In this same study, family support was not associated with adherence to dietary restrictions. Other research suggests that more favorable marital adjustment among center hemodialysis patients and their spouses may be related to better fluid-intake but not dietary adherence (Somer and Tucker, 1988, 1992). In one of the few available studies involving social or familial factors and adherence among pediatric ESRD patients, Davis et al. (1996) reported better post-transplantation adherence among patients whose parents were classified as having better verbal and nonverbal communication skills.

Other studies have found that social support was not related to adherence among ESRD patients (Boyer et al., 1990; Cummings et al., 1982; Hitchcock et al., 1992; Rudman et al., 1999). At least one study has found that the association of social support and adherence is moderated by patient gender. Kimmel et al. (1995) reported a significant association between greater perceived support and more favorable medication adherence among males, but no association among females. Finally, the results of a study of 56 center hemodialysis patients (Moran et al., 1997) suggested that the association between support and adherence is moderated by individual differences in trait conscientiousness. Clearly, additional research is needed to clarify what seems to be a complex association between social and family support and patient adherence.

Patient X Treatment Interactions and Adherence

We have previously argued that the association between individual patient differences and adherence can be clarified by considering the interactive association of patient characteristics with features of the illness and medical treatment context (i.e., the "patient by context interactive framework") (Christensen, 2000). From this perspective, adherence should be best when the patient's characteristic or preferred style of coping with illness-related stress is consistent with the contextual features or demands of the particular type of medical intervention the patient is undergoing. For example, in two studies comparing samples of staff-treated center dialysis and self-treated home dialysis patients, we found that adherence was maximized in cases in which the patients' preferred styles of coping matched the requirements or demands of the type of dialysis treatment received (Christensen et al., 1990, 1994a). That is, patients with highly active or vigilant coping styles exhibited better adherence when undergoing renal treatment that is primarily patient controlled and carried out at home (i.e., CAPD or home hemodialysis). Patients with less active or more avoidant styles of dealing with stress exhibited more favorable adherence when undergoing staff-administered treatment in a hospital or clinic (i.e., center hemodialysis).

In our own ongoing research we have begun identifying patients at an early, asymptomatic stage in the progression of chronic renal failure, and then following them as they approach renal failure and ESRD. This provides a unique opportunity to prospectively test hypotheses concerning the prediction of adherence to a future regimen. Our initial work using this methodology examined 69 patients first assessed in the early stages of renal insufficiency (Christensen et al., 1999b). All patients had a form of progressive renal disease and were identified based on routine screening of renal function (i.e., serum creatinine levels > 3.0 mg/dl). Patients' degree of "information vigilance" was assessed using a composite measure consisting of the information preference subscale from the Krantz Health Opinion Survey (Krantz et al., 1980), the Internal Health Locus of Control scale from the Multidimensional Health Locus of Control scales (Wallston et al., 1978), and the monitoring subscale from the Miller Behavioral Style Scale (Miller, 1987). Higher information vigilance scores were defined by higher scores on each of these measures. Patients were reassessed approximately 2 years after this pre-ESRD assessment. Results indicated that among home dialysis patients, individuals reporting higher information vigilance scores displayed better fluid-intake adherence than low information vigilance patients once dialysis treatment was actually initiated. Among center hemodialysis patients, those possessing a more information-vigilant style displayed poorer adherence (higher IWG) when undergoing the provider-directed, hospital-based treatment. Thus, consistent with the interactive framework, regimen adherence was best predicted by the degree of congruence between patients' coping style and the demands or requirement of the type of dialysis eventually prescribed.

Psychological Distress and Disorder in ESRD patients

Chronic physical disease often challenges individuals with serious lifestyle disruptions, role loss, substantial uncertainty about the future, and pain or physical discomfort. Given this degree of stress, it should not be surprising that higher rates of psychiatric illness have been documented among patients with a chronic physical illnesses than in the population at large (Rodin and Voshart, 1986; Taylor and Aspinwall, 1990). ESRD patients are no exception to this association. In fact, recent epidemiologic evidence suggests that the rate of psychiatric disorders in the ESRD population is substantially higher than that observed in many other chronic medical conditions (Kimmel et al., 1998c). Kimmel and colleagues reported that hospitalization rates for psychiatric disorders were over twice as high for ESRD patients as for non-ESRD patients with diabetes, heart disease, or cerebrovascular disease. Mood disorders, dementia, and substance-use disorders were the most common psychiatric illnesses among ESRD patients. Various studies have reported variable rates in the estimated prevalence of depressive disorders in this population, suggesting that 12–40 percent of ESRD patients meet diagnostic criteria for a depressive disorder (Craven et al., 1987, 1988; Hinrichson et al., 1989; Lowry and Atcherson, 1980). Although these estimates vary, they are consistently higher than the 2–9 percent prevalence of depressive disorders observed in the general population (American Psychiatric Association, 1994).

The substantial variation in depression estimates across various studies is likely the product of heterogeneity in diagnostic criteria. One significant challenge in the assessment of depression in this population involves the overlap or confounding between somatic signs and symptoms of depression, and analogous symptoms associated with renal failure. The neurovegetative symptoms of depression, such as fatiguability, cognitive deficits, decreased appetite, sleep difficulties, and loss of libido can all occur secondary to chronic renal failure and in the absence of a depressive syndrome. Additionally, conditions associated with ESRD, such as anemia, electrolyte disturbances, and underlying systemic disease (e.g., diabetes), may also imitate depressive symptoms. Craven et al. (1987) reported that only one somatic indicator – appetite and weight change – showed a specific relationship to major depression among ESRD patients. Other somatic symptoms (e.g., loss of energy, decreased sexual interest) were so common in their entire hemodialysis patient sample that they were not useful in distinguishing depressed from nondepressed individuals.

The manner in which somatic symptoms are considered in the context of a depression assessment can have a substantial influence on the conclusions reached. For example, O'Donnell and Chung (1997) found that rates of major depression varied from 6 to 34 percent among hemodialysis patients, depending on the criteria that were used. When somatic depression symptoms were excluded (given the overlap with uremic symptoms), only 6 percent of the sample met DSM-IV criteria for a depressive disorder. However, when all DSM-IV-endorsed somatic symptoms were considered the rate of major depression rose to 34 percent.

Differences in Distress for Transplantation versus Dialysis

There is some indication that depression symptoms are highest among patients treated with center hemodialysis and somewhat lower among those with a functioning renal graft (Christensen et al., 1991; Evans et al., 1985). In fact, improvement in patient quality of life (including a reduction in emotional distress) is considered a central goal of transplantation as a treatment for ESRD (Dew et al., 1997). However, the findings involving differences in patient wellbeing for transplantation versus dialysis are not entirely consistent. Whereas some studies (e.g., Christensen et al., 1991) have reported less emotional distress following transplantation, others have reported no such differences between transplant and dialysis patients (e.g., Devins et al., 1990a; Kalman et al., 1983).

Christensen and Moran (1998) have suggested that whether or not renal transplantation is associated with an improvement in patient quality of life may depend upon individual patient differences. Christensen et al. (2000) further argued that because the post-transplant period is marked by a transition toward greater independence and greater responsibility for monitoring and managing one's own health, differences in patient coping style may influence adaptation. Consistent with this perspective, we found that among patients receiving a renal transplant, those classified as having a high preference for seeking and receiving health-related information prior to transplantation exhibited significantly improved emotional wellbeing (lower depression) afterwards. However, the improvement in quality of life following successful transplantation did not extend to all patients in the sample. Those patients who showed a relatively low preference for information actually showed a slight, though nonsignificant, increase in depression after transplantation. Among waiting-list patients who were not transplanted during the follow-up period, preference for information had little effect on depression (Christensen et al., 2000).

Emotional Distress in Pediatric Patients

Although there has been less research examining psychological distress among pediatric ESRD patients, previous reports have detailed a wide range of psychological and behavioral problems among such children (Brownbridge and Fielding, 1994; Eisenhauer et al., 1988; Fukunishi and Kudo, 1995). For example, Fukunishi and Kudo (1995) examined the prevalence of psychiatric problems in a total of 53 children with ESRD (26 on CAPD and 27 with a kidney transplant) compared to a control group of 27 healthy children. A significantly higher number of children on dialysis met the criteria for separation anxiety disorder: 65 percent, compared to 18 percent of transplanted children and only 3 percent of healthy children. Interestingly, adjustment disorder was significantly more common in the transplanted group than in CAPD children, and there was no evidence of adjustment disorder in the control group. Moreover, Eisenhauer and colleagues (1988) compared the prevalence of psychiatric disorders in children with earlier-stage chronic renal disease relative to children with end-stage renal disease. Depression was the most common disorder in children with ESRD, whereas anxiety disorders were more common in those with less advanced renal disease.

Depression Influences Survival in ESRD

The high prevalence of depression in the ESRD population seems even more troubling in the context of evidence that depression may be related to earlier patient mortality (Burton et al., 1986; Kimmel et al., 2000a; Peterson et al., 1991; Shulman et al., 1988). Peterson et al. (1991) reported that a cognitive item subset from the BDI (somatic items were eliminated to avoid confounding with disease severity) significantly predicted hemodialysis patient mortality over a 2-year period. Other studies have failed to replicate a relationship between depression and survival (Christensen et al., 1994b; Devins et al., 1990b; Husebye et al., 1987; Kimmel et al., 1998a). In the most recently published study, Kimmel et al. (2000a) reported that initially assessed depression failed to predict mortality in a sample of 295 hemodialysis patients after controlling for demographic and medical risk factors. However, by obtaining six repeated assessments of depression over an average 39-month follow-up period, Kimmel and colleagues were able to treat BDI scores as a time-varying covariate. Using this strategy, depression changes did significantly predict patient survival. Specifically, a one-standard deviation (SD) increase in BDI-assessed depression from one assessment period to the next was associated with a 32 percent increase in mortality risk. This pattern suggests that an acute worsening (or a transitory improvement) in mood may have particularly important implications for patient mortality.

Using a different perspective, Christensen et al. (2001) examined the potential effect of trait differences in neuroticism or chronic negative affectivity on mortality among patients with chronic renal disease. Neuroticism scores obtained using the NEO Five Factor Inventory (Costa and McCrae, 1992) uniquely and significantly predicted survival across an average 49-month follow-up period, after controlling for the significant effects of age, diabetic status, renal replacement status, and anemia (hemoglobin level). One novel aspect of the study was that personality was assessed in the very early stages of chronic renal impairment, before treatment for renal failure was required. The estimated mortality rate for patients with trait neuroticism scores 1 SD above the mean was 40.7 percent higher than for patients with average scores on this dimension. A significant independent effect was also obtained for the conscientiousness trait. For patients with relatively low trait conscientiousness scores the estimated mortality rate was 46.5 percent higher relative to average scorers.

Mediating Influences

Several potential mediating processes have been proposed that might explain or account for the apparently deleterious effect of depression on patient mortality (see review by Kimmel et al., 1993). Regimen nonadherence is one such process. This proposition seems reasonable, given that motivational deficits are commonly seen in individuals with a depressive disorder. However, research to date has generally failed to find an association between symptoms of depression, or negative mood more generally, and patient adherence (Christensen et al., 1994b; Friend et al., 1997a; Simoni et al., 1997). A second behaviorally mediated process that may partly account for an association between depression and earlier mortality involves the influence of depression on nutritional status. Malnutrition is known to be a significant risk factor for increased morbidity and mortality among ESRD patients (Leavy et al., 1998). Moreover, there is evidence that depressed mood in this population may contribute to undernourishment and malnutrition. Friend et al. (1997b) reported that higher BDI scores predicted significant reductions in serum albumin levels (an indicator of nutritional adequacy) over a 6-month follow-up period. This association remained significant in an analysis examining only nonsomatic symptoms of depression.

An increasingly common cause of death among ESRD patients treated with renal dialysis is patient withdrawal from treatment. Earlier reports indicated that 11–22 percent of such deaths are due to a decision to withdraw from treatment (Neu and Kjellstrand, 1986; Port et al., 1989). More recent reports suggest this number may be increasing. Bordenave et al. (1998) reported that 44 percent of the 120 deaths on their hemodialysis unit from 1990 to 1996 were due to the cessation of dialysis. The reasons underlying withdrawal are not entirely clear, but, not surprisingly, patients who stop treatment tend to be older and have more severe physical impairments (Bordenave et al., 1998). Other characteristics distinguishing patients who cease dialysis are more puzzling, and suggest that nonmedical factors play a role. For example, withdrawal is higher among females and among Caucasians than among most other ethnic groups (Leggat et al., 1997). Depression seems likely to play a role in influencing patient decisions to terminate dialysis treatment. However, we are aware of no data examining the extent to which symptoms of depression contribute to this process, or the extent to which the successful treatment of depression might influence such a decision. Given the likelihood that depression (or other forms of psychological distress or disorder) and sociocultural factors play a role in influencing patient and provider judgments about treatment termination, this issue clearly warrants additional attention from behavioral medicine clinicians and researchers.

Immunologic factors may also play an important role in influencing mortality among ESRD patients (Kimmel et al., 1998a). Substantial data indicate that patients receiving renal dialysis show immunocompromise on both enumerative and functional indicators of cell-mediated immunity (Haag-Weber and Horl, 1993; Kay and Raij, 1986). Moreover, the nature of the dialysis process itself (e.g., frequent access to the patient's vascular system) increases patient exposure to infectious agents. In the case of patients receiving renal transplants, induced immunosuppression is the central aim of the post-transplantation medication regimen. The reduced immunocompetence observed in this population, coupled with increased exposure to pathogens, has clear consequences for outcomes. Infection is, in fact, the third leading cause of death in the general ESRD population (USRDS, 2000).

Evidence from the general psychoneuroimmunology literature suggests that depression and emotional distress are associated with reduced immunocompetence (O'Leary, 1990). This raises the possibility that reductions in immunocompetence due to depression, in an already immunocompromised ESRD population, may play a role in mediating an association between depression and mortality. This possibility has not yet been examined in the ESRD population and is in need of investigation.

Psychological Intervention in ESRD

Whereas research documenting the prevalence of emotional (e.g., depression) and behavioral (e.g., nonadherence) dysfunction among ESRD patients is common, studies examining interventions designed to ameliorate these problems are few. Hener et al. (1996) reported that couples-oriented supportive psychotherapy and cognitive–behavioral therapy were both more effective than a no-treatment control group in reducing symptoms of depression and anxiety among hemodialysis patients. The two intervention groups did not differ in terms of outcome. In a novel test of the effects of manipulated self-presentations, Leake et al. (1999) found that patients randomly assigned to selectively present themselves as successful copers during a videotaped interview reported significantly reduced depression up to 1 month following the study. Depression levels among control group patients were unchanged. Participation in the strategic self-presentation exercise may have facilitated patients' problem-solving skills and enhanced their self-efficacy to deal with the disease.

Evidence involving the utility of pharmacologic treatment for depression in this population is mixed. Early studies involving tricyclic antidepressant medications reported modest success when these medications were used with ESRD patients with a diagnosed mood disorder (see review by Kimmel et al., 1993). A limiting factor in the use of tricyclic medications involves the side-effects, which may not be well tolerated by ESRD patients. There have been few controlled trials examining the effect of the newer selective serotonin reuptake inhibitor (SSRI) antidepressants in this population. However, the available evidence suggests these medications are both well tolerated and effective (Blumenfield et al., 1997).

Most intervention studies targeting ESRD patient regimen adherence have used behaviorally oriented techniques. There is modest evidence to suggest that behavioral strategies (e.g., self-monitoring, behavioral contracting and positive reinforcement) are associated with improved adherence among hemodialysis patients (Barnes, 1976; Brantley et al., 1990; Carton and Schweitzer, 1996; Christensen and Lawton, 1997; Cummings et al., 1981; Hart, 1979; Hegel et al., 1992; Keane et al., 1981). However, most past studies have been limited to small n or single-subject designs. Further research involving large patient samples and a broader range of intervention techniques is clearly needed before the most effective strategies in this population can be determined.

Neuropsychological Effects of ESRD

End-stage renal disease and the uremic state that results from renal failure are known to have profound effects on the central nervous system. In past decades serious CNS disturbances, including dialysis-associated dementia, uremic delirium, and other encephalopathic syndromes, posed a substantial threat to the wellbeing of the ESRD patient (Fraser and Arieff, 1988). Contemporary advances in the dialysis procedure and earlier initiation of treatment have greatly reduced the incidence of these major CNS complications. However, ESRD continues to be associated with a variety of changes in neuropsychological functioning. Mild to moderate impairments in psychomotor speed, attention and concentration, verbal and nonverbal memory, and constructional ability have been observed in ESRD patients (Baker et al., 1989; Bremer et al., 1997; English et al., 1978; Hart and Kreutzer, 1988; Southeaver et al., 1982). The most salient deficits in these studies have seemed to appear in tasks that require sustained attention or psychomotor speed. Bremer et al. (1997) reported that 37 percent of renal failure patients showed signs of mild impairment in one or more areas of cognitive functioning, compared to 15 percent of nonrenal-impaired control subjects. Moreover, this study reported that decrements in vocational functioning among dialysis patients may be due partly to these impairments in cognitive ability.

The degree of neurocognitive impairment appears to be greatest among patients with advanced renal failure but who have not yet begun dialysis treatment (Hart et al., 1983; McKee et al., 1982). Moreover, an improvement in cognitive functioning is generally observed among dialysis patients who undergo successful renal transplantation (Fennell et al., 1984; Kramer et al., 1996).

In contrast to research reporting cognitive deficits in ESRD samples, two recent studies have failed to identify differences in the neurocognitive functioning of chronic hemodialysis patients, compared with matched medical controls having normal renal function (Pliskin et al., 1996; Umans and Pliskin, 1998). Pliskin and colleagues have suggested that neuropsychological deficits reported for other samples may have been due, in part, to inadequate dialysis treatment in study participants (e.g., inadequate dialysis time or delivery), or to a failure to appropriately match control subjects on important demographic characteristics (e.g., education level) or clinical variables (e.g., medical co-morbidity). Additional study of neurocognitive changes over time as renal failure progresses, as well as across variations in renal treatment modality, is clearly needed before firm conclusions about the neurocognitive effects of ESRD and its treatment can be drawn.

Clinical Implications and Conclusions

Behavioral medicine research and practice seems poised to make increasingly significant contributions to the care of patients with ESRD. Although psychiatric and psychological consultation has long played a role in the management of these patients, until recently there was little empirical foundation for clinicians to draw on when making assessment and treatment decisions. This review suggests that several target problems or issues that are central to the care of the ESRD patient can be more effectively addressed through a melding of behavioral medicine research and practice.

First, substantial advances have been made in the assessment, diagnosis, and treatment of mood disorders in this population. In our own clinical health psychology consultation service, over a 12-month period the most common referral request from our renal dialysis and transplantation programs involved the assessment and treatment of depression (45 percent of ESRD patient referrals). Recent research has underscored the importance of modifying the administration or interpretation of diagnostic assessments to better recognize the overlap of physical signs and symptoms of renal disease with the neuro-vegetative symptoms of depression. Studies examining the efficacy or effectiveness of psychological treatments for mood disorders in the ESRD population are still scarce. The available data suggest that various psychotherapeutic approaches (e.g., cognitive–behavioral, supportive) can significantly, and with relatively equal efficacy, reduce emotional dysfunction in this population. Given the added complexities involved in utilizing pharmacologic depression treatments in patients with chronic renal impairment, there is an even greater need for more careful evaluation of nonpharmacological alternatives.

Patient nonadherence to some aspect of the prescribed medical regimen reflects the second most common reason (25 percent of referrals to our service) for psychological consultation in this population. Considerable progress has been made in the ESRD research literature in identifying patient factors predictive of problematic adherence behavior. Our own research in this area suggests that a consideration of patients' coping preferences or personality may be useful in selecting the most appropriate renal treatment modality for a particular individual. Adherence intervention research has, unfortunately, lagged behind assessment-based research. Additional attention to the design and implementation of effective adherence behavior intervention protocols is an essential part of enhancing patient outcomes.

Approximately 20 percent of the referrals to our service involved concerns about cognitive impairment as the primary complaint. The neuropsychological impact of renal failure has received somewhat less attention in the research literature, and the factors influencing the neurocognitive performance of these patients are not well understood. On balance, the research and clinical reports that are available suggest that mild to moderate decline in certain areas of cognitive function is common in this population, and that the potential consequences of these impairments on patient lifestyle may be substantial. The neuropsychology of renal failure is clearly in need of further study.

We firmly believe that behavioral medicine research and practice has much to offer to the care of patients with end-stage renal disease. In a reciprocal sense, we also believe that research involving this relatively understudied population can inform behavioral medicine theory and practice more broadly. It is our hope that this chapter will spark additional interest in the behavioral medicine community to address the many clinical challenges and theoretically intriguing issues posed by this chronic, potentially debilitating condition.

References

American Psychiatric Association (1994). *Diagnostic and Statistical Manual of Mental Disorders* (4th ed.). Washington D.C.: American Psychiatric Association.

Armstrong, S. H., and Weiner, M. F. (1981). Noncompliance with post-transplantation immunosuppression. *International Journal of Psychiatry in Medicine*, 11, 89–93.

Baker, L. R. I., Brown, A. L., Byrne, J., Charlesworth, M., Jackson, M., Roe, C. J., and Warrington, E. K. (1989). Head scan appearances and cognitive function in renal failure. *Clinical Nephrology*, 32, 242–248.

Bame, S. I., Petersen, N., and Wray, N. P. (1993). Variation in hemodialysis patient compliance according to demographic characteristics. *Social Science in Medicine*, 37, 1035–1043.

Barnes, M. R. (1976). Token economy control of fluid overload in a patient receiving hemodialysis. *Journal of Behavior Therapy and Experimental Psychiatry*, 7, 305–306.

Bell, F. (2000). Post-renal transplant compliance. *Journal of Child Health Care*, 4, 5–9.

Blowey, D. L., Hebert, D., Arbus, G. S., Pool, R., Korus, M., and Koren, G. (1997). Compliance with cyclosporine in adolescent renal transplant patients. *Pediatric Nephrology*, 11, 547–551.

Blumenfield, M., Levy, N. B., Spinowitz, B., Charytan, C., Beasley, C. M., Dubey, A. K., Solomon, R. J., Todd, R., Goodman, A., and Bergstrom, R. F. (1997). Fluoxetine in depressed patients on dialysis. *International Journal of Psychiatry in Medicine*, 27, 71–80.

Bordenave, K., Tzamaloukas, A. H., Conneen, S., Adler, K., Keller, L. K., and Murata, G. H. (1998). Twenty-one year mortality in a dialysis unit: Changing effect of withdrawal from dialysis. *ASAIO Journal*, 44, 194–198.

Boyer, C. B., Friend, R., Chlouverakis, G., and Kaloyanides, G. (1990). Social support and demographic factors influencing compliance in hemodialysis patients. *Journal of Applied Social Psychology*, 20, 1902–1918.

Brady, B. A., Tucker, C. M., Alfino, P. A., Tarrant, D. G., and Finlayson, G. C. (1997). An investigation of factors associated with fluid adherence among hemodialysis patients: A self-efficacy theory based approach. *Annals of Behavioral Medicine*, 19, 339–343.

Brantley, P. J., Mosley, T. H., Bruce, B. K., McKnight, G. T., and Jones, G. N. (1990). Efficacy of behavioral management and patient education on vascular access cleansing compliance in hemodialysis patients. *Health Psychology*, 9, 103–113.

Bremer, B. A., Wert, K. M., Durica, A. L., and Weaver, A. W. (1997). Neuropsychological, physical, and psychosocial functioning of individuals with end-stage renal disease. *Annals of Behavioral Medicine*, 19, 348–352.

Brown, J., and Fitzpatrick, R. (1988). Factors influencing compliance with dietary restrictions in dialysis patients. *Journal of Psychosomatic Research*, 32, 191–196.

Brownbridge, G., and Fielding, D. M. (1994). Psychosocial adjustment and adherence to dialysis treatment regimes. *Pediatric Nephrology*, 8, 744–749.

Burton, H. J., Kline, S. A., Lindsay, R. M., and Heidenheim, P. A. (1986). The relationship of depression to survival in chronic renal failure. *Psychosomatic Medicine*, 48, 261–269.

Carton, J. S., and Schweitzer, J. B. (1996). Use of a token economy to increase compliance during hemodialysis. *Journal of Applied Behavioral Analysis*, 29, 111–113.

Christensen, A. J. (2000). Patient X treatment context interaction in chronic disease: A conceptual framework for the study of patient adherence. *Psychosomatic Medicine*, 62, 435–443.

Christensen, A. J., and Ehlers, S. E. (in press). Psychological factors in end stage renal disease: An emerging context for behavioral medicine research. *Journal of Consulting and Clinical Psychology*.

Christensen, A. J., Moran, P. J., and Ehlers, S. E. (1999b). *Prediction of Future Dialysis Regimen Adherence: A Longitudinal Test of the Patient by Treatment Interactive Model*. Presented at the annual meeting of the Society of Behavioral Medicine, San Diego, CA.

Christensen, A. J.; and Smith, T. W. (1995). Personality and patient adherence: Correlates of the five-factor model in renal dialysis. *Journal of Behavioral Medicine,* 18, 305–313.

Christensen, A. J., and Lawton, W. J. (1997). *Behavioral Modification of Fluid Intake in Non-Adherent Hemodialysis Patients.* Presented at the annual meeting of the American Society of Nephrology, San Antonio, TX.

Christensen, A. J., and Moran, P. J. (1998). The role of psychosomatic research in the management of end-stage renal disease: A framework for matching patient to treatment. *Journal of Psychosomatic Research,* 44, 523–528.

Christensen, A. J., Wiebe, J. S., Smith, T. W., and Turner, C. W. (1994b). Predictors of survival among hemodialysis patients: Effect of perceived family support. *Health Psychology,* 13, 521–525.

Christensen, A. J., Ehlers, S. L., Raichle, K. A., Bertolatus, J. A., and Lawton, W. J. (2000). Predicting change in depression following renal transplantation: Effect of patient coping preferences. *Health Psychology,* 19, 348–353.

Christensen, A. J., Ehlers, S. L., Raichle, K. A., Ferneyough, K., and Lawton, W. J. (2001). *Patient Personality Predicts Mortality in Chronic Renal Insufficiency: A Four-Year Prospective Examination.* Under review.

Christensen, A. J., Holman, J. M., Turner, C. W., Smith, T. W., and Grant, M. K. (1991). A prospective examination of quality of life in end-stage renal disease. *Clinical Transplantation,* 5, 46–53.

Christensen, A. J., Moran, P. J., and Wiebe, J. S. (1999a). Assessment of irrational health beliefs: Relation to health practices and medical regimen adherence. *Health Psychology,* 18, 169–176.

Christensen, A. J., Smith, T. W., Turner, C. W., and Cundick, K. E. (1994a). Patient adherence and adjustment in renal dialysis: A person by treatment interactional approach. *Journal of Behavioral Medicine,* 17, 549–566.

Christensen, A. J., Smith, T. W., Turner, C. W., Holman, J. M., and Gregory, M. C. (1990). Type of hemodialysis and preference for behavioral involvement: Interactive effects on adherence in end-stage renal disease. *Health Psychology,* 9, 225–236.

Christensen, A. J., Smith, T. W., Turner, C. W., Holman, J. M., Gregory, M. C., and Rich, M. A. (1992). Family support, physical impairment, and adherence in hemodialysis: An investigation of main and buffering effects. *Journal of Behavioral Medicine,* 15, 313–325.

Christensen, A. J., Wiebe, J. S., and Lawton, W. J. (1997). Cynical hostility, expectancies about health care providers, and patient adherence in hemodialysis. *Psychosomatic Medicine,* 59, 307–312.

Christensen, A. J., Wiebe, J. S., Benotsch, E. G., and Lawton, W. J. (1996). Perceived health competence, health locus of control, and patient adherence in renal dialysis. *Cognitive Therapy and Research,* 20, 411–421.

Comty, C. (1969). Selection of patients for long-term hemodialysis. *Pennsylvania Medicine,* 72, 72–73.

Cook, W. W., and Medley, D. M. (1954). Proposed hostility and pharisaic-virtue scales for the MMPI. *Journal of Applied Social Psychology,* 13, 99–125.

Costa, P. T., and McCrae, R. R. (1992). *NEO PI-R Professional Manual.* Odessa, FL: Psychological Assessment Resources, Inc.

Craven, J. L., Rodin, G. M., and Johnson, L. (1987). The diagnosis of major depression in renal dialysis patients. *Psychosomatic Medicine,* 49, 482–492.

Craven, J. L., Rodin, G. M., and Littlefield, C. H. (1988). The Beck Depression Inventory as a screening device for major depression in renal dialysis patients. *International Journal of Psychiatry in Medicine,* 18, 373–382.

Cummings, M. K., Becker, M. H., Kirscht, J. P., and Levin, N. W. (1981). Intervention strategies to improve compliance with medical regimens by ambulatory hemodialysis patients. *Journal of Behavioral Medicine*, 4, 111–127.

Cummings, M. K., Becker, M. H., Kirscht, J. P., and Levin, N. W. (1982). Psychosocial factors affecting adherence to medical regimens in a group of hemodialysis patients. *Medical Care*, 20, 567–580.

Davis, M. C., Tucker, C. M., and Fennell, R. S. (1996). Family behavior, adaptation, and treatment adherence of pediatric nephrology patients. *Pediatric Nephrology*, 10, 160–166.

Davison, A. M. (1996). Options in renal replacement therapy. In C. Jacobs, C. Kjellstrand, K. Koch, and J. Winchester (Eds.), *Replacement of Renal Function by Dialysis* (4th ed., pp. 1304–1315). Boston: Kluwer Academic.

De Geest, S., Borgermans, L., Gemoets, H., Abraham, I., Vlaminck, H., Evers, G., and Vanrenterghem, Y. (1995). Incidence, determinants, and consequences of subclinical noncompliance with immunosuppressive therapy in renal transplant recipients. *Transplantation*, 59, 340–347.

Devins, G. M., Mandin, H., Hons, R. B., Burgess, E. D., Klassen, J., Taub, K., Schorr, S., Letourneau, P. K. and Buckle, S. (1990a). Illness intrusiveness and quality of life in end-stage renal disease: Comparison and stability across treatment modalities. *Health Psychology*, 9, 117–142.

Devins, G. M., Mann, J., Mandin, H., Paul, L. C., Hons, R. B., Burgess, E. D., Taub, K., Schorr, S., Letourneau, P. K., and Buckle, S. (1990b). Psychosocial predictors of survival in end-stage renal disease. *Journal of Nervous and Mental Disease*, 178, 127–133.

Dew, M. A., Switzer, G. E., Goycoolea, J. M., Allen, A. S., DiMartini, A., Kormos, R. L., and Griffith, B. P. (1997). Does transplantation produce quality of life benefits? A quantitative review of the literature. *Transplantation*, 64, 1261–1273.

Diaz-Buxo, J. A., Plahey, K., and Walker, S. (1999). Memory card: A tool to assess patient compliance in peritoneal dialysis. *Artificial Organs*, 23, 956–958.

Didlake, R. H., Dreyfus, K., Kerman, R. H., Van Buren, C. T., Kahan, B. D. (1988). Patient noncompliance: A major cause of late graft failure in cyclosporine treated renal transplants. *Transplantation Proceedings*, 20, 63–69.

Eisenhauer, G. L., Arnold, W. C., and Livingston, R. L. (1988). Identifying psychiatric disorders in children with renal disease. *Southern Medical Journal*, 81, 572–576.

Eitel, P., Friend, R., Griffin, K. W., and Wadhwa, N. K. (1998). Cognitive control and consistency in compliance. *Psychology and Health*, 13, 953–973.

English, A., Savage, R. D., Britton, P. G., Ward, M. K., and Kerr, D. N. S. (1978). Intellectual impairment in chronic renal failure. *British Medical Journal*, 1, 888–890.

Ettenger, R. B., Rosenthal, J. T., Marik, J. L., Malekzadeh, M., Forsythe, S. B., Kaimil, E. S., Salusky, I. B., and Fine, R. N. (1991). Improved cadaveric renal transplant outcome in children. *Pediatric Nephrology*, 5, 137–142.

Evans, R. W., Manninen, D. L., Garrison, L. P., Hart, L. G., Blagg, C. R., Gutman, R. A., Hull A. R., and Lowrie, E. G. (1985). The quality of life of patients with end-stage renal disease. *New England Journal of Medicine*, 312, 553–559.

Fennell, R. S., III, Rasbury W. C., Fennell, E. B., and Morris, M. K. (1984). Effects of kidney transplantation on cognitive performance in a pediatric population. *Pediatrics*, 74, 273–278.

Fraser, C. L., and Arieff, A. I. (1988). Nervous system complications in Uremia. *Annals of Internal Medicine*, 15, 143–153.

Friend, R., Hatchett, L., Schneider, M. S., and Wadhwa, N. K. (1997a). A comparison of attributions, health beliefs, and negative emotions as predictors of fluid adherence in renal dialysis patients: A prospective analysis. *Annals of Behavioral Medicine*, 19, 344–347.

Friend, R., Hatchett, L., Wadhwa, N. K., and Suh, H. (1997b). Serum albumin and depression in end-stage renal disease. *Advances in Peritoneal Dialysis*, 13, 155–157.

Fukunishi, I., and Kudo, H. (1995). Psychiatric problems of pediatric end-stage renal failure. *General Hospital Psychiatry*, 17, 32–36.

Haag-Weber, M., and Hörl, W. H. (1993). Uremia and infection: mechanisms of impaired cellular host defense. *Nephron*, 63, 125–131.

Hart R. P., Pederson J. A., Czerwinski A. W., and Adams R. L. (1983). Chronic renal failure, dialysis, and neuropsychological function. *Journal of Clinical Neuropsychology*, 5, 301–12.

Hart, R. (1979). Utilization of token economy within a chronic dialysis unit. *Journal of Consulting and Clinical Psychology*, 47, 646–648.

Hart, R. P., and Kreutzer, J. S. (1998). Renal system. In R. E. Tarter, D. H. Van Thiel et al. (Eds.), *Medical Neuropsychology: The Impact of Disease on Behavior. Critical Issues in Neuropsychology* (pp. 99–120). New York: Plenum Press.

Hartman, P. E., and Becker, M. H. (1978). Noncompliance with prescribed regimen among hemodialysis patients: A method of prediction and educational diagnosis. *Dialysis and Transplantation*, 7, 978–989.

Haynes, R. B. (1979). Determinants of compliance: The disease and the mechanics of treatment. In R. B. Haynes, D. W. Taylor, and D. L. Sackett (Eds.), *Compliance in Health Care* (pp. 49–62). Baltimore: Johns Hopkins University Press.

Hegel, M. T., Ayllon, T., Thiel, G., and Oulton, B. (1992). Improving adherence to fluid restrictions in male hemodialysis patients: A comparison of cognitive and behavioral approaches. *Health Psychology*, 11, 324–330.

Hener, T., Weisenberg, M., and Har-Even, D. (1996). Supportive versus cognitive–behavioral intervention programs in achieving adjustment to home peritoneal kidney dialysis. *Journal of Consulting and Clinical Psychology*, 64, 731–741.

Hinrichsen, G. A., Lieberman, J. A., Pollack, S., and Sternberg, H. (1989). Depression in hemodialysis patients. *Psychosomatics*, 30, 284–289.

Hitchcock, P. B., Brantley, P. J., Jones, G. N., and McKnight, G. T. (1992). Stress and social support as predictors of dietary compliance in hemodialysis patients. *Behavioral Medicine*, 18, 13–20.

Horne, R., and Weinman, J. (1999). Patients' beliefs about prescribed medicines and their role in adherence to treatment in chronic physical illness. *Journal of Psychosomatic Research*, 47, 555–567.

Husebye, D. G., Westlie, L., Styrovosky, T. J., and Kjellstrand, C. M. (1987). Psychological, social, and somatic prognostic indicators in old patients undergoing long-term dialysis. *Archives of Internal Medicine*, 147, 1921–1924.

Johnson, E. M., Canafax, D. M., Gillingham, K. J., Humar, A., Pandian, K., Kerr, S. R., Najarian, J. S., and Matas, A. J. (1997). Effect of early cyclosporine levels on kidney allograft rejection. *Clinical Transplantation*, 11, 552–557.

Kalman, T. P., Wilson, P. G., and Kalman, C. M. (1983). Psychiatric morbidity in long-term renal transplant recipients and patients undergoing hemodialysis. *Journal of the American Medical Association*, 250, 55–58.

Kaplan, R. M., and Simon, H. J. (1990). Compliance in medical care: Reconsideration of self-predictions. *Annals of Behavioral Medicine*, 12, 66–71.

Kaplan-DeNour, A., and Czaczkes, J. W. (1972). Personality factors in chronic hemodialysis patients causing noncompliance with medical regimen. *Psychosomatic Medicine*, 34, 333–344.

Kay, N. E., and Raij, L. R. (1986). Immune abnormalities in renal failure and hemodialysis. *Blood Purification*, 4, 120–129.

Keane, T. M., Prue, D. M., and Collins, F. L. (1981). Behavioral contracting to improve dietary compliance in chronic renal dialysis patients. *Journal of Behavior Therapy and Experimental Psychiatry*, 12, 63–67.

Kiley, D. J., Lam, C. S., and Pollak, R. (1993). A study of treatment compliance following kidney transplantation. *Transplantation*, 55, 51–56.

Kimmel, P. L., Peterson, R. A., Weihs, K. L., Simmens, S. J., Alleyne, S., Cruz, I., and Veis, J. H. (2000a). Multiple measurements of depression predict mortality in a longitudinal study of chronic hemodialysis outpatients. *Kidney International*, 57, 2093–2098.

Kimmel, P. L., Peterson, R. A., Weihs, K. L., Simmens, S. J., Alleyene, S., Cruz, I., and Veis, J. H. (1998a). Psychosocial factors, behavioral compliance and survival in urban hemodialysis patients. *Kidney International*, 54, 245–254.

Kimmel, P. L., Peterson, R. A., Weihs, K. L., Simmens, S. J., Boyle, D. H., Verme, D., Umana, W. O., Veis, J. H., Alleyne, S., and Cruz, I. (1995). Behavioral compliance with dialysis prescription in hemodialysis patients. *Journal of the American Society of Nephrology*, 5, 1826–1834.

Kimmel, P. L., Phillips, T. M., Simmens, S. J., Peterson, R. A., Weihs, K. L., Alleyne, S., Cruz, I., Yanovski, J. A., and Veis, J. H. (1998b). Immunologic function and survival in hemodialysis patients. *Kidney International*, 54, 236–244.

Kimmel, P. L., Thamer, M., Rochard, C. M., and Ray, N. F. (1998c). Psychiatric illness in patients with end-stage renal disease. *American Journal of Medicine*, 105, 214–221.

Kimmel, P. L., Varela, M. P., Peterson, R. A., Weihs, K. L., Simmens, S. J., Alleyne, S., Amarshinge, A., Mishkin G. J., Cruz, I., and Veis, J. H. (2000b). Interdialytic weight gain and survival in hemodialysis patients: Effects of duration of ESRD and diabetes mellitus. *Kidney International*, 57, 1141–1151.

Kimmel, P. L., Weihs, K. L., and Peterson, R. A. (1993). Survival in hemodialysis patients: The role of depression. *Journal of the American Society of Nephrology*, 4, 12–27.

Kramer, L., Madl, C., Stockenhuber, F., Yeganehfar, W., Eisenhuber, E., Derfler, K., Lenz, K., Schneider, B., and Grimm, G. (1996). Beneficial effect of renal transplantation on cognitive brain function. *Kidney International*, 49, 833–838.

Krantz, D. S., Baum, A., and Wideman, M. V. (1980). Assessment of preferences for self-treatment and information in health care. *Journal of Personality and Social Psychology*, 39, 977–990.

Leake, R., Friend, R., and Wadhwa, N. (1999). Improving adjustment to chronic illness through strategic self-presentation: An experimental study on a renal dialysis unit. *Health Psychology*, 18, 54–62.

Leavey, S. F., Strawderman, R. L., Jones, C. A., Port, F. K., and Held, P. J. (1998). Simple nutritional indicators as independent predictors of mortality in hemodialysis patients. *American Journal of Kidney Diseases*, 31, 997–1006.

Leggat, J. E., Bloembergen, W. E., Levine, G., Hulbert-Shearon, T. E., and Port, F. K. (1997). An analysis of risk factors for withdrawal from dialysis before death. *Journal of the American Society of Nephrology*, 8, 1755–1763.

Lowry, M. R., and Atcherson, E. (1980). A short-term follow-up of patients with depressive disorder on entry into home dialysis training. *Journal of Affective Disorders*, 2, 219–227.

Manley, M., and Sweeney, J. (1986). Assessment of compliance in hemodialysis adaptation. *Journal of Psychosomatic Research*, 30, 153–161.

McKee, D. C., Burnett, G. B., Raft, D. D., Batten, P. G., and Bain, K. P. (1982). Longitudinal study of neuropsychological functioning in patients on chronic hemodialysis: A preliminary report. *Journal of Psychosomatic Research*, 26, 511–518.

Miller, S. M. (1987). Monitoring and blunting: Validation of a questionnaire to assess styles of information-seeking under threat. *Journal of Personality and Social Psychology*, 52, 345–353.

Moran, P. J., Christensen, A. J., and Lawton, W. J. (1997). Conscientiousness, social support, and adaptation to chronic illness. *Annals of Behavioral Medicine*, 19, 333–338.

Morduchowicz, G., Sulkes, J., Aizic, S., Gabbay, U., Winkler, J., and Boner, G. (1993). Compliance in hemodialysis patients: A multivariate regression analysis. *Nephron*, 64, 365–368.

Neu, S., and Kjellstrand, C. M. (1986). Stopping long-term hemodialysis: An empirical study of withdrawal of life-supporting treatment. *New England Journal of Medicine*, 314, 14–20.

O'Leary, A. (1990). Stress, emotion, and human immune function. *Psychological Bulletin*, 106, 363–382.

O'Donnell, K., and Chung, J. Y. (1997). The diagnosis of major depression in end-stage renal disease. *Psychotherapy and Psychosomatics*, 66, 38–43.

Oldenburg, B., MacDonald, G. J., and Perkins, R. J. (1988). Factors influencing excessive thirst and fluid intake in dialysis patients. *Dialysis and Transplantation*, 17, 21–40.

Peterson, R. A., Kimmel, P. L., Sacks, C. R., Mesquita, M. L., Simmens, S. J., and Reiss, D. (1991). Depression, perception of illness and mortality in patients with end-stage renal disease. *International Journal of Psychiatry in Medicine*, 21, 343–354.

Pliskin, N. H., Yurk, H. M., Ho, L. T., and Umans, J. G. (1996). Neurocognitive function in chronic hemodialysis patients. *Kidney International*, 19, 1435–1440.

Plough, A. L., and Salem, S. (1992). Social and contextual factors in the analyses of mortality in end-stage renal disease: Implications for health policy. *American Journal of Public Health*, 72, 1293–1295.

Poll, I. B., and Kaplan De-Nour, A. (1980). Locus of control and adjustment to chronic hemodialysis. *Psychological Medicine*, 10, 153–157.

Port, F. K., Wolfe, R. A., Hawthorne, V. M., Ferguson, C. W. (1989). Discontinuation of dialysis therapy as a cause of death. *American Journal of Nephrology*, 9, 145–149.

Raiz, L. R., Kilty, K. M., Henry, M. L., and Ferguson, R. M. (1999). Medication compliance following renal transplantation. *Transplantation*, 68, 51–55.

Rettig, R. A., and Levinsky, N. G. (1991). *Kidney Failure and the Federal Government*. Washington DC: National Academy Press.

Rodin, G., and Voshart, K. (1986). Depression in the medically ill: An overview. *American Journal of Psychiatry*, 143, 696–705.

Rosenbaum, M., and Ben-Ari Smira, K. (1986). Cognitive and personality factors in the delay of gratification in hemodialysis patients. *Journal of Personality and Social Psychology*, 51, 357–364.

Rosenstock, I. M. (1966). Why people use health services. *Millbank Memorial Fund Quarterly*, 44, 94–127.

Rovelli, M., Palmeri, D., Vossier, E., Bartus, S., Hull, D., and Schweizer, R. (1989). Noncompliance in organ transplant recipients. *Transplantation Proceedings*, 21, 833–834.

Rudman, L. A., Gonzales, M. H., and Borgida, E. (1999). Mishandling the gift of life: Noncompliance in renal transplant patients. *Journal of Applied Social Psychology*, 29, 834–851.

Schneider, M. S., Friend, R., Whitaker, P., and Wadhwa, N. K. (1991). Fluid noncompliance and symptomatology in end-stage renal disease: Cognitive and emotional variables. *Health Psychology*, 10, 209–215.

Schupak, E., Sullivan, J. F., and Lee, D. Y. (1967). Chronic hemodialysis in "unselected" patients. *Annals of Internal Medicine*, 67, 708–717.

Sherbourne, C. D., Hays, R. D., Ordway, L., DiMatteo, M. R., and Kravitz, R. L. (1992). Antecedents of adherence to medical recommendations: Results from the medical outcomes study. *Journal of Behavioral Medicine*, 15, 447–468.

Shulman, R., Price, J. D. E., and Spinelli, J. (1988). Biopsychosocial aspects of long-term survival on end-stage renal failure therapy. *Psychological Medicine*, 19, 945–954.

Siegal, B. R., and Greenstein, S. M. (1997). Postrenal transplant compliance from the perspective of African-Americans, Hispanic Americans, and Anglo-Americans. *Advances in Renal Replacement Therapy*, 4, 46–49.

Siegel, B., and Greenstein, S. M. (1999). Profiles of noncompliance in patients with a functioning renal transplant: A multicenter study. *Transplantation Proceedings*, 31, 1326–1327.

Simoni, J. M., Asarnow, J. R., Munford, P. R., Koprowski, C. M., Belin, T. R., and Salusky, I. B. (1997). Psychological distress and treatment adherence among children on dialysis. *Pediatric Nephrology*, 11, 604–606.

Sketris I., Waite, N., Grobler, K., West, M., and Gerus S. (1994). Factors affecting compliance with cyclosporine in adult renal transplant patients. *Transplant Proceedings*, 26, 2538.

Somer, E., and Tucker, C. M. (1988). Patient life engagement, spouse marital adjustment, and dietary adherence of hemodialysis patients. *Journal of Compliance in Health Care*, 3, 57–65.

Somer, E., and Tucker, C. M. (1992). Spouse–marital adjustment and patient dietary adherence in chronic hemodialysis: A comparison of Afroamericans and Caucasians. *Psychology and Health*, 6, 69–76.

Southeaver, G. T., Ryan, J. J., and DeWolfe, A. S. (1982). Neuropsychological patterns in uremia. *Journal of Clinical Psychology*, 38, 490–496.

Stanton, A. L. (1987). Determinants of adherence to medical regimens by hypertensive patients. *Journal of Behavioral Medicine*, 10, 377–394.

Taylor, S. E., and Aspinwall, L. G. (1990). Psychological aspects of chronic illness. In G. R. VandenBos and P. T. Costa, Jr. (Eds.), *Psychological Aspects of Serious Illness*. Washington D.C.: American Psychological Association.

U.S. Renal Data System (2000). *USRDS Annual Report*. Bethesda, MD: The National Institutes of Health, National Institute of Diabetes and Digestive and Kidney Diseases.

Umans, J. G., and Pliskin, N. H. (1998). Attention and mental processing speed in hemodialysis patients. *American Journal of Kidney Diseases*, 32, 749–751.

Wallston, K. A., Wallston, B. S., and DeVellis, R. (1978). Development of the multidimensional health locus of control scales. *Health Education Monographs*, 6, 160–170.

Weed-Collins, M., and Hogan, R. (1989). Knowledge and health beliefs regarding phosphate-binding medication in predicting compliance. *ANNA Journal*, 16, 278–283.

Wiebe, J. S., and Christensen, A. J. (1996). Patient adherence in chronic illness: Personality and coping in context. *Journal of Personality*, 64, 815–835.

Wiebe, J. S., and Christensen, A. J. (1997). Conscientiousness, health beliefs, and patient adherence in renal dialysis. *Annals of Behavioral Medicine*, 19, 30–35.

Wittenberg, S. H., Blanchard, E. B., Suls, J., Tennen, H., McCoy, G., and McGoldrick, M. D. (1983). Perceptions of control and causality as predictors of compliance and coping in hemodialysis. *Basic and Applied Social Psychology*, 4, 319–336.

Wolcott, D. W., Maida, C. A., Diamond, R., and Nissenson, A. R. (1986). Treatment compliance in end-stage renal disease patients on dialysis. *American Journal of Nephrology*, 6, 329–338.

CHAPTER 11

Asthma

Bruce G. Bender

University of Colorado/National Jewish Medical and Research Center

and

Thomas L. Creer

Ohio University

Introduction

Attempts to solve the puzzle of asthma have not suffered from a lack of effort by various groups, including medical and behavioral scientists. What has occurred, however, can best be described by considering the metaphor of a darkened stage, where a spotlight jumps from one player to another, focusing, sometimes briefly and erratically, on individual topics such as emotions, physiology, psychology, immunology, genetics, biology, and biochemistry. Each topic has held the limelight with respect to asthma; indeed, adherents of each field can marshal evidence, to one degree or another, in support of a link between their specialty and asthma. Shifting the focus from one topic to another, however, has not advanced our knowledge of the causes of asthma, nor of how the condition can be controlled. Indeed, focusing separate spotlights on each player at once, as occurs in a multidisciplinary approach, has likely hindered our understanding. All this approach has done is generate a considerable amount of babble and discord among scientists, along with isolated pockets of knowledge that may or may not have value in treating patients with asthma. Only on raising the stage lights to reveal all the different players working together to perform the play does a sense of unity emerge. It is this

Correspondence concerning this chapter should be addressed to Bruce Bender Ph.D. Department of Psychology, University of Colorado, National Jewish Medical and Research Center, 1400 Jackson Street, Denver, Colorado 80206.

interdisciplinary team approach, with continual reciprocal interactions among all players, including patients, that has forged the growing body of knowledge and expertise we have regarding asthma and its management.

Interdisciplinary Approach to Asthma Management

A major shift in the treatment of chronic disorders entails moving away from a multidisciplinary approach towards an interdisciplinary one. As suggested by the metaphor, multidisciplinary refers to activities independently taken by professionals representing a number of disciplines who work with a patient in an uncoordinated fashion. In the case of asthma, for example, we bring expertise in assessment and behavioral change procedures to a treatment team, but may lack knowledge of how other members of the team, particularly physicians and other healthcare providers, treat the patient. For their part, physicians and nurses know what medications to prescribe for a patient, but may be unaware of how we might assist them to enhance compliance with the treatment regimen they prescribe. The interdisciplinary approach assumes that physicians, psychologists, nurses, health educators, physical therapists, social workers, and other healthcare professionals have a working knowledge of each other's skills and expertise. We do not wish to duplicate the knowledge and actions of others: that would be redundant and provide no benefit either to patients or to ourselves. Rather, we need to know how and why other healthcare providers act as they do. In the best of circumstances, the interdisciplinary approach "is synergistic, integrating the knowledge and skills from the various disciplines into a coordinated plan for patient care" (Varni, 1983, p. 5).

Initially, an interdisciplinary model for asthma that included behavioral scientists was grudgingly accepted by some medical personnel. The latter's behavior was understandable given earlier thought, particularly that emanating from psychoanalysis, which labeled asthma as a psychological problem resulting from a faulty mother–child relationship (French and Alexander, 1941). However, this perception has faded in the past three decades as healthcare providers have discovered what an interdisciplinary model involving psychologists can achieve. The acceptance of the model in the management of asthma is exemplified by treatment guidelines for the condition.

Treatment Guidelines for Asthma

Treatment guidelines for different conditions are often reluctantly accepted by healthcare professionals, including psychologists (e.g., Clay, 2000). Driven by converging trends of cost containment and evidence-based medicine, the guidelines recommend specific strategies that should be followed in treating given diseases or disorders. Under the best of circumstances, treatment guidelines are a bittersweet pill. They are based on traditional linear thinking, in that, if event A occurs the response should be B; if event C occurs the response should be D, etc. (Ackoff, 1994). Yet, nonlinear variables, including a patient's psychological reactions, frequently enter into the sequence of treatment events and alter outcomes. Other nonlinear events range from a physician applying his or her unique experiences, knowledge, and imagination – factors that comprise the art of medicine – to a naturally occurring physical change – spontaneous remission of symptoms – which can significantly alter the course of asthma. Creer (in press) described how, in a number of asthma studies, nonlinear variables produced as significant an outcome as did the manipulation of independent variables. The specter of healthcare providers being asked to treat asthma in a rote manner, without consideration of the unique nonlinear variables present in the treatment context, is frightening.

On the other hand, treatment guidelines for asthma (National Institutes of Health, 1991; 1997) benefit and enhance the work of psychologists. This is illustrated by the following: first, guidelines lay out treatment options precisely, including the types and doses of medications that should be prescribed. This may seem minor, but unless medical personnel follow treatment guidelines, psychologists and other behavioral scientists may find themselves attempting to improve patient compliance with a useless or potentially harmful treatment regimen (Creer and Levstek, 1996). As asthma medications become more potent and specific in their action, the value of a common blueprint shared by all members of the interdisciplinary treatment team is a necessity. Second, treatment guidelines for asthma carve out a role for both psychologists and patients. Key points in the most recent set of treatment guidelines include the following (National Institutes of Health, 1997): (a) patient education, beginning at the time of diagnosis and integrated into every step of asthma care; (b) patient education provided by all members of the team; (c) teaching asthma self-management skills by tailoring information and a treatment approach to fit the needs of each patient; (d) teaching and reinforcing such behavioral skills as inhaler use, self-monitoring, and environmental control; (e) joint development of treatment plans by team members and patients; (f) encouragement of an active partnership by providing written self-management and individualized asthma action plans to patients; and (g) encouraging adherence to the treatment plan. Another highlight of the guidelines is referral of patients to psychologists, psychiatrists, social workers, or other mental health professionals when the existence of a psychological problem prevents or interferes with successful treatment.

We will spend most of this chapter discussing the application of the interdisciplinary model to asthma. Before launching into a discussion of the significance of the interdisciplinary team approach to asthma management, however, we wish to highlight pertinent epidemiological data, the definition of asthma, and characteristics of the disorder. We will point out why the information is important to psychologists and other members of an interdisciplinary treatment team.

Epidemiology of Asthma

A mass of epidemiological data has been accumulated regarding asthma (Gergen and Mitchell, in press) and offers a number of uses to psychologists. First, epidemiological data help the clinician detect any behavioral problems that are apt to be exhibited by a patient with asthma. Knowing that children with asthma experience a high rate of school absenteeism, for example, alerts one to look for academic problems or deficits in social skills normally acquired in regular school attendance. Second, epidemiological information are invaluable in serving as the basis for clinical decisions (Garb, 1998). Garb emphasized that a shortcoming of clinical practice is a disregard or underuse of information about base rates. If base rates for a disorder vary as a function of patient variables, e.g., race, social class, gender, or age, or of dependent variables such as school absenteeism or attack context, these factors will affect the diagnosis and treatment of that condition.

Prevalence

In 1993–94, an estimated 13.7 million people in the United States reportedly had asthma; from 1980 to 1994 the prevalence of self-reported asthma in the US increased 75 percent (Centers for Disease Control, 1998a). In 1998, a state-specific estimate of asthma reported that the disorder affected an estimated 17,299,000 people in the US. This estimate represents an increase from 6.7 million people with asthma in 1980, and indicates that 6.4 percent of the population in the US experienced asthma in 1998 (Centers for Disease Control, 1998b).

The prevalence of asthma provides a baseline for the analysis and interpretation of data. Prevalence data alone, for example, have been used to support the contention that work-related asthma is underestimated (Jajosky et al., 1999), a conclusion that warrants a more intensive approach to identify those with the condition and, in turn, making needed changes in the workplace environment. On the other hand, data on the prevalence of asthma may result in a totally different interpretation. Keely and Silverman (1999), for example, suggested that pediatric asthma is overdiagnosed, urging that the indiscriminate application of the asthma label, and the consequences that accompany such a diagnosis, be avoided. For behavioral scientists, prevalence data assist us to make decisions regarding treatment options for asthma patients (Garb, 1998).

Mortality

For most of the 20th century deaths from asthma were rare. Both patients and healthcare providers regarded as a truism the oft-quoted statement by Sir William Osler (1892) that "the asthmatic patient pants into old age." The implication was that although people with asthma may have recurring episodes of the disorder throughout their lives, few died from the condition. Thought regarding asthma mortality changed in the 1960s, however, with an abrupt and significant increase in deaths from asthma, particularly in New Zealand and Australia. Although no agreement was reached on the exact cause of this increase, several factors, including the introduction of new inhaled drugs, changes in disease classification, improved accuracy of death certificates, and advances in diagnostic procedures for confirming asthma, were correlated with the trend (Pearce et al., 1998).

Rates of death from asthma in the United States sharply increased from 0.8 per 100,000 general population in 1977–78 to 2.0 in 1989; they remained at this level until a slight increase in deaths to 2.1 was reported in 1994 (Sly and O'Donnell, 1997). Nevertheless, these mortality rates are 50 percent higher than those found in 1979. The exact number of deaths from asthma in the US ranged from 1674 in 1977 to 5487 in 1994. Rates of death, Sly and O'Donnell noted, were higher for blacks than whites; rates among whites increased more for females than for males. Despite being low compared to other diseases or disorders, such as heart conditions, cancer, and chronic obstructive pulmonary disease (COPD), almost all deaths from asthma are inexcusable given the fact that the disease can almost always be controlled.

Morbidity

The major impact of asthma is found in analyzing morbidity data. Pediatric asthma is the major cause of school absenteeism because of chronic physical conditions, and is the leading cause of hospitalizations in children. In 1990 alone, children between the ages of 5 and 17 years missed more than 10 million days of school, experienced 160,000 hospitalizations, and made 860,000 emergency room (ER) visits because of asthma (Weiss et al., 1992). Newacheck and Halfon (2000) recently described prevalence, impact, and other trends in childhood disability due to asthma. They noted that a small but significant proportion of youngsters, approximately 1.4 percent of all US children, experienced some degree of disability due to asthma in 1994–95. Prevalence of disability due to asthma was higher for adolescents, black youngsters, and children from low-income and single-parent families. Disabling asthma resulted in 20 restricted activity days, including 10 days absent from school, and was almost twice the burden experienced by children with other types of chronic disability. Newacheck and Halfon concluded that disabling asthma, as found in the National Health Interview Survey, had increased by 232 percent since 1969.

Fewer morbidity data are available with respect to adults. However, there is ample evidence that the magnitude of occupational asthma is widely underestimated (Blanc et al., 1999; Jajosky et al., 1999), that hospitalization for patients over the age of 45 is expensive (Stanford et al., 1999), and that there is a low probability that asthma can be reversed in older patients (Reed, 1999). More data on the impact of asthma in adults should be gathered and reported, suggested Pearce and his colleagues (1998), given the increase in pollution and work-site triggers of the disorder.

Finally, the cost of asthma continues to escalate. Weiss et al. (1992) found that the estimated economic costs of asthma in the US were $6.2 billion in 1990. Recent estimates by others (e.g., Smith et al., 1997) reinforce these findings. Asthma is an expensive disorder not only to patients and their families but, as with all chronic health conditions, to society.

Definition and Characteristics of Asthma

Asthma has proved elusive to define, although accurate descriptions extend back to Hippocrates (e.g., Pearce et al., 1998). A reason for this elusiveness is that, as Busse and Reed (1988) emphasize, those working with asthma define the disorder according to their specific needs. Clinicians, for example, want a different definition than epidemiologists, who study patient populations, or immunologists, who investigate the pathogenesis of the condition. Despite difficulties in definition, groups composed of asthma experts have issued guidelines for treatment of the disorder. A definition of asthma that has unified interdisciplinary healthcare teams was provided by the initial set of treatment guidelines developed and disseminated for asthma in the United States (National Institutes of Health, 1991): "Asthma is a lung disease with the following characteristics: (1) airway obstruction (or airway narrowing) that is reversible (but not completely so in some patients) either spontaneously or with treatment; (2) airway inflammation; and (3) airway hyperresponsiveness to a variety of stimuli" (p. 1). Pertinent characteristics of asthma are incorporated into this definition. The significance to behavioral scientists of these characteristics is described below.

Intermittency

The frequency of attacks varies from patient to patient and, for a given patient, from time to time. Intermittency of attacks presents several problems to behavioral scientists (Creer and Bender, 1995). First, the unique pattern of each patient's asthma can make it difficult to generate and implement decisions on how to treat that patient. As we are uncertain about the outcome of a decision, we must consider treatment options within a probabilistic framework. We hope that a given treatment strategy will provide optimal asthma control, but it may fail to do so. Uncertainty surrounding treatment decisions plagues healthcare providers who treat asthma and undermines the confidence of patients (Creer, 2000a,b). Second, the intermittency of asthma makes it difficult both to recruit and to maintain patients in research studies. Patients can be enthusiastic volunteers when experiencing symptoms of asthma; when asymptomatic, however, they lose interest. Finally, the intermittency of attacks generates a wide range of expectations in patients (Renne and Creer, 1985). Patients with persistent or perennial asthma, for example, know they are likely to experience asthma throughout the year; hence, they may be more adherent to a treatment regimen. Depending upon the frequency of attacks, patients with intermittent asthma may go long periods between episodes. Consequently, they often forget how to treat an attack and are unprepared to manage one when it occurs. For this reason, the classification of a patient's asthma – whether regarded as mild, moderate, or severe – must never be the basis for recruiting participants for an asthma self-management program. Because of the variability of asthma, as well as the capriciousness of behaviors correlated with that variability, all patients with the disorder must be taught self-management skills (Creer, 1979).

Severity

This term refers to the severity both of a patient's asthma and of discrete attacks. Use of the term has often been ambiguous; thus, one may not always know what is meant when it is said that a person has mild, moderate, or severe asthma. Patients rely on how they are breathing at any moment to label attacks. If the patient has what healthcare personnel refer to as mild asthma but is experiencing airway obstruction, he is apt to say that he has severe asthma. The patient is not breathing normally, and although he has not had an attack for several months, the episode is severe to him.

On the other hand, a patient who takes a controller drug to prevent asthma and as-needed medications to control exacerbations might, if queried, reveal that she is not experiencing any breathing problems at that moment; further-more, as she has not had any exacerbations for some time, she might say she has mild asthma. In both cases the patient is correct because they defined their asthma according to (a) how they are breathing at a given moment; (b) how long it has been since they experienced an episode; and (c) the degree to which their asthma is controlled. Healthcare personnel, however, use a different approach: they operationally define asthma severity into four categories – mild intermittent, mild persistent, moderate persistent, and severe persistent – based on their assessment of three factors: symptoms, nighttime symptoms, and lung function. A stepwise treatment strategy, using this classi-fication scheme, is incorporated into treatment guidelines for asthma (National Institutes of Health, 1991, 1997). The way patients and healthcare providers perceive asthma severity often leads to behavioral problems that require psy-chological intervention. The most fundamental problem centers on how best to control asthma. On the one hand, physicians and other healthcare pro-viders seek to prevent asthma attacks when possible. To achieve this goal, they recommend that patients with moderate persistent or severe persistent asthma take a controller drug daily, usually an inhaled corticosteroid, the aim being to establish and maintain control over the asthma. Patients, on the other hand, often balk at taking a daily medication for asthma, particularly when they are asymptomatic. Differing perceptions of asthma and its control often lead to patient noncompliance, although, as will be described, this is just one factor contributing to medication adherence.

Reversibility

As noted, asthma is characterized by symptoms that remit either spontan-eously or with treatment. The ability of airway obstruction to abate is generally considered as distinguishing asthma from other chronic airway disorders, par-ticularly emphysema and chronic bronchitis. There are, however, two excep-tions to the criteria of reversibility (Creer and Bender, 1995): First, reversibility may be relative. Complete reversibility occurs in most asthma patients who receive proper treatment; other patients, on the other hand, do not achieve complete reversibility even with intensive treatment (Loren et al., 1978). This clouds the picture in attempting to make an accurate diagnosis of asthma, particularly in adults, who may have both asthma and chronic bronchitis. Second, the fact that attacks remit spontaneously makes it impossible to prove definitively a cause–effect relationship between changes in a patient's asthma and treatment for the condition. There is always a chance that spontaneous reversibility unrelated to a medical treatment has accounted for changes observed in a patient's asthma (Creer, 1982). The problem can be illustrated by describing a long-term follow-up study of asthma self-management (Caplin and Creer, in press). A surprisingly high number of patients reported that their asthma was in remission and that they were asymptomatic. The investigators suggested the findings occurred because optimal self-management by patients was coupled with optimal medical care provided by skilled asthma specialists. Although this synthesis of skills likely did produce the positive change, the period of time since the patients received self-management training – 7 years – does not exclude the possibility of naturally occurring remission contributing to the results.

Airway Hyperresponsiveness

Airway hyperreactivity or hyperresponsiveness is ubiquitous in asthma. This is an exaggerated airway response, referred to as bronchoconstriction, which occurs when airways are exposed to a number and variety of stimuli that trigger asthma exacerbations in individual patients. Bronchoconstriction constitutes an asthma attack or episode; it consists of a reduction in airway size caused by small muscle spasm, mucosal swelling or edema, mucosal inflammation, increased mucus secretion, or a combination of these factors. Stimuli that produce bronchconstriction include: (a) viral respiratory infections; (b) allergens, such as pollens, dust mites, molds, cat dander, and cockroach parts; (c) irritants such as tobacco smoke, air pollution, or strong odors; (d) aspirin; (e) exercise; (f) weather changes; and (g) emotional reactions, such as laughing too hard or crying. Behavioral scientists may be asked to teach patients to avoid exposing themselves to stimuli that produce bronchoconstriction, and thereby prevent asthma attacks. As environmental manipulation is a staple of behavioral change procedures, we are increasingly asked to assist patients to perform and maintain behaviors required to produce environmental change. In particular, our skills can significantly help patients reduce household stimuli that trigger asthma, including dust mites, cockroach parts, mold and mildew, and cigarette smoke. Thus far, however, the removal of such environmental stimuli has generally been unsuccessful (Jadad et al., 2000).

Airway Inflammation

Although airway inflammation has been recognized as a factor in asthma since the 1800s (Pearce et al., 1998), how inflammation occurs and interacts with bronchial hyperresponsiveness remains unknown. It is believed, however, that inflammation is not caused by a single cell or single inflammatory mediator, but results from complex interactions among inflammatory cells, mediators, and cells and tissues present in the airways (National Institutes of Health, 1991). Airway inflammation can be controlled through the taking of controller drugs, such as inhaled corticosteroids, cromolyn sodium or necromil sodium, long-lasting β-agonists, and antileukotriene drugs.

For behavioral scientists, the challenge of managing airway inflammation can often be summed up in two words: medication compliance. Problems with compliance or adherence to treatment regimens have grown as a direct function of the increase in inhaled controller drugs prescribed for asthma. As noted, these drugs are prescribed for daily use by patients with moderate persistent or severe persistent asthma, regardless of the current status of their condition, e.g., whether they are symptomatic or not. The problem is comparable to that when patients are asked to take a daily medication to control hypertension. Such patients likely do not experience any physical symptoms of hypertension, but are nevertheless asked to adhere to taking drugs prescribed for them. However, the situation is more complicated in prescribing drugs for asthma, as is shown by the following.

First, two distinct types of medication may be prescribed for a patient's asthma (National Institutes of Health, 1997). One is referred to as a quick-relief or rescue medication and is dispensed via an inhaler to manage an acute attack or an exacerbation of asthma. Quick-relief medications, however, will not prevent attacks. The second type of drug is a controller medication taken to prevent asthma exacerbations; it, too, is often taken via an inhaler. Controller drugs will not, however, abort an asthma attack. The distinction between quick-relief and controller drugs is often unclear to patients; consequently, they may fail to comply with their healthcare provider's advice. Because quick-relief drugs produce an immediate effect, adherence is often greater than with controller medications. The downside of this behavior, however, may be the overuse of quick-relief drugs (Milgrom et al., 1996).

Second, inhaled asthma medications are effective only when taken in the proper manner. If they are not inhaled correctly, the medications may fail to reach the airways and lungs to control inflammation. Unfortunately, not all patients use their inhalers correctly. There are several reasons for this (Creer and Levstek, 1996): (a) patients are not taught to use the inhaler in the appropriate manner; (b) healthcare providers do not know how to use the inhalers appropriately, and therefore do not teach their patients how to take their drugs correctly; and (c) healthcare providers fail to monitor patients to be certain that they continue to use an inhaler correctly over time. When any of these situations exists, the patient is likely to be noncompliant.

Third, reports find that controller or preventive medications, particularly inhaled corticosteroids, are underprescribed for the treatment of asthma (e.g., Diette et al., 1999). These studies suggest that if more patients took a controller drug this would reduce their reliance on as-needed quick-relief drugs and, as is often the case, hospital ER visits.

Finally, problems occur when two or more controller drugs are prescribed to be taken concurrently by a patient. Excluding the costs of a polydrug regimen – a problem for most individuals – some patients have complained that taking two or more controller drugs concomitantly has the paradoxical effect of masking the onset of an asthma exacerbation. These patients often say that they feel more comfortable relying on a quick-relief drug taken as needed, rather than using multiple controller medications (Creer et al., 1999).

Role of the Psychologist in the Interdisciplinary Team

Because psychological disorders are increased in the high-risk asthma group (Todd, 1995) and often interfere with medical management (Bender and Klinnert, 1998), psychological assessment and intervention must be included in an interdisciplinary asthma program. In response to the healthcare revolution that is taking place in the US, significant changes are occurring in how asthma patients are treated. These have required that psychology redefine its place in healthcare settings.

The relationship between psychological disorders and chronic disease is complex and interactive. At first glance, it seems obvious that the imposition of chronic disease represents a potent stressor which can induce psychological difficulty, particularly depression (e.g., Yellowless et al., 1988). However, the causal relationship is bidirectional. The pre-existence of a psychological disorder can also contribute to poorly controlled and consequently severe disease. Nonadherence to medical advice in particular can generate psychological difficulties in patients or their families, thereby exacerbating the illness and causing excessive, inappropriate, and expensive overuse of healthcare services.

Although pharmacological tools for effective asthma management are readily available, treatment failure, excessive ER visits, and hospitalizations occur largely because of patient nonadherence to their treatment regimens. In some cases, treatment nonadherence is directly related to a psychological disorder. Studies employing state-of-the-art microchip technologies – recording the exact date and time when patients use aerosolized medications – reveal that prescribed medication is often not taken as directed (Milgrom and Bender, 1995). As physicians increase the frequency of prescribed dosing to gain better control of the disease, patients become less compliant (Coutts et al., 1992). Children from dysfunctional families are more nonadherent than other patients in their use of asthma medications (Bender et al., 1998). However, even seemingly stable and cooperative patients can be markedly nonadherent with medications essential for the control of their asthma (Milgrom et al., 1995). The absence of necessary healthcare behaviors, therefore, contributes to out-of-control asthma, a finding particularly prevalent among inner-city African-Americans (Greineder et al., 1995; Apter et al., 1998). The most serious consequence of this type of asthma is death (Strunk et al., 1985).

Delivery of Psychological Services in the Treatment of Asthma

An advantage of tertiary care facilities is that they have the critical mass of experienced health and behavioral professionals needed to diagnose and treat respiratory disorders efficiently and effectively. Psychological services are but one essential component of interdisciplinary disease management in these settings. Mental health professionals with behavioral and psychological expertise, and knowledge and skills regarding respiratory disorders, effectively provide such services in these environments. When these services are provided in collaboration with medical caregivers, the result is likely to be a positive change in a patient's health, healthcare behaviors, and quality of life. Such results are less likely to occur in settings that provide less comprehensive and limited interdisciplinarian assistance with respect to healthcare (Bender and Milgrom, in press; Bender et al., 2000). Interdisciplinary approaches to asthma treatment are characterized by the following case examples.

First, working with contentious families where a child's asthma is poorly controlled requires that the psychologist understand what behaviors are required for optimal self-management. The psychologist must not only be knowledgeable and skilled at reducing familial conflict, but know the best approach to take in helping families share responsibility for executing the necessary components of effective asthma management.

Second, where a depressed adolescent refuses to adhere to a medication regimen, the psychologist must have an understanding of the effects and side-effects of various asthma medications, assist in removing sources of resistance, and help the adolescent plan to take medications at times and places that avoid personal embarrassment. In these situations, it is usually the psychologist who directs the interdisciplinary treatment team to resolve such problems.

Third, an adult with COPD and asthma may complain that a particular medication causes depression. The unique skills of the psychologist can assess whether the medication or other disease-related factors are contributing to the affective concerns, and discuss alternative medications with the patient's physician.

Fourth, when a 4-year-old child becomes anxious about an invasive procedure necessary for evaluating lung damage, a psychologist knowledgeable about the procedure can help alleviate the anxiety. A variety of psychological or behavioral techniques are available, such as enabling the child to practice the procedure with a doll; advising the parents about topics they might discuss with their child in the days leading up to the procedure; and, time permitting, teaching the child relaxation procedures, accompanied by systematic desensitization by reciprocal inhibition (Creer, 1979; Creer and Christian, 1976).

Finally, some patients appear to lose some memory and motor skills in the period immediately following a severe respiratory arrest. The psychologist may be asked to evaluate the neurological and functional implications of this event, and to help plan a program of remediation. An interdisciplinary treatment team must rely upon such expertise for evaluation and program development.

Assessing Psychological Interventions on Disease Outcome

Over the years, a number of psychological and behavioral techniques have been used with asthma patients. Many of these were developed and tested in a tertiary treatment center for the disorder (Creer, 1979; Creer and Christian, 1976). They are categorized as follows.

Interventions for Specific Problems

For high-risk asthma patients, the higher frequency of psychological disorders and the widespread failure to adhere to health-promoting self-care techniques underscore the need for direct psychological services. Psychological techniques and interventions must be tailored specifically to the disease population if they are to efficiently change healthcare behavior. A variety of behavioral techniques have been developed and applied to alter problems specific to individual asthma patients; these include relaxation training (Lehrer et al., 1986), biofeedback (Kotses et al., 1991; Murphy et al., 1989), relaxation coupled with biofeedback (Miklich et al., 1977), hypnosis (Mussell and Harley, 1988), and time-out procedures to reduce unnecessary hospital stays (Creer, 1970; Hochstadt et al., 1980). These techniques have often been added as components to asthma self-management programs.

Family Therapy

Improved asthma symptoms have been demonstrated in response to family therapy (e.g., Gustafsson et al., 1987; Lask and Matthew, 1979). In the treatment of children with severe, poorly controlled asthma, psychological interventions focus on the entire family. This requires families to be taught a spectrum of behaviors required for effective management of childhood asthma (Bender and Klinnert, 1998). Adherence to an asthma treatment regimen involves patients not only taking medications appropriately, but working in partnership with an interdisciplinary team to establish environmental control over asthma triggers, and recognizing and treating symptoms when they occur. For many families of children with out-of-control asthma, problems in daily living take precedence over the specific needs of the child. These families are often markedly dysfunctional, with a gamut of financial, social, and psychological needs. Intervention requires the involvement of mental health providers who can address a range of problems faced by all members of these units. With such families, intervention must concentrate on specific, manageable problems, and provide an area within which to address the family's motivation to change. Discussion of family problems and interactions occurs within the context established by behaviors required for the asthmatic child's care, the cost of medications, shared responsibilities of family members, and actions that must be performed when exacerbations of asthma symptoms occur. When lines of communication and clarification of responsibilities regarding the asthmatic child are addressed directly, the intervention is likely to improve the effective and efficient management of the condition.

Patient Education

A number of asthma education programs have been conducted to determine the effects of increased patient knowledge on the morbidity of the disorder. Some support can be found for the effect of education on reducing healthcare use (Bolton et al., 1991; Osman et al., 1994). These studies are the exception, however, in that teaching patients about asthma without including behavioral or psychological intervention components has generally been found to be insufficient to induce behavioral change. For example, it has been reported that asthma education alone is ineffective in changing healthcare behavior, or in reducing morbidity from asthma (Tattersell, 1993; Rubin et al., 1989).

The best and most reliable conclusion regarding the role of limited – information-only – patient education programs for adults with asthma was provided by the Cochrane Airways Group of the Cochrane Library. In what is fast becoming the gold standard for the evaluation of treatment programs for asthma, the Cochrane Airways Group provides systematic reviews updated on a regular basis. The Group recently assessed 11 randomized and controlled trials of individual asthma education for adults over 16 years of age (Gibson et al., 2000a). Their conclusion was that limited asthma education does not improve health outcomes in adults with asthma. The use of such education in the ER may be effective, although the Airways Group cautioned that this needs further evaluation.

Psychoeducational Interventions

Although asthma education programs alone are generally insufficient in changing healthcare behavior and related outcomes, education is a necessary component of interdisciplinary efforts to improve asthma self-management. When asthma education is combined with other psychological approaches to behavioral change, the intervention often becomes effective. Several psychoeducational interventions embed asthma education within individually tailored programs administered by a healthcare giver, usually a nurse or health educator. The introduction of a caregiver sympathetic to the patient had a powerful influence on healthcare behavior. Fifty-three high-risk asthmatic children with histories of repeated ER visits and hospitalizations were enrolled in an intensive self-management program (Greineder et al., 1995). In addition to direct asthma education, the children and their families met individually with and received regular telephone calls from an outreach nurse. This intervention, distinct from other education programs in its inclusion of a caregiver available only to patients in the program, resulted in an 79 percent reduction in emergency room visits, an 86 percent reduction in hospitalizations, and an average savings of over $1,600 for each patient. Because all patients received medical care from the same health maintenance organization before, during, and after the program, the changes were attributed solely to the psycho-educational intervention. In another study, 47 adult asthmatics with varied hospitalization histories were randomly assigned either to a routine care control group or to an intervention group who received intensive, individual counseling and education on self-management strategies (Mayo et al., 1990). The intervention group alone demonstrated a dramatic reduction in hospitalizations. Although both programs were presented as educational interventions, they included an educator/counselor who played a central role in advising, encouraging, instructing, and motivating patients. Given the convincing evidence that offering factual information to chronically ill patients does not by itself change behavior (e.g., Gibson et al., 2000a; Tattersell, 1993), the importance of the therapeutic healthcare provider should not be underestimated.

Self-Management

The psychological components of other psychoeducational intervention programs have been more clearly recognized and labeled. Chief among these approaches has been the development and introduction of self-management programs for asthma. Green (1981) referred to the program developed at a tertiary treatment center, the National Asthma Center in Denver, as the "grandparent" of all asthma self-management programs. The research that served as the foundation for these programs was rooted at this facility (Creer, 1979; Creer and Christian, 1976; Decker and Kaliner, 1988). A study by Creer and colleagues (1988) described the program developed and tested with pediatric asthma at the National Asthma Center. In the study, 123 children between the ages of 5 and 17 years with confirmed asthma were randomly assigned to self-management or waiting-list control groups. Ten children and their parents or other family members were enrolled in each group. Specific skills taught in an eight-session program included knowledge of asthma and its management, and appropriate self-management skills. The latter included: (a) self-monitoring and self-recording of data; (b) information processing and evaluation; (c) decision-making competencies; and (d) self-instruction, particularly that relevant either to stimulus or to response change. By presenting the program over 8 weeks, both acquisition of knowledge and performance of self-management skills were assessed.

A number of outcome measures were used. Overall, the performance of asthma self-management produced: (a) significant reductions in asthma attacks; (b) improved management of asthma exacerbations; (c) a significant increase in school attendance; (d) significant improvements in peak flow readings over time; (e) significant positive changes in locus of control and self-concept measures; and (f) a 68 percent reduction in health costs for asthma among participants. Perhaps the most important finding of the study, however, was obtained at a 5-year follow-up. These results indicated there was an unexpectedly high rate of quiescence of asthma symptoms in the children – estimated to be as high as 80 percent – and, for those still experiencing the disorder, that their asthma was controlled through continued performance of self-management skills.

Based on the findings obtained with the children, a self-management program for adults was developed and tested. Seventy-six adults with confirmed asthma were randomly assigned to either a treatment group or to a waiting-list control group (Kotses et al., 1995). Patients in the treatment group participated in a 7-week training program that emphasized self-management, stimulus and behavioral control, decision making, relaxation exercises, and problem solving. At a 6-month follow-up, patients were found to experience fewer asthma attacks, reduced medication use, increased self-efficacy, and improved overall self-management skills. In a second report, the investigators demonstrated a significant cost-benefit from this intervention program: the cost of administering the program to each patient was $208, with an average cost savings of $475 (Taital et al., 1995).

Although asthma education programs increase knowledge about asthma and appropriate care for the condition, evidence that self-management significantly alters healthcare behavior has not been accepted by everyone. A meta-analysis performed across 11 education intervention studies, for example, concluded that such programs did not reduce morbidity outcomes, including rate of school absenteeism, frequency of hospitalization, or ER visits (Bernard-Bonnin et al., 1995). However, three factors militate against such a pessimistic outcome.

First, questions have been raised about the accuracy of systematic reviews and meta-analyses in evaluating treatments of asthma. Jadad and co-workers (2000) evaluated 50 systematic reviews and meta-analyses on the topic, and concluded that 40 of them had serious and extensive flaws. Findings with minimal flaws applicable to behavioral scientists include: (a) limited asthma education is, as also suggested by Gibson and his colleagues (2000a), unlikely to improve health outcomes in adults with asthma, and (b) chemical and physical actions taken to reduce exposure to dust mites seem ineffective.

Second, the Cochrane Airways Group has continued to examine asthma self-management programs which, when coupled with regular health practitioner review, influence health outcomes in adults with asthma. In the most recent update (Gibson et al., 2000b), results from 25 self-management trials were examined and compared with usual care as reported in 22 studies. Gibson and his colleagues concluded that asthma self-management training which includes self-monitoring by either peak expiratory flow rates or symptoms, coupled with regular medical review and a written asthma action plan, appears to improve health outcomes for adults with asthma. Furthermore, they continued, training programs that enable people to adjust their medication using a written action plan appear to be more effective than other forms of asthma self-management.

Finally, there is a mass of relevant evidence on the impact of asthma self-management on health outcomes. Pertinent outcome and process data, derived from summaries of the topic (e.g., Creer, 1979, 2000b; Creer and Christian, 1976; Creer and Levstek, 1996; Gibson et al., 2000b), are depicted in table 11.1. It is these outcome data that have spurred experts who write treatment guidelines to insist that self-management skills be taught to patients from the moment their asthma is diagnosed (e.g., National Institutes of Health, 1997).

Table 11.1   Outcome variables changed as a result of asthma self-management

Outcome variables

Positive increases in the following measures

Knowledge about asthma and its management
Acquisition and performance of asthma self-management skills
Higher peak flow rates
Academic attendance
Academic performance
Work attendance
Quality of life
Psychological variables
  Mood
  Self-concept
  Attitudes towards asthma and its management
Medication compliance
  Correct use of prescribed controller or quick relief medications
  Correct taking of inhaled medications
Interactions with healthcare providers
Family involvement with illness and its management
Remission of asthma symptoms

Positive decreases in the following measures

Visits to hospital emergency rooms
Hospital visits
  Duration of hospitalizations
Frequency of symptom days
Nighttime asthma
Medication use (e.g., switch from more potent to less potent drugs, etc.)
Symptom and asthma severity
Activity restriction
Psychological variables
  Depression
  Anxiety and distress
Costs of asthma treatment and management
Relapse in self-management skills

The outcome variables are self-explanatory. It is of interest, however, to note the process variables that have been reported by patients as helping them establish and maintain control over their asthma (Caplin and Creer, in press; Creer et al., 1988; Kotses et al., 1995). They credited the continued performance of four types of behavior as significant to their success: (a) the self-initiation, performance, and refinement of the self-management skills they had acquired; (b) the development and strengthening of self-efficacy regarding their performance; (c) the realization of positive outcome expectations regarding their performance; and (d), perhaps surprisingly, the value of the decision-making skills they acquired and continued to perform during and after participation in the program. The latter were reported by a majority of patients as being invaluable, not only in controlling asthma, but in managing their lives.

The Future of Psychology in Tertiary Care Settings

The impact of psychology in improving the healthcare of asthma patients has been documented. However, healthcare in the US is in such a state of transition that not even experts can predict the future with any certainty (e.g., Plocher, 1997). The future of psychology in tertiary healthcare centers will depend, as in the past, upon our ability to change critical healthcare behaviors and related outcomes. To achieve this goal, we must continue: (1) to be highly knowledgeable about the disease or disorder we are helping to treat; (2) to be active, perhaps even proactive, partners in interdisciplinary treatment teams; and (3) to demonstrate that the services we offer are definable, efficient, and cost-effective.

The managed care preference to contract for psychological services with a mental health provider group separate from medical services, conflicts directly with the model of psychological services integrated into an interdisciplinary healthcare system. The provision of "general practice" psychological services is unlikely to result in significant changes in healthcare behavior, or to alter the course of chronic illness. Such an approach may be less costly in the short term, but ineffective and expensive in the long term. One or two telephone conversations between a psychologist and a physician, perhaps followed by a letter summarizing the mental health consultation, cannot replace ongoing reciprocal interactions and collaboration between psychological and medical caregivers in an interdisciplinary care setting. The mental health practitioner in the treatment facility is positioned to develop psychological interventions that are integrated with other healthcare. As noted, the first comprehensive plans for an asthma self-management program emerged from an interdisciplinary, tertiary healthcare center (Creer and Christian, 1976). Research data gathered from the perspective of this outline served as the genesis of the self-management program developed and evaluated by Creer and his colleagues (1988) described earlier. In another hospital-based asthma program, the psychological intervention included identification of the patient's health beliefs, tailoring of prescribed treatment to specific patient characteristics, negotiating a behavioral contract between patient and physician, and, where indicated, problem-focused family therapy (Weinstein, 1995). Such innovative interdisciplinary programs can only occur when the psychological caregiver understands the disease and its treatment, and has a voice in patient care and treatment planning.

Demonstrating the Cost-Effectiveness of Psychological Services

Cost-effective interventions are those that provide a reasonably effective outcome judged to be worth the cost involved, whereas cost-saving interventions actually result in money being saved (Doubilet et al., 1986). From the per-spective of a disease management planner, therefore, the judgment of cost-effectiveness may depend upon debatable criteria. Nonetheless, the decision as to whether psychological interventions are worth the cost is likely to rest on whether a demonstrable change occurs, and/or whether that change can be achieved within a reasonable period of time or number of sessions. Open-ended psychotherapy sessions that last many months with unspecified goals are likely to be less regarded than interventions with specific objectives and a session- or time-limited length. It is unreasonable to expect that all psycho-logical interventions should necessarily be cost saving, but in some instances this is anticipated. The interventions described above that yielded improved symptom control also resulted in large cost savings. Changing behavior in low- to moderate-risk asthmatics saved an average of $475 per patient (Taitel et al., 1995), whereas the intervention with high-risk, frequently hospitalized patients saved $1642 per patient (Greineder et al., 1995). Although economic benefit cannot be allowed to become the sole criterion for behavioral pro-grams, instances where cost savings are achieved become powerful arguments in their favor (Friedman et al., 1995).

Future Research on Interdisciplinary Interventions

The combination of advances and availability of new and highly effective anti-inflammatory medications, and the development of practitioner guide-lines for the care of asthma, has greatly increased our capacity to effectively control asthma. However, whereas asthma treatments have improved, patient adherence to these treatments has not. Adherence to inhaled anti-inflammatory medications is no better than was adherence to theophylline 10 years ago (Bender et al., 1997). Treatments fail when the patient: (a) does not under-stand the nature of the illness and its treatment; (b) does not perceive airway changes; (c) is overwhelmed by life's other demands; (d) struggles with a psychological disorder; or (e) is shackled by doubts about his ability to bring about change in his disease. Given the large number of factors that interact to determine patient healthcare behavior, it follows that solutions must neces-sarily be multifaceted. No single intervention can resolve the myriad human problems that prevent treatment adherence. Programs that have banked on a singular approach to behavior change – typically through education only – have met with disappointment (Gibson et al., 2000a).

Despite the large number of published studies addressing adherence and compliance with asthma treatment, much remains to be learned about patient behaviors, underlying causes of nonadherence, and interventions to change the pattern. Even the methods of adherence measurement are a work-in-progress, although improvements may lead to increased understanding of the problem. With increased ability to assess the psychosocial factors that prevent a particular patient from engaging in effective self-management, specific inter-ventions may be applied. Patients and families who demonstrate psychological dysfunction also require psychological interventions. When these are provided by mental health practitioners who are knowledgeable about the disease and who work within an interdisciplinary model, they are more likely to result in a change in asthma management behavior (Bender, 1996). However, psychological interventions do not invariably improve the psychological disorder or treatment outcome. Further, other correlates of treatment nonadherence, including poverty, parental psychopathology, and stressful life events, are often the result of complex causal factors and beyond the reach of the individual healthcare provider. Large-scale programs such as the National Cooperative Inner-City Asthma Study, sponsored by the National Institutes of Health, represent attempts to discover broad solutions to these difficult problems. Results from such investigations will add insight into potential solutions, but may not provide immediate, pervasive answers to the problem of high morbidity and mortality among inner-city children with asthma.

Comparison across studies of the effectiveness of various psychological and psychoeducational interventions is difficult because of large methodological variability. Individual studies have been weakened by failure to include appropriate control groups, to clearly define the patient sample or intervention, to employ objective outcome measures, or to extend patient follow-up for a sufficient interval to adequately evaluate outcome (Bender and Klinnert, 1998). Creer et al. (1990) argued that if studies of the impact of self-management interventions on the treatment of asthma are to have the scientific merit necessary to stand up to peer review, and if the results of these investigations are to attain widespread acceptance, they must meet a number of criteria, including: (1) participants recruited in an unbiased fashion, with well-defined asthma and in numbers sufficient to allow appropriate statistical analysis; (2) random assignment to treatment and control groups; (3) use of clearly described and standardized treatments; (4) use of well-defined, valid, and reliable outcome measures; (5) collection of sufficient follow-up data; and (6) appropriate interpretation of data, including distinguishing between statistical and clinical significance.

In conclusion, psychologists are poised to take a leading role in developing and implementing healthcare interventions that will generate more positive outcomes for patients. The research background that defines psychology equips us with the ability to evaluate treatment outcomes, and to determine which combination of psychological and medical interventions results in the most effective and cost-efficient disease control. With specialized knowledge and unique skills, particularly as integrated into interdisciplinary treatment programs, psychologists will be able to design, implement, and study innovative programs that can change healthcare behavior and improve the treatment of chronic disease. Evidence of the potential of our role was noted in the study by Caplin and Creer (in press) described earlier. When followed up 7 years after participating in a self-management program (Kotses et al., 1995), a number of patients reported they no longer had the frequency or severity of asthma attacks that they experienced prior to their participation in the program. Many said they had adopted a monitoring procedure, comprised of watchful waiting, to evaluate their asthma. Furthermore, fully half of those who relapsed in performing self-management skills with the exception of self-monitoring, did so because their asthma was in remission or quiescent. These results indicate that a three-element formula – the use of a variety of potent asthma medications, plus care by healthcare providers skilled in treating asthma, plus the performance of appropriate self-management skills by motivated and confident patients – produce higher rates of asthma remission than has heretofore been observed in studies of the natural history of adult asthma (e.g., Reed, 1999). Although further study is needed to verify these findings, it appears as if the performance of self-management skills, and the psychological consequences of patient performance – namely the self-efficacy and outcome expectations they develop – hold the key to the eventual control of asthma.

References

Ackoff, R. L. (1994). Systems thinking and thinking systems. *System Dynamics Review*, 10, 175–188.

Apter, A. J., Reisine, A. T., Affleck, G., Barrows, E., and ZuWallack, R. L. (1998). Adherence with twice-daily dosing of inhaled steroids. *American Journal of Respiratory and Critical Care Medicine*, 157, 1810–1817.

Bender, B. G., Milgrom, H., Rand, C., and Wamboldt, F. S. (2000). Measurement of treatment nonadherence in children with asthma. In D. Drotar (Ed.), *Promoting Adherence to Medical Treatment in Chronic Childhood Illness*. (pp. 153–171). Mahwah, NJ: Lawrence Erlbaum Associates.

Bender, B. G. (1996). Tertiary care respiratory medicine: Is there a place for psychology in the managed care world? *Health Psychologist*, 18, 10–26.

Bender, B. G., and Klinnert, M. D. (1998). Psychological correlates of asthma severity and treatment outcomes in children. In H. Kotses and A. Harver (Eds.), *Self Management of Asthma* (pp. 63–84). New York: Marcel Dekker.

Bender, B. G., and Milgrom, H. (in press). Neuropsychological and psychiatric side-effects of medications used to treat asthma and allergic rhinitis. In A. A. Kaptein and T. L. Creer (Eds.), *Behavioral Sciences and Respiratory Disorders*. Reading, UK: Harwood Academic Publishers.

Bender, B., Milgrom, H., Bowry, P., Gabriels, R., Ackerson, L., and Rand, C. (1997). Asthmatic children's adherence with aerosolized medications. *American Journal of Respiratory and Critical Care Medicine*, 151, A352,

Bender, B., Milgrom, H., Rand, C., and Ackerson, L. (1998) Psychological factors associated with medication nonadherence in asthmatic children. *Journal of Asthma*, 35, 347–353.

Bender, B., Milgrom, H., Rand, C., and Wamboldt, F. S. (2000). Measurement of treatment nonadherence in children with asthma. In D. Drotat (Ed.) *Promoting Adherence to Medical Treatment in Chronic Childhood Illness: Concepts, Methods, and Interventions*. (pp. 153–172) Mahwah, NJ: Lawrence Erlbaum.

Bernard-Bonnin, A., Stachenko, S., Bonin, D., Charette, C., and Rousseau, E. (1995). Self-management teaching programs and morbidity of pediatric asthma: A meta-analysis. *Journal of Allergy and Clinical Immunology*, 95, 34–41.

Blanc, P. D., Eisner, M. D., Israel, L., and Yelin, E. H. (1999). The association between occupation and asthma in general medical practice. *Chest*, 115, 1259–1264.

Bolton, M. B., Tilley, B. C., Kuder, J., Reeves, T., and Schultz, L. R. (1991). The cost and effectiveness of an education program for adults who have asthma. *Journal of General Internal Medicine*, 6, 401–407.

Busse, W. W., and Reed, C. E. (1988). Asthma: definitions and pathogenesis. In E. Middleton Jr., C. E. Reed, E. F. Ellis, N. F. Adkinson Jr., and J. W. Yunginger (Eds.), *Allergy: Principles and Practice* (3rd ed., pp. 969–989). St. Louis: C. V. Mosby Co.

Caplin, D. L., and Creer, T. L. (in press). A self-management program for adult asthma. Part III. Maintenance and relapse of skills. *Journal of Asthma*.

Centers for Disease Control (April 25, 1998a). Surveillance for asthma – United States, 1960–1995. *Morbidity and Monthly Weekly Report*, 47, No. SS-1.

Centers for Disease Control (December 4, 1998b). Forecasted state-specific estimates of self-reported asthma prevalence – United States, 1998. *Morbidity and Mortality Weekly Report*, 47, 1022–1025.

Clay, R. A. (June, 2000). Treatment guidelines: sorting fact from fiction. *Monitor for Psychology, 31* [Online]. Available: http.//apa.org/monitor/

Coutts, J. A., Gibson, N. A., and Paton, J. Y. (1992). Measuring compliance with inhaled medication in asthma. *Archives of Disease in Childhood*, 67, 332–333.

Creer, T. L. (1970). The use of time-out from positive reinforcement procedure with asthmatic children. *Journal of Psychosomatic Research*, 14, 117–120.

Creer, T. L. (1979). *Asthma Therapy: A Behavioral Health-Care System for Respiratory Disorders*. New York: Springer Publishing Company.

Creer, T. L. (1982). Asthma. *Journal of Consulting and Clinical Psychology*, 50, 912–921.

Creer, T. L. (2000a). Self-management of chronic diseases. In M. Boekaerts, P. R. Pintrich, and M. Zeidner (Eds.), *Self-Regulation: Theory, Research, Applications* (pp. 601–629). Orlando, FL: Academic Press.

Creer, T. L. (2000b). Self-management and the control of chronic pediatric illness. In D. Drotar (Ed.), *Promoting Adherence to Medical Treatment in Chronic Childhood Illness* (pp. 95–129). Mawah, NJ: Lawrence Erlbaum Associates.

Creer, T. L., Backial, M., Burns, K. L., Leung, P., Marion, R. J., Miklich, D. R., Morrill, C., Taplin, P. S., and Ullman, S. (1988). Living with asthma. I. Genesis and development of a self-management program for childhood asthma. *Journal of Asthma*, 25, 335–362.

Creer, T. L., and Bender, B. G. (1995). Pediatric asthma. In M. C. Roberts (Ed.), *Handbook of Pediatric Psychology* (2nd ed., pp. 219–240). New York: Guilford.

Creer, T. L., and Christian, W. P. (1976). *Chronically-Ill and Handicapped Children: Their Management and Rehabilitation*. Champaign, IL: Research Press.

Creer, T. L., and Levstek, D. (1996). Medication compliance and asthma: Overlooking the trees because of the forest. *Journal of Asthma*, 33, 203–211.

Creer, T. L., Wigal, J. K., Kotses, H., and Lewis, P. (1990). A critique of 19 self-management programs for childhood asthma: Part II Comments regarding the scientific merit of the programs. *Pediatric Asthma, Allergy, and Immunology*, 4, 41–55.

Creer, T. L., Winder, J. A., and Tinkelman, D. (1999). Guidelines for the diagnosis and management of asthma: Accepting the challenge. *Journal of Asthma*, 36, 391–407.

Decker, J. J., and Kaliner, M. A. (1988). *Understanding and Managing Asthma*. New York: Avon Press.

Diette, G. B., Wu, A. W., Skinner, E. A., Markson, L., Clark, R. D., McDonald, R. C., Healy, J. P., Jr., Huber, M., and Steinwachs, D. M. (1999). Treatment patterns among adult patients with asthma. Factors associated with overuse of inhaled ß-agonists and underuse of inhaled corticosteroids. *Archives of Internal Medicine*, 159, 2697–2704.

Doubilet, P., Weinstein, M. C., and McNeil, B. J. (1986). Use and misuse of the term "cost effective" in medicine. *New England Journal of Medicine*, 314, 23–25.

French, T. M., and Alexander, F. (1941). Psychogenic factors in bronchial asthma. *Psychosomatic Medicine Monographs*, No. 4.

Friedman, R., Sobel, D., Myers, P., Caudill, M., and Benson, H. (1995). Behavioral medicine, clinical health psychology, and cost offset. *Health Psychology*, 14, 509–518.

Garb, H. N. (1998). *Studying the Clinician. Judgment Research and Psychological Assessment.* Washington, D.C.: American Psychological Association.

Gergen, P. J., and Mitchell, H. E. (in press). Epidemiology of asthma. In A. A. Kaptein and T. L. Creer (Eds.), *Behavioral Sciences and Respiratory Disorders.* Reading, UK: Harwood Academic Publishers.

Gibson, P. G., Coughlan, J., Wilson, A. J., Hensley, M. J., Abramson, M., Brauman, A., and Walters, E. H. (2000a). Limited (information only) patient education programs for adults with asthma (Cochran Review). *The Cochrane Library, Issue 2.* Oxford: Update Software.

Gibson, P. G., Coughlan, J., Wilson, A. J., Hensley, M. J., Abramson, M., Bauman, A., Hensley, M. J., and Walters, E. H. (2000b). Self-management education and regular practitioner review for adults with asthma (Cochrane Review). *The Cochrane Library, Issue 2.* Oxford: Update Software.

Green, L. (1981). Summary and recommendations. *Self-Management Educational Programs for Childhood Asthma:* Volume 2. Bethesda, MD: National Institute of Allergy and Infectious Diseases.

Greineder, D. K., Loane, K. C., and Parks. P. (1995). Reduction in resource utilization by an asthma outreach program. *Archives of Pediatric and Adolescent Medicine*, 149, 415–420.

Gustafsson, P. A., Kjellman, N. M., Ludvigsson, J., and Cederblad, M. (1987). Asthma and family interaction. *Archives of Disease in Childhood*, 62, 258–263.

Hochstadt, N., Shepard, J., and Lulla, S. H. (1980). Reducing hospitalizations of children with asthma. *Journal of Pediatrics*, 97, 1012–1015.

Jadad, A. R., Moher, M., Browman, G. P., Booker, L., Sigouin, C., Fuentes, M., and Stevens, R. (2000). Systematic reviews and meta-analyses on treatment of asthma: Critical evaluation. *British Medical Journal*, 320, 537–540.

Jajosky, R. A., Harrison, R., Reinisch, F., Flattery, J., Chan, J., Tumpowsky, C., Davis, L., Reilly, M. J., Rosenman, K. D., Kalinowski, D., Stanbury, M., Schill, D. P., and Wood, J. (1999). Surveillance of work-related asthma in selected US states using surveillance guidelines for state health departments – California, Massachusetts, Michigan, and New Jersey, 1993–1995. *Morbidity and Mortality Weekly Report, Center for Disease Control Surveillance Summary*, 48, 1–20.

.Keeley, D. J., and Silverman, M. (1999). Issues at the interface between primary and secondary care in the management of common respiratory disease. 2: Are we too ready to diagnose asthma in children? *Thorax*, 54, 625–628.

Kotses, H., Bernstein, I. L., Bernstein, D. I., Reynolds, R. V. C., Korbee, L., Wigal, J. K., Ganson, E., Stout, C., and Creer, T. L. (1995). A self-management program for adult asthma. Part I: Development and evaluation. *Journal of Allergy and Clinical Immunology*, 95, 529–540.

Kotses, H., Harver, A., Segreto, J., Glaus, K. D., Creer, T. L., and Young, G. A. (1991). Long-term effects of biofeedback-induced facial relaxation on measures of asthma severity in children. *Biofeedback and Self Regulation*, 16, 1–22.

Lask, B., and Matthew, D. (1979). Childhood asthma. A controlled trial of family psychotherapy. *Archives of Disease in Childhood*, 54, 116–119.

Lehrer, P. M., Isenberg, S., and Hochron, S. M. (1986). Asthma and emotion: A review. *Journal of Asthma*, 30, 5–21.

Loren, M. L., Leung, P. K., Cooley, R. L., Chai, H., Bell, T. D., and Buck, V. M. (1978). Irreversibility of obstructive changes in severe asthma in children. *Chest*, 74, 126–129.

Mayo, P. H., Richman, J., and Harris, H. W. (1990). Result of a program to reduce admissions for adult asthma. *Annals of Internal Medicine*, 112, 864–871.

Miklich, D. R., Renne, C. M., Creer, T. L., Alexander, A. B., Chai, H., Davis, M. H., Hoffman, A., and Danker-Brown, P. (1977). The clinical utility of behavior therapy as an adjunctive treatment for asthma. *Journal of Allergy and Clinical Immunology*, 60, 285–294.

Milgrom, H., and Bender, B. (1995). Behavioral side effects of medications used in the treatment of children with asthma and allergic rhinitis. *Pediatrics in Review*, 16, 333–337.

Milgrom, H., Bender, B., Ackerson, L., Bowry, P., Smith, B., and Rand, C. (1995). Children's compliance with inhaled asthma medications. *Journal of Allergy and Clinical Immunology*, 95, 217.

Milgrom, H., Bender, B., Ackerson, L., Bowry, P., Smith, B., and Rand, C. (1996). Noncompliance and treatment failure in children with asthma. *Journal of Allergy and Clinical Immunology*, 98, 1051–1057.

Murphy, A. I., Karlin, R., Hochron, S., Lehrer, P. M., Swartzman, L., and McCann, B. (1989). Hypnotic susceptibility and its relationship to outcome in the behavioral treatment of asthma: Some preliminary data. *Psychological Reports*, 65, 691–698.

Mussell, M. J., and Harley, J. P. (1988). Trachea-noise biofeedback in asthma: A comparison of the effect of trachea-noise biofeedback, a bronchodilator, and no treatment on the rate of recovery from exercise- and eucapnic hyperventilation-induced asthma. *Biofeedback and Self Regulation*, 13, 219–234.

National Institutes of Health (1991). *Executive Summary: Guidelines for the Diagnosis and Management of Asthma* (NIH Publication No. 91-3042A). Washington, D.C.: US Department of Health and Human Services.

National Institutes of Health (1997). *Expert Panel Report 2: Guidelines for the Diagnosis and Management of Asthma* (NIH Publication No. 97-4051A). Washington, D.C.: US Department of Health and Human Services.

Newacheck, P. W. and Halfron, N. (2000). Prevalence, impact, and trends in childhood disability due to asthma. *Archives of Pediatric and Adolescent Medicine*, 154, 287–293.

Osler, W. (1862). *The Principles and Practice of Medicine*. New York: D. Appleton.

Osman, L. M., Abdalla, M. I., Beattie, J. A. G., Ross, S. J., Russell, I. T., Friend, J. A., Legge, J. S., and Douglas, J. G. (1994). Reducing hospital admission through computer supported education for asthma patients. *British Medical Journal*, 308, 568–571.

Pearce, N., Beasley, R., Burgess, C., and Crane, J. (1998). *Asthma Epidemiology. Principles and Methods*. New York: Oxford University Press.

Plocher, D. W. (1997). Disease management. In P. R. Kongstevedt (Ed), *Essentials of Managed Healthcare* (2nd ed., pp. 225–236). Gatihersburg, MD: Aspen Publications.

Reed, C. E. (1999). The natural history of asthma in adults: The problem of irreversibility. *Journal of Allergy and Clinical Immunology*, 103, 539–547.

Renne, C. M., and Creer, T. L. (1985). Asthmatic children and their families. In M. L. Walraich and D. K. Routh (Eds.), *Advances in Developmental and Behavioral Pediatrics*, Vol. 6 (pp. 41–81). Greenwich, CN: Jai Press, Inc.

Rubin, D. H., Bauman, L. J., and Lauby, J. L. (1989). The relationship between knowledge and reported behavior in childhood asthma. *Developmental and Behavioral Pediatrics*, 10, 307–312.

Sly, R. M., and O'Donnell, R. (1997). Stabilization of asthma mortality. *Annals of Allergy, Asthma, and Immunology*, 78, 347–354.

Smith, D. H., Malone, D. C., Lawson, K. A., Okamoto, L. J., Battista, C., and Saunders, W. B. (1997). A national estimate of the economic costs of asthma. *American Journal of Respiratory Care and Critical Care Medicine*, 156, 787–893.

Stanford, R., McLaughlin, T., and Okamoto, L. J. (1999). The cost of asthma in the emergency department and hospital. *American Journal of Respiratory and Critical Care Medicine*, 160, 211–215.

Strunk, R. C., Mrazek, D. A., Fuhrmann, G. S., and LaBrecque, J. F. (1985). Physiologic and psychological characteristics associated with deaths due to asthma in childhood: A case controlled study. *Journal of the American Medical Association*, 254, 1193–1198.

Taitel, M. S., Kotses, H., Bernstein, I. L., Bernstein, D. I., and Creer, T. L. (1995). A self-management program for adult asthma. Part II: Cost–benefit analysis. *Journal of Allergy and Clinical Immunology*, 95, 672–676.

Tattersell, M. J. (1993). Asthma patients' knowledge in relation to compliance with drug therapy. *Journal of Advanced Nursing*, 18, 103–113.

Todd, W. E. (1995). New mindsets in asthma: Interventions and disease management. *Journal of Care Management*, 1, 2–8.

Varni, J. W. (1983). *Clinical Behavioral Pediatrics*. New York: Pergamon Press.

Weinstein, A. G. (1995). Clinical management strategies to maintain drug compliance in asthmatic children. *Annals of Allergy, Asthma, and Immunology*, 74, 304–310.

Weiss, K. B., Gergen, P. J., and Hodgson, T. A. (1992). An economic evaluation of asthma in the United States. *New England Journal of Medicine*, 326, 862–866.

Yellowless, P. M., Haynes, S., Potts, N., and Ruffin, R. E. (1988). Psychiatric morbidity in patients with life-threatening asthma: Initial report of a controlled study. *Medical Journal of Australia*, 149, 246–249.

CHAPTER 12

Arthritis

Heather M. Burke, Alex J. Zautra, Amy S. Schultz, John W. Reich and Mary C. Davis

Arizona State University

Introduction

Arthritis and musculoskeletal disorders are the most common sources of disability in the United States (Lawrence et al., 1998). Currently, approximately 40 million Americans suffer from some form of arthritis or musculoskeletal condition (Lawrence et al., 1998). As the population continues to age, this will reach epidemic proportions. The societal and personal impact of these disabling conditions underscores the importance of establishing a clear understanding of the biobehavioral mechanisms that influence course, prognosis, and treatment outcomes. Although improvements in medical technology have, in some cases, been able to stall disease progression and improve quality of life (QOL), there remains a large proportion of disability and suffering untouched by conventional medical treatment. As a result, more comprehensive models of disease and disability need to be employed to better conceptualize these disorders.

The stress–diathesis approach, although initially developed in studies of schizophrenia, has recently been applied to better understand the complex mechanisms underlying other disorders, such as depression and chronic pain (Banks and Kerns, 1996; Monroe and Simons, 1991). In this approach, individuals develop disease as a result of an interaction between a predisposing vulnerability, i.e., diathesis, and a precipitating agent in their environment, i.e., stress. Traditionally, researchers applying the stress–diathesis model to

This research was supported by grants from the National Institute on Aging, 1 F31 AG05850-01 (Heather M. Burke, Predoctoral Fellow) and the Arthritis Foundation (Alex J. Zautra, Principal Investigator).

Correspondence concerning this chapter should be addressed to Alex Zautra, PhD, Department of Psychology, P.O. Box 871104, Arizona State University Tempe, AZ 85287-1104.

arthritis and musculoskeletal conditions have focused on physiological vulnerabilities, such as genetic factors or pre-existing disease. However, Engel (1977) emphasized the importance of considering not only biological, but also psychological and social factors to understand health and disease processes. The introduction of his biopsychosocial model addressed the lack of a one-to-one correspondence between organic disease and subjective symptoms. Only by considering the interacting biological, psychological, and social sources of vulnerability and stress can investigators and clinicians understand the outcomes of chronic illnesses such as arthritis and musculoskeletal conditions. Thus, the purpose of this chapter is to take a diathesis–stress approach to understanding the most common arthritis and musculoskeletal conditions in the United States: osetoarthritis (OA), fibromyalgia (FM), and rheumatoid arthritis (RA). We will provide evidence that: 1) these disorders are best understood within a diathesis–stress framework, and 2) this approach also has important implications for treatment.

Diatheses

According to the stress–diathesis model, the process of adaptation and its health consequences depend upon an individual's vulnerability to the threats to psychological and physical wellbeing posed by stressful circumstances. There exist individual differences in biological, psychological, and social sources of vulnerability, which ultimately interact with stress factors to produce negative outcomes. For instance, individuals with arthritis and musculoskeletal conditions confronted with identical stressors will not experience identical outcomes. Furthermore, despite the fact that these conditions share a common symptomatology and are often treated within the same medical specialty, each disorder varies in its relative contributions from biological, psychological, and social factors. Thus, there are individual and disease-specific sources of variability in biopsychosocial diathesis factors. We will discuss the common biological, psychological, and social sources of diathesis factors for each of these conditions. Although a detailed description of the biological mechanisms that contribute to these conditions is beyond the scope of this chapter, a brief description of the biological nature of each disorder is warranted.

Biological Factors

Rheumatoid Arthritis

Rheumatoid arthritis is a systemic autoiummune disease characterized by multiple joint tenderness, swelling, and pain. As of 1990, more than 2 million Americans suffer from either adult or juvenile rheumatoid arthritis (JRA) (Lawrence et al., 1998). Onset of symptoms before age 16 is diagnosed as JRA. Common symptoms of RA include fatigue, morning stiffness, and joint tenderness and/or swelling (Harris, 1993). Although joint tenderness and/or swelling may initially appear asymmetric, more symmetric involvement occurs as the disease progresses (Harris, 1993). The inflammation surrounding affected joints in RA can be easily observed with radiographic techniques. In addition, there are several blood markers of systemic inflammation.

There is a growing body of evidence to suggest that RA is the end-point of a continuum of psychological, endocrine, and immune dysregulation (Chrousos and Gold, 1992). The hormonal responses intrinsic to psychological stress are thought to trigger a cascade of dysregulated endocrine and immune activity that ultimately results in the inflammation seen in RA. There are several potential endocrine–immune pathways in which this could occur. For instance, stress-sensitive hormones such as prolactin and estradiol activate the components of the immune system that are directly involved in RA disease activity. Thus, at the hormonal–immune level, individuals with RA may be especially vulnerable to the effects of stress.

Several demographic and disease course variables have been associated with poor prognosis in RA. For instance, although the incidence of RA increases with age, there is evidence that an early onset (particularly before age 60) is associated with more aggressive disease (Harris, 1993). Furthermore, younger patients with RA are also more vulnerable to developing depression, which itself is a disabling condition (Wright et al., 1998). Second, the first 2 years of disease activity appear to be the most amenable to treatment effects (Anderson et al., 2000). Thus, age and duration of disease activity serve as diathesis factors contributing to the course and prognosis in individuals with RA.

Osteoarthritis

Like RA, OA has a clear biological component. OA is the most prevalent form of arthritis in the United States, affecting approximately 20.7 million people (Lawrence et al., 1998). Because the prevalence of this condition increases linearly with age, prevalence is expected to rise considerably as the population matures (Mankin, 1993). Common symptoms of OA include pain (often exercise induced), limited range of motion, and morning stiffness of short duration (Keefe et al., 1987; Kraus, 1997). As the disease progresses, joint deformity and inflammation may develop (Mankin, 1993). Although the etiology of OA is unknown, the pathogenesis is characterized primarily by cartilage destruction and bone erosions (Kraus, 1997). Known risk factors for development of OA include increasing age, physical trauma, congenital factors, and obesity (Kraus, 1997).

OA is a progressive condition, but there remains great variability in the subjective experience of the disease. Indeed, some patients with radiographically confirmed advanced disease report few symptoms, whereas some with mild but detectable disease activity report a great deal of pain and activity limitation (Pincus et al., 1984). There is also evidence that younger individuals with OA suffer from more psychological disability and pain, whereas older patients experience more physical disability (Weinberger et al., 1990). Thus, as in RA, the age of the individual serves as a vulnerability factor for an unfavorable course and prognosis.

Fibromyalgia

In contrast to the well-documented disease activity in RA, FM is a chronic pain syndrome of unknown origin that currently affects an estimated 3.7 million Americans. Whereas most OA patients can trace their illness to a regional condition, the FM pain experience is widespread and found in soft tissue instead of the joints. Common symptoms of FM include pain in all four quadrants of the body, pain in specific "tender points," fatigue, stiffness, and nonrefreshing sleep (Bennett, 1993; Wolfe et al., 1990). Approximately 85% of FM patients are women. As with OA, the prevalence of FM appears to increase with age (Lawrence et al., 1998).

Currently, there is no objective test of disease activity in FM. As a result, physicians have to rely entirely on subjective symptoms reported by their patients to make a diagnosis. Further complicating an accurate diagnosis, many individuals with FM often meet criteria for other conditions, such as chronic fatigue syndrome (CFS) (Bennett, 1993), irritable bowel syndrome, Raynaud's phenomenon, and clinical depression (Wolfe et al., 1990). One of the most viable models for FM is a dysregulation of stress responses that most likely originates at the central nervous system level (for a review, see Bennett, 1999). An imbalance of crucial neurotransmitters such as substance P (Russell et al., 1994; Vaeroy et al., 1988) and dysregulation in hypothalamopituitary–adrenal axis activity has been documented (Adler et al., 1999; Catley et al., 2000). However, at present it is difficult to ascertain whether these abnormalities are causes or effects of living in pain.

Because of the lack of a definitive pathophysiological mechanism for FM, there remains controversy surrounding the course and prognosis for this condition. Although FM symptoms tend to be chronic, there is a great deal of individual variability in the course and prognosis of the disease. Whereas some studies of clinic samples of individuals with FM have demonstrated the continued presence of symptoms as long as 10 years after symptom onset (Kennedy and Felson, 1996; Wigers, 1996), other investigators have found better prognoses in community samples. For example, in a community-based longitudinal study of individuals with chronic widespread pain, 35% still had widespread pain, 50% had regional pain, and 15% had no pain at 2-year follow-up (MacFarlane et al., 1996). Similar to patterns observed in RA and OA patients, individuals with FM who continued to have symptoms at follow-up tended to be older and have a longer duration of symptoms, as well as less education, more tender points, and more somatic symptoms.

Psychological Factors

Besides biological vulnerabilities, many psychological factors serve as risk factors for affecting adjustment to arthritis and musculoskeletal conditions, possibly interacting with stress to produce symptoms, disease activity, and/or poor psychological health. Some of the most powerful factors include neuroticism, self-efficacy, coping, and evidence of psychopathology, particularly depression.

Neuroticism

The role of personality factors in the development and progression of, and adaptation to arthritis-related conditions has often been a focus of investigation (Affleck et al., 1992; Stone et al., 1997). Traditionally, attention has focused on identifying personality attributes specific to each condition. More recently, attention has shifted to identifying individual differences in personality within diagnostic groups that contribute to disease course. Neuroticism, the dispositional tendency to experience negative emotions under a variety of situations, is a personality characteristic that has been linked to an increased frequency of stressful experiences in the general population. This may be particularly problematic in RA, as RA disease activity is especially vulnerable to the effects of stress (Zautra et al., 1995a). Consistent with this research, in individuals with RA, neuroticism has been associated with poor self-rated functional status (Radanov et al., 1997a), more intense pain (Affleck et al., 1992), and mental health problems (Fyrand et al., 1997). Although few studies have investigated the role of neuroticism in individuals with OA or FM, it is likely that facets of neurotic disposition account for some of the variability in symptom expression among individuals within each of these conditions. For instance, patients with FM who score high in neuroticism are more frustrated with their physicians than those low in neuroticism (Walker et al., 1997). In one of the few studies investigating the role of neuroticism in adaptation to OA, neuroticism at baseline predicted pain up to 20 years later (Turk-Charles et al., 1999). These results suggest that it may be advantageous to focus on identifying subsets of individuals with certain personality characteristics, particularly neuroticism, within diagnostic groups, in order to more accurately predict outcomes.

Self-Efficacy

Decades of research have demonstrated that high levels of self-efficacy have a positive benefit for health maintenance and recovery. Certainly, chronic illnesses such as arthritis and musculoskeletal conditions represent some of the major challenges in life to freedom of action and general wellbeing. Thus, maintenance of control beliefs is particularly salient to the mental and physical health of individuals with arthritis-related conditions.

Results of cross-sectional studies demonstrate significant positive correlations between self-efficacy and various health outcomes. Higher self-efficacy has been linked to less pain (Buckelew, et al., 1994, 1996; Keefe et al., 1997), improved movement capacity (Rejeski et al., 1996), and less fatigue (Brown and Nicassio, 1987; Riemsma, et al., 1998) in individuals with RA, OA, and FM. These associations have also been demonstrated in longitudinal research studies, where self-efficacy has been significantly related to daily ratings of pain, mood, and coping variables in patients with RA, even over and above medical status variables (Lefebvre et al., 1999). In sum, higher self-efficacy is consistently shown to relate to better health status. However, the mechanism for these effects remains to be elucidated. For example, self-efficacy may directly dampen an individual's stress response, as an individual who feels confident in his/her ability to cope may be less likely to appraise situations as being stressful than an individual without such confidence (Lazarus and Folkman, 1984). Thus, self-efficacy may affect coping responses themselves. Alternatively, low self-efficacy may serve as a proxy for depression and help-lessness, which themselves predict poorer health.

Depression

The documented relationship between chronic pain and depression serves as another powerful illustration of how pain consists of biological, psychological, and social factors (for reviews, see Banks and Kerns, 1996; Romano and Turner, 1985). There is a high prevalence of depression in both RA (Creed et al., Murphy, and Jason, 1990) and FM patient populations (Aaron et al., 1996; Ercolani et al., 1994; Hawley and Wolfe, 1993; Hudson et al., 1985). At issue is the question of whether the experience of chronic pain precedes or is the result of depression. In RA patients, depression has been associated with pain (Affleck et al., 1991; Ferguson and Cotton, 1996; Fifield et al., 1991; Parker and Wright, 1995). Further, some longitudinal studies have even demonstrated that pain precedes depression in patients with RA and FM (Brown, 1990; Morrow et al., 1994; Nicassio and Wallston, 1992; Nicassio et al., 1995a).

The strong relationship between pain and depression has led some investig-ators to hypothesize that FM, which has no known etiology, may be a form of "affective spectrum disorder" (Hudson and Pope, 1989). To investigate this hypothesis, comparisons have been made between depression associated with FM versus other sources of chronic pain. These comparisons have yielded equivocal results. Some studies have found no difference in current or life-time history of major depressive disorder between patient populations with FM and those with RA (Ahles et al., 1991). In contrast, results of other studies have demonstrated that FM patients score higher on measures of psycholo-gical distress (Uveges et al., 1990), depression (Alfici et al., 1989), lifetime prevalence of affective disorder (Walker et al., 1997), and familial prevalence of major affective disorder (Hudson et al., 1985) than their RA counterparts. Compared to patients with other forms of musculoskeletal pain, patients with FM experienced significantly more depression than those with low back pain or lumbar herniation (Krag et al., 1995), but did not differ from myofascial pain patients (Roth and Bachman, 1993). Thus, at this point, although pa-tients with FM experience a high rate of depression, it is not yet clear whether depression is an inherent part of FM.

Social Factors

Just as individual differences in biological and psychological sources of vul-nerability affect outcome in arthritis and musculoskeletal conditions, so too do social factors. Two important social sources of resilience and vulnerability include perceived social support and stigmatization.

Social Support

Traditionally, the effect of social support on health outcomes has been conceptualized in two ways. One is that social support has a direct effect on health. Another is that social support moderates (i.e., buffers) the effects of stress on health outcomes. The latter model has important implications for individuals with arthritis-related conditions. As individuals with chronic pain and disability may be more vulnerable to the effects of stress, social support becomes more important. There is evidence to support the stress-buffering effects of social support in individuals with arthritis and musculoskeletal conditions (Affleck et al., 1988; for review, see Manne and Zautra, 1992). Quality of close relationships has also been associated with greater effectiveness of pain medication (Radanov et al., 1996), less disability (Weinberger et al., 1990), and lower levels of depression (Nicassio et al., 1995b). Because the quality of social relationships appears crucial to many important outcomes, individuals with chronic illnesses who lack adequate support structures may be at particular risk. Indeed, depression, poor coping responses, and other psychological factors may interact to produce negative outcomes. For instance, the tendency of individuals with FM to cope with pain by withdrawing from personal relationships may make them more vulnerable to the negative effects of stress (Zautra et al., 1999).

Stigma

Individuals with chronic pain may be more vulnerable to another social source of stress: stigma. According to several empirical studies, individuals with chronic pain of unknown etiology are more likely than those with pain of known etiology to feel stigmatized and think that others are attributing their symptoms to personality problems (Lennon et al., 1989). Indeed, research focus often shows bias consistent with stigmatization. For example, both the early investigations of RA and more recent studies of FM have focused on personality attributes. Although no data are yet available for the FM population, stigma may be a common source of social stress. For instance, common responses to perceived stigma among those with chronic pain include withdrawal from personal relationships (Osborn and Smith, 1998), and increasing frequency of medical consultations (Lennon et al., 1989). Likewise, individuals with FM have a condition of unknown etiology, tend to withdraw from social relationships (Zautra et al., 1999), and have high medical utilization rates (Kirmayer et al., 1988). Furthermore, perceived stigmatization may not be limited to FM. For instance, the physical disfigurement present in the later stages of RA may also be a source of social sensitivity that deserves greater attention. Thus, greater attention to vulnerability to stigmatization in arthritis and musculoskeletal conditions is warranted.

Biopsychosocial Factors of Stress

According to the diathesis–stress model, stressors in life are seen as provoking agents that challenge adaptation for all, but harm only those who are vulnerable (Banks and Kerns, 1996; Monroe and Simons, 1991). Whereas the biopsychosocial sources of diathesis factors have been extensively investigated, the biopsychosocial aspects of the stress side of the equation have largely been ignored. For example, there are many acute and chronic sources of stress, including stresses that arise from strained interpersonal relationships. Among those with chronic pain, there are other sources of stress as well, including stresses that arise from the illness itself. In our view, research and treatment approaches that fail to distinguish among the many forms of stress may demonstrate an association between general indicators of stress and health, but provide too little specificity to facilitate the development of theory or aid in devising treatments and preventive interventions.

Biological

Much past research focused on two biological components of the stimulus–response stress equation: activation and recovery. On the stimulus side of the equation, stress activation refers to the extent of the initial arousal and threat level. In contrast, on the response side of the equation, recovery refers to the feedback and downregulation of stress hormones. Homeostasis occurs when the two sides of the equation are equivalent. Both the stimulus and the response sides of the stress equation have been implicated in rheumatological conditions.

With regard to stimulus properties, it is widely accepted that uncontrollable and unpredictable situations are perceived as most stressful. As symptom exacerbations of arthritis and musculoskeletal conditions are often unpredictable and uncontrollable, the stimulus properties of stress in chronic pain deserve more empirical attention.

A significant body of research on the biological aspects of stress has focused on the hypothalamopituitary–adrenal (HPA) axis and its role in immune system suppression. Stress activates the central nervous system (CNS), causing the release of prolactin (PRL) and adrenocorticotrophic hormone (ACTH) from the pituitary, which triggers release of cortisol from the adrenal cortex. In the healthy individual, cortisol suppresses cellular immune function, whereas PRL stimulates it. These opposing actions, as well as the action of gonadal steroids, allow for modulation of the immune response around a homeostatic set point. The literature suggests that stress can be both immunostimulatory and immunoinhibitory, depending on the intensity and duration of the stressor (Potter and Zautra, 1997). This suggests that consideration of the temporal aspects of the stress response is imperative to understanding the relationship between stress and health. For instance, unabated stress responses can be harmful to health and wellbeing (McEwen, 1998). Indeed, research from our own laboratory suggests that the duration of the emotional stress response is more predictive of health symptoms than the initial magnitude of the response in women with RA and OA (Burke, 1999). Thus, temporal qualities of the stress response may affect the stress–health relationship in individuals with arthritis and musculoskeletal conditions.

Psychological

Just as biological responses to stress exist, so too do psychological responses. There is little doubt that how an individual copes with a chronic illness is associated with long-term adaptation to the condition.

Coping

The adaptiveness of specific coping strategies may often be context and disease specific (for review, see Manne and Zautra, 1992). There is evidence that those with RA and OA who use active coping strategies have more favorable outcomes than those who use passive coping strategies, which involve retreat in the face of a stressor. In individuals with RA and OA, passive coping, but not active coping, is related to reduced functional status (Affleck et al., 1992; Zautra et al., 1995). In addition, coping strategies such as wishful thinking and catastrophizing account for a significant amount of variability in physical disability, pain, and depression in individuals with RA and OA (Beckham et al., 1991).

There is some evidence that individuals with FM cope differently than those with OA or RA. For example, Zautra et al. (1999) found that FM patients used more avoidant strategies than their OA counterparts. Despite the evidence for an association between active coping and favorable outcomes in individuals with RA and OA, studies focusing on individuals with FM have yielded conflicting results. In individuals with FM, increases in both passive and active coping have been associated with depression (Nicassio et al., 1995a), and more coping effort was associated with increased physical disability (although less psychological disability) (Martin et al., 1996). These results suggest that coping responses that may be adaptive in some conditions (RA and OA) may actually be maladaptive in another (FM).

Social

In addition to the data highlighting the psychological aspects of stress, there is mounting evidence that social stressors are particularly difficult for patients coping with chronic illness. Family conflict has been associated with poor psychological adjustment to RA (Manne and Zautra, 1989). Indeed, patients with chronic illness may be more sensitive than their healthy counterparts to interpersonal conflict with individuals who are major sources of support, such as family and close friends (Revenson et al., 1991). Because chronic illness often leads to severe limitation in the capacity to function independently, a disturbance in supportive relationships threatens to further isolate the patients and thus may increase anxiety and depression.

Outcomes

In this brief review we cannot do justice to the complexities of defining successful outcomes for those with these arthritis-related illnesses. However, we think that it is important to evaluate the course of the lives of those with FM, RA, and OA from a biopsychosocial perspective. These illnesses have different natural courses and trajectories, and awareness of such differences is important in the examination of the quality of life over time of those with one or more of these illnesses.

Biological

Perhaps the most dramatic example of the importance of considering biological aspects of disease in the measurement of outcomes has been the experience of doctors and patients in the use of steroid medications in the treatment of RA. The anti-inflammatory action of cortisol significantly reduces pain and activity limitation, and many patients have stayed on prednisone and other forms of steroid preparations for years as a means of controlling their disease. However, although symptom severity improves, disease progression is not prevented and the chronic steroid use eventually leads to damage in organ systems throughout the body.

Although evaluation of the joint space is a necessary component for tailoring any biological therapy for RA, there are other indicators that may be more appropriately targeted for improvement in psychosocial interventions. Changes in immune function, including the proliferation of proinflammatory cytokines, may well turn out to be good markers of disease-related processes in RA that are directly affected by psychosocial interventions, and which carry or mediate the effects of such treatments on disease progression.

The same markers used in RA ought not to be chosen for OA and FM, however, neither of which is properly classified as an autoimmune disorder. In OA, the mechanics of joint function is one important outcome marker, but may be less critical than perceived wellbeing. There is now mounting evidence that arthroscopic surgeries, as well as other corrective methods directed toward those with OA, may have a large expectation or placebo effect (Moseley et al., 1996). Indeed, the low correlation between joint damage and symptoms of OA should give us pause in the design of any study to evaluate the efficacy of a biologically based treatment for this chronic pain disorder.

In FM the biological markers are not secure, and those that we might contemplate for study, such as substance P, are neuropeptides and not easily obtained. Nevertheless, we may expect technological advancements that will allow us to assess changes in brain chemistry and neural activity as a function of therapies of many kinds, including psychosocial. Once we have learned more about the central neurological processes involved in the chronicity of FM, we may well benefit from the use of the rapidly developing brain imaging technologies in charting its course.

Psychological

If we had adopted a biomedical perspective on these illnesses, then we would stop here in the discussion of outcomes, for only those that mark biological processes would have currency. Yet we know better than that from the substantial literature that has documented the force of psychosocial factors both in the course of illness and in defining the meaning of adaptation for those with a chronic health problem.

What concerns us in outcomes is the QOL of those with RA, FM and OA. It is useful to examine psychological outcomes as QOL in three domains. The containment of negative affective experiences such as pain and suffering that derive from these conditions is certainly first on this list, and there are many studies devoted to understanding the various dimensions of affective health. Among the most important has been the presence of depression and anxiety as well as pain, in terms of both intensity and time to recovery following a pain episode. A second concern is positive affective health. The motivation to engage in life activities derives at least in part from anticipated positive outcomes, and functional impairment has a bidirectional relationship with positive affective experiences. People who cannot find sources of positive engagement in life's activities are likely to be more vulnerable to functional loss, and that loss only leads to more disability over time. Zautra et al. (1995) have shown that these positive affective states are independent markers of outcomes of arthritis, equally important to consider in the evaluation of the quality of life of the chronically ill.

A third aspect of these outcomes that deserves close attention is more cognitive than affective in nature, although that dichotomy is not altogether an accurate depiction of these processes. The beliefs of the person are key components: helplessness and other depressogenic cognitions are likely to be very important to study in the course of adaptation to any chronic illness, including arthritis-like conditions. General self-efficacy and expectations for success from interventions directed by others are beliefs that can be modified by interventions of many types. Another important outcome that is likely to attract increased attention in the future concerns those cognitions that affect the anticipation of pain and stress. Acceptance and other means of construing life experiences that reduce anxiety surrounding pain and limitations are also key processes worthy of study as components of quality of life among chronic pain patients.

Social

Social factors also should not be ignored as important outcomes in chronic pain patients. It is perhaps already well understood that these illnesses do not just affect those afflicted biologically: they also constitute challenges to adaptation among family and in the workplace. Outcomes in quality of life include lessening the burden for those who care for the person with one of these illnesses. Outcomes in the social arena also mean a reduction in the social stigma often associated with such illnesses as FM, where the common refrain is "Isn't this something all in the head?" Some researchers have focused wisely on the solicitousness of the support system, which may inadvertently reinforce illness behavior. We have been interested in pursuing how support might encourage self-reliance versus dependence, and found that whereas in some conditions one is called for, in other situations the other approach may be most beneficial (Reich and Zautra, 1995). The usefulness of these various approaches to support may well vary according to the illness. We urge further work on these and related topics to fully develop a behavioral approach to quality of interpersonal relations for those who need to contend with chronic and painful illnesses among those within their core social network.

Implications for Treatment

Conventional biomedical treatment of arthritis and musculoskeletal conditions typically targets control of disease activity and reduction of symptoms. Furthermore, most pharmacological interventions are disease specific, that is, the drugs used to treat RA disease activity are not always identical to those used to treat OA or FM. In contrast to the specific nature of conventional biomedical treatment, psychosocial interventions have often been "one size fits all." Sometimes a combination of biological and psychological factors has been included in interventions, although not necessarily in a coordinated fashion.

Biological Treatment

In the past, the common pharmacological approach to treating RA was to follow a "pyramidal strategy" by aiming to "first do no harm," and prescribe glucocorticoids and nonsteroidal anti-inflammatory drugs (NSAIDS) to control symptoms and inflammation (McCracken, 1991). However, it soon became clear that, left unchecked, the progressive nature of RA could cause significant disability and mortality (Harris, 1993). As a result, physicians have now attempted to "turn the pyramid upside down," prescribing an aggressive arsenal of pharmaceutical treatments in the earlier stages of the disease (Harris, 1993; Fries, 1990). Included in this arsenal are disease-modifying drugs and biologic response modifiers, as well as the more traditional medications that reduce symptoms and physical impairment, such as NSAIDs, salicylates, and glucocorticoids (Harris, 1993).

As there is no known cure for OA, the primary goal of treatment is symptom relief. Common types of treatment include pharmacological agents such as NSAIDs, analgesics, and topical ointments (Brandt, 1993). Although usually reserved as a treatment of last resort, surgical replacement of joints is often required for severe OA and RA (Brandt, 1993).

Treatment in patients with FM also is targeted to symptom management. Both pharmacological and psychological interventions have yielded conflicting results. Common pharmacological treatment includes tricyclic antidepressants at lower doses than would be prescribed for the treatment of depression. Also, the newer class of selective serotonin reuptake inhibitors is used widely in the treatment of FM pain. These substances incidentally promote slow-wave sleep, something that has often been demonstrated to be deficient in patients with FM (Moldofsky et al., 1975). Unlike OA and RA, FM does not involve an inflammatory process, and so treatment with NSAIDs and corticosteroids is usually ineffective (Bennett, 1993). Furthermore, because of the fear of dependence and addiction, narcotic analgesics have been avoided, even when their use may be warranted. Thus, effective pharmacological treatment of the pain associated with FM remains elusive. However, a recent meta-analysis of common treatments for FM demonstrated that nonpharmacological interventions were more effective than pharmacological treatments for treating the pain (Rossy et al., 1999).

Psychosocial Treatment

Owing to the contributions of biological, psychological, and social factors to RA, OA, and FM, numerous psychosocial interventions have been developed. One of the most common forms of psychosocial treatment is cognitive–behavioral therapy (CBT). Common elements of CBT include biofeedback and relaxation (for reviews, see Anderson et al., 1988; Nicassio and Greenberg, in press). The goal is to improve some aspect of health status, such as pain tolerance, mobility, self-management, and selfefficacy. CBT has been found to decrease pain, lower disease activity, decrease depression, and reduce healthcare use in individuals with RA (Anderson et al., 1988; McCracken, 1991; Nicassio and Greenberg, in press). As in RA patients, common components of CBT therapy in OA patients include exercise treatments (Rejeski et al., 1998) and enhancing coping skills and spousal support (Keefe et al., 1996). Significant improvements in health status and enhancement of self-efficacy were found in these studies. The effect of increased self-efficacy on the health of individuals with RA and OA has also been reported in samples of FM patients (Burckhardt and Bjelle, 1994). Education, exercise, and cognitive and psychoeducational programs have been shown to increase self-esteem and various aspects of health in individuals with FM (Gowans et al., 1999). After a review of the literature, Keefe (1998) suggested that interventions for FM should target increasing self-efficacy to enhance their effectiveness.

Self-help group interventions, such as the Arthritis Self Management Program, have traditionally focused on improving knowledge and increasing health behaviors in individuals with arthritis and musculoskeletal conditions (Lorig et al., 1998). In their review, Nicassio and Greenberg (in press) concluded that these self-help programs effectively increase arthritis knowledge, improve compliance with health behaviors, increase self-efficacy, and reduce pain and healthcare utilization in individuals with RA and OA. Although self-help management programs have recently been applied to FM patients, further research is needed to demonstrate their effectiveness.

Future Directions

From the discussion of RA, OA, and FM, it should be clear that each disorder has unique contributions from biological, psychological, and social factors. However, despite this, psychosocial treatment has not so far been shaped to fit the different needs of those with various forms of chronic pain. We think that future treatments of these conditions should target the specific biopsychosocial qualities unique to each condition. For instance, in RA, a condition with known pathophysiological features and pharmacological treatments, attention to the psychosocial factors that influence compliance with pharmacological treatment may be useful. In addition, interventions designed to address barriers to compliance that utilize existing social systems (i.e., family, peers, and healthcare providers) may also be beneficial.

Compliance with nonpharmacological treatment recommendations could be a target of treatment in OA and FM. As the development of OA is often dependent on preventable factors such as exercise and obesity, treatment addressing compliance with exercise regimens would be especially useful in this population. Similarly, compliance with lifestyle changes would also be a useful target of intervention in FM. Interventions targeting exercise initiation in individuals with FM would best be accomplished with close supervision by trained healthcare professionals who are sensitive to these considerations.

Well-designed treatments should also consider the sources of stress that may be unique to each condition. For instance, we have discussed how unpredictable and uncontrollable events are perceived as the most stressful. Exacerbations of symptoms may be predicted by overexertion and climate changes in OA, and thus may be less stressful than the relatively unpredictable exacerbations of FM and RA. Likewise, the relative lack of symptom relief in FM may make this pain an additional source of stress that may not be as pronounced in OA, where pharmacological agents provide some relief. Thus, treatments that consider the controllability and predictability of stressors and devise ways to affect these qualities may be most effective. Another promising treatment – mindfulness meditation – trains attention deployment and promotes a nonjudgmental acceptance of all life conditions, whether positive or negative (Kabat-Zinn, 1990). Its use with people suffering from arthritis and musculoskeletal conditions is likely to increase as more professionals become aware of its efficacy in enhancing holistic wellbeing.

Treatments that target the social aspects of each condition may have a significant impact on QOL and may be particularly effective. After all, the effects of arthritis and musculoskeletal conditions are not limited to the individual afflicted with the disease. We have discussed evidence that interpersonal stress is particularly damaging to the health of individuals with RA. Thus, interventions that elicit participation from family members and/or spouses of RA patients to improve the quality of their relationships may yield more powerful effects. Manipulation of the social environment of individuals with OA may help them adopt the lifestyle changes (i.e., exercise, weight management) necessary to prevent and treat the disease. In addition, individuals with

FM often react to stress by withdrawing from social relationships, and feel misunderstood by their healthcare providers. Thus, interventions that prompt spouses and family members to continue to engage the patient in their social activities may improve the outcome in these cases. Furthermore, proper training of healthcare professionals to communicate effectively with individuals and be aware of stigmatization factors may reduce the need for "doctor-shopping" among patients with FM.

From the above discussion it should be clear that, although RA, OA, and FM share many common symptoms and forms of treatment, they remain distinct conditions. Consideration of the unique contributions of biological, psychological, and social factors to each of these chronic conditions may yield more comprehensive models and efficacious treatments.

References

Aaron, L. A., Bradley, L. A., Alarcon, G. S., Alexander, R. W., Triana-Alexander, M., Martin, M. Y. and Alberts, K. R. (1996). Psychiatric diagnoses in patients with fibromyalgia are related to health-care seeking behavior rather than to illness. *Arthritis and Rheumatism*, 39, 436–445.

Adler, G. K., Kinsley, B. T., Hurwitz, S., Mossey, C. J., and Goldenberg, D. L. (1999). Reduced hypothalamic–pituitary and sympathoadrenal responses to hypoglycemia in women with fibromyalgia syndrome. *American Journal of Medicine*, 106, 534–543.

Affleck, G., Pfeiffer, C., Tennen, H., and Fifield, J. (1988). Social support and psychosocial adjustment to rheumatoid arthritis: Quantitative and qualitative findings. *Arthritis Care and Research*, 1, 71–77.

Affleck, G., Tennen, H., Urrows, S., and Higgins, P. (1991). Individual differences in the day to day experience of chronic pain: A prospective daily study of rheumatoid arthritis patients. *Health Psychology*, 10, 419–426.

Affleck, G., Tennen, H., Urrows, S., and Higgins, P. (1992). Neuroticism and the pain–mood relation in rheumatoid arthritis: Insights from a prospective daily study. *Journal of Consulting and Clinical Psychology*, 60, 119–126.

Ahles, T. A., Khan, S. A., Yunus, M. B., Spiegel, D. A., and Masi, A. T. (1991). Psychiatric status of patients with primary fibromyalgia, patients with rheumatoid arthritis, and subjects without pain: A blind comparison of DSM-III diagnoses. *American Journal of Psychiatry*, 148, 1721–1726.

Alfici, S., Sigal, M., and Landau, M. (1989). Primary fibromyalgia syndrome: A variant of depressive disorder? *Psychotherapy and Psychosomatics*, 51, 156–161.

Anderson, J. J., Wells, G., Verhoeven, A. C., and Felson, D. T. (2000). Factors predicting response to treatment in rheumatoid arthritis: The importance of disease duration. *Arthritis and Rheumatism*, 43, 22–29.

Anderson, K. O., Bradley, L. A., Young, L. D., McDaniel, L. K., and Wise, C. M. (1988). Rheumatoid arthritis: Review of psychological factors related to etiology, effects, and treatment. *Psychological Bulletin*, 98, 358–387.

Banks, S. M. and Kerns, R. D. (1996). Explaining high rates of depression in chronic pain: A diathesis stress framework. *Psychological Bulletin*, 119, 95–110.

Beckham, J. C., Keefe, F. J., Caldwell, D. S., and Roodman, A. A. (1991). Pain coping strategies in rheumatoid arthritis: Relationships to pain, disability, depression and daily hassles. *Behavior Therapy*, 22, 113–124.

Bennett, R. M. (1993). The fibromyalgia syndrome: Myofascial pain and the chronic fatigue syndrome. In W. N. Kelley, E. D. Harris, S. Ruddy, and C. B. Sledge (Eds.), *Textbook of Rheumatology* (4th ed., pp. 471–483). Philadephia: W.B. Saunders Company.

Bennett, R. M. (1999). Emerging concepts in the neurobiology of chronic pain: Evidence of abnormal sensory processing in fibromyalgia. *Mayo Clinic Proceedings*, 74, 385–398.

Brandt, K. D. (1993). Management of Osteoarthritis. In W. N. Kelley, E. D. Harris, S. Ruddy, and C. B. Sledge (Eds.), *Textbook of Rheumatology* (4th ed., pp. 1385–1399). Philadelphia: W.B. Saunders Company.

Brown, G. K. (1990). A causal analysis of chronic pain and depression. *Journal of Abnormal Psychology*, 22, 127–137.

Brown, G. K., and Nicassio, P. N. (1987). Developments of a questionnaire for the assessment of active and passive coping strategies in chronic pain patients. *Pain*, 31, 53–64.

Buckelew, S. P., Parker, J. C., Keefe, F. J., Deuser, W. E., Crews, T. M., Conway, R., Kay, D. R., and Hewett, J. E. (1994). Self-efficacy and pain behavior among subjects with fibromyalgia. *Pain*, 59, 377–384.

Buckelew, S. P., Huyser, B., Hewett, J. E., Parker, J. C., Johnson, J. C., Conway, R., and Kay, D. R. (1996). Self-efficacy predicting outcome among fibromyalgia subjects. *Arthritis Care and Research*, 9, 97–104.

Burckhardt, C. S., and Bjelle, A. (1994). Perceived control: A comparison of women with fibromyalgia, rheumatold arthritis, and systemic lupus erythematosus using a Swedish version of the Rheumatology Attitudes Index. *Scandinavian Journal of Rheumatology*, 25, 300–306.

Burke, H. M. (1999). *Level and Duration of the Stress Response Predict Health Symptoms in Older Women*. Manuscript submitted for publication.

Catley, D., Kaell, A. T., Kirschbaum, C., and Stone, A. A. (2000). Naturalistic evaluation of cortisol secretion in persons with fibromyalgia and rheumatoid arthritis. *Arthritis Care and Research*, 13, 51–61.

Chrousos, G. P., and Gold, P. W. (1992). The concepts of stress and stress system disorders: Overview of physiological and behavioral homeostasis. *Journal of the American Medical Association*, 267, 1244–1252.

Creed, F., Murphy, S., and Jayson, M. V. (1990). Measurement of psychiatric disorder in rheumatoid arthritis. *Journal of Psychosomatic Research*, 34, 79–87.

Engel, G. L. (1977). The need for a new medical model: A challenge for biomedicine. *Science*, 196, 129–136.

Ercolani, M., Trombini, G., Chattat, R., Cervini, C., Piergiacomi, G., Salaffi, F., Zeni, S., and Marcolongo, R. (1994). Fibromyalgic syndrome: Depression and abnormal illness behavior: Multicenter investigation. *Psychotherapy and Psychosomatics*, 61, 178–186.

Ferguson, S. J., and Cotton, S. (1996). Broken sleep, pain, disability, social activity, and depressive symptoms in rheumatoid arthritis. *Australian Journal of Psychology*, 48, 9–14.

Fifield, J., Reisine, S. T., and Grady, K. E. (1991). Work disability and the experience of pain and depression in rheumatoid arthritis. *Social Science and Medicine*, 33, 579–585.

Fries, J. F. (1990). Reevaluating the therapeutic approach to rheumatoid arthritis: The "Sawtooth" strategy. *Journal of Rheumatology*, 17, 12–15.

Fyrand, L., Wichstrom, L., Moum, T., Glennas, A., and Kvien, T. K. (1997). The impact of personality and social support on mental health for female patients with rheumatoid arthritis. *Social Indicators Research*, 40, 285–298.

Gowans, S. E., deHueck, A., Voss, S., and Richardson, M. (1999). A randomized, controlled trial of exercise and education for individuals with fibromyalgia. *Arthritis Care and Research*, 12, 120–128.

Harris, E. D. (1993). Clinical features of rheumatoid arthritis. In W. N. Kelley, E. D. Harris, S. Ruddy, and C. B. Sledge (Eds.), *Textbook of Rheumatology* (4th ed., pp. 874–911). Philadelphia: W. B. Saunders Company.

Hawley, D. J., and Wolfe, F. (1993). Depression is not more common in rheumatoid arthritis: A 10 year longitudinal study of 6153 patients with rheumatic disease. *Journal of Rheumatology*, 20, 2025–2031.

Hudson, J. I., Hudson, M. S., Pliner, L. F., and Goldenberg, D. L. (1985). Fibromyalgia and major affective disorder: A controlled phenomenology and family history study. *American Journal of Psychiatry*, 142, 441–446.

Hudson, J. I., and Pope, H. G. Jr. (1989). Is fibromyalgia a form of "affective spectrum disorder?" *Journal of Rheumatology*, 19, 15–22.

Kabat-Zinn, J. (1990). *Full Catastrophe Living*. New York: Delacorte.

Keefe, F. J. (1998). Cognitive processes and the pain experience. *Journal of Muscoloskeletal Pain*, 6, 41–45.

Keefe, F. J., Caldwell, D. S., Queen, K. T., Gil, K. M., Martinez, S., Crisson, J. E., Ogden, W. and Nunley, J. (1987). Pain coping strategies in osteoarthritis patients. *Journal of Consulting and Clinical Psychology*, 55, 208–212.

Keefe, F. J., Caldwell, D. S., Baucom, D., Salley, A., Robinson, E., Timmons, K., Beaupre, P., Weisberg, J., and Helms, M. (1996). Spouse-assisted coping skills training in the management of osteoarthritic knee pain. *Arthritis Care and Research*, 9, 279–291.

Keefe, F. J., Affleck, G., Lefebure, J., Starr, K., Caldwell, D., and Tennen, H. (1997). Coping strategies and coping efficacy in rheumatoid arthritis: A daily process analysis. *Pain*, 69, 35–42.

Kennedy, M. F., and Felson, D. T. (1996). A prospective long term study of fibromyalgia syndrome. *Arthritis and Rheumatism*, 39, 682–685.

Kirmayer, L. J., Robbins, J. M., and Kapusta, M. A. (1988). Somatization and depression in fibromyalgia syndrome. *American Journal of Psychiatry*, 145, 950–954.

Krag, N. J., Norregaard, J., Hindberg, I., Larsen, J. K., and Danneskiold-Samsoe, B. (1995). Psychopathology measured by established self-rating scales and correlated to serotonin measures in patients with fibromyalgia. *European Psychiatry*, 10, 404–409.

Kraus, V. B. (1997). Pathogenesis and treatment of osteoarthritis. *Advances in Rheumatology*, 81, 85–104.

Lawrence, R. C., Helmick, C. G., Arnett, F. C., Deyo, R. A., Felson, D. T., Giannini, E. H., Heyse, S. P., Hirsch, R., Hochberg, M. C., Hunder, G. G., Liang, M. H., Pillemer, S. R., Steen, V. D., and Wolfe, F. (1998). Estimates of the prevalence of arthritis and selected musculoskeletal disorders in the United States. *Arthritis and Rheumatism*, 41, 778–799.

Lazarus, R. S., and Folkman, S. (1984). *Stress, Appraisal, and Coping*. New York: Springer.

Lennon, M. C., Link, B. G., Marback, J. J., and Dohrenwend, B. P. (1989). The stigma of chronic facial pain and its impact on social relationships. *Social Problems*, 36, 117–134.

Lefebvre, J. C., Keefe, F. J., Affleck, G., Raezer, L. B., Starr, K., Caldwell, D. S., and Tennen, H. (1999). The relationship of arthritis self-efficacy to daily pain, daily mood, and pain coping in rheumatoid arthritis patients. *Pain*, 80(1–2), 425–435.

Lorig, K., Gonzalez, V. M., Laurent, D. D., Morgan, L., and Laris, B. A. (1998). Arthritis self-management program variations: Three studies. *Arthritis Care and Research*, 11, 448–454.

Macfarlane, G. J., Thomas, E., Papageogiou, A. C., Schollum, J., Croft, P. R., and Silman, A. J. (1996). The natural history of chronic pain in the community: A better prognosis than in the clinic? *Journal of Rheumatology*, 23, 1617–1620.

Mankin, H. J. (1993). Clinical features of osteoarthritis. In W. N. Kelley, E. D. Harris, S. Ruddy, and C. B. Sledge (Eds.), *Textbook of Rheumatology* (4th ed., pp. 1374–1384). Philadelphia: W.B. Saunders Company.

Manne, S. L., and Zautra, A. J. (1989). Spouse criticism and support: Their association with coping and psychological adjustment among women with rheumatoid arthritis. *Journal of Personality and Social Psychology*, 56, 608–617.

Manne, S. L., and Zautra, A. J. (1992). Coping with arthritis. *Arthritis and Rheumatism*, 35, 1273–1280.

Martin, M. Y., Bradley, L. A., Alexander, R. W., Alarcon, G. S., Triana-Alexander, M., Aaron, L. A., and Alberts, K. R. (1996). Coping strategies predict disability in patients with primary fibromyalgia. *Pain*, 68, 45–53.

McCracken, L. M. (1991). Cognitive behavioral treatment of rheumatoid arthritis: A preliminary review of efficacy and methodology. *Annals of Behavioral Medicine*, 13, 57–65.

McEwen, B. S. (1998). Protective and damaging effects of stress mediators. *Seminars in Medicine of the Beth Israel Deaconess Medical Center*, 338, 171–179.

Moldofsky, H., Scarisbrick, P., England, R., and Smythe, H. (1975). Musculoskeletal symptoms and non-REM sleep disturbance in patients with "fibrositis syndrome" and healthy subjects. *Psychosomatic Medicine*, 37, 341–351.

Monroe, S. M., and Simons, A. D. (1991). Diathesis-stress theories in the context of life stress: Implications for the depressive disorders. *Psychological Bulletin*, 110(3), 406–425.

Morrow, K. A., Parker, J. C., and Russell, J. L. (1994). Clinical implications of depression in rheumatoid arthritis. *Arthritis Care and Research*, 7, 58–63.

Moseley, Jr., J. B., Wray, N. P., Kuykrendall, D., Willis, K., and Landon, G. (1996). Arthroscopic treatment of osteoarthritis of the knee: A prospective, randomized, placebo-controlled trial. *American Journal of Sports Medicine*, 24, 28–34.

Nicassio, P. M., and Greenberg, M. A. (2001). The effectiveness of cognitive–behavioral and psychoeducational interventions in the management of arthritis. In M. H. Weisman and J. Louie (Eds.), Treatment of the Rheumatic Diseases (2nd ed.) (pp. 147–161). Orlando, FL: William Saunders.

Nicassio, P. M., and Wallston, K. A. (1992). Longitudinal relationships among pain, sleep problems, and depression in rheumatoid arthritis. *Journal of Abnormal Psychology*, 101, 514–520.

Nicassio, P. M., Schoenfeld-Smith, K., Radojevic, V., and Schuman, C. (1995a). Pain coping mechanisms in fibromyalgia: Relationship to pain and functional outcomes. *Journal of Rheumatology*, 22, 1552–1558.

Nicassio, P. M., Radojevic, V., Schoenfeld-Smith, K., and Dwyer, K. (1995b). The contribution of family cohesion and the pain coping process to depressive symptoms in fibromyalgia. *Annals of Behavioral Medicine*, 17, 349–356.

Osborn, M., and Smith, J. A. (1998). The personal experience of chronic benign lower back pain: An interpretative phenomenological analysis. *British Journal of Health Psychology*, 3, 65–83.

Parker, J. C. and Wright, G. E. (1995). The implications of depression for pain and disability in rheumatoid arthritis. *Arthritis Care and Research*, 8, 279–283.

Pincus, T., Callahan, L., Sale, W., Brooks, A., Psyne, L., and Vaughn, W. (1984). Severe functional declines, work disability, and increased mortality in seventy-five rheumatoid arthritis patients studies over nine years. *Arthritis and Rheumatism*, 27, 864–872.

Potter, P. T., and Zautra, A. J. (1997). Stressful life events' effects on rheumatoid arthritis disease activity. *Journal of Clinical and Consulting Psychology*, 65, 319–323.

Radanov, B. P., Frost, S. A., Schwarz, H. A., and Augustiny, K. F. (1996). Experience of pain in rheumatoid arthritis: An empirical evaluation of the contribution of developmental psychosocial stress. *Acta Psychiatrica Scandinavica*, 93, 482–488.

Reich, J. W., and Zautra, A. J. (1995). Spouse encouragement of self-reliance and other-reliance in rheumatoid arthritis couples. *Journal of Behavioral Medicine*, 18, 249–260.

Rejeski, W. J., Craven, T., Ettinger, W. H., McFarlane, M., Shumaker, S. (1996). Self-efficacy and pain in disability with osteoarthritis of the knee. *Journal of Gerontology*, 51, P24–P29.

Rejeski, W. J., Ettinger, W. H., Martin, K., and Morgan, T. (1998). Treating disability in knee osteoarthritis with exercise therapy: A central role for self-efficacy and pain. *Arthritis Care and Research*, 11, 94–101.

Revenson, T. A., Schiaffino, K. M., Majerovitz, S. D., and Gibofsky, A. (1991). Social support as a double-edged sword: the relation of positive and problematic support to depression among rheumatoid arthritis patients. *Social Science and Medicine*, 33, 807–13.

Riemsma, R. P., Rasker J. J., Taal, E., Griep, E. N., Wouters, J. M., and Wiegman, O. (1998). Fatigue in rheumatoid arthritis: the role of self-efficacy and problematic social support. *British Journal of Rheumatology*, 37, 1042–1046.

Romano, J. M., and Turner, J. A. (1985). Chronic pain and depression: Does the evidence support a relationship? *Psychological Bulletin*, 97, 18–34.

Rossy, L. A., Buckelew, S. P., Dorr, N., Hagglund, K. J., Thayer, J. F., McIntosh, M. J., Hewett, J. E. and Johnson, J. C. (1999). A meta-analysis of fibromyalgia treatment interventions. *Annals of Behavioral Medicine*, 21, 180–191.

Roth, R. S., and Bachman, J. E. (1993). Pain experience, psychological functioning and self reported disability in chronic myofascial pain and fibromyalgia. *Journal of Musculoskeletal Pain*, 1, 209–216.

Russell, I. J., Orr, M. D., Littman, B., Vipraio, G. A., Alboukrek, D., Michalek, J. E., Lopez, Y., and MacKillip, R. (1994). Elevated cerebrospinal fluid levels of substance P in patients with the fibromyalgia syndrome. *Arthritis and Rheumatism*, 37, 1593–1601.

Stone, A. A., Broderick, J. E., Porter, L. S., and Kaell, A. T. (1997). The experience of rheumatoid arthritis pain and fatigue: Examining momentary reports and correlates over one week. *Arthritis Care and Research*, 10, 185–193.

Turk-Charles, S., Gatz, M., Pedersen, N. L., and Dahlberg, L. (1999). Genetic and behavioral risk factors for self-reported joint pain among a population-based sample of Swedish twins. *Health Psychology*, 18, 644–654.

Uveges, K. M., Parker, J. C., Smarr, K. L., McGowan, J. F., Lyon, M. G., Irvin, W. S., Meyer, A. A., Buckelew, S. P., Morgan, R. K., Delmonico, R. L., Hewett, J. E., and Kay, D. R. (1990). Psychological symptoms in primary fibromyalgia syndrome: Relationship to pain, life stress, and sleep disturbance. *Arthritis and Rheumatism*, 33, 1279–1283.

Vaeroy, H., Helle, R., Forre, O., Kass, E., and Terenius, L. (1988). Elevated cerebrospinal fluid levels of substance P and high incidence of Raynaud's phenomenon in patients with fibromyalgia: New features for diagnosis. *Pain*, 32, 21–26.

Walker, E. A., Keegan, D., Gardner, G., Sullivan, M., Katon, W. J., and Bernstein, D. (1997). Psychosocial factors in fibromyalgia compared with rheumatoid arthritis: I. Psychiatric diagnoses and functional disability. *Psychosomatic Medicine*, 59, 565–571.

Weinberger, M., Tierney, W. M., Booher, P., and Hiner, S. L. (1990). Social support, stress and functional status in patients with osteoarthritis. *Social Science and Medicine*, 30, 503–508.

Wigers, S. H. (1996). Fibromyalgia outcome: The predictive values of symptom duration, physical activity, disability pension, and critical life events: A 4.5-year prospective study. *Journal of Psychosomatic Research*, 41, 235–243.

Wolfe, F., Smythe, H. A., Yunus, M. B., Bennett, R. M., Bombardier, C., Goldenberg, D. L., Tugwell, P., Campbell, S. M., Abeles, M., and Clark, P. (1990). The American College of Rheumatology 1990 Criteria for the Classification of Fibromyalgia. *Arthritis and Rheumatism*, 33(2), 160–172.

Wright, G. E., Parker, J. C., Smarr, K. L., Johnson, J. C., Hewett, J. E., and Walker, S. E. (1998). Age, depressive symptoms, and rheumatoid arthritis. *Arthritis and Rheumatism*, 41, 298–305.

Zautra, A. J., Burleson, M. H., Smith, C. A., Blalock, S. J., Wallston, K. A., Devellis, R. F., Devellis, B. M., and Smith, T. W. (1995). Arthritis and perceptions of quality of life: An examination of positive and negative affect in rheumatoid arthritis patients. *Health Psychology*, 14, 399–408.

Zautra, A. J., Hamilton, N. A., and Burke, H. M. (1999). Comparison of stress responses in women with two types of chronic pain: Fibromyalgia and osteoarthritis. *Cognitive Therapy and Research*, 23, 209–230.

Index